# ORGANIZATIONS
rational, natural, and open systems

# ORGANIZATIONS
## rational,
## natural,
## and
SECOND
EDITION
## open systems

**W. RICHARD SCOTT**

*Stanford University*

Prentice-Hall, Inc. *Englewood Cliffs, New Jersey 07632*

*Library of Congress Cataloging-in-Publication Data*

SCOTT, W. RICHARD.
  Organizations : rational, natural, and open systems.

  Bibliography: p. 339
  Includes indexes.
  1. Organization.   I. Title.
  HM131.S385  1987        302.3'5        86-9368
  ISBN 0-13-641820-1

The author wishes to thank the copyright owners for permission to reprint in the text the following figures, tables and quotations:

Fig. 1-1. From Harold J. Leavitt, Applied organizational change in industry: structural, technological and humanistic approaches, in J. G. March (ed.), *Handbook of Organizations,* p. 1145. Copyright © 1965 by Rand McNally College Publishing Company, Chicago, Illinois. Reprinted by permission.

Figs. 4-1 and 4-2. Adapted from Robert L. Swinth, *Organizational Systems for Management,* pp. 18 and 23. Grid, Inc., Columbus, Ohio, 1974. Reprinted by permission.

*continued, page 362*

© 1987, 1981 by Prentice-Hall, Inc.
A division of Simon & Schuster
Englewood Cliffs, New Jersey 07632

Printed in the United States of America

10  9  8  7  6  5  4  3  2  1

Cover design: Wanda Lubelska
Manufacturing buyer: Carol Bystrom

ISBN  0-13-641820-1  01

Prentice-Hall International (UK) Limited, *London*
Prentice-Hall of Australia Pty. Limited, *Sydney*
Prentice-Hall Canada Inc., *Toronto*
Prentice-Hall Hispanoamericana, S.A., *Mexico*
Prentice-Hall of India Private Limited, *New Delhi*
Prentice-Hall of Japan, Inc., *Tokyo*
Prentice-Hall of Southeast Asia Pte. Ltd., *Singapore*
Editora Prentice-Hall do Brasil, Ltda., *Rio de Janeiro*

*aguin for*
*Jennifer, Elliot, and Sydney*

# contents

**2  ORGANIZATIONS
   AS RATIONAL SYSTEMS**    31

**3  ORGANIZATIONS
   AS NATURAL SYSTEMS**    51

**4  ORGANIZATIONS
   AS OPEN SYSTEMS**    76

# preface

When I was invited by a European colleague earlier this year to describe the effects of the current "crisis" in sociology on the state of organization theory, I conjured up this picture of the contemporary scene:

> The dominant cathedral of Rational Structure has been partially dismantled and, although portions are still standing, many of its building blocks have been carted off to be reconfigured into alternative and challenging contructions. More fragile shelters and colorful but perhaps temporary tents have been thrust up in vacant lots. The scene is one of much animation and energy: raw materials and scaffolding are strewn about; lamps in windows and camp fires burn far into the night. The image I wish to convey of the present situation . . . is partly that of crisis and confusion but more that of vigorous controversy and an enriching profusion of competing models and methods. (Scott, 1986)

Though I perhaps became somewhat carried away in the poetry of the moment, I do believe that the overall portrait is substantially correct. The field of organizations has undergone enormous change in the past few decades. It is currently, I believe, the most lively and vigorous area of study within sociology, and perhaps within all of the social sciences. This is a source of both excitement and confusion. Much is happening in the field, and developments are occurring faster than our ability to assimilate them into coherent patterns.

In the first edition of this book, published in 1981, the dominant transformation described was the shift from closed to open system models of organizations. Prior to the 1960s, most of the theorizing and research on organizations looked inside the organization not only for topics of study but also for bases of explanation. Organizations were assumed to be relatively autonomous and complete systems, and understanding was to be found in examining factors and processes within their fixed boundaries. Beginning about 1960, all this changed. The openness of organizations to their environments was recognized, and the linkages among "internal" and "external" objects and events was more likely to be taken into account. Organizations came to be viewed as less internally coherent and more externally connected than formerly assumed.

The first edition also described the revitalization—as well as the renewed criticism—of rational system models and the developing interest in natural system models. Rational system models have continued to grow and flourish, especially the transactions costs version pursued by the new institutional economists. The newer, challenging natural system conceptions could only be sketched or incompletely described six years ago. Now it is possible to present a much fuller account of them. The ecological, resource dependence, Marxist, and institutional approaches are more fully elaborated, and increasingly constitute full-fledged alternatives to rational system arguments. Views emphasizing cultural explanations have also gained much currency in recent years, and we consider these insights as well. Attention is also given in this edition to the recently developing ethnomethodological and interactionist approaches. There is much new work to review.

There was a time, approximately in the mid 1960s, when it appeared as if organizational sociology was in danger of being submerged under administrative science, which addresses the important but narrow issues of rational design and technical efficiency. That danger now appears quite remote. Organizational sociologists have rediscovered their intellectual roots and are enthusiastically addressing the old, central issues of the discipline—the distribution and use of power, the determinants and consequences of inequality, the creation of commitments and of meaning—within a set of new theoretical frameworks. It is a time of great excitement and ferment. This revised edition attempts to reflect this creative agitation. As before, we propose to deal with some of the complexity by showing that it can be understood as reflecting continuing controversies among three theoretical perspectives: the rational, natural, and open systems approaches. This framework is severely tested by the multiplicity of new ideas and concerns, but its seams appear to have held against the onslaught.

In the preface to the first edition, I attempted to acknowledge the help I have received from my former teachers and students and my current colleagues. This list is now too long to enumerate. I know who they are and they know. I hope they also know how grateful I am for all they have taught me.

Among my immediate circle at Stanford, I rely ever more heavily on the wisdom and virtue of Jim March, Jeff Pfeffer, and John Meyer. They are smarter and more productive than I, but gracious enough to treat me as an equal. In the stimulating intellectual community of organizations students on this campus, these three are a major resource for us all.

My wife Joy and our children continue to indulge and support my scholarly activities, even though they cut deeply into our evenings and weekends. The children will settle only for some tangible evidence of my guilt, and have again claimed their place on the dedication page. Joy knows the value of intangibles.

**W. Richard Scott**

*Stanford, California*

# ORGANIZATIONS

rational, natural, and open systems

# PART ONE

# AN INTRODUCTION TO ORGANIZATIONS

Organizations play a leading role in our modern world. Their presence affects—some would insist that the proper term is *infects*—virtually every sector of contemporary social life. Peter Drucker thus observes, "Young people today will have to learn organizations the way their forefathers learned farming." Chapter 1 endeavors to amplify and justify this advice by examining both the practical and theoretical benefits to be gained from a better understanding of organizations.

Part One pursues the two major themes of *commonality* and *diversity*. Organizations share certain features, which serve to differentiate them from other social forms. Students of this field believe that we can understand much about a specific organization from knowing about other organizations. Understanding how a factory functions can illuminate the workings of a hospital; and knowledge of a governmental bureau can help us understand the workings of a union.

Diversity appears in many guises. While organizations may possess common, generic characteristics, they exhibit staggering variety—in size, in structure, and in operating processes. Just as organizations vary, so do those who study them. Students of organizations bring to their task varying interests, tools, and intellectual preconceptions. Of particular importance are differences in the level of analysis employed and in the theoretical perspectives utilized.

Three influential perspectives are introduced in Chapter 1 as competing definitions of organizations. Part Two is devoted to an intensive examination of these perspectives, which have shaped and continue to govern our understanding of organizations.

# the subject is organizations

The recurrent problem in sociology is to conceive of corporate organization, and to study it, in ways that do not anthropomorphize it and do not reduce it to the behavior of individuals or of human aggregates.

Guy E. Swanson (1976)

The philosopher Alfred North Whitehead once suggested that, properly organized, education should proceed through three stages. In the first stage, that of *romance*, the student's interest is aroused: he or she is brought face to face with the object of study in all its power and mystery. If the subject is mechanical engineering, for example, the student could be taken to see a steam locomotive or a steel mill in operation. In the second stage, labeled *discipline*, the student acquires the concepts and methods required to analyze the subject and its parts and processes. And in the third stage, that of *fruition*, the methods and concepts are applied to the subject so that its structure and functioning may be understood and, perhaps, improved (Whitehead, 1929).

Our subject is organizations. We do not need to plan a field trip for students to observe this phenomenon in action: organizations are all around us. Because of their ubiquity, however, they fade into the background, and we need to be reminded of their impact. This chapter begins with a discussion of the practical and the theoretical importance of organizations: we attempt to arouse your interest so that an intellectual courtship can begin. We also begin the task of developing concepts for analyzing organizations; this work will continue throughout the volume. We do not intend to postpone the phase of fruition until the final chapters but will attempt early and often to demonstrate how the use of the concepts and methods can improve our understanding of the structure and functioning of organizations and, in some cases, contribute to their betterment.

## THE IMPORTANCE OF ORGANIZATIONS

There is no need to belabor the assertion that ours is an organizational society—that organizations are a prominent, if not the dominant, characteristic of modern societies. Organizations were present in older civilizations—

Chinese, Greek, Indian—but only in modern industrialized societies do we find large numbers of organizations engaged in performing many highly diverse tasks. To the ancient organizational assignments of soldiering, public administration, and tax collection have been added such varied tasks as discovery (research organizations), child and adult socialization (schools and universities), resocialization (mental hospitals and prisons), production and distribution of goods (industrial firms, wholesale and retail establishments), provision of services (organizations dispensing assistance ranging from laundry and shoe repair to medical care and investment counseling), protection of personal and financial security (police departments, insurance firms, banking and trust companies), preservation of culture (museums, art galleries, universities, libraries), communication (radio and television studios, telephone companies, the post office), and recreation (bowling alleys, pool halls, the National Park Service, professional football teams). Even such a partial listing testifies to the truth of Parsons's statement that "the development of organizations is the principal mechanism by which, in a highly differentiated society, it is possible to 'get things done,' to achieve goals beyond the reach of the individual" (1960:41).

Even though organizations are now ubiquitous, their development has been sufficiently gradual and uncontroversial that they have emerged during the past few centuries almost unnoticed. The spread of public bureaucracies into every sector and the displacement of the family business by the corporation "constitutes a revolution" in social structure, but one little remarked until recently.

> Never much agitated, never even much resisted, a revolution for which no flags were raised, it transformed our lives during those very decades in which, unmindful of what was happening, Americans and Europeans debated instead such issues as socialism, populism, free silver, clericalism, chartism, and colonialism. It now stands as a monument to discrepancy between what men think they are designing and the world they are in fact building. (Lindblom, 1977: 95)

The prevalence of organizations in every arena of social life is one indicator of their importance. Another, rather different index of their significance is the increasing frequency with which organizations are singled out as the source of many of the ills besetting contemporary society. Thus, writing in 1956, C. Wright Mills pointed with alarm to the emergence of a "power elite" whose members occupied the top positions in three overlapping organizational hierarchies: the state bureaucracy, the military, and the larger corporations. At about the same time, Ralf Dahrendorf (1959 trans.) in Germany was engaged in revising and updating Marxist doctrine by insisting that the basis of the class structure was no longer the ownership of the means of production but the occupancy of positions that allowed the wielding of organizational authority. Such views, which remain controversial, focus on the effects of organizations on societal stratification systems, taking account of the changing bases of power and prestige occasioned by the growth in number and size of organizations.

A related criticism concerns the seemingly inexorable growth in public-sector organizations. The two great German sociologists Max Weber (1947 trans.) and Robert Michels (1949 trans.) were among the first to insist that the central political issue for all modern societies was no longer the type of economic structure that prevailed—whether capitalist, socialist, or communist—but the increasing dominance by the public bureaucracy of the ostensible political leaders.

Other criticisms point to the negative consequences of the growth of organizations in virtually *every* area of social existence. Borrowing from and enlarging on a theme pervading the thought of Weber, these critics decry the rationalization of modern life—in Weber's phrase, the "disenchantment of the world" (1946 trans.:51). The essence of this view is graphically captured by Norman Mailer: "Civilization extracts its thousand fees from the best nights of man, but none so cruel as the replacement of the good fairy by the expert, the demon by the rational crisis, and the witch by the neurotic female" (1968:83). Organizations are viewed as the primary vehicle by which, systematically, the areas of our lives are rationalized—planned, articulated, scientized, made more efficient and orderly, and managed by "experts." (See, for example, Mannheim, 1950 trans.; Ellul, 1964 trans.; Goodman, 1968; and Galbraith, 1967.) The dark side of such progress is depicted by Roszak, who defines the technocracy as "that social form in which an industrial society reaches the peak of its organizational integration." He writes, "Under the technocracy we become the most scientific of societies; yet, like Kafka's K., men throughout the 'developed world' become more and more the bewildered dependents of inaccessible castles wherein inscrutable technicians conjure with their fate" (1969: 5, 13).

A new generation of feminist critics reminds us that it is not just "men" who are trapped in organizational cages. Like Roszak, Glennon (1979) decries the growth of technocracy, but on the feminist grounds that it feeds the "dualism of private-expressive and public-instrumental selves and worlds" and engenders a bureaucratic rationality that extends instrumental and administrative orientations into everyday— including private—life. Ferguson (1984: 203) is even more direct in her criticism:

> The organizational forms and discourse of bureaucratic capitalism institutionalize modes of domination that recreate the very patterns of oppression that feminism arose to combat.

These critics thus add their voices to others who have called attention to the ways in which organizational structures damage the personalities and psyches of their participants. Alienation, overconformity, and stunting of normal personality development are among the consequences attributed, not to such special cases as prisons and concentration camps, but to everyday, garden-variety organizations (see Argyris, 1957; Maslow, 1954; Whyte, 1956).

We attempt to evaluate such criticisms of organizations at appropriate points throughout this volume. Here we simply note that these negative views towards organizations provide further testimony to their importance in the modern world.

In addition to their being mechanisms for accomplishing a great variety of objectives and, perhaps as a necessary consequence, the source of many of our current difficulties, organizations have yet another important effect on our collective lives. This effect is more subtle and less widely recognized, but it may be quite profound in its implications. It is, perhaps best introduced by an analogy: "The medium is the message." This twentieth-century aphorism was coined by Marshall McLuhan (1964) to focus attention on the characteristics of the mass media themselves—print, radio, movies, television—in contrast with the content transmitted by these media. McLuhan defines media very broadly as "any extension of ourselves"; elaborating his thesis, he notes, "The message of any medium is the change in scale or pace or pattern that it introduces into human affairs" (1964: 23, 24).

McLuhan's thesis appears to be more clearly applicable to our subject—organizations—than to any specific media of communication. First, like media, organizations represent extensions of ourselves. Organizations can achieve goals that are quite beyond the reach of any individual—from building skyscrapers and dams to putting a person on the moon. But to focus on what organizations *do* may conceal from us the more basic and far-reaching effects that occur because organizations are the *mechanisms*—the media—by which those goals are pursued. A few examples may suggest some of these unanticipated organizational effects:

•In his crucial decision on how to react to the installation of Russian missiles in Cuba, President Kennedy had to select from among a naval blockade, a "surgical" air strike, and a massive land invasion, not because these were the only conceivable responses, but because these were the principal organizational routines that had been worked out by the Pentagon (see Allison, 1971).

•Although we seek "health" when we visit the clinic or the hospital, what we get is "medical care." Clients are encouraged to view these outputs as synonymous although there may be no relation between them. In some cases, the relation can even be negative: more care can result in poorer health (see Illich, 1976).

•Products manufactured by organizations reflect the manufacturing process. They often reflect the need to subdivide work and to simplify tasks, and the manufacturing pressures toward standardization of parts and personnel (Veblen, 1904). Customization—in the genuine sense, not in the Detroit sense—becomes prohibitively expensive. Metal replaces wood and plastic replaces metal in many products to satisfy organizational, not consumer, needs.

To suggest that our organizational tools shape in unanticipated ways the products and services they produce would appear to be a relatively sweeping and unsettling generalization on which we might be content to rest our case. However, our arguments concerning the importance of organizations are not quite finished: we give the screw one final turn.

We will fail to perceive the importance of organizations for our own lives if we view them merely as tools for achieving goals. Organizations must also be viewed as actors in their own right, as *corporate persons,* to use Coleman's phrase (1974). They can take actions, utilize resources, enter into contracts, and own property. Coleman describes how these rights have gradually developed since the Middle Ages to the point where now it is accurate to speak of two kinds of persons—*natural* persons (such as you and me) and corporate or *juristic* persons (such as the Red Cross and

General Motors). The social structure of the modern society can no longer be described accurately as consisting only of relations among natural persons: our understanding must be stretched to include as well those relations between natural and corporate persons, and between corporate and corporate persons. In short, we must come to "the recognition that the society has changed over the past few centuries in the very structural elements of which it is composed" (Coleman, 1974: 13).

A different kind of rationale for justifying the study of organizations as a basic social science pursuit is suggested by the following statement of Homans: "The fact is that the organization of the large formal enterprises, governmental or private, in modern society is modeled on, is a rationalization of, tendencies that exist in all human groups" (1950: 186–87). To say that organizations exhibit "tendencies that exist in all human groups" is to suggest that organizations provide the setting for a wide variety of basic social processes, such as socialization, communication, ranking, the formation of norms, the exercise of power, and goal setting and attainment. If these generic social processes operate in organizations, then we can add as much to our knowledge of the principles that govern their behavior by studying organizations as by studying any other specific type of social system. But Homans asserts something more.

To say that we can perceive in organizations "a rationalization of tendencies that exist in all human groups" is to suggest that organizations are characterized by somewhat distinctive structural arrangements that affect the operation of the processes occurring within them. For example, social control processes occur within all social groups, but there are some forms or mechanisms of control—for instance, a hierarchical authority structure—that are best studied in organizations, since it is within these systems that they appear in their most highly developed form.[1] The processes of interest can occur at various levels of analysis, as will be discussed in the following section. Also, decidedly, one of the important tasks is to spell out clearly what is meant by *distinctive structural arrangements*. We will begin this task in the present chapter but will find it sufficiently challenging that we will need to keep it before us throughout this volume.

At this point, however, we assert our belief that the study of organizations can contribute to basic sociological knowledge by increasing our understanding of how generic social processes operate within distinctive social structures.

## ORGANIZATIONS AS AN AREA OF STUDY

### Emergence of the Area

The study of organizations is both a specialized field of inquiry within the discipline of sociology and an increasingly recognized focus of

---

[1]This general argument has been elaborated elsewhere (Scott, 1970). The basic premise is that a set of generic social processes—such as socialization, integration, status, power, adaptation—may be identified in all social structures. However, each of these processes operates differently depending on the structural context in which it is acting so that, for example, the process of integration is effected in a small group differently than in an organization, and both differ from the same process occurring within a community, and so on.

multidisciplinary research and training. It is impossible to determine with precision the moment of its appearance, but it is safe to conclude that until the late 1940s, organizations did not exist as a distinct field of sociological inquiry. Precursors may be indentified, but each lacked some critical feature. Thus, there was some empirical research on organizations by, for example, criminologists who studied prisons (for example, Clemmer, 1940), political analysts who examined party structures (for example, Gosnell, 1937), and industrial sociologists who studied factories and labor unions (for example, Whyte, 1946). But these investigators rarely attempted to generalize beyond the specific organizational form they were studying. The subject was prisons or parties or factories or unions—not organizations. Similarly, in the neighboring disciplines, political scientists were examining the functioning of legislative bodies or public agencies, and economists were developing their theory of the firm, but they were not attempting to generalize beyond these specific forms.

Industrial psychologists did pursue such general problems as low morale, fatigue, and turnover within several types of organizational settings, but they did not attempt to determine systematically how the varying characteristics of different organizational contexts influenced these worker reactions. And although, from early in this century, administrative and management theorists such as Fayol (1949 trans.) and Gulick and Urwick (1937) did concentrate on the development of general principles concerning administrative arrangements, their approach was more often prescriptive than empirical. That is, they were interested in determining what "should be" in the interests of maximizing efficiency and effectiveness rather than in examining and explaining organizational arrangements as they existed.

Within sociology, the emergence of the field of organizations may be roughly dated from the translation into English of Weber's (1946 trans., 1947 trans.) and, to a lesser extent, Michels's (1949 trans.) analyses of bureaucracy. Shortly after these classic statements became accessible to American sociologists, Robert K. Merton and his students at Columbia University attempted to outline the boundaries of this new field of inquiry by compiling theoretical and empirical materials dealing with various aspects of organizations (Merton et al., 1952). Equally important, a series of pathbreaking and influential case studies of diverse types of organizations was launched under Merton's influence, including an examination of the Tennessee Valley Authority (Selznick, 1949), a gypsum mine and factory (Gouldner, 1954), a state employment agency and a federal law-enforcement agency (Blau, 1955), and a union (Lipset, Trow, and Coleman, 1956). For the first time, sociologists were engaged in the development and empirical testing of generalizations dealing with the structure and functioning of organizations viewed as organizations.

In a similar fashion, analysts working in other social science traditions focused increasingly on general organizational issues. After World War II, students of industrial psychology, public administration, social anthropology, and institutional economics began to pay less attention to divergent backgrounds and more to common interests. Intellectual ancestors, such as Machiavelli, St. Simon, Weber, and Frederick Winslow Taylor, were uncovered, and more recent academic forbears, such as Elton Mayo (1945) and Chester Barnard (1938; 1948), were rediscovered and reprinted. Even a couple of token women contributors were identified, in the persons of Lillian M. Gilbreth—who collaborated with her husband in finding ways to improve work efficiency in factories but also applied the techniques at home and whose feats are celebrated in the book and movie *Cheaper by the Dozen* (see Gilbreth and Gilbreth, 1917)—and Mary Parker Follett (1942), an early student of management and change working in the human relations tradition. After about a decade of empirical research and theory development, three textbook-treatises—March and Simon (1958), Likert (1961), and Blau and Scott (1962)—provided needed integration and heightened interest in the field. Also, a new journal, *Administrative Science Quarterly*, founded in 1956, emphasized the interdisciplinary character of the field.[2]

### Common and Divergent Interests

What features do all organizations exhibit in common? What are the general organizational issues analysts began to perceive among the great diversity of specific goals and structural arrangements? Most analysts have conceived of organizations as social structures created by individuals to support the collaborative pursuit of specified goals. Given this conception, all organizations confront a number of common problems. All must define (and redefine) their objectives; all must induce participants to contribute services; all must control and coordinate these contributions; resources must be garnered from the environment and products or services dispensed; participants must be selected, trained, and replaced; and some sort of working accommodation with the neighbors must be achieved.

In addition to these common operational requirements, some analysts have also emphasized that all organizations are beset by a common curse. A high proportion of the resources utilized by any organization is expended in maintaining the organization itself rather than in achieving the specified goals. Although organizations are viewed as means to accomplish ends, the means themselves absorb much energy, and in the extreme (but perhaps not rare) case become ends in themselves.

There is a convergence of interest around these common features, but we must not overlook the many bases of divergence. Most obvious, organizations come in a bewildering variety of sizes and shapes. The largest of them are very large: General Motors employed 690,000 persons in 1985; American Telephone and Telegraph, before divestiture, counted more than 3 million stockholders. Most workers in this country are employees of someone else: only about 8 percent of the work force is self-employed. And more workers are employed by fewer and larger companies: by 1975, 3 percent of the employing organizations accounted for 55 percent of the employed, and about one quarter of the total work force was employed by firms with more than 1000 employees. Still, small organizations remain the most common type: 51 percent of all employing organizations in 1975 employed 3 or fewer individuals. (U.S. Department of Labor, 1979) And the predominant ownership form remains the sole proprietorship, with

[2]Other brief histories of the development of organizations as an identifiable field of inquiry are provided by March (1965: ix–xvi) and Pfeffer (1982: 23–33). An entertaining, if jaundiced, view of the evolution of organization theory can be found in Perrow (1973).

more than 12 million establishments, compared with about 2.8 million corporations and about 1.5 million partnerships. Of course, the corporation far outstrips the other forms in assets, employees, and earnings. (U.S. Bureau of the Census, 1984) These employment organizations also vary greatly in the types of goods and services provided: from coal mining to computers, from fortune-telling to futures forecasting.

Large and growing numbers of people are employed in the public sector. In 1984, over 16 million individuals—about one fifth of the number working in the private sector—were employed in federal, state, and local governments. The number of units or agencies involved is difficult to determine because of the nested character of governmental forms. *The United States Government Manual* (U.S. Office of the Federal Register, 1984) provides organizational charts and brief descriptions of the principal agencies. It currently numbers almost 1000 pages! It is well to recognize that federal employees make up only about 20 percent of all governmental officials, the vast majority of whom are employed at the state (3.8 million) and local levels (9.3 million), where there is great variation in organizational arrangements.

Employing organizations do not exhaust the list of organizational forms. Verba and Nie (1972) estimate that about two thirds of adult Americans belong to one or more voluntary associations, not counting churches. The number and variety of such forms is large, and includes labor unions, political parties, professional societies, business and trade associations, fraternities and sororities, civic service associations, reform and activist groups, and neighborhood organizations. Two "slices" into this world suggest how diverse it is. A vertical slice, extracting only one occupational group, doctors of medicine, reveals over 380 specialty associations listed in the *Directory of Medical Specialists*. A horizontal slice, an attempt to compile a detailed list of all voluntary associations in Birmingham, England, reported 4264 such organizations. (Newman, 1975)

In addition to size and sector, organizations vary greatly in structural characteristics. The relatively flat authority and control structure found in many voluntary associations stands in sharp contrast with the multilayer hierarchy of a military unit or a civil service bureaucracy. And both seem relatively clean and simple in comparison with the project team or matrix structures (discussed in Chapter 9) found in an advanced research and development unit of a space exploration company. Some organizations are capital-intensive, placing most of their resources in machinery and automated equipment. Others invest heavily in the "human capital" of their work force, selecting highly qualified personnel, underwriting their further specialized training, and then struggling to keep them from taking their expertise to some other company. Organizations vary in these but also in many other important ways, as we will see.

Another basis for divergence resides not in the organizations themselves but in the interests, training, and employment setting of those who investigate them. As implied earlier, researchers from different disciplines vary to some extent in the kinds of organizations they choose to study. Political scientists continue to focus on political parties and state administrative structures, economists on business firms, sociologists on voluntary associations and on agencies engaged in social welfare and social control functions, and anthropologists on comparative administration in primitive, colonial, and developing societies. Disciplinary differences remain even when a single type of organization is selected for study: specialists tend to look not only at different objects but also at different aspects of the same object. Thus, the political scientist will be likely to emphasize power processes and decision making within the organization; the economist will examine the acquisition and allocation of scarce resources within the organization and will attend to such issues as productivity and efficiency; the sociologist has quite varied interests but if there is a focus it will likely be on status orderings and on the effect of norms and sentiments on behavior; the psychologist will be interested in variations in perception, learning, and motivation among participants; and the anthropologist will call attention to the effects of diverse cultural values on the functioning of the system and its members. The study of organizations embraces all these interests, and students of organizations work to develop conceptual frameworks within which all of these topics and their interrelations may be examined. And, increasingly, organizational analysts attempt to specify what is distinctive about power, or status, or motivation, because that process is carried on within the context of organizations.

Cutting across these disciplinary divisions is another, more general basis of divergence among those who study organizations: the adoption of a *basic* versus an *applied* research orientation. Some studies are aimed primarily at accurately describing existing features and relations of organizations in order simply to better understand their nature and operation. Others seek knowledge in order to solve specific problems or to bring about desired changes in these sytems. Of course, there is not a hard-and-fast line between these interests. Basic research, particularly in the long run, can lead to practical applications and applied research often contributes importantly to our general knowledge. Both rest on interests and values: neither is value-free and the same investigators often conduct both basic and applied studies.

Still, there are important differences in these orientations. Basic research is driven more by theory—in its choice both of problems and of variables. Particular concepts—authority, legitimacy, institutionalization—are of interest because of their place in theoretical arguments, not because of their practical significance. Basic research is more likely to focus on the independent variables—on understanding the effects of certain concepts of interest—than on the dependent variables. Conversely, applied research is driven by an interest in solving some identified problem—low morale or productivity, high turnover—and is willing to incorporate any factors, whether economic, psychological, or technical, that may shed light on it. Thus, applied studies are much more likely to be interdisciplinary: practical problems do not respect disciplinary boundaries.

Although there are many exceptions, applied research is more likely to be conducted by researchers located in nonacademic settings: in governmental bureaus, research units of corporations, consulting firms, or policy-research organizations. The results of these studies are less likely to be published in scholarly journals; often they result in no publications at all, only a report to the client group and/or chief executive officer. Basic research is conducted largely within the academic departments of colleges and universities. This work is either unfunded—and hence subsidized by the academic institution (which may, for example, permit low teaching loads and reward faculty for their research productivity)—or is funded largely through research grants from government sources or private foundations.[3] These organizations support research primarily because of "public interest" arguments: it is better to know than not to know, and all benefit from the discovery of new knowledge.

An intermediate group of scholars "swing" both ways. These scholars are faculty members in professional schools: business, educational administration, public administration, public health, engineering management, social-work administration, and so forth. These faculty are more likely to engage in consulting work for private companies or public organizations than those located in academic departments, and they are generally more likely to carry out applied studies, in part because of pressures from their students—past (alumni) and present—who are interested in usable practical information and in skills that will affect the "bottom line," e.g., profits. At the same time, these faculty are confronted by demands from their school and university to contribute to basic knowledge—that is, to publish in scholarly journals. As faculty members of a university, they are subject to the academic culture and its requirements, although these pressures vary from campus to campus and school to school.

Both the basic and the applied-science orientations have made and may be expected to continue to make important contributions to our knowledge of organizations—what they are and how they work. In the long run, each orientation depends on and complements the other, and a healthy scientific enterprise requires that both types of research receive attention and support.

### Levels of Analysis

Although organizations furnish a common locus of research for many social scientists, by no means are all investigators interested in finding answers to the same questions. Even apart from the variety of conceptual schemes and orientations that guide inquiry and the differences in methodological tools, investigators differ in the level of analysis at which they choose to work (see Blau, 1957). For present purposes, the level of analysis is determined by the nature of the dependent variable—that is, by whether the phenomenon to be explained is (1) the behavior or attributes of individual participants within organizations, (2) the functioning or characteristics of some aspect or segment of organizational structure, or (3) the characteristics or actions of the organization viewed as a collective entity. We will briefly discuss each of these levels.

Some investigators are interested in explaining individual behavior within an organization. At this level, organizational characteristics are viewed as context or environment, and the investigator attempts to explore their impact on the attitudes or behavior of individuals. Such a perspective is labeled *social psychological* and is exemplified by the work of March and Simon (1958) and Porter, Lawler, and Hackman (1975).

---

[3]Increasingly, however, scholars within academic departments are also affiliating with other organizational units—laboratories, centers, institutes—both within the university and outside. These organizations serve as a research base for studies that are often applied in character.

At the second level, the major concern is to explain the structural features and social processes that characterize organizations and their subdivisions. The investigator working at this level may focus on the various subunits that make up the organization (for example, work groups, departments, authority ranks) or may examine various analytical components (for example, specialization, communication networks, hierarchy), attempting in both cases to account for their characteristics and to explore their interrelations. This level of analysis is labeled the *structural,* and examples of its use are found in the works of Udy (1959*b*) and Blau and Schoenherr (1971).

At the third level of analysis, the focus is on the organization as a collective actor functioning in a larger system of relations. Within this approach, the analyst may choose either to examine the relation between a specific organization or class of organizations and the environment (for example, Selznick, 1949; Pugh et al., 1969) or to examine the relations that develop among a number of organizations viewed as an interdependent system (for example, Aiken and Hage, 1968; Warren, 1967). This level of analysis is labeled *ecological.*

Admittedly, distinguishing among these three levels of analysis is somewhat arbitrary and ambiguous. Many levels of analytical complexity can be identified as one moves from organizational-individual to societal-organizational relations.[4] Nevertheless, if only to remind us of the complexity of the subject matter and the variety of aims and interests with which analysts approach it, the three types can prove useful as a rough gauge for distinguishing among broad categories of studies.

Of course, the level of analysis at which we choose to examine organizational behavior also affects somewhat the types of data gathered and how they are treated. We cannot provide in this volume a detailed discussion of research methods used in the study of organizations,[5] but one set of methodological distinctions is of particular significance to this discussion of levels of analysis. Lazarsfeld and his colleagues (Lazarsfeld, 1959; Lazarsfeld and Menzel, 1961) have developed a typology of measures that usefully illustrates ways in which information gathered at one level may be employed in analyses at a different level. They begin by distinguishing between two generalized units: *members* and *collectives*—units at different levels in the sense that members are defined as parts of collectives. The subjects of interest may vary. For example, for one type of analysis, the members may be persons and the collectives, departments; for another, the members may be departments and the collectives, organizations.

*Members* may be characterized by a number of different types of properties:

---

[4]In Chapter 6 we introduce and define several additional levels of analysis, all of which are distinctions made within the ecological level.

[5]Survey chapters discussing simulation techniques, field methods, and laboratory methods applied to the study of organizations are contained in March (1965). Research techniques and instruments appropriate for analyzing individual jobs, the structure of subunits, and the structure and performance of entire organizations are described in Van de Ven and Ferry (1980). And a review of methods and instruments for assessing interorganizational relations, with an emphasis on professional service organizations, is provided by Morrissey, Hall, and Lindsey (1982).

1. *Absolute:* properties based solely on information concerning the member—for example, the age or sex of an individual.
2. *Relational:* properties obtained from information about relationships among the members—for example, sociometric (preference) choices given or received by an individual.
3. *Comparative:* properties based on information obtained from comparing the member's value on some property with the distribution of values on that property over the collective—for example, the relative seniority of an individual worker.
4. *Contextual:* properties based on information about the collective to which the member belongs—for example, an individual being characterized as an employee of a large versus a small department. (Lazarsfeld and Menzel, 1961: 431–33)

Note that the fourth measure differs from the first three in that it is based on information gathered at a different level: a property of a collective is used to characterize its members. In reverse fashion, information based on members can be combined and used to characterize a collective. The first two of the following three measures of *collectives* are of this type:

1. *Analytical:* properties based on a summary measure of some property of each member of the collective—for example, the average age of the members of a department.
2. *Structural:* properties based on a summary measure of the relationships among members—for example a measure of cohesion based on the relative number of sociometric choices directed by members to others within the collective as compared with those directed outside.
3. *Global:* properties of collectives not based on information concerning individual members or their relationships—for example, the assets of a company. (Lazarsfeld and Menzel, 1961: 426–29)

Although the formal definitions of the various properties are based on the source of the data, the full schema reflects the important fact that level of analysis is determined not by the *source* of the information but by the *use* to which that information is put. An analytical property of a collective, for example, is based on information obtained from members but is used to characterize the collective.

Perhaps it is apparent that these measures were spawned in the effort by survey analysts to find ways to utilize survey data obtained from individual respondents to characterize structural features of groups (see Kendall and Lazarsfeld, 1950). These innovations, and their codification in the typology proposed by Lazarsfeld and Menzel, were instrumental in shifting the attention of analysts from the social psychological characteristics of participants to the structural properties of collectives such as organizations. They ushered in a wave of studies that examined the impact of the properties of organizations (collectives) on individual (member) behavior (for example, Lazarsfeld and Thielens, 1958; Lipset, Trow, and Coleman, 1956; Blau, 1960), and they paved the way for later work that focused on the interrelations of structural features within organizations (collectives).

Early research on organizations was conducted almost exclusively at the social psychological level. The structural level of analysis became prominent in the early 1960s and continues to be heavily utilized by sociologists. The ecological level was the last to develop, emerging in the late 1960s, and continues to acquire adherents.

## THE ELEMENTS OF ORGANIZATIONS

Organizations are highly varied and often highly complex, so it may be helpful to begin with a simplifying model allowing us to focus on basic characteristics. The proposed model shown in Figure 1–1 is adapted from Leavitt (1965).[6] Let us briefly consider each element.

### Social Structure

*Social structure* refers to the patterned or regularized aspects of the relationships existing among participants in an organization. The social structure of any human grouping can be analytically separated into two components. As Kingsley Davis (1949: 52) suggests,

> ... always in human society there is what may be called a double reality—on the one hand a normative sytem embodying what *ought* to be, and on the other a factual order embodying what is.... these two orders cannot be completely identical, nor can they be completely disparate.

We shall refer to Davis's first component as the *normative structure;* this component includes values, norms, and role expectations. Briefly, *values* are the criteria employed in selecting the goals of behavior; *norms* are the generalized rules governing behavior that specify, in particular, appropriate means for pursuing goals; and *roles* are expectations for or evaluative standards employed in assessing the behavior of occupants of specific social positions. A social position is simply a location in a system of

[6]Leavitt identifies the four "internal" elements but does not include the environment as a separate factor. As will be obvious from our discussion, we regard the environment as an indispensable ingredient in any organizational model.

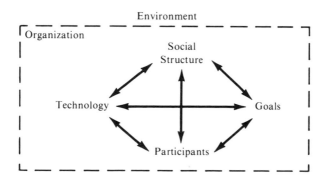

**FIGURE 1–1**   Leavitt's Diamond: A Model of an Organization. *Source:* Adapted from Leavitt (1965), Figure I, p. 1145.

social relationships. (For a basic formulation of positions and roles, see Gross, Mason, and McEachern, 1958.) In any social grouping, values, norms, and roles are not randomly arranged, but are organized so as to constitute a relatively coherent and consistent set of beliefs and prescriptions governing the behavior of participants. It is for this reason that we speak of a normative *structure*.

The second component, which Davis refers to as "a factual order," we will call the *behavioral structure*. This component focuses on actual behavior rather than on prescriptions for behavior. Homans's (1950: 33–40) well-known classification of social behavior into activities, interactions, and sentiments suggests the types of elements that constitute the behavioral structure. Because our concern is with the analysis of behavioral *structure*, rather than simply behavior, we focus on those activities, interactions, and sentiments that exhibit some degree of regularity—the recurrent behavior of a given individual or similarities in the behavior of a class of individuals. Such actions, exhibiting some consistency and constancy in their general characteristics, are themselves arranged into larger patterns or networks of behavior. For example, we may observe in a group over a period of time which individuals attempt to influence others and with what degree of success, and in this way obtain a description of the power structure within that group. Or by observing the patterning of sentiments among group members—who is attracted to or rejected by whom—we can describe the sociometric structure of the group. Both the power structure and the sociometric structure are specific instances of behavioral structures.

As the passage from Davis reminds us, the normative structure and the behavioral structure of a social group are neither independent nor identical, but are to varying degrees interrelated. The normative structure imposes an important set of constraints on the behavioral structure, shaping and channeling behavior and helping to account for much of the regularity and patterning that exist. On the other hand, much behavior departs from the normative structure and is an important source of additions to and changes in that structure. Behavior shapes norms just as norms shape behavior. Groups vary in the extent to which their normative and behavioral structures are aligned. In some situations precept corresponds closely to practice: this appears to be the case in many utopian communities or communes—at least in their early stages of development (see Kanter, 1972). In other situations a sizable gulf appears between professed beliefs and behavior. Reports suggest that Victorian England might represent an instance of this situation with respect to sexual morality versus practice. In any case, the normative and behavioral structures are always in a state of dynamic tension—each existing and changing somewhat independently of the other at the same time each exerts continuing force on the other.

All social groups—or *collectivities*, to use the more general term—are characterized by a normative structure applicable to the participants and by a behavioral structure linking participants in a common network or pattern of activities, interactions, and sentiments. These two interrelated structures constitute the *social structure* of a collectivity.[7]

Organizational participants are likely to emphasize the amount of

[7]For a more extensive discussion of normative, behavioral, and social structures, see Scott, 1970:102–10.

confusion, the indeterminacy, and the unpredictability of the actions of their co-workers, in part because such matters draw their attention and require their energies. However, to focus on the social structure of organizations is to emphasize the impressive amount of order exhibited by the behavior of participants in organizations. Every day hundreds or thousands of persons in organizations perform millions of individual acts, yet the outcome is not bedlam, not total confusion or chaos, but a reasonable approximation of order. This phenomenon deserves our attention.

Emphasizing the importance of the social structure of organizations does not commit us to the view that relations among participants are all sweetness and light: social structure does not connote social harmony. Conflict is always possible and usually present among participants in any social structure. An emphasis on social structure should enable us to see that much of whatever conflict is present in the organization is patterned, in the sense that it is built into the structure of relations between individuals and groups and is not due to innately aggressive individual participants. Not only stability and order but tension and stress, deviance and change can often be attributed to structural factors. (See Merton, 1957: 131–60)

The social structure of an organization varies in the extent to which it is formalized. A *formal* social structure is one in which the social positions and the relationships among them have been explicitly specified and are defined independently of the personal characteristics of the participants occupying these positions. By contrast, in an *informal* social structure, it is impossible to distinguish between the characteristics of the positions and the characteristics of the participants. In an informal structure, when specific participants leave or enter the system, their roles and relationships develop and change as a function of their personal characteristics and the interactions that occur among them.[8]

### Participants

Organizational participants are those individuals who, in return for a variety of inducements, make contributions to the organization (Barnard, 1938; Simon, 1957). All individuals participate in more than one organization, and the extent and intensiveness of their involvement may vary greatly; the decision as to who is to be regarded as a participant is thus often a difficult one and may legitimately vary with the issue at hand. For example, a single individual may simultaneously be an employee of an industrial firm, a member of a union, a church member, a member of a fraternal lodge or sorority; a "member" of a political party, a citizen of the state, a client of a group medical practice, a stockholder in one or more companies, and a customer in numerous retail and service organiza-

---

[8]Of course, at any given point in the history of a particular structure, new jobs are being created around the particular skills and interests of specific individuals. Miner (1985) has labeled these positions *idiosyncratic jobs* and notes two subtypes: *evolved jobs,* created around current organizational members, and *opportunistic hires,* created around people outside the organization. The number of such positions appears to vary considerably by type of organization, as does the extent to which such informal positions become codified and formalized. Informal job redefinition followed by codification appears to be a significant form of mobility in some organizations. (See also Miner and Estler, 1985.)

tions. Analysts disagree, as we shall see, on the extent to which organizations do and should incorporate facets of participants. How much of the personality and personal characteristics of individual participants is relevant to the functioning of the organization also varies from one type of organization and role to another: consider the situation of a novice in a religious order versus that of an occasional customer in a supermarket.

The demographic characteristics of participants—for example, their age, gender, ethnic distributions—have important consequences for many aspects of organizational structure and functioning; we will explore those implications in Chapter 7. And the structural features of organizations—the opportunities they create and the sorting rules they use for selection and retention and promotion—have equally fateful consequences for participants, as we discuss in Chapter 8.

### Goals

The concept of organizational goals is among the most important—and most controversial—concepts to be confronted in the study of organizations. Some analysts insist that goals are indispensable to the understanding of organizations; others question whether goals perform any function other than to justify past actions. Then, too, behaviorialists are fond of pointing out that only individuals have goals; collectivities, such as organizations, do not. We will not attempt to tackle these prickly issues here but promise not to duck them indefinitely.

For most analysts, goals constitute a central point of reference in the analysis of organizations. Goals are tentatively defined as *conceptions of desired ends*—conditions that participants attempt to effect through their performance of task activities.

Since goals figure prominently in some definitions of organizations, we will consider them further in the following section, and we will discuss the major issues and problems bearing on their analysis in Chapter 11.

### Technology

To focus on the technology of an organization is to view the organization as a place where some type of work is done, as a location where energy is applied to the transformation of materials, as a mechanism for transforming inputs into outputs. The connotations of the term *technology* are narrow and hard, but we will insist that every organization does work and possesses a technology for doing that work. Some organizations process material inputs and fabricate new equipment and hardware. Others "process" people, their products consisting of more knowledgeable individuals, in the case of effective school systems, or healthier individuals, in the case of effective medical clinics. Still others process primarily symbolic materials, such as information or music. Technologies consist in part of machines and mechanical equipment but also comprise the technical knowledge and skills of participants.

All organizations possess technologies, but organizations vary in the extent to which these techniques are understood, or routinized, or efficacious. Some of the most interesting theoretical and empirical work in recent years has focused on the relation between the characteristics of technology and the structural features of organizations. This work is described and evaluated in Chapter 9.

### Environment

Every organization exists in a specific physical, technological, cultural, and social environment to which it must adapt. No organization is self-sufficient; all depend for survival on the types of relations they establish with the larger systems of which they are a part. Early analysts of organizations, as we will see, tended to overlook or underestimate the importance of organization-environmental linkages, but recent work places great emphasis on these connections. And, indeed, the number and variety of these connections are impressive. Let us briefly reconsider each of the four organizational components in this light.

Very few organizations assume full responsibility for the socialization and training of their participants. Employees come to the organization with heavy cultural and social baggage obtained from interactions in other social contexts. With very few exceptions—such as inmates in "total institutions" (Goffman, 1961)—participants are involved in more than one organization at any given time. These outside interests and commitments inevitably constrain the behavior of participants in any given organization and, in some instances, strongly influence it. To regard participants as completely contained by the organization is to misperceive one of the fundamental characteristics of organizations: that they are systems built on the *partial involvement* of their members.

Similarly, few organizations create their own technologies; rather, they import them from the environment in the form of mechanical equipment, packaged programs and sets of instructions, and trained workers. Any specific organization must also adapt to the larger occupational structure—e.g., union rules or professional norms—in the selection and deployment of workers within the organization. Moreover, the environment is the source of the inputs to be processed by the organization, just as it is the "sink" to which all outputs are delivered—as products to be sold, clients restored to function, or waste materials to be eliminated.

Parsons (1960) has called attention to the important relation between an organization's goals and the larger societal environment. What is termed a goal or objective by a specific organization is, from the point of view of the larger society, its specialized function. An organization may thus expect societal support for its activities to reflect the relative value society places on those functions: if health represents a strong positive value for a society, for example, then those organizations that supply health care may expect to receive a disproportional share of resources supporting their work.

Last, the social structure of the organization will reflect important features borrowed from or impressed upon it by the environment. Structural forms, no less than technologies, are rarely invented and are usually borrowed from the environment. Part Three of this volume explores the thesis that environmental complexity tends to be incorporated within and reflected by the structural features of organizations. These incorporations may give rise to formal components such as rules or offices or departments, or they may form the basis for informal cliques or for work patterns not sanctioned by the formal structure. Both formal and informal structures can have their roots in the environment.

While insisting on the pervasive and critical importance of environmental influences on organizational forms and operations, we must not assume that the causal processes work in only one direction. Organizations not only are influenced by but also affect their environments. Although modern theorists differ in their views of the relative importance of these casual connections, as we will discuss in later chapters, they generally agree that the relations between organizations and environments are vital, complex, and interdependent.

Each of these organizational elements—social structure, participants, goals, technology, environment—represents an important component of all organizations. Indeed, each element has been regarded as of surpassing importance by one or more analysts of organizations. However, the chief value of Leavitt's diamond is as a graphic reminder that no one element is so dominant as to be safely considered in isolation from the others. Organizations are, first and foremost, *systems* of elements, each of which affects and is affected by the others. Goals are not *the* key to understanding the nature and functioning of organizations, no more than are the participants, the technology, or the social structure. And no organization can be understood in isolation from the larger environment. We will miss the essence of organization if we insist on focusing on any single feature to the exclusion of all others.

## DEFINING THE CONCEPT OF ORGANIZATION

Consistent with the objectives of this volume, not one but three definitions of organizations will be presented. These definitions pave the way for our description and evaluation in Part Two of three major perspectives employed in the analysis of organizations. Thus, we leave to later chapters the considerable task of spelling out the implications of these differing definitions. We give special attention here to the first definition—actually, several related definitions will be discussed—both because it has tended until recently to dominate the field and because it has served to establish organizations as a distinctive field of study. This definition is most consistent with a *rational system* perspective on organization. Two other definitions—one associated with the *natural system* perspective and the other with the *open systems* perspective—will be briefly described here and examined more fully in later chapters.

### A Rational System Definition

Since a primary function of a definition is to help us to distinguish one phenomenon from another, most definitions of organizations emphasize the distinctive features of organizations—those that help to distinguish them from related social forms. Many analysts have attempted to formulate such definitions, and their views appear similar, as illustrated by the following four influential definitions.

According to Barnard (1938: 4),

formal organization is that kind of coöperation among men that is conscious, deliberate, purposeful.

According to March and Simon (1958: 4)

> organizations are assemblages of interacting human beings and they are the largest assemblages in our society that have anything resembling a central coordinative system. . . . The high specificity of structure and coordination within organizations—as contrasted with the diffuse and variable relations *among* organizations and among unorganized individuals—marks off the individual organization as a sociological unit comparable in significance to the individual organism in biology.

According to Blau and Scott (1962: 5),

> since the distinctive characteristic of . . . organizations is that they have been formally established for the explicit purpose of achieving certain goals, the term "formal organizations" is used to designate them (Blau and Scott, 1962: 5).[9]

And, according to Etzioni (1964: 3),

> organizations are social units (or human groupings) deliberately constructed and reconstructed to seek specific goals.

All of these definitions point to the existence of two structural features that distinguish organizations from other types of collectivities.

> •Organizations are collectivities oriented to the pursuit of relatively specific goals. They are "purposeful" in the sense that the activities and interactions of participants are centrally coordinated to achieve specified goals. Goals are *specific* to the extent that they are explicit, are clearly defined, and provide unambiguous criteria for selecting among alternative activities.
> •Organizations are collectivities that exhibit a relatively high degree of formalization. The cooperation among participants is "conscious" and "deliberate"; the structure of relations is made explicit and can be "deliberately constructed and reconstructed." As previously defined, a structure is *formalized* to the extent that the rules governing behavior are precisely and explicitly formulated and to the extent that roles and role relations are prescribed independently of the personal attributes of individuals occupying positions in the structure.

It is the combination of relatively high goal specificity and relatively high formalization that distinguishes organizations from other types of collectivities. Note that both goal specificity and formalization are viewed as variables: organizations may be characterized by higher or lower levels

---

[9]This definition, which I developed with Blau a good many years ago, now strikes me as somewhat misleading. Emphasis is placed on the conditions present at the founding of the organization: on whether the unit was "formally established for the explicit purpose of achieving certain goals." The wording suggests that factors associated with the founding of the unit—in particular, the intent of the founders—are of critical importance. Such historical considerations seem much less important to me now than the current state of the system—that is, the extent of goal specificity and of formalization.

of each. Nevertheless, as a structural type, organizations are expected to exhibit higher levels of formalization and goal specificity than other types of collectivities, such as primary groups, families, communities, and social movements. In general—there certainly are exceptions—families and kinship structures tend to rank relatively high on formalization but low on goal specificity (Litwak, 1968; Litwak and Meyer, 1966); social movements tend to exhibit low levels of formalization combined with higher levels of goal specificity,[10] although the specificity of goals varies greatly from movement to movement and from time to time (Gusfield, 1968); and communities are characterized by low levels of both goal specificity and formalization (Hillery, 1968: 145–52; and Moe, 1959).

We arrive, then, at the first definition: *organizations are collectivities oriented to the pursuit of relatively specific goals and exhibiting relatively highly formalized social structures.* Note that this definition focuses not only on the distinctive characteristics of organizations but also on their normative structure. It is compatible with the rational system perspective.

### A Natural System Definition

Gouldner (1959) reminds us that the distinguishing features of a phenomenon are not its only characteristics and, indeed, may not be the most important ones. Although organizations often—not always—espouse specific goals, the behavior of participants is frequently not guided by them, nor can they be safely used to predict organizational actions. Similarly, formal role definitions and written rules may have been developed, but they sometimes provide few if any restrictions on the behavior of members. Thus, if the behavioral structure is attended to, rather than the normative structure, the first definition of organizations can be quite misleading.

It is of interest that although many conventional organizations, such as public schools and government mental-health services, have felt the need to develop explicit goal statements and formalized job titles and procedures, other organizations have decided to do away with such superfluous decorations and camouflage. Such appears to be the case with a set of organizational forms labeled *collectivist* organizations (Rothschild-Whitt, 1979). These organizations include many recently developed innovative forms, particularly in the service sector—for example, free medical clinics, alternative schools, rape-counseling centers, and legal collectives—as well as some earlier forms, such as food and producer cooperatives. Some of these organizations clearly are pursuing relatively broad and diffuse objectives, such as societal reform or the promotion of more open and authentic relations among their participants. Others have defined relatively specific objectives. However, virtually all of them eschew formalization as a structural characteristic. Rothschild-Whitt's (1979) survey of the structural features of collectivist organizations suggests that many go to

---

[10]In recent years, analysts of movements have placed more emphasis on their organizational features—for example, the extent to which they are guided by a full-time, paid staff and have regularized mechanisms for obtaining resources and recruits and for setting goals. (See Zald and Ash, 1966; McCarthy and Zald, 1973.) It would appear that this shift in emphasis reflects both changes in the perspectives employed by social analysts, who are increasingly sensitive to organizational features, and changes in the nature of social movements, which are more likely to adopt organizational models.

great lengths to eliminate or reduce formalization. They deny the authority of office, seek to minimize the promulgation of rules and procedures, attempt to eliminate status gradations among participants, and do away with role differentiation and specialization of function. Great stress is laid on equality in decision making, and differences in interests and preferences among individual members are deemed of great importance. The personal qualities of members do matter! Thus, if our first definition of organization is used, collectivities such as these are excluded.[11]

A natural system conception of organizations is not entirely based on what organizations are not, although this is an important ingredient in the perspective. Positive attention is devoted to examining the way in which organizations—like all collectivities—attend to the needs or requirements of their own system. Organizations are viewed as organic systems imbued with a strong drive to survive, to maintain themselves as systems. The development of informal structures and distinctive cultures is regarded as an important means to this end. These structures grow out of the natural abilities and interests of participants and enable the collectivity to benefit from the human resources of its membership.

Hence, a second definition of organizations, useful for viewing them as natural systems, is proposed: *organizations are collectivities whose participants share a common interest in the survival of the system and who engage in collective activities, informally structured, to secure this end.*

### An Open System Definition

The previous definitions tend to view the organization as a closed system, separate from its environment and comprising a set of stable and easily identified participants. However, organizations are not closed systems, sealed off from their environments, but are open to and dependent on flows of personnel and resources from outside. Also, if an organization is to survive, it must induce participants to contribute resources, energy, and time to it. Individuals have different interests and value various inducements: they join and leave the organization depending on the bargains they can strike—the relative advantage to be had from staying or going. Thus, rather than viewing the organization as a coherent system of relations oriented to the pursuit of specific goals, we might view it more accurately as an opportunistic collection of divergent interest groups temporarily banded together.

We arrive, then, at a third definition, useful for viewing organizations as open systems: *organizations are coalitions of shifting interest groups that develop goals by negotiation; the structure of the coalition, its activities, and its outcomes are strongly influenced by environmental factors.*

---

[11]We would argue, however, that although these forms are excluded by the rational system definition, they are also illuminated by it. Collectivist forms do not simply exhibit relatively low levels of formalization; they are characterized by active hostility to formalization. They are self-consciously and energetically antiformal in practice and, more important, in their ideologies and normative systems. Indeed, much of the interest and energy they generate among their participants can be directly attributed to the ideological battle they wage against the more conventional formalized and hierarchical models. They are organized in opposition to the prevailing model of organizations—a model so widely shared that its *negation* can serve as a potent basis of organization.

It is no doubt unsettling to be confronted so early with three such diverse views of organizations. But better to know the worst at the outset! The definitions are quite different in that they not only encompass somewhat divergent types of collectivities but also emphasize different facets of a given organization. But this is precisely why they are useful. It is essential to remember that definitions are neither true nor false but are only more or less helpful in calling attention to certain aspects of the phenomenon under study. With the help of these definitions, and the more general perspectives with which they are associated, we can expect to see and learn more about organizations than would be possible were we to employ a single point of view. As we proceed, we will call attention to the stimulating vistas and profound depths charted by each of the conceptions. Each has its own charms (as well as its own blemishes), and each carries its own truth (as well as its own biases).

### A Note on Bureaucracy

The term *bureaucracy* will come up again and again throughout this volume, and so we would do well to confront this concept head-on at an early stage. The term is a problem because, although frequently used by students of organizations, it is defined in many ways. The term also carries with it a great deal of emotional freight. For many the terms bureaucracy and bureaucrat are epithets—accusations connoting rule-encumbered inefficiency and mindless overconformity. (See, e.g., Mises, 1944; Parkinson, 1957.) Indeed, these are probably the most common views of bureaucracy held by the people in this society. By contrast, the foremost student of bureaucracy, Max Weber, used the term to refer to that form of administrative organization that, in his view, was capable of attaining the highest level of efficiency! (Weber, 1947 trans.: 339).

If we set aside for the moment its pejorative uses, we can see that organizational analysts employ the concept descriptively in at least three different ways. Some use the term bureaucracy as a general synonym for organization; others reserve it for public organizations or the administrative units of the nation-state; and still others, most notably Weber, use the term to designate a particular type of administrative structure. All of this can be very confusing, not only to beginning students but to all of us who attempt to study organizations. Although we cannot dispel all of the confusion, we will try to be clear about how we propose to use the concept, and we can suggest how our own usage relates to some of the other definitions.

Our definition of bureaucracy is indebted to the work of Bendix, who writes: "Seen historically, bureaucratization may be interpreted as the increasing subdivision of the functions which the owner-managers of the early enterprises had performed personally in the course of their daily routine" (1956: 211–12). Such functions include supervision, personnel selection and management, accounting and financial management, record keeping, job design, and long-range planning. In this sense, bureaucracy refers to the middle layer of the organization: the head of the organization—whether president, dictator, owner, or leader—is excluded, as are the lower levels—for example, the production workers. A useful way of thinking about a bureaucracy is that it consists of those positions (or activities) whose function is to maintain the organization itself. In short, *bureaucracy* is defined as the existence of a specialized administrative staff.

Like formalization and goal specificity, bureaucracy should be viewed as a variable: organizations vary in terms of how much of their personnel resources are devoted to administrative, as opposed to production, activities. Bendix, following Melman (1951), has proposed that for industrial organizations a crude but serviceable index of the degree of bureaucratization is the ratio of administrative (salaried) to production (wage) employees. Data compiled by Bendix (1956: 214) from several sources show that for a number of Western countries the ratio of administrative to production workers in industry steadily increased from under 1:10 in 1900 to over 1:5 by 1950. And there is evidence that the rate of bureaucratic expansion may be increasing. Edwards (1979: 135) reports that one important component of the bureaucracy, the proportion of foremen in manufacturing companies, increased at a rate of 15 percent between 1910 and 1940 but jumped to a rate of 67 percent between 1940 and 1970. The causes of increased bureaucratization will be discussed in Part Three of this volume.

Although the precise identification of bureaucratic positions or activities may often pose problems to the investigator, the conceptual distinction suggested by Bendix seems clear in the case of industrial or commercial organizations. Unfortunately, this is not the case for public organizations. Consider the Internal Revenue Service of the State Department of our federal government. In the case of these units, the entire organization is devoted to administrative activities! We believe that our conception of bureaucracy can encompass these situations, but only if we are clear about the level of analysis at which we approach such systems.

If we choose the ecological level and focus on the State Department as an organization within a larger system of organizations, as a specialized administrative arm of the executive office of the president, then it is consistent with our definition to view the entire department as a bureaucracy. These "bureaus" and their officials may appropriately be seen as working to maintain our nation. On the other hand, if we choose the structural level of analysis, concentrating on the internal structures and processes of the State Department, then we will observe that there is within this bureau a specialized administrative staff that assists the secretary of state in the administration of the department. Each bureau has its own internal bureaucracy: a group of officials who do not directly carry out the work of the agency but supervise, regulate, and support those who do (see Downs, 1967).

Weber's conception differs from our own. As noted, he defines bureaucracy as a special type of administrative structure—the structures that developed in association with a rational-legal mode of authority relation. The distinctive characteristics of these structures include a clear differentiation of responsibilities among officials, the hierarchical arrangement of offices, the use of technical criteria of recruitment, and impersonal norms governing the relations among officials. Weber argued that these bureaucratic structures—present in both private and public organizations—were gradually replacing administrative systems based on traditional authority relations. His conception of these structures and the processes leading to their ascendancy will be discussed in more detail in Chapter 2. We introduce it here merely to distinguish it from our own definition of bureaucracy.

It is of interest that from all three points of view described, the level of bureaucratization is increasing. If we define bureaucratization at the structural level as an increase in the proportion of resources devoted to administrative compared with production activities, then, as we have seen, bureaucracy is increasing. If we define bureaucratization at the ecological level as an increase in the size of the administrative machinery of the nation-state, then in virtually all contemporary societies bureaucracy is increasing. It is in this sense that Jacoby (1973 trans.) writes of *The Bureaucratization of the World*. And if we adopt Weber's definition and view bureaucracy as a special type of administrative structure, then he is clearly correct that in most modernizing societies over the past century, bureaucracies have been replacing more traditional administrative forms. It is with reference to Weber's definition of bureaucracy that some analysts, such as Bennis (Bennis and Slater, 1968), assert that the most advanced organizations are currently moving toward the development of *postbureaucratic* forms. These developments will be described and evaluated in Chapter 9.

Finally, although we will not ourselves employ the term bureaucracy as a pejorative label for stagnant, incompetent administration, we will want to consider the causes of administrative pathology and, in particular, to struggle to understand how it is that arrangements created and adopted to ensure efficient and responsive administrative performance sometimes—indeed, all too often—result in the exact opposite. These questions are addressed in Chapter 12.

## SUMMARY

Organizations are important objects of study and concern for many reasons. They are vital mechanisms for pursuing collective goals in modern societies. They are not neutral tools because they affect what they produce; they function as collective actors that independently possess certain rights and powers. Both as mechanisms and as actors, organizations are alleged to be the source of some of contemporary society's most serious problems. Organizations encompass generic social processes but carry them out by means of distinctive structural arrangements.

Although an interest in organizational forms and processes may be traced far back in history, a distinctive field of sociological inquiry focusing on the creation and empirical testing of generalized knowledge concerning organizations did not develop until after 1950. This development was linked with and greatly stimulated by the translation into English of Max Weber's historical and comparative studies of administrative organizations, conducted during the first two decades of this century. The field of organizational studies is becoming increasingly interdisciplinary. Among the bases on which studies vary is the level at which analysis is carried out: some research occurs at the social psychological level and emphasizes the interaction of individuals and groups within organizations and the impact of organizational characteristics on these processes; other studies are conducted at the structural level and attempt to account for variations in the patterned features of organizations; and still other research is focused at the ecological level, viewing the organization as an actor or subunit in a more comprehensive system of relationships.

Three contrasting definitions of organizations are presented. Each is associated with one of three perspectives on organizations to be elaborated in Part Two: the rational system, the natural system, and the open system perspectives. The first definition views organizations as highly formalized collectivities oriented to the pursuit of specific goals. The second definition views organizations as collectivities seeking to survive. And the third definition views organizations as coalitions of interest groups highly influenced by their environments. Each of these definitions is viewed as opening up a useful, if partial, view of organizations.

# PART TWO

# THREE PERSPECTIVES ON ORGANIZATIONS

In this century, three more or less distinct perspectives have been employed in the study of organizational structure. The term *perspective* is used advisedly since we will be dealing in each case not with a single, unified model of organizational structure but rather with a number of varying approaches that bear a strong family resemblance. Thus, our concern will be with three types of approaches or three schools of thought, the notion of perspective serving as a conceptual umbrella under which we may gather the related views. To add further to the complexity, the three perspectives partially conflict, partially overlap, and partially complement one another.

An understanding of these perspectives is valuable for several reasons. It is very difficult to comprehend or to fully utilize the large literature on organizations without knowledge of the differing perspectives underlying this work. Why does one analyst concentrate on one type of problem while another completely ignores it? Why do some investigators emphasize historical materials while others deal exclusively with contemporary data? These are the sorts of questions we can begin to answer by examining the perspectives employed. Also, we should expect to receive help not only in making sense out of past studies but in examining the current efforts of organizational analysts. For although these perspectives emerged at different times, later perspectives have not succeeded in supplanting earlier ones: the three perspectives continue to coexist and to claim their share of advocates.

Although we devote some effort to describing the history of each perspective, the perspectives are not primarily of historical interest. They are analytical models intended to guide—and to interpret—empirical research. They have changed over time as one school has replaced another within each of the traditions, but to a surprising extent, the general outlines of the three perspectives have remained reasonably clear.

In their pure form, the perspectives share many of the features of *paradigms* as described by Kuhn in his influential essay on scientific revolutions. Kuhn describes paradigms as "models from which spring particular coherent traditions of scientific research" (1962: 10).

The three perspectives to be considered are the rational, the natural, and the open system perspectives. They are considered in the order of their emergence. For each, we first discuss the basic model that forms its core. Then we consider three or four representative theorists or schools within that tradition. Each discussion concludes with an evaluation of the contributions and limitations of the perspective. Chapter 2 reviews the rational system perspective, following its development from Weber to Simon. In Chapter 3, we describe the natural system perspective, beginning with Michels and ending with Parsons. And Chapter 4 reviews the open system perspective, from its origins in the general systems theory as advanced by Bertalanffy through its application to organizations by analysts ranging from Boulding to Weick. Most of the work reviewed in these introductory chapters extends only up to the 1960s. These chapters provide the first, not the last word on perspectives on organizations.

Beyond this point, matters become more complex and, we think, more interesting. There have been a number of attempts to combine the perspectives into more complex models. In Chapter 5 we review three of these efforts by other theorists and propose a fourth of our own. Combining the perspectives provides a framework that enables us to conceptually "place" a number of the more important, recent theoretical developments, including transactions costs, resource dependency, population ecology, Marxist approaches, and institutionalization theory.

# 2
# organizations as rational systems

A well-designed machine is an instance of total organization, that is, a series of interrelated means contrived to achieve a single end. The machine consists always of particular parts that have no meaning and no function separate from the organized entity to which they contribute. A machine consists of a coherent bringing together of all parts toward the highest possible efficiency of the functioning whole, or interrelationships marshalled wholly toward a given result. In the ideal machine, there can be no extraneous part, no extraneous movement; all is set, part for part, motion for motion, toward the functioning of the whole. The machine is, then, a perfect instance of total rationalization of a field of action and of total organization. This is perhaps even more quickly evident in that larger machine, the assembly line.

John William Ward (1964)

From the rational system perspective, organizations are instruments designed to attain specified goals. How blunt or fine an instrument they are depends on many factors that are summarized by the concept of rationality of structure. The term *rationality* in this context is used in the narrow sense of *technical* or *functional* rationality (Mannheim, 1950 trans.: 53) and refers to the extent to which a series of actions is organized in such a way as to lead to predetermined goals with maximum efficiency. Thus, rationality refers not to the selection of goals but to their implementation. Indeed, it is perfectly possible to pursue irrational or foolish goals by rational means. Captain Ahab in Melville's classic *Moby Dick* chases the white whale across the seven seas musing, "All my means are sane, my motive and my object mad." Nazi Germany provides a more terrible, nonfiction example. Adolf Hitler's insane objective of eradicating Europe's Jewish population was efficiently pursued by hosts of functionaries who, like Adolph Eichmann, took the goal as given and worked faithfully to rationally bring it about. (Arendt, 1963) It is essential to keep in mind the restricted definition of *rationality* used within the rational system perspective.

## THE DEFINING CHARACTERISTICS

From the standpoint of the rational system perspective, the behavior of organizations is viewed as actions performed by purposeful and coordinated agents. The language employed connotes this image of rational calculation: such terms as *information, efficiency, optimization, implementation,* and *design* occur frequently. But another somewhat different set of terms also occurs within this perspective; it indicates the cognitive limitations of the individual decision maker and the effects of the organizational context in which rational choices are made. These terms—*constraints, authority, rules, directives, jurisdiction, performance programs, coordination*—imply that the rationality of behavior within organizations takes place within (some analysts would argue, because of) clearly specified limits.

It is no accident that the key features of organizations emphasized by rational system theorists are the very characteristics that have been noted to distinguish organizations from other types of collectivities. Rational system theorists stress goal specificity and formalization because each of these elements makes an important contribution to the rationality of organizational action.

### Goal Specificity

Goals are conceptions of desired ends. These conceptions vary in the precision and specificity of their criteria of desirability. Specific goals provide unambiguous criteria for selecting among alternative activities. As viewed by economists or by decision theorists, goals are translated into a set of preference or utility functions that represent the value of alternative sets of consequences. Without clear preference orderings among alternatives, rational assessment and choice are not possible.

Specific goals not only supply criteria for choosing among alternative activities; they guide decisions about how the organization structure itself is to be designed. They specify what tasks are to be performed, what kinds of personnel are to be hired, how resources are to be allocated among participants. The more general or diffuse the goals, the more difficult it is to design a structure to pursue them.

It is important to note that some organizations espouse quite vague and general goals, but in their actual daily operation are guided by relatively specific goals that do provide criteria for choosing among alternative activities and for designing the organization structure itself. Consider the case of education. Although both educators and laypeople will argue endlessly about the true function of education and about the virtues of liberal arts versus more practical types of programs, within a given school there will be considerable agreement on such matters as what disciplines should be represented among the faculty, what courses will count toward graduation, and how many units are required for a student to graduate. With agreement on such matters as these, administrators can safely allow the faculty occasionally to debate the ultimate aims of education. Similarly, although physicians cannot agree on abstract definitions of health or illness, they do successfully organize their work around such proximate outcomes as relieving pain and prolonging life.

Vague goals do not provide a solid basis for formal organizations.

Either the goals become more specific and limited over time, as often happens, or the structures developed are likely to be unstable and amorphous. Collective movements such as radical political sects or protest groups may temporarily succeed in mobilizing resources and participants around vague concepts such as liberation or ecology. Indeed, their generality may broaden their appeal and enlist the support of diverse groups. But unless more specific and delimited goals emerge, we would not expect such movements to give rise to formal organizations.

The most precise description of the manner in which specific goals support rational behavior in organizations is that developed by Herbert Simon, whose classic, *Administrative Behavior,* first appeared in 1945. His ideas on this subject will be summarized later in this chapter as an example of one of the major contributions to the rational system perspective.

### Formalization

All rational system theorists assume the existence and presume the importance of a formalized structure, but few make explicit the contributions that formalization makes to rationality of behavior in organizations. Let us attempt to do so.

Recall that a structure is formalized to the extent that the rules governing behavior are precisely and explicitly formulated and to the extent that roles and role relations are prescribed independently of the personal attributes of individuals occupying positions in the structure. Formalization may be viewed as an attempt to make behavior more predictable by standardizing and regulating it. This, in turn, permits "stable expectations to be formed by each member of the group as to the behavior of the other members under specified conditions. Such stable expectations are an essential precondition to a rational consideration of the consequences of action in a social group." (Simon, 1957: 100)

Formalization may also be viewed as an attempt to make more explicit and visible the structure of relationships among a set of roles and the principles that govern behavior in the system. It becomes possible to diagram the organization's structure or work flow and then consciously to study and manipulate it—to design and redesign the division of responsibilities, the flow of information or materials, or the ways in which participants report to one another. As Gouldner (1959: 405) notes,

> fundamentally, the rational model implies a "mechanical" model, in that it views the organization as a structure of manipulable parts, each of which is separately modifiable with a view to enhancing the efficiency of the whole. Individual organizational elements are seen as subject to successful and planned modification, enactable by deliberate decision.

Thus, in a fundamental sense, the organizational structure is viewed as a means, as an instrument, which can be modified as necessary to improve performance. Organizational designers and managers draw and redraw the organizational chart; coaches attempt to improve performance by diagraming plays and giving chalk talks; and consultants are employed to recommend better arrangements for achieving business goals. In recent years, highly technical managerial systems, such as management by objectives (MBO), planning, programming, and budgeting systems (PPBS), program evaluation review techniques (PERT)—all designed to provide greater visibility and, hence, greater accountability for the critical work flows—have been developed and widely adopted to facilitate rational decision making within complex organizational systems. (See Haberstroh, 1965; Odione, 1965; Drucker, 1976; Wildavsky, 1979: 26–40.)

Formalization can contribute to rationality in other, less obvious ways. In addition to making behavior more available for conscious design, the structuring of expectations prior to interaction carries with it another distinct advantage. Laboratory research by Bales (1953) documents the strains and tensions generated when a status structure begins to emerge among individuals who entered the situation as presumed status-equals. These status battles and their associated interpersonal tensions are reduced by the prestructuring of differentiated role expectations in which an individual is assigned a role prior to his or her participation. Thus, in an experimental study, Carter and his colleagues (1953) found that group leaders who had been appointed to their position by the experimenter spent less time attempting to assert their power and defend their position and encountered less resistance to their leadership efforts than leaders who emerged on their own. (See also Verba, 1961: 161–72.)

Formalization also serves to objectify the structure—to make the definitions of roles and relationships appear to be both objective and external to the participating actors. These qualities contribute substantially to the efficacy of these systems in controlling behavior. A series of experiments conducted by Zucker (1977) demonstrates this effect. Subjects placed in an ambiguous situation were much more likely to accept influence from another when that person was defined as holding a specified organizational position (not, by the way, a position of authority but simply a named office) than when the person was described simply as "another person."

The social cement that binds and regulates activities and interactions in informal groups is the sociometric structure—the patterning of affective ties among participants. The creation of a formal structure constitutes an important functional alternative to the sociometric structure. With formalization, the smooth functioning of the organization is to some degree made independent of the feelings—negative or positive—that particular members have for one another. As Merton (1957: 195) notes, "formality facilitates the interaction of the occupants of offices despite their (possibly hostile) private attitudes toward one another." Indeed, many organizations discourage the development of positive sentiments among their members for fear that such emotional ties will undermine discipline and judgment and interfere with attempts to deploy participants rationally.

Formalization makes allowances for the finitude of humans. The process of succession—the movement of individuals into and out of offices—can be routinized and regularized so that one appropriately trained person can replace another with minimal disturbance to the functioning of the organization. In this sense, organizations can—although few actually do—achieve a kind of immortality. The Roman Catholic church may be cited as a particularly successful example.

Formalized structures are thus rendered independent of the participation of any particular individual; a related consequence is that it becomes less essential to recruit unusually gifted individuals for the key positions. The power and influence of leaders can be determined in part by the definition of their offices and not made a function of their personal qualities—their charisma. Referring to political structures, MacIver notes, "The man who commands may be no wiser, no abler, may be, in some sense no better than the average of his fellows; sometimes, by any intrinsic standard, he is inferior to them. Here is the magic of government." (1947: 13) More generally, here is the magic of formalization. To explain more clearly the alchemy of this process, Wolin (1960: 383) draws an analogy between the formalization of structure and scientific method:

> Method, like organization, is the salvation of puny men, the compensatory device for individual foibles, the gadget which allows mediocrity to transcend its limitations. . . . organization, by simplifying and routinizing procedures, eliminates the need for surpassing talent. It is predicated on "average human beings."

In the highly formalized organization, the innovating entrepreneur is supplanted by a corps of administrators and technical specialists. Leadership, even innovation, is routinized and regularized by being incorporated into the formal structure. (See Schumpeter, 1947; Galbraith, 1967.)

We have reviewed some of the major contributions that formalization of structure can make to rational functioning of the organization. We must note here, however, that we have discussed only the *form* of a formalized structure; nothing has been said about its *content*. That is, we have stated that in a formalized structure positions are specified, roles are defined, and role relationships are prescribed independently of the personal attributes of participants, and we have indicated certain advantages that stem from such arrangements. But we have not concerned ourselves with the content of these specifications, definitions, and prescriptions. The content of the formal structure has also been of great concern to certain rational system theorists, as we will see when we discuss their contributions in the next section.

## SELECTED SCHOOLS

The preceding discussion represents an effort to distill the central elements characterizing the rational system perspective. This perspective does not reflect a unitary position but includes a set of somewhat varied, historically distinct approaches. Before briefly characterizing some of these major schools, we must first acknowledge that only one of them— that associated with Simon's work—explicitly emphasizes goal specificity. The rest assume its presence. And few concern themselves with formalization per se but consider specific ways in which organizations can or should be designed to attain maximum effectiveness. That is, most of the advocates of the rational system position assume the importance of formal structure and concern themselves with specifying the nature or content of that structure. Four schools will be briefly described: Taylor's scientific management; attempts by Fayol and others to formulate administrative principles; Weber's theory of bureaucracy; and Simon's discussion of administrative behavior.

### Taylor's Scientific Management

The scientific management approach received its primary impetus from the work of Frederick W. Taylor (1911) in the late nineteenth and early twentieth centuries but was carried forward by the contributions of others, such as Frank and Lillian Gilbreth, Henry Gantt, and Charles Bedeaux. Taylor and his followers insisted that it was possible to scientifically analyze tasks performed by individual workers in order to discover those procedures that would produce the maximum output with the minimum input of energies and resources. Efforts were concentrated on analyzing individual tasks, but attempts to rationalize labor at the level of the individual worker inevitably led to changes in the entire structure of work arrangements. Ward (1964) describes the sequence of changes that resulted from Taylor's efforts to improve the efficiency of performing such menial tasks as shoveling coal and iron ore in a steel mill:

> First, a variety of kinds of shovels had to be designed to handle different kinds of materials. That also meant building shovel rooms in the various parts of the yard, so that a gang would have the proper tools at hand. To eliminate the waste motion of wandering about so large a yard, it meant, as Taylor said, "organizing and planning work at least a day in advance," so that when men checked in, they would be at that day's work. This meant, Taylor reported, building a labor office for a planning staff—a bureaucracy, as we would say. Large maps of the yard were then necessary to show at a glance the location of different kinds of work and the location of men. Furthermore, the installation of a telephone network was essential for more effective interior communication. Once the yard was mapped so that one could see at a glance the relationships in time and sequence between different jobs, it led, naturally enough, to the reorganization of the yard itself, so that materials could be delivered or dumped in a more logical sequence.
>   One can see readily enough what happened. Taylor's attempt to make the crudest physical act of labor efficient led inexorably to a further organization of every aspect of the production process. (Ward, 1964: 64–65)

It was not only, or even primarily, the lot of workers that was to be altered by the introduction of scientific management: the role of management was also to be transformed. Taylor aspired to replace the arbitrary and capricious activities of managers with analytical, scientific procedures:

> Under scientific management arbitrary power, arbitrary dictation, ceases; and every single subject, large and small, becomes the question for scientific investigation, for reduction to law. . . .
>   The man at the head of the business under scientific management is governed by rules and laws which have been developed through hundreds of experiments just as much as the workman is, and the standards which have been developed are equitable. (Taylor, 1947: 211, 189)

The activities of both managers and workers were to be rationalized; both were equally subject to the regimen of science.

Taylor believed that the adoption of scientific management principles by industrial concerns would usher in a new era of industrial peace. The interests of labor and management would be rendered compatible. Workers would be scientifically selected to perform those tasks for which they were best suited. Scientifically determined procedures would allow them to work at peak efficiency, in return for which they would receive top wages. "Once work was scientifically plotted, Taylor felt, there could be no disputes about how hard one should work or the pay one should receive for labor. 'As reasonably might we insist on bargaining about the time and place of the rising and setting sun,' he once said." (Bell, 1960: 228) Managers would cooperate with workers in devising appropriate work arrangements and pay scales and would enjoy the fruits of maximum profits.

The underlying spirit of Taylor's approach—an amalgam of the Protestant ethic, social Darwinism, and a view of human beings as motivated exclusively by economic incentives—found widespread acceptance among American managers at the turn of the century. However, many were disquieted by Taylor's vision of their own new role: "After all, Taylor had questioned their good judgment and superior ability which had been the subject of public celebration for many years. Hence, many employers regarded his methods as an unwarranted interference with managerial prerogatives." (Bendix, 1956: 280) Workers for their part resisted time-study procedures and attempts to standardize every aspect of their performance and rejected incentive sytems requiring them to perform continuously at a peak level of efficiency. Nevertheless scientific management has had a profound and lasting effect on industrial practice and on theoretical conceptions of work organization.[1]

### Administrative Theory

A second approach, developing concurrently with scientific management, emphasized management functions and attempted to generate broad administrative principles that would serve as guidelines for the rationalization of organizational activities. Whereas Taylor and his disciples proposed to rationalize the organization from the "bottom up"— changes in the performance of individual tasks affecting the larger structure of work relations—the administrative management theorists worked to rationalize the organization from the "top down." Henri Fayol, a French industrialist writing in the early part of this century, was probably the earliest exponent of this approach, but his ideas did not become widely available in this country until 1949, when his major work was translated. Influential participants in this movement in the United States included two General Motors executives, Mooney and Reiley (1939), whose treatise on management principles gained a wide following, and

---

[1]Perhaps the most useful overview of Taylor's conception is contained in his testimony before the Special House Committee to Investigate the Taylor and Other Systems of Shop Management in 1912. This testimony is reprinted in Taylor (1947). Summaries of and commentaries on his contribution will be found in Bell (1960: 222–37), Bendix (1956: 274–81), and Mouzelis (1968: 78–87). A severe critique of Taylor's work from a Marxist perspective is provided by Braverman (1974: 85–138).

Gulick and Urwick, who in 1937 collaborated to edit the volume *Papers on the Science of Administration.*

The various contributors to this perspective did not reach agreement as to the number of principles required or the precise formulation of many specific principles, but there was considerable consensus on the importance of two types of activities: coordination and specialization (Massie, 1965; Tausky, 1970). The major principles developed to guide coordination activities include the scalar principle, which emphasizes the hierarchical organizational form in which all participants are linked into a single pyramidal structure of control relations; the unity-of-command principle, specifying that no organizational participants should receive orders from more than one superior; the span-of-control principle, which emphasizes that no superior should have more subordinates than can be effectively overseen (theorists were unable to agree on the precise number of subordinates who could be supervised); and the exception principle, which recommends that all routine matters be handled by subordinates and that the superior be free to deal with exceptional situations to which existing rules are inapplicable. Specialization issues include decisions both about how various activities are to be distributed among organizational positions and about how such positions can most effectively be grouped into work units or departments. Among the principles espoused to guide these types of decisions is the departmentalization principle, which maintains that activities should be grouped so as to combine homogeneous or related activities within the same organizational unit. Homogeneity might be based on similarity of purpose (activities contributing to the same subgoal—for example, marketing), process (activities requiring similar operations—for example, typing), clientele (activities performed on the same set of recipients—for example, a medical team organized around the care of a specific group of patients), or place (for example, services provided to individuals in a given regional territory). Also proposed is the line-staff principle, by which all activities directly concerned with achieving organizational goals are designated as line functions, to be distinguished from staff activities, which consist primarily of advice, service, or support. Staff units are to be segregated from the scalar organization of power and responsible and subordinate to appropriate line units.

Note the heavy emphasis on formalization implicit in these principles. Careful specification of work activities and concern for their grouping and coordination is the hallmark of the formalized structure. Mooney (1937: 92) makes explicit this call for formalization by distinguishing between jobs (positions) and the person on the job:

> In every organization there is a collective job to be done, consisting always of the sum of many individual jobs, and the task of administration, operating through management, is the co-ordination of all the human effort necessary to this end. Such co-ordination, however, always presupposes the jobs to be coordinated. The job as such is therefore antecedent to the man on the job, and the sound co-ordination of these jobs, considered simply as jobs, must be the first and necessary condition in the effective co-ordination of the human factor.

The more astute administrative theorists recognized that their managerial principles furnished at best only broad guidelines for decision making. Thus, Fayol (1949 trans.: 19) reminds practitioners,

> The soundness and good working order of the body corporate depends on a certain number of conditions termed indiscriminately principles, laws, rules. For preference I shall adopt the term principles whilst dissociating it from any suggestion of rigidity, for there is nothing rigid or absolute in management affairs, it is all a question of proportion. Seldom do we have to apply the same principle twice in identical conditions; allowance must be made for different changing cirumstances.

And Gulick (Gulick and Urwick, 1937: 31) cautions,

> Students of administration have long sought a single principle of effective departmentalization just as alchemists sought the philosopher's stone. But they have sought in vain. There is apparently no one most effective system of departmentalism.

In spite of such disclaimers, the managerial principles enunciated by the administrative theorists came under increasing attack. Three types of criticisms have been made: (1) that the principles are mere truisms or common-sense pronouncements; (2) that the principles are based on questionable premises; and (3) that the principles occur in pairs or clusters of contradictory statements with little guidance for application to a given situation. (See Massie, 1965: 406.) With respect to the first type of criticism, it is quite correct that many of the proposed administrative principles are primarily definitional, outlining the characteristics of a hierarchically structured formal organization, whereas others are sufficiently vague and imprecise to be of little help to practitioners or researchers. In regard to the second, Massie (1965: 405) has provided a lengthy listing of questionable premises, including the assumption that individuals are motivated primarily by economic interest, that they prefer the security of a definite assignment to the freedom of discretionary activity, that they prefer not to work and so must be constrained to do so, and that managers are capable of predicting work needs in advance and establishing effective arrangements for work and its coordination. The problem is not that these assumptions are inevitably false, but that they are not made explicit enough to serve as specifications for the application of the principles. The third type of criticism has been given greatest currency by Simon, whose influential text on administration commenced with "an indictment of much current writing about administrative matters" (1957: 36). Simon, examining one after another principle, concluded variously that they involved inconsistencies, lack of specification, or "a deceptive simplicity—a simplicity that conceals fundamental ambiguities" (1957: 21).

Without gainsaying any of these criticisms, we can admire what the administrative theorists attempted to do. They were pioneers in identifying the fundamental features of formal organizational structure, audaciously clinging to the view that all organizations contain certain common structural characteristics. With the improved vision of hindsight, it is now apparent that their search was confounded not so much by their inadequate theory of motivation or by the prescriptive cast of their propositions as by their failure to develop conditional generalizations—statements that specify the limits of their applicability to particular situations or types of organizations.[2]

### Weber's Theory of Bureaucracy

Contemporaneous with and yet independent of the scientific management school and those who attempted to formulate administrative principles was the work of Max Weber, the influential German sociologist writing at the turn of the century. Weber's analysis of administrative structures was only a limited aspect of his much larger interest in accounting for the unique features of Western civilization. (See Bendix, 1960.) In his view, what was distinctive was the growth of rationality in the West, and his active mind roamed across legal, religious, political, and economic systems, as well as administrative structures, as he searched for materials to test and extend his notions by comparing and contrasting differing cultures and historical periods. Weber's analysis of administrative systems can be fully appreciated only if it is seen in this larger context, since his listing of the structural characteristics of bureaucracy was generated in an attempt to differentiate this more rational form from earlier forms.

In his justly famous typology, Weber (1947 trans.: 328) distinguishes three types of authority:

•*Traditional authority*—resting on an established belief in the sanctity of immemorial traditions and the legitimacy of those exercising authority under them

•*Rational-legal authority*—resting on a belief in the "legality" of patterns of normative rules and the right of those elevated to authority under such rules to issue commands

•*Charismatic authority*—resting on devotion to the specific and exceptional sanctity, heroism or exemplary character of an individual person, and of the normative patterns or order revealed or ordained by him.

Clearly, the basis for the typology is differences in the beliefs by which legitimacy is attributed to an authority relation. Associated with each authority type is a distinctive administrative structure. Traditional authority gives rise to the particularistic and diffuse structures exemplified by patrimonialism and its various manifestations, including gerontocracy, patriarchalism, and feudalism. (See Delany, 1963; Dibble, 1965.) The simplest way to visualize a *patrimonial* system is as a household writ large: an estate or production organization governed by a ruler-owner who in managing the enterprise relies for assistance on a variety of dependents, ranging from slaves to serfs to sons. Rational-legal authority provides the basis for the more specific and universalistic structures of which the most highly developed form is the bureaucracy. And charismatic authority is associated with the "strictly personal" relations linking an impressive leader with his devoted coterie of followers or disciples.

[2]This is the major insight that underlies the *contingency theory* of organizations, described in Chapter 4.

In Weber's view, only traditional and rational-legal authority relations are sufficiently stable to provide the basis for the formation of permanent administrative structures. And, during recent centuries, particularly in Western societies, traditional structures are viewed as gradually giving way to rational-legal structures, most notably in "the modern state" and in "the most advanced institutions of capitalism," due to their "purely technical superiority over any other form of organization." (Weber, 1946 trans.: 196, 214) Charismatic forms arise in periods of instability and crisis when extraordinary measures are called for and seemingly offered by individuals perceived as possessing uncommon gifts of spirit and mind. Lenin, Hitler, Gandhi, and Mao are only a few recent examples of such charismatic leaders, ilustrating their diversity and their power to inspire the fanatical devotion of others around their personal vision of "reform." However, for such movements to persist, they must move in the direction of one or the other stable forms, by establishing "new" traditional structures[3] or new bureaucratic structures. Charisma becomes routinized: the circle of adherents expands to include more but less committed participants; systematic sources of support replace voluntary and heartfelt, but irregular, contributions; personal ties between leader and followers are replaced by more orderly but impersonal arrangements; and rules of succession are developed in recognition of the truth that no one lives forever—not even a superhuman leader (Weber, 1947 trans.: 358–73).

Weber's typology of authority is of interest not only because it underlies his conception of basic changes occurring in administrative systems over time. The distinction between traditional and rational-legal forms also serves as the basis for his influential conception of the characteristics of bureaucratic structures. In many presentations of Weber's work, this model is depicted as a simple list of administrative characteristics present in bureaucratic forms, characteristics such as these:

- a fixed division of labor among participants
- a hierarchy of offices
- a set of general rules that govern performance
- a separation of personal from official property and rights
- selection of personnel on the basis of technical qualifications
- employment viewed as a career by participants

However, his contribution can be better appreciated if these bureaucratic elements are described in relation to the traditional features they supplanted. Thus, according to Weber (1946 trans.: 196–204; 1947 trans.: 329–36), bureaucratic systems are distinguished from traditional administrative forms by the following features:

1. Jurisdictional areas are clearly specified: the regular activities required of personnel are distributed in a fixed way as official duties (in contrast with the patrimonial arrangement, in which the division of labor is not firm or regular but depends on assignments made by the leader, which can be changed at any time).

[3]The art of "inventing" traditions is described by Hobsbawm and Ranger (1983).

2. The organization of offices follows the principle of hierarchy: each lower office is controlled and supervised by a higher one. However, the scope of authority of superiors over subordinates is circumscribed, and lower offices enjoy a right of appeal (in contrast with the patrimonial form, where authority relations are more diffuse, being based on personal loyalty, and are not ordered into clear hierarchies).

3. An intentionally established system of abstract rules governs official decisions and actions. These rules are relatively stable and exhaustive, and can be learned. Decisions are recorded in permanent files. (In patrimonial systems, general rules of administration either do not exist or are vaguely stated, ill-defined, and subject to change at the whim of the leader. No attempt is made to keep permanent records of transactions.)

4. The "means of production or administration"—for example, tools and equipment or rights and privileges—belong to the office, not the office-holder, and may not be appropriated. Personal property is clearly separated from official property, and working space from living quarters. (Such distinctions are not maintained in patrimonial administrative systems since there is no separation of the ruler's personal household business from the larger "public" business under his direction.)

5. Officials are personally free, selected on the basis of technical qualifications, appointed to office (not elected), and compensated by salary. (In more traditional administrative systems, officials are often selected from among those who are personally dependent on the leader—for example, slaves, serfs, relatives. Selection is governed by particularistic criteria, and compensation often takes the form of benefices—rights granted to individuals that for example, allow them access to the stores of the ruler or give them grants of land from which they can appropriate the fees or taxes. Benefices, like fiefs in feudalistic systems, may become hereditary and sometimes are bought and sold.)

6. Employment by the organization constitutes a career for officials. An official is a full-time employee and looks forward to a lifelong career in the agency. After a trial period he or she gains tenure of position and is protected against arbitrary dismissal. (In patrimonial systems, officials serve at the pleasure of the leader and so lack clear expectations about the future and security of tenure.)

When we thus juxtapose Weber's list of bureaucratic characteristics and the related aspects of patrimonial systems, a clearer view emerges of Weber's central message. He viewed each bureaucratic element as the *solution* to a problem or defect contained within the earlier administrative systems. Further, each element operates not in isolation but as part of a system of elements that, in combination, were expected to provide more effective and efficient administration. To capture both the notions of distinctive elements and their interrelation, Weber employed what is termed an *ideal-type* construct. This approach attempts to isolate those elements regarded as most characteristic of the phenomenon to be explored. The term "ideal-type" is somewhat misleading, since it does not refer to a normatively preferred type but rather to the construction of a simplified model that focuses attention on the most salient or distinctive features.

Even though Weber's model of administrative systems emphasized that they were composed of many, interrelated factors, in his own analysis he focused primarily on the type of authority relation between superiors and subordinates in the administrative structure. In contrasting the rational-legal with the other two (nonrational) types, he stressed two seemingly contradictory points. First, the rational-legal form provides the basis for a more stable and predictable administrative structure for both superiors and subordinates. The behavior of subordinates is rendered more reliable by the specificity of their role obligations, the clarity of hierarchical connections, and their continuing dependence on the hierarchy in the short run for income and in the longer term for career progression. And superiors are prevented from behaving arbitrarily or capriciously in their demands made on subordinates.

On the other hand, the rational-legal structure permits subordinates to exercise "relatively greater independence and discretion" than is possible in the other types of administrative systems (Smith and Ross, 1978). Because obedience is owed not to a person—whether a traditional chief or a charismatic leader—but to a set of impersonal principles, subordinates in bureaucratic systems have a stronger basis for independent action, guided by their interpretation of the principles. They also have a clear basis for questioning the directives of superiors, whose actions are presumably constrained by the same impersonal framework of rules. By supporting increased independence and discretion among lower administrative officials constrained by general administrative policies and specified procedures, bureaucratic systems are capable of handling more complex administrative tasks than traditional systems. (This general argument will be amplified in Chapter 10.)

Weber was no Pollyanna, believing in costless progress. He was quite ambivalent about the developments he charted, observing that bureaucratic forms appeared capable of growing with an inexorable logic of their own, concentrating great power in the hands of their masters, reducing individual participants to the status of "cog in an ever-moving mechanism" and imprisoning humanity in an "iron cage" (1946 trans.: 228; 1958 trans.: 181). Bureaucracy's greatest fan was at the same time one of its most severe critics. We consider these and related problems associated with the growth of bureaucracy in later chapters, particularly Chapter 12.

Weber's analysis of bureaucratic structure, while influential, has also been controversial. We briefly review two important criticisms. Since type of authority relation goes a long way toward determining the nature of administrative structures, in Weber's conception, criticisms of his views of the type of authority prevailing in bureaucratic systems take on special significance. Both Parsons and Gouldner have suggested that Weber tended to confuse two analytically distinguishable bases of authority. On the one hand, in his discussion of the administrative hierarchy of bureaucracies, Weber notes that authority rests on "incumbency in a legally defined office." On the other hand, in his discussion of criteria for recruitment and advancement, Weber appears to argue that authority is based on "technical competence." (Parsons, 1947: 58–60) Indeed, at one point Weber states, "Bureaucratic administration means fundamentally the exercise of control on the basis of knowledge" (1947 trans.: 339). Gouldner (1954: 22–23) underlines the contradiction:

> Weber, then, thought of bureaucracy as a Janus-faced organization, looking two ways at once. On the one side, it was administration based on discipline. In the first emphasis, obedience is invoked as a means to an end; an individ-

ual obeys because the rule or order is felt to be the best known method of realizing some goal.

In his second conception, Weber held that bureaucracy was a mode of administration in which obedience was an end in itself. The individual obeys the order, setting aside judgments either of its rationality or morality, primarily because of the *position* occupied by the person commanding. The content of the order is not examinable.

One might defend Weber by insisting that there is a high positive correlation between a person's position in the hierarchy and his or her degree of technical competence. Such may have been the case in Weber's day, when on-the-job experience was a major source of technical competence, but seems far off the mark in today's world of minute specialization supported by prolonged and esoteric training in institutions separated from the work setting. Thompson (1961: 47) convincingly portrays the ever-widening gap between ability and authority in modern organizations, asserting that

> authority is centralized, but ability is inherently decentralized because it comes from practice and training rather than from definition. Whereas the boss retains his full *rights* to make all decisions, he has less and less *ability* to do so because of the advance of science and technology.

Staff-line arrangements, in which the positional authority of the line administrator is distinguished from the technical expertise of the staff specialist, appear to be not so much a solution to the difficulty—see studies by Dalton (1950; 1959) and others on staff-line conflict—as a structural recognition of the distinctiveness of the two sources of authority sloughed over in Weber's analysis.

A second criticism of Weber's formulation is that his ideal-type construct of bureaucracy is "an admixture of a conceptual scheme and a set of hypotheses" (Blau and Scott, 1962: 33), the difficulty being that Weber does not clearly distinguish definitions from propositions in his model. Weber's conception not only calls attention to what he regards as the key elements of bureaucracy—a set of characteristics—but also contains numerous propositions linking the various elements. For example, it is implied that organizations having a well-developed hierarchy of authority also attempt to standardize the performance of tasks by applying rules and formalized procedures, and that these same organizations also employ technical criteria in recruiting and promoting personnel, and so on. Weber's conception contains numerous propositions about the interrelations of structural characteristics in organizations, some explicit but many implicit. For a long time sociologists following in Weber's footsteps took as given the interrelations posited in his schema.

Udy (1959a; 1959b) was among the first to suggest that Weber's model could be regarded as identifying a set of structural variables whose interrelations should not be taken as a matter of definition but as a subject for empirical exploration. His lead was quickly followed by numerous others, including Hall (1963; 1968), Pugh and colleagues (1968; 1976), and Blau and associates (1966; 1971), all of whom documented the great variety exhibited by structural systems. Perhaps of greatest interest, studies by Udy (1959*a*) questioned Weber's assertion that bureaucratic organizations (in Weber's sense) were necessarily also rational in form. Employing a sample of 150 organizations from 150 nonindustrial societies (settings that afford greater variation in structural features), Udy distinguished the "bureaucratic" attributes of these organizations, including such features as a hierarchical authority structure and a specialized administrative staff, from their "rational" attributes, including specified, limited objectives and the distribution of rewards based on performance.[4] Although structural features within each of the two clusters were positively interrelated, Udy found no association between the two sets of variables: organizations that possessed more bureaucratic features were not more likely than organizations lacking them to exhibit rational features. Similarly, studies by Hall (1963; 1968) of samples of United States organizations found that an emphasis on technical qualifications was negatively correlated with other bureaucratic features, such as a hierarchy of authority, emphasis on rules, and a division of labor. This finding not only challenges Weber's ideal-type conception of bureaucracy and supports the earlier criticism that Weber confused authority of office with authority of expertise, it raises the interesting question of when—under what conditions—bureaucratic structures are rational structures. This central query is addressed in many of the following chapters.

Although it is clearly possible to criticize and improve upon many specific aspects of Weber's formulation, he remains the acknowledged master of organization theory: the intellectual giant whose conceptions continue to shape definitions of the central elements of administrative systems, and whose historical and comparative vision continues to challenge and inform our understanding of organizational forms and their evolution.[5]

### Simon's Theory of Administrative Behavior

Herbert Simon, both in his early work on administration[6] and in his later collaborative work with March, has clarified the processes by which goal specificity and formalization contribute to rational behavior in organizations. (See Simon, 1957, 1964; March and Simon, 1958.) We have already observed that Simon was critical of the platitudes developed by Fayol and others searching for management principles. He also criticized the assumptions made by Taylor and other early theorists about the actors in organizations. For the "economic man" motivated by self-interest and completely informed about all available alternatives, Simon proposed to

[4]Although we have no quarrel with the specific organizational features selected by Udy to represent "rational" characteristics, we are uncomfortable with the assumption that any given organizational feature can be regarded as rational irrespective of the circumstances in which it operates. In short, we believe that it is much preferable to view rationality as applicable to the *relation* between means and ends rather than to either means or ends viewed in isolation.

[5]Summaries and critical reviews of Weber's contributions to organization theory are provided by Albrow (1970), Bendix (1960), and Mouzelis (1968).

[6]Simon's basic work, *Administrative Behavior*, first appeared in 1945. However, all our references are to the second edition of this work, published in 1957, which contains an extensive new introduction.

substitute a more human "administrative man," who seeks to pursue his self-interests but does not always know what they are, is aware of only a few of all the possible alternatives, and is willing to settle for an adequate solution in contrast with an optimal one.

Following the lead of Barnard (1938), Simon distinguishes between (1) an individual's decisions to join and to continue to participate in an organization and (2) the decisions an individual is asked to make as a participant in the organization. Only the latter set of decisions is of interest in the present context.[7] A scientifically relevant description of an organization, according to Simon (1957: 37), details what decisions individuals make as organizational participants and the influences to which they are subject in making these decisions. In general, in Simon's view, organizations both simplify decisions and support participants in the decisions they need to make.

A primary way in which organizations simplify participants' decisions is to restrict the ends toward which activity is directed. Simon points out that goals affect behavior only as they enter into decisions about how to behave. Goals supply the value premises that underlie decisions. *Value premises* are assumptions about what ends are preferred or desirable. They are combined in decisions with *factual premises*—assumptions about the observable world and the way in which it operates. The more precise and specific the value premises, the greater their impact on the resulting decisions, since specific goals clearly distinguish acceptable from unacceptable (or more from less acceptable) alternatives. Typically, participants higher in the hierarchy make decisions with a large value component, whereas lower participants are more apt to make decisions having a larger factual component. Those closer to the top make decisions about what the organization is going to do; those in lower positions are more likely to be allowed to make choices as to how the organization can best carry out its tasks. Simon (1957: 45–56) insists that quite different criteria of correctness underlie these two classes of decisions: choice of ends can be validated only by fiat or consensus; choice of means can be validated empirically.

Ultimate goals served by organizations are frequently somewhat vague and imprecise. Some organizations exist to develop and transmit knowledge, others to maintain public order, and others to care for and cure patients. Such general goals in themselves provide few cues for guiding the behavior of participants. However, as March and Simon (1958: 191) argue, they can serve as the starting point for the contruction of *means-ends chains* that involve

> (1) starting with the general goal to be achieved, (2) discovering a set of means, very generally specific, for accomplishing this goal, (3) taking each of these means, in turn, as a new subgoal and discovering a set of more detailed means for achieving it, etc.

In this manner, there is established a hierarchy of goals in which each level is

---

[7]Factors affecting the first type of decision—decisions to participate—are discussed in Chapter 7 of this volume. See also March and Simon (1958: 52–111.)

considered as an end relative to the levels below it and as a means relative to the levels above it. Through the hierarchical structure of ends, behavior attains integration and consistency, for each member of a set of behavior alternatives is then weighted in terms of a comprehensive scale of values— the "ultimate" ends. (Simon,1957: 63)

For example, in a manufacturing organization, an assignment to an individual worker to constuct a specific component of a piece of equipment such as an engine provides that worker with an end toward which to direct his or her activities. This end, viewed from the level of his or her supervisor, is only a means toward the creation of the engine. The supervisor's end is to ensure that all parts are available when needed and are correctly assembled to produce the engine. However, this objective, when viewed from the next higher level, is only a means to the end of completing the final product, such as a lawn mower, containing the engine. The completion of all parts and assembly operations required to produce the lawn mower, while an end for the manufacturing division, is only a means at a higher level to the ultimate end of selling the lawn mower for profit to retail outlets. Viewed from the bottom up, the rationality of individual decisions and activities can be eveluted only as they relate to higher-order decisions; each subgoal can be assessed only in terms of its consistency or congruency with more general goals. Viewed from the top down, the factoring of general purposes into specific subgoals that can then be assigned to organizational subunits (individuals or departments) enhances the possibility of rational behavior by specifying value premises and hence simplifying the required decisions at every level. From this perspective, then, an organization's hierarchy can be viewed as a congealed set of means-ends chains promoting consistency of decisions and activities throughout the organization.

The ultimate goals—making a profit, achieving growth, prolonging life—are those that, by definition, are not viewed as means to ends but as ends in themselves. They may be determined by consensus or by decree. In either case, any challenge to these ultimate objectives is likely to be met with strong resistance. Physicians, for example, often refuse to consider the merits of euthanasia, and capitalists react with righteous indignation to any questions concerning their rights to profits. Apart from any considerations of self-interest, such emotional reactions are partly caused by the half-conscious realization that any challenge to the ultimate objectives calls into question the premises around which the entire enterprise is structured.

Organizations also support participants in the decisions they must make. A formalized structure supports rational decision making by dividing responsibilities among participants and providing them with the necessary means to handle them: resources, information, equipment. Specialized roles and rules, information channels, training programs, standard operating procedures—all may be viewed as mechanisms both for restricting the range of decisions each participant makes and for assisting the participant in making appropriate decisions within that range. As Perrow (1979: 149–53) notes, Simon's model of organizational influence stresses unobtrusive control of participants: training and channeling of information and attention play a larger role in producing dependable behavior than do commands or sanctions.

Underlying Simon's model of organizational decision making is a conception of cognitive limits on individual decision makers.[8] Simon (1957: 79) stresses that

> it is impossible for the behavior of a single, isolated individual to reach any high degree of rationality. The number of alternatives he must explore is too great, the information he would need to evaluate them so vast that even an approximation to objective rationality is hard to conceive. Individual choice takes place in an environment of "givens"—premises that are accepted by the subject as bases for his choice; and behavior is adaptive only within the limits set by these "givens."

By providing integrated subgoals, stable expectations, required information, necessary facilities, routine-performance programs, and in general a set of constraints within which required decisions can be made, organizations supply these "givens" to individual participants. This is the sense in which March and Simon (1958: 169–71) intend the concept *bounded rationality*—a concept that both summarizes and integrates the two key elements of the rational system perspective: goal specificity and formalization.[9]

The model developed by Simon also can be used to explain how the very structures developed to promote rationality can, under some conditions, have the opposite effect. These and other sources of organizational pathologies will be discussed in Chapter 12.

## SUMMARY AND TENTATIVE CONCLUSIONS

Any conclusions reached at this point must be tentative; it is difficult to appraise the strengths and limitations of any one perspective in isolation from the others. Nevertheless, a few general observations on the rational system approach can be made at this time.

From the rational system perspective, structural arrangements within organizations are conceived as tools deliberately designed for the efficient realization of ends. As Gouldner (1959: 404–5) notes, "the focus is, therefore, on the legally prescribed structures—i.e., the formally 'blue-printed' patterns—since these are more largely subject to deliberate inspection and rational manipulation." All theorists utilizing this perspective focus on the normative structure of organizations: on the specificity of goals and the formalization of rules and roles. There are, however, important differences among the various schools considered in their approach to the normative structure.

[8]More recent studies by cognitive psychologists have pursued in detail the types of cognitive biases and errors that commonly afflict individual decision makers. These researchers have given primary attention to the types of *heuristics* employed by individuals when confronting uncertainty. (See Tversky and Kahneman, 1974; Nisbett and Ross, 1980; Kahneman, Slovic, and Tversky, 1982.) Simon's work should stimulate organizational researchers to examine more closely the ways in which structural arrangements within organizations overcome or amplify the biases of individual actors.

[9]A good overview of Simon's contributions to the analysis of decision making in organizations is provided by Taylor (1965). An interesting critique of Simon's work is provided by Krupp (1961), and useful applications and extensions of Simon's framework are carried out by Allison (1971) and Steinbruner (1974).

Taylor was highly pragmatic in his approach, placing his faith in a method by which, beginning with individual jobs, superior work procedures could be developed and appropriate arrangements devised for articulating the various tasks to be performed. Work planning was distinguished from work performance, the former becoming the responsibility of management. Taylor was concerned primarily with devising methods for the planning of work and working arrangements. The administrative theory group was less pragmatic and more prescriptive in its approach. They believed that general principles of management could be devised to guide managers as they designed their organizations, and so they busied themselves constructing lists of "do's and dont's" as guides to managerial decision making. Weber was less concerned with discovering ways— whether pragmatic or prescriptive—for improving organizations than with attempting to develop a parsimonious descriptive portrait of the characteristics of the newly emerging bureaucratic structures. Like Weber, Simon was also descriptive in his approach, examining the effect of structural features on individual decision makers within the organization. Simon's conception, in particular, enables us to understand better how thousands and even hundreds of thousands of individual decisions and actions can be integrated in the service of complex goals. Such rational, purposeful collective behavior requires the support of an organizational framework.

The four types of theorists also differ in the level of analysis at which they work. Taylor and Simon operate primarily at the social psychological level, focusing on individual participants as they perform tasks or make decisions; they treat structural features as contexts affecting these behaviors. By contrast, the administrative theorists and Weber work at the structural level, attempting to conceptualize and analyze the characteristics of organizational forms.

Thompson (1967: 54) provides a simple summary of the general argument underlying the rational system perspective: "structure is a fundamental vehicle by which organizations achieve bounded rationality." The specification of positions, role definitions, procedural rules and regulations, value and factual inputs that guide decision making—all function to canalize behavior in the service of predetermined goals. Individuals can behave rationally because their alternatives are limited and their choices circumscribed.

In a larger sense, however, rationality resides in the structure itself, not in the individual participants—in rules that assure participants will behave in ways calculated to achieve desired objectives, in control arrangements that evaluate performance and detect deviance, in reward systems that motivate participants to carry out prescribed tasks, and in the set of criteria by which participants are selected, replaced, and promoted. Because of its emphasis on the characteristics of structure rather than the characteristics of participants, Bennis has dubbed the rational system perspective one of "organizations without people" (1959: 263).[10]

[10]Consistent with this conclusion, Boguslaw (1965: 2) has pointed out that whereas the classical utopians strove to achieve their end of the perfect social system by "populating their social systems with perfect human beings," the "new utopians"—systems engineers and control-systems experts—have become impatient with human imperfections, so that "the theo-

Let us not forget, however, that the conception of rationality employed by this perspective is limited. At the top of the organization, the value premises that govern the entire structure of decision making fall outside the system: as long as they are specific enough to provide clear criteria for choice, these premises can support a "rational" structure no matter how monstrous or perverted their content. And at the bottom of the organization, "rational" behavior often consists in turning off one's mind and one's critical intellectual judgment and blindly conforming to the performance program specified by the job description (see Veblen, 1904).

We have noted the great emphasis the rational system places on control—the determination of the behavior of one subset of participants by the other. Decision making tends to be centralized, and most participants are excluded from discretion or from exercising control over their own behavior. Most rational system theorists justify these arrangements as being in the service of rationality: control is the means of channeling and coordinating behavior so as to achieve specified goals. Few perceive the possibility that interpersonal control may be an end in itself—that one function of elaborate hierarchies and extensive divisions of labor is to allow some participants to control others. The critical or Marxist perspective calls attention to these possibilities. We will examine this critique in more detail in Chapter 7.

None of these rational system theorists took much notice of the effect of the larger social, cultural, and technological context on the structure of the organization. Although Weber attempted to account for the emergence and growth of bureaucratic structures by pointing to larger societal changes (see Chapter 7), he did not examine variations in structure among bureaucratic organizations and relate these to differences in social context.

Also, by concentrating on the normative structure, rational system analysts have virtually ignored the behavioral structure of organizations. We learn much from these theorists about plans and programs and premises, about roles and rules and regulations, but very little indeed about the actual behavior of organizational participants. The implication is that if planning is good, if decisions are sound, implementation will take care of itself. Others note the need to motivate and control participants so that their actions will coincide with design, but these theorists—Taylor, for example—are criticized for holding an oversimplified view of human beings and for having inadequate knowledge of what factors will and will not prove effective in motivating behavior.

These and related criticisms gave rise to alternative perspectives on organizations. The second perspective to be considered, the natural system perspective, developed specifically in opposition to the rational system model and was designed to correct its oversimplified conception of organizational structure and its naïve conception of individual participants.

---

retical and practical solutions they seek call increasingly for decreases in the number and in the scope of responsibility of human beings within the operating structures of their new machines systems.

. . . the new utopians are concerned with non-people and with people-substitutes."

# 3

# organizations as natural systems

To administer a social organization according to purely technical criteria of rationality is irrational, because it ignores the nonrational aspects of social conduct.

Peter M. Blau (1956)

The natural system perspective developed in large measure from critical reactions to the inadequacies of the rational system model. And in our own discussion, we shall make frequent references to these criticisms. However, the natural system perspective should not be seen as merely providing a critique of another perspective. Rather, it defines a novel and interesting view of organizations that deserves to be considered and evaluated in its own right. As with our discussion of the rational system approach, we will first attempt to isolate those more general or basic ideas common to most natural system advocates and then briefly examine selected schools within this perspective.

## IMPORTANT VERSUS DISTINCTIVE CHARACTERISTICS

Whereas the rational system theorists conceive of organizations as collectivities deliberately constructed to seek specific goals, natural system advocates emphasize that organizations are, first and foremost, collectivities. Thus, the rational system perspective stresses those features of organizations that distinguish them from other types of social groups, but the natural system theorists remind us that these distinguishing characteristics are not their only characteristics (Gouldner, 1959: 406). Indeed, they may not even be the most important characteristics.

We have already seen that much is made by rational system theorists of goal specificity and formalization as characteristics differentiating organizations from other types of collectivities. Natural system theorists generally acknowledge the existence of these attributes but argue that other characteristics—characteristics shared with all social groups—are of greater significance. Take first the matter of organizational goals and goal specificity.

### Goal Complexity

Organizational goals and their relation to the behavior of participants seem much more problematic to the natural than to the rational
system theorist. This is largely because natural system analysts pay more
attention to behavior and hence worry more about the complex interconnections between the normative and the behavioral structures of organizations. Two general themes characterize their views of organizational goals.
First, there is frequently a disparity between the stated and the "real"
goals pursued by organizations—between the professed or official goals
that are announced and the actual or operative goals that can be observed
to govern the activities of participants. Second, natural system analysts
emphasize that even when the stated goals are actually being pursued,
they are never the only goals governing participants' behavior. They point
out that all organizations must pursue *support* or "maintenance" goals in
addition to their *output* goals (Gross, 1968; Perrow, 1970: 135). No organization can devote its full resources to producing products or services;
each must expend energies maintaining itself.

These distinctions, though useful, do not go quite far enough. They
do not capture the most profound difference between these two perspectives on organizational goals. The whole thrust of the natural system view
is that organizations are more than instruments for attaining narrowly
defined goals; they are, fundamentally, social groups attempting to adapt
and survive in their particular circumstances. Thus, formal organizations,
like all other social groups, are governed by one overriding goal: survival.
Gouldner (1959: 405) emphasizes this implication of the natural system
perspective:

> The organization, according to this model, strives to survive and to maintain
> its equilibrium, and this striving may persist even after its explicitly held
> goals have been successfully attained. This strain toward survival may even
> on occasion lead to the neglect or distortion of the organization's goals.

Under many conditions, organizations have been observed to modify
their goals so as to achieve a more favorable adjustment. If their survival
is at stake, organizations will abandon the pursuit of their avowed objectives in order to save themselves. It is because of such tendencies that organizations are not to be viewed primarily as means for achieving specified ends, but as ends in themselves.

Two types of explanations have been proposed to account for the
survival instincts of organizations. The first, and more elaborate, argues
that the organizations are *social systems* characterized by a number of needs
that must be satisfied if they are to survive. This view is linked to a
broader theoretical framework known as functional analysis, which we
will briefly describe later in this chapter. Other theorists reject such assumptions as being anthropomorphic at worst and unnecessary at best.
They suggest instead that one does not have to posit a survival need for
the collectivity itself. It is sufficient to assume that some participants will
have a vested interest in the survival of the organization. Because it is a
source of power, or resources, or prestige, or pleasure, they wish to see it

preserved and will include among their own goals as participants that the organization itself be protected and, if possible, strengthened.

One of the earliest analyses, and in many ways still the best, of how some participants may seek to preserve an organization even at the sacrifice of the goals for which it was originally established is that provided by Robert Michels (1949 trans.), a contemporary of Weber's writing in pre–World War I Germany. His analysis of the changes that occurred in the largest socialist party in Europe, Germany's Social Democratic party, is rightly regarded as a classic. This work is most famous for its formulation of "the iron law of oligarchy," which equates the processes by which complex administrative work is carried out in an organization with the processes by which power shifts from the rank-and-file members to a small group of leaders. "Who says organization says oligarchy" (see Chapter 12). Of greater interest for present purposes are Michels's views on the consequences of these oligarchical tendencies for the professed goals of the organization. The leaders of the party continue to give lip service to its revolutionary objectives, but over time become increasingly conservative, reluctant to risk the gains they have achieved or to endanger the party, which is their source of strength. Michels (1949 trans.: 390) gloomily concludes,

> Thus, from a means, organization becomes an end. To the institutions and qualities which at the outset were destined simply to ensure the good working of the party machine (subordination, the harmonious cooperation of individual members, hierarchical relationships, discretion, propriety of conduct), a greater importance comes ultimately to be attached than to the productivity of the machine. Henceforward the sole preoccupation is to avoid anything which may clog the machinery.

Another way of viewing differences in the uses of goals by rational and natural system analysts is suggested by Brunsson (1985). He argues that the rational system decision-making model is in fact rational only if attention is focused on the decision as outcome. If instead we attend to actions (goal implementation) as outcome, then a more "irrational" decision process produces better results. Irrational decision processes speedily remove alternative possibilities and overestimate probabilities of success attached to the chosen alternative in order to structure participants' expectations, eliminate conflicts, and mold commitment to the selected course of action. Rational system theorists emphasize the normative structure and so focus on decisions—designs or proposals for action—as if they were the principal outcomes. Natural system theorists stress the behavioral structure and are more interested in examining what is done rather than what is decided or planned. Commitment and motivation loom as more salient variables than search and calculation if action rather than decision is the focus.

### Informal Structure

If the ends that organizations are designed to serve are not pure and simple and specific in the view of the natural system analysts, neither are the structures that exist to attain them. The natural system theorists do not deny the existence of highly formalized structures within organizations, but they do question their importance, in particular their impact on the behavior of participants. Formal structures purposefully designed to regulate behavior in the service of specific goals are seen to be greatly affected—supplemented, eroded, transformed—by the emergence of *informal* structures.

While there is widespread agreement as to the importance of informal structure, there is little consensus on how it is to be defined. Indeed, the distinction between formal and informal is quite confusing since so many superficially related but different meanings have been associated with this dichotomy. Some analysts equate the formal structure with the normative system designed by management—the "blueprint" for behavior—and the informal structure with the behavioral system—the actual behavior of participants. Roethlisberger and Dickson (1939: 558–62), founders of the human relations school discussed in more detail below, come rather close to this position in their pioneering discussion of these concepts. They propose that

> the patterns of human interrelations, as defined by the systems, rules, policies, and regulations of the company, constitute the formal organization. . . . It includes the systems, policies, rules, and regulations of the plant which express what the relations of one person to another are supposed to be in order to achieve effectively the task of technical production. (1939: 558)

By contrast, the informal organization is described as follows:

> Many of the actually existing patterns of human interaction have no representation in the formal organization at all, and others are inadequately represented by the formal organization. . . . Too often it is assumed that the organization of a company corresponds to a blueprint plan or organization chart. Actually, it never does. (1939: 559)

Most analysts, however, view informal structures as encompassing both normative and behavioral dimensions, so that it is possible to speak of formal norms *and* formal patterns of behavior, and of informal norms *and* informal patterns of behavior. Still, there is disagreement about the basis for distinguishing between the two types of structures. Some analysts tend to equate this dichotomy with such earlier distinctions as primary–secondary and *gemeinschaft–gesellschaft* relations (see Dubin, 1968: 104), but Blau (1955: 143) argues that relations within organizations are "clearly distinct" from either of these polar types. Another definition of these concepts is supplied by Litterer (1963: 10), who suggests that "by formal is meant those aspects of organizations which have been, or possibly might be, consciously planned" whereas "the informal organization is conceived of as being the aspects of organization that are not formally planned but that more or less spontaneously evolve from the needs of people."

All of these conceptions of the distinction between formal and informal are different from the one we propose. As first discussed in Chapter 1, we find it useful to equate formal structures with those norms and behavior patterns that exist regardless of the characteristics of the individual actors. Informal structures are those based on the personal characteristics or resources of the specific participants. Thus, for example, formal authority refers to those control rights that are available to and exercised by all incumbents of a given position, such as supervisor or teacher; informal authority would indicate those rights that become available to a particular supervisor or teacher because of his or her special qualities or individual resources. Obviously, one of the clearest ways to distinguish empirically between the formal and the informal elements in a given situation is to observe what happens to beliefs and behaviors when there is a change in personnel.

Regardless of differences in the specific conceptions, all natural system analysts emphasize that there is more to organizational structure than the prescribed rules, the job descriptions, and the associated regularities in the behavior of participants. Individual participants are never merely "hired hands" but bring along their heads and hearts: they enter the organization with individually shaped ideas, expectations, and agendas, and they bring with them differing values, interests, and abilities.

Expressed through interaction, these factors come together to create a reasonably stable informal structure. One of the most important insights of the natural system perspective is that the social structure of an organization does not consist of the formal structure plus the idiosyncratic beliefs and behaviors of individual participants but rather of a formal structure and an informal structure: informal life is itself structured and orderly. Participants within formal organizations generate informal norms and behavior patterns: status and power systems, communication networks, sociometric structures, and working arrangements.

In the early studies exploring informal structures, it was presumed that they characterized only the lower strata of the organization: managers and executives were immune to such developments. But empirical studies by Dalton (1959) and others dispelled such notions. Also, early studies emphasized the dysfunctional consequences of the informal structures as private and "irrational" concerns that impeded the implementation of the elegant formal design. Thus, Roethlisberger and Dickson decided that the formal structure expresses the "logic of cost and efficiency" whereas the informal structure embraces the "logic of sentiments" (1939: 562–64). Increasingly, however, analysts have emphasized the positive functions performed by informal structures—in increasing the ease of communication, facilitating trust, and correcting for the inadequacies of the formal systems (see Gross, 1953).

Greater appreciation for the functions of informal systems was coupled with increasing skepticism that formalization was conducive to rationality. Natural system analysts emphasize that formalization places heavy and often intolerable burdens on those responsible for the design and management of an organization. No planners are so farseeing or omniscient as to be able to anticipate all the possible contingencies that might confront each position in the organization. Attempts to program in advance the behavior of participants are often misguided, if not foolhardy. Such programming can easily become maladaptive and lead to behaviors both ineffective and inefficient, giving rise to the "trained incapacity" that Veblen (1904) called attention to long ago and for which some organizations have become notorious. (See also Merton, 1957: 197–200.) Further, formal arrangements that curtail individual problem solving and the use of discretion undermine participants' initiative and self-confidence, causing them to become alienated and apathetic. Such restrictive arrangements not only damage participants' self-esteem and mental health but prevent them from effectively contributing their talents and energies to the larger enterprise (Argyris, 1957; McGregor, 1960). In sum, natural system analysts insist that highly centralized and formalized structures are doomed to be ineffective and irrational in that they waste the organization's most precious resource: the intelligence and initiative of its participants.

### Functional Analysis

Functional analysis has served as an important underpinning for the work of some of the most influential natural system analysts. The origins of this widely used model are to be found in the work of a group of British social anthropologists, most notably Malinowski (1939) and Radcliffe-Brown (1952). Merton's essay (1957: 19–84) has become the most influential statement of this approach in sociology. The paradigm is complex, and there are many variants; nevertheless, its central features can be quickly summarized. The model assumes that the social unit, in our case the organization, has certain needs or requirements that must be met if it is to persist in its present form. As we will see when specific schools are discussed, analysts vary in how explicit they are in formulating the set of functional prerequisites. The specific structures that constitute the organization are analyzed in terms of the needs they meet, the functions they perform in ensuring the survival of the system. By analogy, if the human body is to survive, a continuing flow of oxygen must be supplied to the blood; the lungs perform this function. Similarly, if the organization is to survive, information about salient changes in its environment must be communicated to decision makers; the internal communication system performs this function. Showing that a given structure meets a functional need constitutes a functional "explanation" for that structure. The existence of an element is explained in terms of its consequences—the functions it performs—rather than by reference to its origins. "Final" causes are emphasized over "efficient" causes.[1] The model also emphasizes that the structural elements are themselves interdependent, so that variation in one causes modification in the others. Such systems are often viewed as tending toward a state of equilibrium; such views follow the work of Pareto as interpreted by Henderson (1935). (See Buckley, 1967: 11–17.)

Many aspects of the functionalist paradigm are problematic. In the case of social systems, unlike biological systems, it is difficult to specify the essential needs; indeed, it is often difficult to specify what is meant by survival of the system. It is also not easy to link a specific structure to a particular need. As Parsons (1966: 24–25) notes, social structures vary in their degree of differentiation: some are highly developed, so that each

---

[1]Blau (1955: 9–10) suggests that this theoretical postulate of the functional model can be accounted for by its distinctive historical origin: social anthropologists studying primitive societies could not test historical explanations for particular structural features since there were no historical documents. To overcome this limitation, they developed a different type of explanation, one that emphasized the contemporary contribution made by the element to the maintenance of the larger social system. Attention shifted from a focus on origins to a concern with the persistence of a particular structural feature.

structural unit performs a highly specialized function, whereas others are much less developed, each structure performing a range of functions. Further, a given function may be performed by more than one type of structure—the concept of *functional equivalents or substitutes*—so that a functional explanation may not be sufficient to account for the development of a specific structural form.[2] Finally, organizational forms are not as highly interdependent and as tightly coupled as biological systems, a point to be amplified in the next chapter.

In spite of all these problems and reservations, functionalism provided the dominant model for organizational (and, more generally, sociological) analysis from the 1930s into the 1960s. Many of our most important insights and generalizations concerning organizations are products of this tradition; despite its flaws, it remains a popular and useful perspective from which to examine organizations.

## SELECTED SCHOOLS

As with the rational system perspective, the natural system perspective is an umbrella under which a number of rather diverse approaches can be gathered. While they share certain generic features, they differ in important particulars. We will be content to discuss briefly four influential variants: Mayo and the human relations school, Barnard's conception of cooperative systems, Selznick's institutional approach, and Parsons's social system model.

### Mayo and the Human Relations School

We will not recount in detail the famous series of studies and experiments conducted at the Hawthorne plant of the Western Electric Company outside Chicago during the late 1920s and early 1930s. This research is meticulously described by Roethlisberger and Dickson (1939) and given its most influential interpretation by Elton Mayo (1945). Mayo, along with Roethlisberger, was a member of the Harvard Business School faculty. He was trained as an industrial psychologist, and his early work grew out of the research tradition established by Frederick W. Taylor. Like Taylor, Mayo studied individual factors such as fatigue in an attempt to determine the optimum length and spacing of rest periods for maximizing productivity. The early work in the Hawthorne plant followed the scientific management approach: the researchers set about to determine the optimal level of illumination for the assembly of telephone relay equipment. Mayo (1945: 69) summarizes the surprising results:

> The conditions of scientific experiment had apparently been fulfilled—experimental room, control room; changes introduced one at a time; all other conditions held steady. And the results were perplexing. . . . Lighting improved in the experimental room, production went up; but it rose also in the control room. The opposite of this: lighting diminished from 10 to 3

[2]In addition to these theoretical and empirical problems, certain logical difficulties attend the use of this model (see Nagel, 1961: 520–35). But if carefully employed, it can be of value in analyzing self-regulating systems (see Hempel, 1959).

foot-candles in the experimental room and the production again went up; simultaneously in the control room, with illumination constant, production also rose.

The researchers were in confusion. Other conditions were run with similar inexplicable results. In desperation, they asked the workers themselves what was going on and learned that the workers were so pleased to be singled out for special attention that they had tried to do the best they could for the researchers and for the company! The "Hawthorne effect" was discovered.

Additional studies carried out by the Harvard group—the second relay-assembly group, the mica-splitting test room, the bank-wiring observation room—all served to call into question the simple motivational assumptions on which the prevailing rational models rested. Individual workers did not behave as "rational" economic actors but as complex beings with multiple motives and values;[3] they were driven as much by feelings and sentiments as by facts and interests; and they did not behave as individual, isolated actors but as members of social groups exhibiting commitments and loyalties stronger than their individualistic self-interests. Thus, in the bank-wiring observation room, workers were observed to set and conform to daily work quotas—group norms restricting production—at the expense of their own higher earnings. And informal status hierarchies and leadership patterns developed that challenged the formal systems designed by managers (see Roethlisberger and Dickson, 1939: 379–447; and Homans, 1950: 48–155). At the social psychological level, the Hawthorne studies pointed to a more complex model of worker motivation based on a social psychological rather than an economic conception of man; at the structural level, the studies discovered and demonstrated the importance of informal organization.

The Hawthorne trunk has given rise to numerous research and reform offshoots, each of which has produced many individual branches. The major research issues pursued include studies of the work groups in the organizational environment, leadership behavior, and the impact of worker background and personality attributes on organizational behavior. Reform attempts include the use of personnel counselors, leadership training, job redefinition, and participation in decision making. Each of these interests merits a brief description; all of them are still flourishing.

The discovery of informal group processes in organizational settings both stimulated and received impetus from the study of small-group behavior carried on by social psychologists and sociologists. Among the former, Maier (1952) and Katz (Katz, Maccoby, and Morse, 1950; Katz et al., 1951) were particularly influential; among the latter, Homans (1950) and Whyte (1951; 1959) were effective in analyzing group processes in organizational settings. A few analysts, such as Sayles (1958), attempted to understand how organizational factors affected the number, types, and

[3]After inspecting the results of the bank-wiring observation room study at the Hawthorne plant, Mayo (1945: 43) concluded, "It is unfortunate for economic theory that it applies chiefly to persons of less, rather than greater, normality of social relationships. Must we conclude that economics is a study of human behavior in non-normal situations, or alternatively, a study of non-normal human behavior in ordinary situations?"

tactics of groups that emerged; most focused not on the determinants but on the consequences of group membership—for example, the impact of group cohesiveness on individual conformity to production norms (Roy, 1952; Seashore, 1954).

From the human relations perspective, leadership is conceived primarily as a mechanism for influencing the behavior of individual participants. Early studies sought a set of leadership traits or characteristics that would stimulate individual performance in the service of organizational goals. Thus, studies by White and Lippitt (1953) reported that participants in experimental task groups performed more effectively under "democratic" than "laissez-faire" or "authoritarian" leaders. Later research stressed the relational aspects of leadership. For example, a series of studies conducted at Ohio State (Stogdill and Coons, 1957) isolated two basic dimensions of leadership behavior: *consideration,* the extent to which trust, friendship, and respect mark the relation between the supervisor and his or her workers, and *initiating structure,* the degree to which the supervisor is a good organizer who can "get the work out." These dimensions were observed to vary independently, and in general, the more effective leaders—that is, the leaders whose subordinates performed better and had higher morale—were those who scored high on both dimensions.

Later efforts emphasized that leadership characteristics vary with the nature of the situation (Fiedler, 1964; 1971) and the specific needs or motivations of the individual subordinates (Cartwright, 1965). Studies by Pelz (1952) suggested that a supervisor's relation to his or her own superior—specifically, the extent of his or her influence upward—is a powerful determinant of the supervisor's influence over his or her own subordinates. Likert (1961) built on this finding to create his model of the supervisor's critical function as a "linking pin" relating lower to higher levels of the hierarchy. Most of these leadership studies ignored the effects of incumbency in a formal office on an individual's influence, either by overlooking this aspect of the situation or by deliberately holding it constant—for example, by studying differences in leadership behavior among all first-line supervisors in a given office or factory situation (see Katz and Kahn, 1952). Blau (1964: 210) has pointed out that "although managerial authority in organizations contains important leadership elements, its distinctive characteristic, which differentiates it from informal leadership, is that it is rooted in the formal powers and sanctions the organization bestows upon managers". It is in keeping with the natural system perspective to ignore this distinctive component of leadership in formal organizations. (We ourselves will focus on it in Chapter 11).

From the very beginning, human relations analysts have emphasized the great variability of individual characteristics and behaviors and have insisted on the relevance of these differences in understanding organizational behavior. Early research demonstrated that such officially irrelevant differences as race (Collins, 1946), class (Warner and Low, 1947), and cultural background (Dalton, 1950) had strong effects on allocation to work roles and organizational behavior. These studies are important forerunners of the more recent interest in the relation between stratification and organizations, which we discuss in Chapter 8.

The human relations school has also given rise to much effort directed at changing organizations—modifying and improving them as social environments. The original Hawthorne researchers were themselves interested in pursuing practical applications of their findings. Stressing the positive relation in their studies between worker satisfaction and productivity, they sought techniques to improve the adjustment and morale of individual workers. One approach involved the introduction of a set of personnel counselors, distinct from the line hierarchy, whose task it was to listen sympathetically to workers' complaints (Roethlisberger and Dickson, 1939: 189–376, 590–604). The interviewing techniques devised for this program contributed to the development of nondirective counseling techniques now in wide use.

Another change strategy devised by the human relations school stressed the importance of supervisory skills in promoting worker morale. Supervisors required special training if they were to become more sensitive to the psychological and social needs of their subordinates. Mayo (1945), influenced in part by Barnard, stressed the important role to be performed by supervisors and managers whose social function it was to elicit cooperation among workers—cooperation that could no longer be assumed to be automatic (see Bendix and Fisher, 1949). Thus, the human relations approach helped to spawn many diverse efforts in leadership training, from simple attitude-change efforts to more intensive Bethel-type sensitivity or T-group training. (See, for example, Argyris, 1962; Blake and Mouton, 1964; National Training Laboratories, 1953.)

Yet another reform approach focused on the need to redefine and enlarge the role definitions specified for workers. Contrary to the assumptions of the rational system model, the human relations group stressed the dangers of excessive formalization with its emphasis on extreme functional specialization. Job enlargement or, at least, job rotation, was advocated as a method of reducing the alienation and increasing the commitment and satisfaction of workers performing routine work (see Argyris, 1957).

Still other reformers stressed the importance of worker participation in decision making within the organization, particularly decisions directly affecting them. Although the notion of linking participation to motivation and commitment was given encouragement by the Hawthorne studies, more direct support has come from the experimental and theoretical work of Lewin (1948) and his colleagues (for example, Coch and French, 1948). Presently, participation by workers in managerial decision making is given much more emphasis in certain European countries than in the United States (see Blumberg, 1968; Tannenbaum et al., 1974; Hofstede, 1984).

Virtually all of these applications of the human relations movement have come under severe criticism on both ideological and empirical grounds. Paradoxically, the human relations movement, ostensibly developed to humanize the cold and calculating rationality of the factory and shop, rapidly came under attack on the grounds that it represented simply a more subtle and refined form of exploitation. Critics charged that workers' legitimate economic interests were being inappropriately deemphasized; that actual conflicts of interest were denied and "therapeutically" managed; and that the roles attributed to managers represented a new brand of elitism. The entire movement was branded as "cow sociology": just as contented cows were alleged to produce more milk, satisfied workers were expected to produce more output (see Bell, 1960: 238–44; Bendix, 1956: 308–40; Landsberger, 1958; Braverman, 1974: 139–51).

The ideological criticisms were the first to erupt, but reservations raised by researchers on the basis of empirical evidence may in the long run prove to be more devastating. Several decades of research have demonstrated no clear relation between worker satisfaction and productivity (see Brayfield and Crockett, 1955; Schwab and Cummings, 1970); no clear relation between supervisory behavior or leadership style and worker productivity (see Hollander and Julian, 1969); no clear relation between job enlargement and worker satisfaction or productivity (see Hulin and Blood, 1968); and no clear relation between participation in decision making and satisfaction or productivity (see Vroom, 1969: 227–39). Where positive relations among these variables have been observed, the direction may be opposite to that predicted: productivity producing satisfaction (Porter and Lawler, 1968) or productivity influencing supervisory style (Lowin and Craig, 1968), rather than vice versa. Even the original Hawthorne results have been reanalyzed and questioned (see Carey, 1967; Sykes, 1965).

Our brief survey of the human relations school cannot do justice to the variety of theoretical implications, empirical studies, and practical reform efforts it has generated. It is only a small exaggeration to suggest that the academic field of industrial sociology first saw the light of day at the Hawthorne plant, with Mayo serving as midwife. Moreover, sociological work on organizations well into the 1950s was shaped primarily by the human relations model—whether it was attempting to fill in the model's missing pieces or attacking its shortcomings and biases. And all of the thousands of studies concerned with motivation, morale, and leadership either have been directly stimulated by or are indirectly beholden to a tiny group of workers who kept increasing their output even though the lights were growing dimmer.[4]

### Barnard's Cooperative System

At the same time that Mayo and his associates were conducting their studies and extrapolating from them to underline the importance of interpersonal processes and informal structures, Chester I. Barnard was expanding his own views of the nature of organizations. Barnard was not a researcher but an executive, president of New Jersey Bell Telephone company. Although Barnard's major book, *The Functions of the Executive* (1938),[5] was a very personal work reflecting his rather distinctive views and concerns, he was in regular contact with the human relations group at Harvard, including Mayo, Roethlisberger, and Henderson. Barnard's influence on the field was great, in part because his treatise was one of the first systematic attempts to outline a theory of organization available to U.S. readers, Weber's work not yet having been translated. Barnard's ideas contributed to human relations approaches and provided a basis for both Selznick's institutionalist views and for Simon's theory of decision making.

---

[4]For a more detailed summary and a highly critical assessment of the human relations school, see Perrow (1979: 90–138).

[5]Unless otherwise indicated, all references in this section are to this work.

Barnard stressed that organizations are essentially cooperative systems, integrating the contributions of their individual participants. As already reported in our review of organizational definitions in Chapter 1, Barnard defined a formal organization as "that kind of coöperation among men that is conscious, deliberate, purposeful" (p. 4).[6] Two separable ideas are embedded in this definition. First, organizations rely on the *willingness* of participants to make contributions. Participants must be induced to make contributions—a variety of incentives can be used to motivate them to do so, including material rewards, opportunities for distinction, prestige, personal power, and associational attractions—and make them in sufficient quantities, or the organization cannot survive.[7] Second, whatever the specific motives that procure cooperation in the enterprise, efforts must be directed toward a common *purpose*. "The inculcation of belief in the real existence of a common purpose is an essential executive function" (p. 87).

Thus, Barnard attempts to combine and reconcile two somewhat contradictory ideas: goals are imposed from the top down while their attainment depends on willing compliance from the bottom up. This view of accepted direction is developed most fully in Barnard's conception of authority. He argues that it is a "fiction that authority comes down from above" (p. 170), noting the many situations in which leaders claim authority but fail to win compliance. This is because authority depends ultimately on its validation from the response of those subject to it: "the decision as to whether an order has authority or not lies with the persons to whom it is addressed, and does not reside in 'persons of authority' or those who issue these orders" (p. 163). Still, some types of orders have a greater "potentiality of assent of those to whom they are sent" (p. 173). These are orders that are products of a well-ordered and integrated communications system that links all contributors in a purposeful cooperative framework.

> At first thought it may seem that the element of communication in organization is only in part related to authority; but more thorough consideration leads to the understanding that communication, authority, specialization, and purpose are all aspects comprehended in coördination. All communication relates to the formulation of purpose and the transmission of coördinating prescriptions for action and so rests upon the ability to communicate with those willing to coöperate. (p. 184)

This conception of an organization as a purposefully coordinated system of communications linking all participants in such a manner that the purposes of superordinates are accepted as the basis for the actions of subordinates became the foundation for Simon's theory of decision making, as described in Chapter 2.

Barnard's views thus contain many ideas that are consistent with a

[6] Like many natural system theorists, Barnard defined organizations so as to emphasize their rational system features—their distinguishing features—but then concentrated on other, more generic aspects in his analysis.

[7] Simon later adopted and elaborated upon Barnard's "contributions-inducements" theory of organizational equilibrium. We review these developments in Chapter 7.

rational system conception of organizations. What sets them apart is his insistence on the nonmaterial, informal, interpersonal, and, indeed, moral basis of cooperation. Material rewards are viewed as "weak incentives" that must be buttressed by other types of psychological and social motivations if cooperative effort is to be sustained. As for informal organization, Barnard argued that "formal organizations arise out of and are necessary to informal organization; but when formal organizations come into operation, they create and require informal organizations" (p. 120). Informal structures facilitate communication, maintain cohesiveness, and undergird "the willingness to serve and the stability of objective authority" (p. 122). Interpersonal ties at their best create a "condition of communion": "the opportunity for commandership, for mutual support" forming the "basis of informal organization that is essential to the operation of every formal organization" (p. 148).

But the most critical ingredient to successful organization is the formation of a collective purpose that becomes morally binding on participants. This is the distinctive function of the executive.

> The distinguishing mark of the executive responsibility is that it requires not merely conformance to a complex code of morals but also the creation of moral codes for others. The most generally recognized aspect of this function is called securing, creating, inspiring of "morale" in an organization. This is the process of inculcating points of view, fundamental attitudes, loyalties, to the organization or coöperative system, and to the system of objective authority, that will result in subordinating individual interest and the minor dictates of personal codes to the good of the coöperative whole. (p. 279)

On the one hand such views sound quaint and hopelessly old-fashioned; they have been subjected to scathing attack by critics such as Perrow (1979: 70–89), who scoff at Barnard's moral imperialism and point out the duplicity inherent in "willing" cooperation that is managed from above. On the other hand, many of these themes have again become highly fashionable as students of organizations rediscover the importance of organizational cultures shaped by zealous managers supplying strongly held values to their members.[8] (See, e.g., Peters and Waterman, 1982.) We discuss these neo-Barnardian views in Chapters 9 and 11.

Consistent with the natural system framework, however, Barnard recognized the existence of organizational forces even more powerful than purpose:

> Finally it should be noted that, once established, organizations change their unifying purposes. They tend to perpetuate themselves; and in the effort to survive may change the reasons for existence. (p. 89)

The necessity of survival can override the morality of purpose.

---

[8]This aspect of Barnard's work no doubt accounts for his enormous popularity among students of organizations in Japan, where many "Barnard Societies" are still active.

### Selznick's Institutional Approach

Philip Selznick, a student of bureaucracy under Merton at Columbia, but an intellectual descendant of Michels and Barnard, has developed his own unique natural system model. Selznick's work has been applied and extended by several of his students, including Burton Clark, Charles Perrow, and Mayer Zald. More recently, his framework has been adapted and elaborated to constitute a major school of organizational theory and research. We restrict attention here to Selznick's seminal early contributions and to the work of his immediate intellectual followers.[9] Unlike Barnard, Selznick has not systematically presented his approach in any single source, but has scattered his ideas through several books and articles. We will attempt to provide a short but coherent sketch of his approach.

For Selznick, "the most important thing about organizations is that, though they are tools, each nevertheless has a life of its own" (1949: 10). He agrees with the rational system analyst that the distinguishing characteristic of formal organizations is that they are rationally ordered instruments designed to attain goals. However, these formal structures can "never succeed in conquering the nonrational dimensions of organizational behavior" (1948: 25). The sources of these nonrational features are (1) individuals, who participate in the organization as "wholes" and do not act merely in terms of their formal roles within the system; and (2) the fact that the formal structure is only one aspect of the concrete social structure that must adjust in various ways to the pressures of its institutional environment. In short, organizational rationality is constrained by "the recalcitrance of the tools of action": persons bring certain characteristics to the organization and develop other commitments as members that restrict their capacity for rational action; organizational procedures become valued as ends in themselves; the organization strikes bargains with its environment that compromise present objectives and limit future possibilities (1949: 253–59).

As I have noted elsewhere,

> if the organization as conceived by Weber operates like a smoothly functioning professional football team, Selznick's image corresponds more closely to Alice's efforts at croquet with equipment and competition provided by the Queen of Hearts. Alice swings her flamingo mallet but the bird may duck his head before the hedgehog-ball is struck; just so, the manager issues his directives but they may be neither understood nor followed by his subordinates. (Scott, 1964: 511)

Selznick views orgnizational structure as an adaptive organism shaped in reaction to the characteristics and commitments of participants as well as to influences from the external environment. He explicitly embraces a functional form of analysis, explaining,

> This means that a given empirical system is deemed to have basic needs, essentially related to self-maintenance; the system develops repetitive means of self-defense; and day-to-day activity is interpreted in terms of the func-

---

[9]Later contributions to the institutional approach are first discussed in Chapter 5 and reappear throughout the rest of the volume.

tion served by that activity for the maintenance and defense of the system (1948: 29).

Insisting that the overriding need of all systems "is the maintenance of the integrity and continuity of the system itself," Selznick attempts to spell out certain more specific "derived imperatives," including the security of the organization as a whole in relation to its environment, the stability of lines of authority and communication, the stability of informal relations within the organization, and a homogeneity of outlook toward the meaning and role of the organization. However, he regards the list as suggestive, not definitive. Acknowledging its vagueness, Selznick defends the concept of organizational need because it directs attention to the internal relevance of organizational behavior, including behaviors that are ostensibly directed outward (1948: 29–30).

To this point Selznick's model appears to be a rather conventional version of the more general natural system model described early in this chapter, but its development takes an unexpected turn. He proposes that we will learn more interesting things about organizations if we do not attempt to examine the satisfaction of all needs of the organism but, like Freud, focus on those needs "which cannot be fulfilled within approved avenues of expression" (1948: 32). Thus, attention is directed away from the formal structures and procedures, insofar as they are functioning smoothly and toward those features created to deal in irregular ways with unmet needs. Such mechanisms include informal structures, ideologies, and co-optation.

Selznick has described this same approach in slightly different language. He argues that rather than following the lead of experimental psychologists who study routine psychological processes, we should imitate the clinical psychologists who examine the dynamic adaptation of the organism over time. Instead of focusing on the day-to-day decisions made in organizations, we should concentrate on those critical decisions that, once made, result in a change in the structure itself. The pattern of these critical decisions, viewed over time, results in the development of a distinctive character structure for each organization, just as an individual's critical decisions and typical mode of coping with problems give rise to the development of a distinctive personality (Selznick, 1957).

Selznick refers to the process by which an organization develops a distinctive character structure as *institutionalization*. As Selznick uses the term, to become institutionalized is to become "infused with value beyond the technical requirements of the task at hand" (1957: 17). In his view

> the term "organization" thus suggests a certain bareness, a lean, no-nonsense system of consciously co-ordinated activities. It refers to an expendable tool, a rational instrument engineered to do a job. An "institution," on the other hand, is more nearly a natural product of social needs and pressures—a responsive, adaptive organism. (1957: 5)

Institutional commitments develop over time as the organization confronts external constraints and pressures from its environment as well as changes in the composition of its personnel, their interests, and their informal relations. No organization is completely immune from these external and internal pressures, although the extent of institutionalization varies from one organization to another.

Following Barnard, Selznick believes that leadership can play a critical role in this evolutionary process. Leaders must define the mission of the enterprise: it is their responsibility to choose and to protect its distinctive values and "to create a social structure which embodies them" (1957: 60). Among the critical decisions confronting any enterprise are the selection of a social base—what clientele, what market to serve; the building of an institutional core—the selection of central personnel; and the determination of the nature and timing of formalization of stucture and procedures (1957: 102–7).

Selznick thus invites us to observe the process by which organizations develop distinctive structures, capacities, and liabilities; he proposes, in sum, a natural history of organizations.

If we examine some of the empirical work stimulated by Selznick's institutional model, we will obtain a clearer picture of both the strengths and weaknesses of the proposed approach. Selznick's most famous study is of the Tennessee Valley Authority (TVA), a decentralized government agency created during the depression to improve the economic status of the entire Tennessee Valley, a chronically depressed, flood-ravaged region. Massive federal funds—at least by the standards of the 1930s—were provided to support a broad-gauged attack on the problems of the area. Flood control, hydroelectric power, and soil conservation efforts were to be provided in an integrated manner. Top agency officials were located at the site, not in far-off Washington, so that officials would not be inclined to impose solutions from above but would work with the local inhabitants in developing acceptable projects (see Lilienthal, 1944).

As we would expect, Selznick (1949) focuses on the "internal relevance"—the consequences for the agency—of these strategies. He points out that the democratic ideology not only served to recruit and motivate talented participants but also enabled the New Deal agency to gain access to a suspicious and conservative area. Agency officials employed co-optation as a strategy to gain legitimacy and political support. *Co-optation* is a mechanism by which external elements are incorporated into the decision-making structures of an organization: in the case of the TVA, local leaders were recruited to participate in the agency's decision-making and advisory bodies. This tactic ensured that the agency would enjoy local political support for its programs, but such support always comes at a price: local leaders exchanged support for a measure of influence on the agency's programs and goals. As a consequence, some public interest goals were subverted to serve private interests. For example, improved land values surrounding water projects that were supposed to benefit the public often fell into private hands, and reforested land intended as watershed was taken over by lumber interests.

Selznick's analysis set the pattern for a number of similar studies that examined the ways in which the original goals of an organization can be displaced or undermined. Thus, Clark's (1956) study of an adult education program in Los Angeles argues that its professed goals of providing cultural and intellectual programs could not be realized because of its marginal organizational and institutional status. Because the program lacked full legitimacy, only those parts of it that could attract large numbers of students were retained, with other academically valuable but less popular offerings losing out to the "enrollment economy." Messinger's (1955) analysis of the Townsend movement, a pressure group developed in the 1930s to represent the economic interests of the elderly, records how the movement attempted to survive by transforming its original radical political objectives into noncontroversial recreational programs. And Zald and Denton (1963) describe the transformation of the YMCA from a religious organization performing rehabilitative and welfare services for the urban poor into a social and recreational center for suburban and middle-class young people.

These and related studies exhibit several common features. The analyst focuses on the administrative history of the organization: the structural features and programs of the organization are viewed as changing over time in response to changing conditions. The methodology employed tends to be that of the case study, and heavy reliance is placed on the analysis of organizational documents and interviews with informants knowledgeable about the organization's history. Given this approach, most of the organizations selected for study have been relatively recently founded. Selznick (1957: 142) insists that he is interested not in recounting the history of any given organization for its own sake but in seeking "to discover the characteristic ways in which types of institutions respond to types of circumstances." However, this interest in generalization is somewhat at odds with the intensive case-study approach. As Cohen (1972: 402) notes, "As the desire to explain more and more aspects of a single study, situation, or phenomenon increases, the possibility of using this explanation outside the situation for which it was created approaches the vanishing point."

Thus, in these earlier uses of the institutional approach, a rather consistent pattern emerges. Fundamentally, analysts sought to explain changes in the goals of the organization—not the professed goals, but the ends actually pursued, the operative goals. The general mode of explanation was similar to that offered by Michels: to increase their own security, organizational participants modify controversial goals in the face of hostile environments. As Perrow notes, the literature spawned by the approach—to which Perrow himself has contributed (see Perrow, 1961)—takes on an "exposé" character: "The major message is that the organization has sold out its goals in order to survive or grow" (1979: 182). Although cynicism seems often justified, this early work stimulated by Selznick's conception appears to go out of its way to inspect the seamy side of organizational life. The studies tend to focus on the forces that undermine the organization's principles and subvert its formal ends to narrow interests. The work seems tinted by a "metaphysical pathos" (Gouldner, 1955). There is no doubt that these accounts of "friction, dilemma, doubt, and ruin" (Selznick, 1948: 25) served as a useful antidote to the paean to organizational rationality being sung during this era by some overexuberant rational system theorists. But it also is the case that Selznick and company were acting as "clinical sociologists" of organizations, and like their role models, the clinical psychologists, they chose to focus primarily on deviance and abnormality.

However, with time, this strongly negative emphasis has been tempered by more constructive concerns about how precarious values can be protected. Selznick himself, as we have noted, began to emphasize that leaders could and should act to defend and, if necessary, reinterpret and renew the mission of their organization (1957). And Clark (1970; 1972) turned his attention to how such "distinctive" and successful colleges as Antioch, Reed, and Swarthmore managed to survive and to preserve their special character. This somewhat redefined and broadened research agenda has gained many adherents. Not only is Selznick's work recognized as providing the underpinnings for the institutionalist perspective, but his concern for the role of leaders in making critical decisions and in defining institutional values has contributed to the current interest in strategic decision making and the creation of organizational cultures. We will consider these developments in later Chapters.

### Parsons's Social System

More so than other analysts working within the natural system tradition, Talcott Parsons has developed a very explicit model detailing the needs that must be met if a system is to survive. Parsons's approach is the product of a lifetime devoted to perfecting a general analytic model suitable for the analysis for all types of collectivities—from small, primary groups to entire societies (see Parsons, 1951; Parsons, Bales, and Shils, 1953; Parsons, 1966). He first applied the model to formal organizations in two papers published in the late 1950s and collected in his book on societies (1960).

Parsons' model is identified by the acronym AGIL, which represents the four basic functions that all social systems must perform if they are to persist:

> A*daptation:* the problem of acquiring sufficient resources.
>
> G*oal attainment:* the problem of setting and implementing goals.
>
> I*ntegration:* the problem of maintaining solidarity or coordination among the subunits of the system.
>
> L*atency:* the problem of creating, preserving, and transmitting the system's distinctive culture and values.

In addition to being applicable to all types of social systems, the schema may be applied at more than one level in analyzing a given type of system. Thus, Parsons applies his model to organizations at the ecological, the structural, and the social psychological levels. Linkages across these levels are also stressed.

First, at the ecological level, Parsons relates organizations to the functioning of the larger society. Applying the AGIL at the societal level, Parsons suggests that subordinate social units such as organizations can be classified according to their societal function (see Table 3–1). For example, economic organizations such as firms are said to serve the adaptive needs of the larger society. As Parsons (1960: 19) points out,

> what from the point of view of the organization is its specified goal is, from the point of view of the larger system of which it is a differentiated part or subsystem, a specialized or differentiated function.

Because of this functional linkage, the place or role of the subsystem is legitimated, and it may expect to receive societal approval and resources

**TABLE 3-1 Parsons's Typology Based on Societal Functions**

| SOCIETAL FUNCTION | ORGANIZATIONAL TYPE | EXAMPLES |
|---|---|---|
| Adaptation | Organizations oriented to economic production | Business firms |
| Goal attainment | Organizations oriented to political goals | Government agencies<br>Other organizations that allocate power, such as banks |
| Integration | Integrative organizations | Courts and the legal profession<br>Political parties<br>Social-control agencies |
| Latency | Pattern-maintenance organizations | Cultural organizations, such as museums<br>Educational organizations<br>Religious organizations |

in accordance with the value placed in the society on the particular functions it performs.

Shifting to the structural level of analysis, Parsons notes that each formal organization may also be analyzed as a social system in its own right, and each must develop its own differentiated subsystems to satisfy the four basic needs. Thus, each organization must develop structures that enable it to adapt to its environment and must mobilize resources needed for its continued operation. Arrangements are also needed to enable the organization to set and implement its goals. To solve its integrative problems, an organization must find ways to command the loyalties of its members, enlist their effort, and coordinate the operations of its various sectors. And mechanisms must be developed to cope with latency problems, to promote consensus on the values that define and legitimate the organization's output and system goals.

While Parsons does not insist that a specific structural unit will develop to manage each of these functional needs, he does argue that structural differentiation will tend to occur along these divisions. Functional imperatives generate the fault lines along which a social structure becomes differentiated. The explanation for this linkage between functional requirements and structural arrangements is simply that the various functional needs are somewhat in conflict, so that efforts directed at solving one functional problem interfere with efforts directed toward the others.[10] Specifically, energies devoted to adapting the organization to its

[10]Parsons's reasoning at this point is illuminated by knowledge of the intellectual origins of the AGIL schema. His conception of these system problems grew out of his work on the *pattern variables*—basic value dichotomies representing the dimensions along which structures are arranged. The pairs of opposing values—universalism–particularism, affectivity–affective neutrality, ascription–achievement, and specificity–diffuseness—were cross-classified, producing the four system needs. Thus, values identified as most appropriate for solving the problem of adaptation are universalism, affective neutrality, specificity, and achievement; at the opposite extreme, values appropriate for improving integration are particularism, affectivity, diffuseness, and ascription (see Parsons, 1951; Parsons, Bales, and Shils, 1953).

environment partially conflict with efforts toward goal attainment—a problem emphasized by Selznick and his colleagues—and efforts directed toward integration—a tension emphasized by Bales (1953)—and so on.

A structural "solution" to these tensions is to create roles and subsystems focused on each problem area. For example, Bales and his colleagues argue that in informal groups the inherent tensions involved in goal attainment (for example, winning the game) versus integration (for example, providing satisfaction for all participants) is partially resolved by the emergence of a "task" leader, who specializes in directing and controlling goal attainment activities, and a "socio-emotional" leader, who specializes in motivating members and reducing tensions (Bales, 1953; Slater, 1955). And in formal organizations, specialized departments and roles—supervisors, maintenance workers, personnel counselors, inspectors—emerge to carry out the multiple, and somewhat conflicting, functions.

This solution only simplifies the definitions of individual roles and subsystems and does not, of course, eliminate the incompatibilities: these are merely pushed to a higher level of the system for resolution. For example, at the level of the informal group, Bales (1953) argues that the differentiated leader roles provide a stable basis for group functioning only if the two leaders form a coalition of mutual support. At the organizational level, Lawrence and Lorsch (1967) have argued that organizations characterized by a higher level of structural differentiation are in greater need of integrative and conflict-resolution mechanisms.

In moving toward a more micro or social psychological level, Parsons again employs the AGIL schema, arguing that each subsystem within the organization itself comprises finer subdivisions that can be distinguished in terms of the functional requirements. For example, within the goal attainment (G) subsystem—that part of the organization with the power to set and mobilize resources for goal attainment—Parsons distinguishes four kinds of decisions:

> *Policy decisions:* decisions concerning what goals are to be pursued and how they are to be attained (the Gg subsector—the goal attainment subsector of the goal attainment subsystem);
>
> *Allocative decisions:* lower-level decisions regarding the allocation of responsibilities and resources among personnel (the Ga subsector);
>
> *Coordinative decisions:* decisions about how personnel are to be motivated and their contributions coordinated (the Gi subsector);
>
> *Supporting values:* values that serve to legitimate and authorize the decision-making rights within this subsystem (the Gl subsector).

Parsons outlines how each of the other subsystems is also differentiated into the appropriate subsectors. Finally, he also uses the four system problems as a means of describing the relationships—in his terms, boundary processes—between systems and subsystems (see Parsons, 1960: 22–41; see also Landsberger, 1961: 227–31).

Like many natural system models, Parsons' framework emphasizes a set of functional needs that all social systems must satisfy in order to survive. As noted, this approach emphasizes the similarities between organizations and other types of social systems. But unlike other natural system models, Parsons's formulation also provides a clear basis for distinguishing between organizations and other social systems. Parsons states, "As a formal analytical point of reference, primacy of orientation to the attainment of a specific goal is used as the defining characteristic of an organization which distinguishes it from other types of social systems" (1960: 17). Within the Parsonian framework, this definition implies more than the widely shared view that organizations tend to pursue specific goals. Parsons calls attention to the relative importance placed on the goal-attainment subsystem in organizations. That is, organizations are social systems placing greater priority on those processes by which goals are set and resources are mobilized for goal attainment than is the case in other social systems.

We cannot hope to summarize all of Parsons's ideas on organizations—his framework rapidly becomes exceedingly complex—but we will review one other useful set of distinctions. In addition to his analysis of the functional differentiation that occurs along a horizontal axis at any given level of analysis, Parsons also distinguishes three major levels of organizational structure. At the bottom layer is the *technical* system, where the actual "product" of the organization is processed. This level is exemplified by the activities of workers on assembly lines, scientists in the laboratory, and teachers in the classroom. Above the technical level is the *managerial* system, whose primary functions are to mediate between the organization and the immediate task environment, including those who consume the organization's products and supply its raw materials, and to administer the organization's internal affairs. At the top of the organization is the *institutional* system, whose function is to relate the organization to the larger society; "the source of the 'meaning,' legitimation, or higher-level support which makes the implementation of the organization's goals possible" (Parsons, 1960: 63–64). Parsons makes the interesting point that there exists a "qualitative break" in the line-authority relation at the two points where the three systems are linked (p. 65). (This distinction among levels anticipates some of the concerns of open system theorists, described in Chapter 4. The significance of the break between levels is discussed in Chapter 10.)

Parsons' theoretical model has been employed by some, but not many, researchers to guide their empirical studies of organizations. Georgopoulos (1972; Georgopoulos and Matejko, 1967) has adapted it in his analysis of hospitals, and Lyden (1975) makes use of it in his study of public organizations. Of course, Parsons's generalized social system paradigm has had considerable impact on the work of sociologists, and many of his specific concepts and ideas have influenced work in the area of organizations. We will limit ourselves to only a few general comments in assessing Parsons' contributions. On the positive side, his work attempts to develop and perfect a limited set of abstract concepts that can then be adapted for use in examining the structure and functioning of diverse social groupings. Using the same generic concepts helps us to see similarities in social structure and process across systems that appear to be quite different. Also, more than those of other natural system theorists, Parsons's framework is quite comprehensive, encompassing the formal and rational aspects of organizations as well as the informal. Further, Parsons is more explicit than others in defining the system needs that must be served for survival.

Problems with the Parsonian framework are numerous. They include the difficulty in translating his analytic concepts into operational variables. For example, although it is reasonably easy to give examples of roles designed to increase integration, it is often difficult to assign a given structural feature such as a role or subunit to any single function (Morse, 1961). Landsberger (1961: 232) is correct that we should not expect concrete social structures to match closely analytical distinctions, but we do need to have a clearer set of rules for relating one to the other than Parsons provides. Finally, as many others have noted, Parsons's formulation tends to be more of a theoretical framework than a substantive theory. We are provided with numerous concepts that help us to see interesting distinctions, but given relatively few testable propositions. The functionalist paradigm underlying the approach does provide some implicit hypotheses—such as, unless the system needs are met the organization will not survive—but as already noted, such predictions are difficult to test.[11]

## SUMMARY AND TENTATIVE CONCLUSIONS

Whereas the rational system model focuses on features of organizations that distinguish them from other social groupings, the natural system model emphasizes commonalities among organizations and other systems. The natural system theorists do not deny that organizations have distinctive features, but they argue that these are overshadowed by the more generic systems and processes. Thus, the specific output goals of organizations are often undermined or distorted by energies devoted to the pursuit of system goals, chief among which is the concern to survive. And the formal aspects of organizational structure that receive so much attention from the rational system analysts are treated as faded backdrops for the "real" informal structures. More generally, whereas the rational system model stresses the normative structure of organizations, the natural system model places more emphasis on the behavioral structure. And where the rational system perspective stresses the importance of structure over the characteristics of participants, the natural system perspective reverses these priorities—so much so that Bennis (1959: 266) labels this orientation as one of "people without organizations."

Most of the early theorists who shaped the natural system perspective embrace a functional model of analysis, although they vary considerably in how explicitly and how fully they pursue its development. The human relations analysts tend to be less overt and less complete in their use of this model than is Barnard or Selznick or Parsons. All schools within the natural system framework presume the existence of certain needs that must be met if the system is to survive, and all direct attention to discovering the mechanisms by which these needs are satisfied.

Varying views of the environment appear to be associated with the natural system theorists. Most of the human relations analysts simply overlook it as a factor. Like the rational system theorists, they concentrate on

[11]A useful general discussion of Parsons' social system model will be found in Morse (1961). Landsberger (1961) provides an excellent description and critique of Parsons' model as it applies to organizations.

the internal organizational arrangements and their effects on participants, treating the organization as a closed system. This neglect is especially striking in the case of the Hawthorne studies, which were conducted during the 1930s, in the depths of the Great Depression. In the bank-wiring observation room study, for example, the workers' efforts to restrict production were viewed as irrational conformity to group norms. Given the larger economic situation, however, these activities may instead have been a highly rational response to the threat of being laid off (see Landsberger, 1958: 58; Blau and Scott, 1962: 92–93). Indeed, during the period of the research there were many layoffs at the Hawthorne plant; in fact, the bank-wiring room study had to be discontinued because so many workers were let go! (Roethlisberger and Dickson, 1939: 395.)

Barnard takes somewhat more account of the environment than the human relations group. He shows awareness that organizations must attract participants by providing them with inducements, indeed must compete with other organizations that are attempting to attract their services and loyalties. Moreover, he recognizes that a given individual participates in many cooperative groups simultaneously, so that his involvement in any single organization is both partial and intermittent. It is undoubtedly such insights that cause Barnard to put such emphasis on obtaining contributions and inspiring commitment. However, Barnard does not attempt to explicitly conceptualize the environment or to examine the extent to which organizations vary in their environment locations.

Selznick and his students, by contrast, do explicitly consider the environment in their analyses of organizations. However, their view is a highly selective one: the environment is perceived primarily as an enemy, as a source of pressures and problems. In most of the earlier studies in this tradition, the organization is viewed as capitulating to a tyrannical and hostile environment as the price of its survival.

In the work of Parsons we begin to have a more balanced view of the environment. Great stress is placed on the importance of the organization-environment relation, the organization being viewed as a subsystem within a more comprehensive social unit, and the environment seen more as a stabilizing element sustaining and legitimating the organization in its special mission than as a source of resistance. In these ways, Parsons anticipates the view of the open systems theorists in his treatment of the environment.

Two quite different perspectives on organizations have now been described. How could two such different viewpoints have arisen? Several explanations have been proposed. Since each sheds additional light on the subject, they will be briefly reviewed.

Lawrence and Lorsch (1967: 163–84) propose that some of the differences in perspective may have been produced by variations in the experience and background of the analysts themselves. They point out that among the rational or *classical* theorists, as they label them, Fayol, Mooney, and Urwick were all practical men with managerial experience. Taylor's training was as an industrial engineer. By contrast, among the natural systems theorists, Mayo, Roethlisberger, Selznick, McGregor, and Parsons were all from academic backgrounds with experience largely in the university. (Exceptions to this division were, on the one side, Weber, who was a university professor—however, in terms of life-style and experience he is more accurately described as a recluse scholar—and Gulick, who was also an academic. On the other side, of course, was Barnard, a company executive.) Lawrence and Lorsch argue that divergent backgrounds shaped the reactions of these analysts to organizations. Coming from the relatively unstructured arrangements of a university, the natural system analysts would be prone to react negatively to the formalism of an industrial plant, and might even be inclined to attribute their own needs for autonomy to workers in this situation.

A second explanation offered is that the analysts concentrated on different types of organizations. The rational system analysts were more likely to investigate industrial firms and state bureaucracies, while the natural system analysts tended to focus on service and professional organizations—schools, hospitals, and the YMCA. Since the degree of formalization and of goal specificity clearly varies greatly across the spectrum of organizations, it is quite possible that the rational system analysts concentrated on the relatively highly structured end of the continuum and the natural system analysts on the less structured end.

A third but related explanation for the differences between the two perspectives also comes from Lawrence and Lorsch, who suggest that organizational forms may vary as a function of their environments: "In simplified terms, the classical [rational] theory tends to hold in more stable environments, while the human relations [natural] theory is more appropriate to dynamic situations" (1967: 183). This important thesis is simply introduced at this point; it will be explored throughout the next several chapters.

Although differences in the analysts' backgrounds or in the particular organization on which they chose to focus may account for some of the variance in these two perspectives, it is our view that these points of view represent more fundamental divisions than are suggested by these explanations. Underlying the perspectives are quite basic divergences in moral and philosophical viewpoints.

The natural and the rational system theorists tend to hold differing conceptions of the actual and the proper relation of individual participants to organizations. Thus, the rational system theorists argue that only selected behaviors of participants are relevant as far as the organization is concerned and that only these "task-related" behaviors are at issue. The natural system theorists tend to expand the definition of organizationally relevant behavior to include more and more aspects of the individual's activities and attitudes. They have done so on two grounds: that such behaviors do in fact have an impact on the task behavior of participants, and thus are *empirically* relevant to an understanding of organizational behavior, and that organizations as social contexts affect the participant's well-being, a relation that has *normative* significance to anyone concerned with bettering the human condition. Many of these theorists point to the dysfunctions arising from the partial inclusion of participants and argue, partly on moral grounds, that organizations should take more responsibility for the "whole person." These arguments are not without merit, but all of the morality is not on one side. It is important to recognize that formal organizations developed in part to place limits on the demands superiors could make on their subordinates. The development of formal role definitions—definitions of the limits of a participant's obligations—was an important step in increasing the freedom of individuals. Whether the organization's purview should incorporate more or fewer facets of the lives of its participants is a basic philosophical difference separating the two perspectives.

Finally, the two approaches are characterized by quite divergent views of the fundamental nature of social systems. These differences are reflected in the contrasting imagery or metaphors employed by the two schools. For the mechanistic model of structure of the rational system perspective, the natural system substitutes an organic model. Rational systems are designed, but natural systems evolve; the former develop by conscious design, the latter by natural growth; rational systems are characterized by calculation, natural by spontaneity. Lest we regard these images of social structure as being of recent vintage, Wolin (1960: 352–434) reminds us that they have a long history in political and social thought. The view of organizations as economic, technological, efficient instruments is associated with the work of such social theorists as Hobbes, Lenin, and Saint-Simon—the precursors of Taylor, Weber, Fayol, and Simon. The view of organizations as communitarian, natural, antirational, organic systems may be traced back to the social theories of Rousseau, Proudhon, Burke, and Durkheim, the intellectual ancestors of Mayo, Barnard, and Selznick. With such lengthy and distinguished pedigrees, it is unlikely that either of these two lines of thought will soon end, or that their differences will be quickly resolved.

# organizations as open systems

That a system is open means, not simply that it engages in interchanges with the environment, but that this interchange is an essential factor underlying the system's viability.

Walter Buckley (1967)

The open system perspective emerged as a part of the intellectual ferment following World War II, although its roots are much older. This general intellectual movement created new areas of study, such as cybernetics and information theory; stimulated new applications, such as systems engineering and operations research; transformed existing disciplines, including the study of organizations; and proposed closer linkages among scientific disciplines. The latter interest has been fostered especially by general systems theory. Its founder, biologist Ludwig von Bertalanffy, was concerned about the growing compartmentalization of science: "The physicist, the biologist, the psychologist and the social scientist are, so to speak, encapsulated in a private universe, and it is difficult to get word from one cocoon to another" (Bertalanffy, 1956:1). Bertalanffy and his associates argued that certain general ideas could have relevance across a broad spectrum of disciplines. In particular, they endeavored to show that many of the most important entities studied by scientists—nuclear particles, atoms, molecules, cells, organs, organisms, ecological communities, groups, organizations, societies, solar systems—are all subsumable under the general rubic of *system*.[1]

All systems are characterized by an assemblage or combination of parts whose relations make them interdependent. While these features underlie the similarities exhibited by all systems, they also suggest the bases for the differences among them. The parts of which all systems are composed vary from being quite simple in structure to very complex, from being highly stable in their state to highly variable, and from being relatively impervious to system forces to being highly reactive to the workings of the system to which they belong. As we move from mechanical through

---

[1]In his monumental book *Living Systems*, Miller (1978) identifies seven basic levels: the cell, the organ, the organism, the group, the organization, the society, and the supranational system.

organic to social systems, the parts of which systems are composed become more complex and variable. Similarly, the nature of the relations among the parts varies from one type of system to another. In this connection, Norbert Wiener, the founder of cybernetics, notes "Organization we must consider as something in which there is an interdependence between the several organized parts but in which this interdependence has degrees" (1956: 322). In mechanistic systems, the interdependence among the parts is such that their behavior is highly constrained and limited. The structure is relatively rigid and the system of relations determinant. In organic systems, the connections among the interdependent parts are somewhat less constrained, allowing for more flexibility of response. In social systems, such as groups and organizations, the connections among the interacting parts become relatively loose: less constraint is placed on the behavior of one element by the condition of the others. Social organizations, in contrast with physical or mechanical structures, are *loosely coupled* systems (see Ashby, 1968; Buckley, 1967: 82–83).

Also, as we progress from simple to complex systems, the nature and relative importance of the various flows among the system elements and between the system and its environment change. The major types of system flows are those of materials, energy, and information. And, as Buckley (1967: 47) notes;

> whereas the relations among components of mechanical systems are a function primarily of spatial and temporal considerations and the transmission of energy from one component to another, the interrelations characterizing higher levels come to depend more and more on the transmission of information.

The notion of types or levels of systems that vary both in the complexity of their parts and in the nature of the relations among the parts has been usefully elaborated by Boulding, who has proposed a classification of systems by their level of complexity. Briefly, Boulding identifies the following system types:

1. *Frameworks:* systems comprising static structures, such as the arrangements of atoms in a crystal or the anatomy of an animal.
2. *Clockworks:* simple dynamic systems with predetermined motions, such as the clock and the solar system.
3. *Cybernetic systems:* systems capable of self-regulation in terms of some externally prescribed target or criterion, such as a thermostat.
4. *Open systems:* systems capable of self-maintenance based on a throughput of resources from its environment, such as a living cell.
5. *Blueprinted-growth systems:* systems that reproduce not by duplication but by the production of seeds or eggs containing preprogrammed instructions for development, such as the acorn–oak system or the egg–chicken system.
6. *Internal-image systems:* systems capable of a detailed awareness of the environment in which information is received and organized into an image or knowledge structure of the environment as a whole, a level at which animals function.
7. *Symbol-processing systems:* systems that possess self-consciousness and so are capable of using language. Humans function at this level.

8. *Social systems:* multi-cephalous systems comprising actors functioning at level 7 who share a common social order and culture. Social organizations operate at this level.

9. *Transcendental systems:* systems composed of the "absolutes and the inescapable unknowables." (Boulding, 1956: 200–207)

Boulding's typology is illuminating in several respects. It quickly persuades us of the great range and variety of the systems present in the world. Levels 1 to 3 encompass the physical systems, levels 4 to 6 the biological systems, and levels 7 and 8 the human and social systems. From levels 1 to 8, systems become progressively more complex, more loosely coupled, more dependent on information flows, more capable of self-maintenance and renewal, more able to grow and change, and more open to the environment. Boulding adds level 9 so that his classification will not be closed but open to new possibilities not yet envisioned.

Although the nine levels can be distinctly identified and associated with specific existing systems, they are not meant to be mutually exclusive. Indeed, each higher-level system incorporates the features of those below it. For example, it is possible to analyze a social organization as a framework, a clockwork, a cybernetic system, and so on up to level 8, the level that captures the most complex, the higher-level, processes occurring in organizations. Boulding argues that because each level incorporates those below it, "much valuable information and insights can be obtained by applying low-level systems to high-level subject matter." At the same time, Boulding reminds us that "most of the theoretical schemes of the social sciences are still at level 2, just rising now to 3, although the subject matter clearly involves level 8" (1956: 208). This is an important criticism of theoretical models of organizations, one we need to keep before us as we review more recent attempts to develop open systems models.

## SPECIAL EMPHASES

Broadly speaking, the contributions of the general systems perspective to organization theory up to this time have been to raise the level of our theoretical models up to level 3, where organizations are viewed as cybernetic systems, and to level 4, where they are viewed as open systems. Although Boulding's typology suggests we still have a long way to go before our models capture the complexity of organizational behavior, the insights obtained by moving to levels 3 and 4 are of great value. Along with our consideration of organizations as cybernetic and as open systems, we also take note of two other concepts emphasized by this perspective: organizations as loosely coupled systems and organizations as hierarchical systems.

### Organizations as Cybernetic Systems

Systems functioning at Boulding's level 3 are capable of self-regulation. This important feat is attained through the development of specialized parts or subsystems related by certain processes or flows. Consider the mechanical example of the thermostat related to a source of heat. The

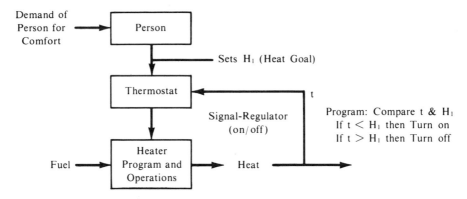

**FIGURE 4-1** Illustration of a Cybernetic System: The Thermostat and the Heater. *Source:* Swinth (1974), Figure 2-1 (p. 18).

system contains three parts: (1) a mechanism for converting inputs into outputs—in this case, a heater that converts fuel into heat; (2) a mechanism for comparing the level of outputs with some desired target level and issuing instructions to the first mechanism based on any discrepancy—in our case, a thermostat that compares the temperature in the room with a desired level and switches the heater on or off accordingly; and (3) a mechanism for setting the desired target level that governs the activity of the second mechanism—in our example, a person who determines the desired temperature for the room and sets the level of the thermostat. Figure 4-1 depicts these three parts and the flows among them for the thermostat example.

Figure 4-2 diagrams the same type of system, but at a more general or abstract level. To view an organization as a cybernetic system is to emphasize the importance of the operations, the control, and the policy centers and to analyze the flows among them (Swinth, 1974). The policy center sets the goals for the system. This activity occurs in response to demands or preferences from the environment (flow 1 in figure 4-2); some of the preferences take the form of specific orders (flow 2). Note that the setting of organizational goals is based on information about preferences in the environment so that exchanges between the environment and the organization can occur. The flows out of the policy center (flow 3) are the goals of the system itself. The control center monitors the performance of the operations level, keeping its outputs in line with the goals established by the policy center. The control center also obtains information about the outputs of the operations level (flow 4). This information is compared with the standards prescribed by the goals issued by the policy center and results in a set of instructions or directives to the operations unit (flow 5). As Buckley emphasizes, such feedback-controlled arrangements result in behavior that is "goal-*directed,* and not merely goal-*oriented,* since it is the deviations from the goal-state itself that direct the behavior of the system, rather than some predetermined internal mechanism that aims blindly" (1967: 53). Further, a feedback mechanism detects departures from the established goals no matter what their cause, an important control characteristic as systems become so complex that all the

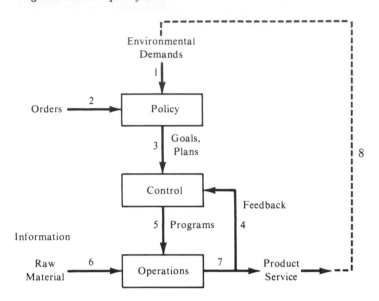

**FIGURE 4–2**    Abstract Model of Cybernetic System. *Source:* Swinth (1974), Figure 2–4 (p. 23).

potential sources of disturbance cannot be identified in advance (see Beer, 1964: 29–30).

The operations unit receives the raw materials (flow 6) and transforms them into products or outputs that are distributed outside the system (flow 7). The cybernetic model places great emphasis on the operational level of the organization—the level at which the production processes of the system are carried out. The analysis of these technical flows—inputs, throughouts, and outputs—is regarded as vital to an understanding of the system; indeed, the control and policy centers are examined chiefly in terms of their impact on these technical flows.

This analytic framework can be applied to the organization as a whole or to any of its subsystems. It can be used, for example, to analyze the operation of a company's personnel subsystem, which must meet the demands of other subsystems for trained employees and must control the recruitment and training of new workers and monitor their turnover (see Carzo and Yanouzas (1967: 345–47)). Or it can be used to examine the working of an entire company, which responds to demands from its marketplace and oversees the production and marketing of desired products for external customers (see Clough, 1963).

While cybernetic mechanisms involving feedback loops are readily discernible in organizations, we must be aware that our discussion of them (like others in this literature) has carried us far above Boulding's level 3 model. Level 3 is that of the thermostat that regulates temperature to a given value; our discussion has included *within* the system a mechanism for selecting the desired value: the policy center. To the extent that this center takes into account the system's past behavior, we then have a second feedback loop (flow 8). Ashby (1952) points out that in such double feedback systems the primary loop handles disturbances in "degree," applying existing decision rules, while the secondary loop handles disturbances in "kind," determining whether or not it is necessary to redefine the rules controlling the operating levels. Monitoring environmental feedback on the system's past behavior—for instance a company's keeping records on sales by product lines—is an important mechanism of adaptation for any open system.

### Organizations as Loosely Coupled Systems

The cybernetic model gives the impression of a taut system—an arrangement of parts such that each is highly responsive to changes in the others. Such system elements are certainly found within organizations, but we should guard against overgeneralization. One of the main contributions of the open systems perspective is the recognition that many systems—especially social systems—contain elements that are only slightly related with other elements and that are capable of fairly autonomous actions (see Ashby, 1968; Glassman, 1973).

This insight can be applied to many different components or elements of organizations and their participants. Thus, we have seen that from the standpoint of the natural system analysts, the normative structure of an organization is only loosely coupled with its behavioral structure. Rules do not always govern actions: a rule may change without affecting behavior, and vice versa. A similar observation has been made at the social psychological level. Some analysts have noted that an individual's goals or intentions may be only weakly, linked to his or her actions (see March and Olsen, 1976; and Chapter 11). The concept of loose coupling can also be applied to the relationship among structural units such as work groups or departments. Inspection of official organizational charts may lend the impression that these units are all highly interrelated and closely coordinated, whereas observation of their actual behavior may reveal that they are slightly and occasionally connected.

A particularly important application of the loose coupling image is that proposed by Cyert and March (1963) and adopted by Pfeffer and Salancik (1978). As noted in Chapter 1 in the open system definition of the concept of organization, these theorists propose to view the key participants in organizations not as a unitary hierarchy or as an organic entity, but as a loosely linked *coalition* of shifting interest groups. According to Pfeffer and Salancik (1978: 36);

> the organization is a coalition of groups and interests, each attempting to obtain something from the collectivity by interacting with others, and each with its own preferences and objectives.

Rather than being oriented to the pursuit of consistent, common objectives, these coalitions change

> their purpose and domains to accommodate new interests, sloughing off parts of themselves to avoid some interests, and when necessary become involved in activities far afield from their stated purposes (1978: 24).

Contrary to first impressions and to rational system assumptions, open system theorists insist that loose coupling in structural arrangements can be highly adaptive for the system as a whole (see Weick, 1976; Pfeffer and Salancik, 1978; see also Chapter 10). It appears that loose coupling need not signify either low moral or low managerial standards.

### The Characteristics of Open Systems

Organizations may be analyzed as cybernetic systems, but they also function at higher levels of complexity (recall Boulding's typology). They operate as open systems. Open systems are capable of self-maintenance on the basis of a throughput of resources from the environment. As Buckley (1967: 50) notes, this throughput is essential to the system's viability. Some analysts have mistakenly characterized an open system as having the capacity for self-maintenance *despite* the presence of throughput from the environment; their assumption is that because organizations are open, they must defend themselves against the environment. This view is misleading, since interaction with the environment is essential for open system functioning. As Pondy and Mitroff (1979: 7) argue, rather than suggesting that organizational systems be protected "against environmental complexity," one should realize that "it is precisely the throughput of nonuniformity that preserves the differential structure of an open system."

This is not to say that open systems do not have boundaries. They do, of course, and must expend energy in boundary maintenance. But it is of equal importance that energies be devoted to activities that span boundaries. Because of the openness of organizations, determining their boundaries is always difficult and sometimes appears to be a quite arbitrary decision. Does a university include within its boundary its students? Its alumni? Faculty during the summer? The spouses of students in university housing? Pfeffer and Salancik (1978: 30) propose to resolve this type of problem by reminding us that individual persons are not enclosed within the boundaries of organizations, only certain of their activities and behaviors. Although this interpretation helps, we all know that many actions have relevance for more than one system simultaneously. For example, a sale from the standpoint of one system is a purchase when viewed from another, and what is an act of conformity for one system can be an act of deviance for another. Moreover, as will be emphasized, all systems are made up of subsystems and are themselves subsumed in larger systems—an arrangement that creates linkages across systems and confounds the attempt to erect clear boundaries among them. Finally, our determination of whether a system is open is itself a matter of how the boundaries of the system are defined. As Hall and Fagen note, "whether a given system is open or closed depends on how much of the universe is included in the system and how much in the environment. By adjoining to the system the part of the environment with which an exchange takes place, the system becomes closed." (1956: 23)

General systems theorists elaborate the distinction between closed and open systems by employing the concept of *entropy:* energy loss or energy that cannot be turned into work. According to the second law of thermodynamics, all closed systems move toward a state of entropy—a random arrangement of their elements, a dissolution of their differentiated structures, a state of maximum disorder. By contrast, open systems, because they are capable of importing energy from their environment, can experience *negative entropy,* or negentropy. By acquiring inputs of greater complexity than their outputs, open systems restore their own energy and repair breakdowns in their own organization. Bertalanffy (1962: 7) concludes, "Hence, such systems can maintain themselves at a high level, and even evolve toward an increase of order and complexity."[2]

To emphasize these twin properties of open systems, Buckley (1967: 58–62) distinguishes between two basic sets of system processes: morphostasis and morphogenesis. The term *morphostasis* is applied to those processes that tend to preserve or maintain a system's given form, structure, or state. Morphostatic processes in biological systems would include circulation and respiration; in social systems, socialization and control activities. *Morphogenesis* is applied to those processes that elaborate or change the system—for example, growth, learning, and differentiation. In adapting to the external environment, all open systems typically become more differentiated in form, more elaborate in structure. Thus, in biological systems, organs whose sensitivities to external stimuli are coarse and broad are succeeded by more specialized receptors capable of responding to a wider range and finer gradations of stimuli. Biological organisms move toward greater complexity through the process of evolution: individual organisms are little affected, but over time, as mutations occur and are selected for their survival value, species are gradually transformed. Social organizations, more variable and loosely coupled than biological systems, can and do fundamentally change their structural characteristics over time. The General Motors of today bears little if any structural resemblance to the company of the same name of fifty years ago. Indeed, social organizations exhibit such an amazing capacity to change their basic structural features that researchers who study organizations over time have difficulty determining when the units they are studying are the same organizations with reorganized structures and when they represent the birth of new organizations.

To repeat, the source of system diversity and variety is the environment. From an open systems point of view, there is a close connection between the condition of the environment and the characteristics of the systems within it: a complex system could not maintain its complexity in a simple environment. Open systems are subject to what is termed the *law of limited variety:* "A system will exhibit no more variety than the variety to

---

[2]It is interesting to note that some information theorists posit a close relation between the concepts of organization and entropy: they are viewed, in effect, as opposite states. If entropy is a state of randomness, or zero organization, it is also the state that provides maximum variety, maximum information, to someone observing a set of elements. As organization develops, constraints and limitations grow, restricting the number of states that may be present among the elements. Miller elaborates this point:

> A well-organized system is predictable—you know what it is going to do before it happens. When a well-organized system does something, you learn little that you didn't already know—you acquire little information. A perfectly organized system is completely predictable and its behavior provides no information at all. The more disorganized and unpredictable a system is, the more information you get by watching it. (Miller, 1953: 3)

Based on such reasoning, information theorists Shannon and Weaver (1963) have proposed a measure of information, $H,$ which assesses the amount of entropy present in a set of elements—their variation, their relative frequency of occurrence, and their interdependence. The higher the $H$ level, the more information and the less organization is present (see also Buckley, 1967: 82–89).

which it has been exposed in its environment" (Pondy and Mitroff, 1979: 7). Although the processes by which such "laws" operate are not clearly understood, Part Three of this volume is devoted to explicating and illustrating the interdependence of organizations and environments.

### Organizations as Hierarchical Systems

General systems theorists also stress that hierarchy is a fundamental feature of complex systems—not so much hierarchy in the sense of status or power differences, but hierarchy in the form of clustering and levels. Systems are composed of multiple subsystems, and systems are themselves contained within suprasystems. This is such a common feature of virtually all complex systems that it is easily overlooked. Books like this one are made of parts, chapters, sections, paragraphs, words, letters. The U.S. political system is constituted of precincts, counties, states, and regions, all contained within the nation-state. And organizations are made up of roles contained within work groups, within departments, within divisions; many organizations are themselves subsystems of larger systems: corporate structures, or associations, or the executive branch of the government. (A diagram illustrating the major clusters to be found in a modern corporate organization will be found in Figure 10–1 of this book.)

Combining the notion of hierarchy with that of loose coupling, we note a common feature of complex systems: the connections and interdependencies within a system component are likely to be tighter and greater than those between system components. In a well-written book, for example, the ideas expressed in a single paragraph should be more closely interrelated than those expressed in different paragraphs. Similarly, interactions within a given academic department within a university are likely to be more frequent and more intense than those occurring between departments. Indeed, as will be discussed in Chapter 9, this tendency provides the basis for an important principle of organizational design.

When subsystems take the form of "stable subassemblies"—units capable of retaining their form without constant attention from superior units—then hierarchical forms have an important survival advantage over other systems (Simon, 1962). Many seemingly complex organizational systems are made up of, and depend for their stability on, units that are highly similar and capable of relatively autonomous functioning—for examples, similarly organized work teams or departments; franchise units; and chain stores. From this perspective, the apparent complexity of many systems becomes simpler: everything is *not* connected to everything else; there are loose connections and missing connections; and many components of systems are identical or nearly so. (See Aldrich, 1979: 75–80.)

To this point, we have emphasized that all systems are composed of subsystems. Let us briefly comment on the significance of the fact that all systems are also subsumed by other, more encompassing systems. This suggests that to understand the operation of a system, it may be as important to look outside the system at its context as to look inside the system at its component units. Schwab (1960) has termed this perspective *rationalism,* the opposite of reductionism. Rationalism occurs when explanation comes by looking outside an entity to the environment or a higher system in which it is embedded. (See also McKelvey, 1982: 5.) In many ways, the open systems perspective points to the significance of the wider environment.

## SELECTED SCHOOLS

As with the previous perspectives, we turn now to several schools that exemplify the open systems approach. We will briefly describe the systems design approach; contingency theory, which can be regarded as a school growing out of the systems design approach; and Weick's social psychological model of organizing. Although open systems approaches to organizations were the last of the three perspectives to emerge, they have spread very rapidly and have had an enormous effect on organization theory. We discuss in this section only a few early developments; in Chapter 5 and later chapters we will consider other approaches embodying open systems assumptions and insights.

### Systems Design

A large and growing number of organization theorists look to general systems theory as a source of ideas to improve the design of organizations—determining proper work flows, control systems, and planning mechanisms, and their interrelations—for carrying out their designated functions (see Carzo and Yanouzas, 1967; Khandwalla, 1977; Swinth, 1974; Mintzberg, 1979). Unlike some of the schools devoted to the study of organizations, the orientation of this group is pragmatic and applied: they seek to change and improve organizations as viewed from a managerial perspective, not simply to describe and understand them.

Many of the analysts attempting to apply systems ideas to organizations are aware both of the great complexity of organizations as one type of system and of the danger of misapplying or overextending analogies based on the operation of other, less complex systems. Beer (1964) proposes a classification of systems ranging from those that are both simple and deterministic, such as the behavior of a block and tackle system, to those that are complex and probabilistic, such as the operation of an assembly line in a factory, to those that are "exceedingly complex" and probabilistic, such as an entire organization (for example, a company). Complex probabilistic systems, whose behavior can be generally described and predicted with statistical procedures, are the province of operations research; exceedingly complex probabilistic systems have given rise to the fields of cybernetics and systems design (Beer, 1964: 18). Because of their great complexity, the latter systems currently defy conventional mathematical modeling approaches. Instead, the most widely employed technique of analysis is to simulate the operation of the system. "Here, all the variables and relationships of interest are linked as understood into a model and then the manager-analyst-researcher manipulates certain ones and observes how others change as the simulation of the system plays itself out" (Swinth, 1974: 11). Note that this approach emphasizes the importance of treating the system as a system.

Complex systems cannot be understood by an analysis that attempts to decompose the system into its individual parts in order to examine each part and relationship in turn. This approach, according to Ashby (1956: 36), one of the founders of the general systems movement,

> gives us only a vast number of separate parts or items of information, the results of whose interactions no one can predict. If we take such a system to pieces, we find that we cannot reassemble it!

Simulation techniques are popular with systems analysts because they are consistent with this image of a unit whose behavior can be understood only as the resultant of complex and probabilistic interactions among its parts. They also support the systems view that to understand organizations one must focus on the operational level of the organization. Thus, a systems design analyst would be more interested in obtaining charts depicting the flows of information, energy, and materials throughout the organization than in inspecting the formal table of organization. In examining a football team as a social system, for example, such an analyst would rather inspect the play books governing the activities of the various players during the course of a game than the formal authority arrangements among the players, coaches, managers, and owners of the club.

It is consistent with the holistic emphasis of the systems analyst that the approach deals with objects or parts of systems, the detailed structure of which is unknown or regarded as irrelevant. These basic units are the so-called black boxes, the smallest elements of the system under study (Haberstroh, 1965: 1174). For the purposes of systems analysis, all the information that is required is a description of the inputs to and the outputs from each of the basic elements (or the relation between the inputs and the outputs). It is not necessary to know the internal working of these system components to understand or simulate the workings of the larger system.

An important characteristic of exceedingly complex, probabilistic systems is that the whole is more than the sum of its parts, in the pragmatic sense that given the properties of the parts and the laws of their interaction, it is not a trivial matter to infer the behavior of the larger system. As a consequence, it is virtually impossible to predict and protect against all the ways in which such systems can fail. Perrow has labeled such failures *normal accidents:* normal because the accidents emerge "from the characteristics of the systems themselves" (1982: 1; see also Perrow, 1984). From an in-depth analysis of the near disaster at the Three Mile Island nuclear plant in Pennsylvania, Perrow notes the more obvious and ever-present problems of design and equipment failures and operator error but emphasizes the role played by "negative synergy."

> "Synergy" is a buzz word in business management circles, indicating that the whole is more than the sum of its parts, or in their congenial familiarity, two plus two equals five. But minus two plus minus two can equal minus five thousand in tightly-coupled, complex, high risk military and industrial systems . . . where complex, unanticipated, unperceived and incomprehensible interactions of off-standard components (equipment, design, and operator actions) threaten disaster. (Perrow, 1982: 18)

Gall (1978: 97) identifies concisely the dilemma posed by these systems: "When a fail-safe system fails, it fails by failing to fail safe."

Among the various flows connecting system elements, the flow of information is the most critical. The gathering, transmission, storage, and retrieval of information are among the most fateful activities of organizations, and design theorists devote much attention to them. (See Sage, 1981.) We have already described in Chapter 2 Simon's views on the cognitive limits of decision makers. From the perspective of systems design, Simon is pointing out the limitations of individuals as information processors.[3] Viewing individuals in this manner, Haberstroh asserts that they exhibit "low channel capacity, lack of reliability, and poor computational ability." On the other hand, individuals possess some desirable features: "The strong points of a human element are its large memory capacity, its large repertory of responses, its flexibility in relating these responses to information inputs, and its ability to react creatively when the unexpected is encountered" (Haberstroh, 1965: 1176). The challenge facing the systems designers is how to create structures that will overcome the limitations and exploit the strengths of each system component, including the individual participants.

Of course, not all environments place the same demands on organizations and their participants for information processing. Recognition of this important point has given rise to a special perspective known as *contingency theory*, which we will briefly summarize next. More generally, a number of theorists argue that the very existence of organizations is explained by the information-processing limitations of individuals confronted by complex situations. These arguments, developed by Arrow (1974) and Williamson (1975), are reviewed in Chapter 7.

### Contingency Analysis

Jay Galbraith (1973:2) states the two assumptions underlying contingency theory most succinctly:

•There is no one best way to organize.
•Any way of organizing is not equally effective.

The first assumption challenges the conventional wisdom of those administrative theorists who have sought to develop general principles applicable to organizations in all times and places. Such a quest not only overlooks the vast diversity of existing organizational forms but also fails to recognize the great variety of tasks undertaken by organizations. The second assumption challenges the "know-nothing" position that the complexity and variety of organizations are such that it is futile to search for any underlying principles to guide their design. A third assumption can be formulated to represent the position of the contingency theorist:

•The best way to organize depends on the nature of the environment to which the organization relates.

---

[3]Simon's contributions to organizations relate as closely to these concerns of systems design as to the rational model of organizations (see Simon, 1960; 1962).

As a branch of systems design, contingency theory emphasizes that design decisions depend—are contingent—on environmental conditions.

Contingency theory is guided by the general orienting hypothesis that organizations whose internal features best match the demands of their environments will achieve the best adaptation. The challenge facing those who embrace this orientation is to be clear about what is meant by "the organization's internal features," "the demands of their environments," "best adaptation," and, most difficult of all, "best match." Details of attempted answers to these questions are best postponed to Part Three, but two general approaches can be briefly described to illustrate the directions pursued within this theoretical tradition.

Lawrence and Lorsch (1967), who coined the label *contingency theory,* argue that different environments place differing requirements on organizations: specifically, environments characterized by uncertainty and rapid rates of change in market conditions or technologies present different demands—both constraints and opportunities—on organizations than do placid and stable environments. They conducted empirical studies of organizations in the plastics, food processing, and standardized container industries to assess the relation between these environments—ranging from high to low uncertainty—and the internal features of each type of organization. They also suggest that different segments of subunits within a given type of organization may confront different external demands. Thus, within plastics manufacturing companies, the research and development units face a more uncertain and more rapidly changing environment than the production departments. To cope with these varying environments, organizations and their subunits develop differentiated characteristics. For example, the normative structure may be more or less highly formalized, or the time orientation of participants may be focused on long- or short-range outcomes. The more varied the types of environments confronted by a given organization type, the more differentiated the organization structure needs to be. Moreover, the more differentiated the structure, the more effort that must be devoted to the integration of the various subunits. In sum, Lawrence and Lorsch propose that the match or coalignment of an organization with its environment occurs on at least two levels: (1) the structural features of each organizational subunit should be suited to the specific environment to which it relates; and (2) the differentiation and mode of integration characterizing the larger organization should be suited to the overall environment within which the organization must operate (see Chapter 10).

Galbraith's (1973; 1977) version of contingency theory is similar to the systems design school in its stress on information processing. As in Lawrence and Lorsch's view, the environment is characterized in terms of the amount of uncertainty it poses for the organization. Galbraith connects the concepts of environmental uncertainty and information processing in the following useful manner: uncertainty enters the organization by affecting the work or tasks that organizations perform, and "the greater the task uncertainty, the greater the amount of information that must be processed among decision makers during task execution in order to achieve a given level of performance" (1977: 36). Various structural arrangements, including rules, hierarchy, and decentralization, may be viewed as mechanisms determining the information-processing capacity of the system. The design challenge is to select a structural arrangement appropriate for the information-processing requirements of the tasks to be performed. We will consider Galbraith's specific arguments in more detail in Chapter 9.

### Weick's Model of Organizing

While the design and contingency theorists have developed their version of the open systems approach at the structural level of analysis, Karl Weick has attempted to pursue some of the implications of this approach at the social psychological level (1969; rev. 1979). We cannot do justice to his subtle and imaginative ideas in this overview but will note some of his lines of argument and attempt to capture the flavor of his work.

Weick cites with approval Bateson's (1972: 334) motto "stamp out nouns." He argues,

> The word, organization, is a noun and it is also a myth. If one looks for an organization one will not find it. What will be found is that there are events, linked together, that transpire within concrete walls and these sequences, their pathways, their timing, are the forms we erroneously make into substances when we talk about an organization. (Weick, 1974: 358)

Rather than talking about organizations, the focus of our attention should be "organizing." This is a very explicit example of the manner in which the systems perspective attempts to shift attention from structure to process.

Weick defines organizing as "the resolving of equivocality in an enacted environment by means of interlocked behaviors embedded in conditionally related processes" (1969: 91). We will attempt to unpack this dense definition. Weick argues that organizing is directed toward information processing generally and, in particular, toward removing its equivocality. He explains that

> the basic raw materials on which organizations operate are informational inputs that are ambiguous, uncertain, equivocal. Whether the information is embedded in tangible raw materials, recalcitrant customers, assigned tasks, or union demands, there are many possibilities, or sets of outcomes that might occur. Organizing serves to narrow the range of possibilities, to reduce the number of "might occurs." The activities of organizing are directed toward the establishment of a workable level of certainty. (Weick, 1969: 40)

This work is carried out by sets of "interlocked behaviors"—"repetitive, reciprocal, contingent behaviors that develop and are maintained between two or more actors" (1969: 91). The activities are carried on in three stages: enactment, selection, and retention. It is important to note that these three stages are Weick's translation of the three phases of natural selection or evolution as developed by Campbell (1969). (See Chapter 5.) Weick substitutes the term *enactment* for Campbell's label of *variations* for the first stage to emphasize the more active role organizational participants carry out in defining the environments they confront. Individual information processors *create* the environment to which the system then adapts (Weick, 1979: 147–69). The process of enactment introduces information (variety) into the system, which is dealt with according to organizational rules or routines: the greater the equivocality in the information introduced, the smaller the number of rules that will be activated to deal with the input. If the input is highly equivocal, only a small number of general rules are used to attempt to structure the input; however, if the input is better understood, a greater number of rules can be applied in responding to it (1969: 73). The application of the rules reduces (by selection) the equivocality of the information. The final phase of information processing determines what information is to be retained for future reference. Although the entire process operates to reduce equivocality, some equivocal features do and must remain if the organization is to be able to survive into a new and different future. In other words, "organizations continue to exist only if they maintain a balance between flexibility and stability" (Weick, 1979: 215). The information received and selected by the organization must be both credited (retained) and discredited or questioned if the organization is to safely face a future that may resemble, but must inevitably differ from, its past.

Weick's major concern is to spell out the implications of the open systems perspective when applied to the level of individual participants and the relationships among them. The semiautonomy of the individual actors is stressed: the looseness and conditionality of the relationships linking them is emphasized. Further, familiar social psychological processes become more problematic when viewed through the lens of a systems analyst. Where the conventional view would stress the use of perceptual sets that give continuity and stability to individual responses, Weick emphasizes the importance of "attention" processes that are more variable because they take into account situational factors—the "particular here and now" that determines what is selected out and what neglected from the available cues (1969: 39). Similarly, whereas conventional wisdom asserts that goals precede activities, that intention precedes action, Weick (1969: 37) insists that behavior often occurs first and then is interpreted—given meaning. The view of interpersonal processes such as coordination and control is similarly affected: such "interlocked behaviors" are viewed as loosely coupled systems allowing individual performers great latitude in interpreting and implementing directions (Weick, 1976). More generally, in his view of causation, Weick embraces and applies many of the most basic concepts of the systems analyst—for example, the concept of *equifinality*, which asserts that a given outcome may be the result of quite different processes, and the concept of *causal arc*, which insists on the likelihood of reciprocal rather than unilateral causation (Weick, 1974; see also Buckley, 1967). In these and related ways, Weick has attempted to "open up" our conception of organizational structure and behavior.

A number of other theories that draw heavily on open system insights have recently appeared, but we reserve discussion of them to later chapters.

## SUMMARY AND TENTATIVE CONCLUSIONS

The open systems perspective developed later than the rational and natural system views, but it has gained adherents rapidly and has profoundly altered our conception of organizations and their central features and processes. The open systems view of organizational structure stresses the

complexity and variability of the individual parts—both individual participants and subgroups—as well as the looseness of connections among
them. Parts are viewed as capable of semiautonomous action; many parts
are viewed as, at best loosely coupled to other parts. Further, in human
organizations, as Boulding emphasizes, the system is multi-cephalous:
many heads are present to receive information, make decisions, direct
performance. Individuals and subgroups form and leave coalitions. Coordination and control become problematic. Also, system boundaries are
seen as amorphous; the assignment of actors or actions to either the
organization or the environment often seems arbitrary and varies depending on what aspect of systemic functioning is under consideration.

Open systems imagery does not simply blur the more conventional
views of the structural features of organizations: it shifts attention from
structure to process. Whether viewed at the more abstract level through
concepts such as enacting, selecting, and retaining processes, or at the
more concrete level with concepts such as input, throughput, and output
production flows and feedback-control loops, the emphasis is on organizing as against organization. Maintaining these flows and preserving these
processes are viewed as problematic. As Weick insists, "processes are repetitive only if this repetitiveness is continuously accomplished" (1969:
36). Both morphostatic and morphogenetic processes are of interest: the
former emphasize self-maintenance and stability, the latter, development
and elaboration of structure. A process view is taken not only of the
internal operations of the organization but of the organization itself as a
system persisting over time. The organization as an arrangement of roles
and relationships is not the same today as it was yesterday or will be
tomorrow: to survive is to adapt, and to adapt is to change. As Leavitt and
his colleagues conclude:

> the complex organization is more like a modern weapons system than like
> old-fashioned fixed fortifications, more like a mobile than a static sculpture,
> more like a computer than an adding machine. In short, the organization is
> a dynamic system. (Leavitt, Dill, and Eyring, 1973: 4)

The interdependence of the organization and its environment receives primary attention in the open systems perspective. Rather than
overlooking the environment, as tends to be true of the rational system
perspective, or viewing it as alien and hostile, as is characteristic of the
natural system perspective, the open systems model stresses the reciprocal
ties that bind and relate the organization with those elements that sur-
round and penetrate it. The environment is perceived to be the ultimate
source of materials, energy, and information, all of which are vital to the
continuation of the system. Indeed, the environment is even seen to be
the source of order itself.

It seems premature to attempt even a tentative assessment of the
open systems perspective at this time. The general systems approach—the
mother ship—was itself launched only about three decades ago, and although its applicability to social organizations has been underscored from
the very beginning, the working out of its specific implications is still
underway. Some problems and dangers are already apparent. There is a
strong tendency to work from analogy, applying insights from one type of

system to another—for example, from the thermostat-heater system to the control system of an organization. While insights can be generated by such analogies, so can errors and misconceptions. Also, more so than the other perspectives, the open systems approach seems to carry with it a large number of highly abstract and often abstruse new concepts and labels, such as cybernetics, morphogenesis, equifinality. New concepts appropriately understood and applied can open our eyes to new facets of reality, but sometimes open systems theorists seem bedazzled by the richness of their new vocabularies and appear to be content simply to relabel the various components of the organizational system under study.

Such problems, however, often accompany new intellectual developments. In general, it seems clear that the open systems perspective brings with it a much-needed dimension to—if not a reorientation of—previously existing viewpoints. After the emergence of the open systems perspective, the old image of a closed, self-contained, self-sufficient system will be difficult to resurrect. The doors and windows of the organization have been opened, and we are more than ever aware of the vital flows and linkages that relate the organization to other systems. Further, we see more clearly now that organizations are processes as well as structures, and that some of these processes are not recurrent cycles but forces changing the existing structures.

# 5 combining the perspectives

Political revolutions aim to change political institutions in ways that those institutions themselves prohibit. Their success therefore necessitates the partial relinquishment of one set of institutions in favor of another.
Like the choice between competing political institutions, that between competing paradigms proves to be a choice between incompatible modes of community life. Because it has that character, the choice is not and cannot be determined merely by the evaluative procedures characteristic of normal science, for these depend in part upon a particular paradigm, and that paradigm is at issue. When paradigms enter, as they must, into a debate about paradigm choice, their role is necessarily circular. Each group uses its own paradigm to argue in that paradigm's defense.

Thomas S. Kuhn (1962)

The three preceding chapters have described and illustrated three perspectives on organizations. We have attempted to present these perspectives succinctly but fairly, discussing examples of work from each, and assessing their strengths and limitations. We have sought to avoid treating these viewpoints as caricatures or as approaches having only historical interest. In our opinion, each is valuable: each focuses on a set of significant and enduring features of organizations.

In this chapter, we begin by reviewing three important attempts to combine and reconcile these three perspectives. Then we propose an alternative combination. The latter approach is used both to briefly review theories previously discussed as well as to introduce new conceptions developed during the past two decades. Since there has been a flurry of theoretical activity during this period, the catalog of new approaches is embarrassingly long: too many ideas are covered too quickly. But, fortunately for the sake of comprehension and utility, the objective is only to introduce the theories that will be considered in more detail in Parts Three and Four of this volume. Each theory is briefly set out in one place so that it can be more easily compared with others, and easily located for review as needed.

As noted in Chapter 1, the three perspectives operate as paradigms, as Kuhn (1962) defines this concept. Functioning as conceptual frameworks and as sets of assumptions guiding empirical investigations, paradigms are not themselves subject to verification. A paradigm is not so much disproved as it is dislodged or supplanted by a different paradigm providing a new map of the territory—indeed, not only a new map but new directions for map making. As Kuhn (1962: 108) observes,

> in learning a paradigm the scientist acquires theory, methods, and standards together, usually in an inextricable mixture. Therefore, when paradigms change, there are usually significant shifts in the criteria determining the legitimacy both of problems and of proposed solutions.

Thus in some respects the differences between competing paradigms cannot be completely resolved by scientific evidence or argumentation.

Nevertheless, noting the selectivity of the perspectives, a number of theorists have attempted to develop more encompassing formulations, combining selected portions of the earlier traditions. We will briefly review three of these synthetic frameworks: the models of Etzioni, of Lawrence and Lorsch, and of Thompson.

## THREE ATTEMPTS AT INTEGRATION

### Etzioni's Structuralist Model

Etzioni (1964) has proposed a "structuralist" approach as a synthesis of the classical (rational) schools and the human relations (natural) schools. (See also, Gross and Etzioni, 1985: 65–88) In contrast with our view, Etzioni does not regard Weber as a contributor to the classical approach but argues that Weber together with Marx provides the basis for the synthetic structuralist model. Marx and Weber both believed that regardless of the best efforts of managers and workers, their economic and social interests are inevitably in conflict. Marx (1972 trans.) viewed factory workers as alienated from their work since they owned neither the means of production nor the product of their labor. Weber (1946 trans.: 221–24) generalized this assertion, noting that soldiers in modern armies did not own their weapons, nor did research scientists own their equipment and supplies. Both assumed that those who owned the means of production could control their use. In this sense, all employees in large organizations can be viewed as alienated from their labor (see Chapter 12). Thus, for Etzioni, control becomes the fundamental issue in understanding organization, and both the rational and the natural system theorists have important, and different, things to say about control systems within organizations. The rational system theorists contribute to the analysis of control by focusing on the distribution of power among organizational positions; the natural system theorists make their contribution by insisting that naked power only alienates, that power must be acceptable to the subordinates in the power relation if control attempts are to be effective, as Barnard (1938) insisted.[1] Weber, according to Etzioni, combines both of these points of view in his examination of the distribution of power, on the one hand, and of the bases on which it is seen to be legitimate by participants in the system, on the other (Etzioni, 1964: 50–51; 1961; Weber, 1947 trans: 324–29).[2]

In addition to combining the rational and natural perspectives in the analysis of the central issue of power, Etzioni proposes that the structuralist model gives equal attention to formal and informal structures, and in particular to the relations between them; to the scope of informal groups and the relations between such groups both inside and outside the organization; to both social and material rewards and their interrelation; and to the interaction of the organization and its environment (Etzioni, 1964: 41–49). In approaching all of these matters, however, the structuralist point of view recognizes fully

> the organizational dilemma: the inevitable strains—which can be reduced but not eliminated—between organizational needs and personal needs; between rationality and non-rationality; between discipline and autonomy; between formal and informal relations; between management and workers, or more generically, between ranks and divisions (Etzioni, 1964: 41).

In sum, the structuralist model suggests that the rational and the natural system perspectives are complementary. Each view represents a partial truth. If the perspectives seem at times to conflict, this is because the organizational elements to which they point sometimes conflict. The recognition of such conflicts is an important part of the "whole" truth about organizations, their structural features, and their functioning.

### Lawrence and Lorsch's Contingency Model

We have already reported Lawrence and Lorsch's various proposals for reconciling the rational and natural system perspectives (Chapter 3) and described their contingency model of organizations (Chapter 4). We briefly review these ideas at this point to emphasize that they suggest a basis on which all three perspectives can be reconciled.

In essence, Lawrence and Lorsch (1967) argue that if an open system perspective is taken—so that any given organization is viewed not in isolation but in relation to its specific environment—then the rational and the natural system perspectives may be seen to identify different organizational types which vary because they have adapted to different types of environments. The rational and natural system perspectives are at variance because each focuses on a different end of a single continuum representing the range of organizational forms. At one extreme, some organizations are highly formalized, are centralized, and pursue clearly specified goals; at the other extreme, some organizations are less formalized, rely greatly on the personal qualities of participants, and lack consensus on

---

[1]Hopkins (1961) has proposed a quite similar basis for reconciliation of the two points of view.

[2]These matters involving power, authority, legitimacy, and control will be more fully discussed in Chapter 11.

goals. The two extreme types depicted by the rational and the natural systems models should not be viewed as differing aspects of the same organization—as, for example, Etzioni's structuralist model would suggest—but rather as different forms of organizations. And, as emphasized by the open systems perspective, the nature of the form is determined by the type of environment to which the organization must relate. Specifically, the more homogeneous and stable the environment, the more appropriate will be the formalized and hierarchical form. And the more diverse and changing the task environment, the more appropriate will be the less formalized and more organic form.

Thus we arrive at the contingency argument: there is no one best organizational form but several, and their suitability is determined by the extent of the match between the form of the organization and the demands of the environment. The general form of this argument is ecological; the argument assumes that different systems are more or less well adapted to differing environments. Environmental conditions determine which systems survive and thrive: those best adapted are most likely to prosper.[3] By this argument, Lawrence and Lorsch attempt to account for the different forms of organizations and for the different theoretical perspectives that have developed to characterize them. Note that their views can also explain why the rational system perspective preceded in time the natural system perspective if it is assumed, as most open system analysts would contend, that the environments of organizations were more stable in the past and have become progressively more volatile.

The open systems perspective is viewed by Lawrence and Lorsch as the more comprehensive framework within which the rational and natural system perspectives may be housed, since each of the latter constitutes only a partial view depicting particular organizational adaptations to differing environmental conditions.

### Thompson's Levels Model

Simultaneously with the emergence of Lawrence and Lorsch's contingency model, James D. Thompson (1967) developed a somewhat different basis for reconciling the three perspectives. In his influential work *Organizations in Action,* Thompson argues that analysts should be mentally flexible enough to admit the possibility that all three perspectives are essentially correct and applicable to all organizations. However, they do not all apply with equal force to all organizational locations. Thompson borrows the distinctions proposed by Parsons (1960: 60–65), summarized in Chapter 3, identifying three organizational levels: the technical level, that part of the organization carrying on the production functions; the managerial, comprising those activities relating to the control of the production functions and the procurement of inputs and the disposition of outputs; and the institutional level, consisting of those activities relating the organization to the larger community and institutional sectors. Thompson's argument is that the three perspectives apply differentially to the three levels of organizations.

---

[3]These arguments are most fully developed in the population ecology approach, described in more detail later in this chapter.

Thompson's model in a nutshell is that organizations strive to be rational although they are natural and open systems. It is in the interest of administrators—those who design and manage organizations—that the work of the organization be carried out as effectively and efficiently as possible. Since technical rationality presumes a closed system, Thompson (1967: 10–13) argues that organizations will attempt to seal off their technical level, protecting it from external uncertainties to the extent possible.[4] Thus, it is the level of the core technology—the assembly line in the automobile factory, the patient care wards and treatment rooms in the hospital—that we would expect the rational system perspective to apply with the most force. At the opposite extreme, the institutional level, if it is to perform its functions, must be open to the environment. It is at this level, where the environment must be enacted or adapted to, that the open systems perspective is most relevant. In the middle is the managerial level, which must mediate between the relatively open institutional and the closed technical levels. To do so effectively requires the flexibility that is associated with the less formalized and more politicized activities depicted by the natural system theorists. It is also the managers—whose power and status are most intimately linked to the fate of the organization—who have the greatest stake in the survival of the organization as a system.

There is much to be said for, and learned from, each of these efforts to reconcile the three perspectives. In a real sense, they are all true, or what may be more important, useful: Etzioni is surely correct that all organizations embody conflicting tendencies between the formal and informal, rational and nonrational aspects of their structures; Lawrence and Lorsch are correct that some types of organizations exhibit higher formalization and goal specificity than other types and that these differences are associated with environmental conditions; and Thompson is correct that some segments or levels of the organization are more closed or open than others. These combinations and applications of the three original perspectives have illuminated additional facets of organizations, and in this way, the utility of the perspectives has been reinforced for a new generation of students of organziations.

## CROSS-CLASSIFYING THE PERSPECTIVES

There is yet another sense in which the three perspectives may be seen as persisting up to the present time, albeit in new combinations. Our introduction to the perspectives in earlier chapters suggested that they fell into a neat time order with the rational perspective preceding the natural system view, and the open system perspective developing most recently. We will suggest now a slightly more complex view—namely, that there have been not three but four phases, created by cross-classifying the three perspectives.

At the risk of considerable oversimplification, we suggest that theoretical models of organizations underwent a major shift about 1960, at the

---

[4]Specific mechanisms, termed *buffering strategies,* used to seal off the technical core are described in Chapter 8.

time open systems perspectives supplanted closed system models. Analyses focusing primarily on the internal characteristics of organizations gave way at approximately that date to approaches emphasizing the importance for the organization of events and processes external to it. After 1960, the environments of organizations, conceived in terms of economic, political, cultural, social, technological, and interorganizational elements, figure prominently in attempts to explain organizational structure and behavior.

On both sides of this watershed representing the transition from closed to open system models, a second trend can be identified: a shift from rational to natural system models of analysis. It appears that this shift has occurred twice! It occurred for the closed system models in the late 1930s and early 1940s, as we have already described in Chapters 2 and 3—the rational system formulations of Weber and Taylor giving way to the natural system approaches of Mayo and Barnard—and it appears to be occurring again for the open systems models at the present time, in ways to be discussed in this chapter.

That is, we suggest that the dominant theoretical model for analyzing organizations up to the late 1930s was the closed rational system model (type I). This model was succeeded by the closed natural system model (type II), which held sway through the 1950s. The open systems models came into prominence during the 1960s. However, this perspective was quickly combined in the work of several major theorists with a resurgence of the rational system model. Open rational systems models (type III) dominated the field well into the 1970s. Recently however, the most prominent theoretical contributions appear to represent a revival of the natural system perspective, but now combined with the open system model (type IV). Although it is possible to thus identify a dominant theoretical orientation for each period, that is not to say that all of the important work associated with that orientation was produced during that period or that important work associated with the alternative orientations was not taking place. The time periods identified are not absolute; and all combinations of theoretical work are active up to the present time.

In addition to varying in their dominant perspective, the approaches reviewed also differ in level of analysis, as we have noted throughout. Closed system models, whether rational or natural, restricted attention (by definition) to the internal characteristics of organizations, but did vary in focus between social psychological and structural properties of organizations. With the advent of open systems models, ecological analyses became an important new source of theorizing about the determinants of organizational behavior and structure. A great deal of the recent theoretical work in organizations has occurred at the ecological level. (Indeed, as will be discussed in Chapter 6, several varying layers of analysis have emerged within this level.)

Table 5–1 summarizes this pattern and lists representative theories and theorists associated with each type of perspective. While there are important similarities between types I and III, the rational systems models, and between types II and IV, the natural systems models, the differences generated by the transition from closed to open models are at least as important. A brief discussion of each type can highlight these similarities and differences. Before reviewing each type, however, we note the relation of these four types to the organization of the present volume. To this point, our discussions of the rational and the natural systems models have emphasized their closed-system versions, types I and II. Although we have stressed the differences between a closed and an open systems perspective, we have deliberately refrained from serious attention to the new generations of rational and natural systems models, types III and IV, which have emerged since the development of the open systems perspective. These most recent contributions receive primary attention in succeeding chapters. Hence, our discussion of types I and II will serve as a brief review of the work of major theorists prior to 1960, as described in Part Two of this volume. And our discussion of types III and IV will serve to preview the work of major theorists since 1960, to be discussed in greater detail in Part Three.

### Type I: Closed Rational System Models

The representative theories and theorists listed in table 5–1 for the closed rational systems models should by this time look very familiar: Taylor, Weber, Fayol, and Gulick and Urwick are old friends. Simon represents a transitional case: his early work (Simon, 1957, first published in 1945) is more closely related to type III models. As emphasized in Chapter 2, all of these theories portray organizations as tools designed to achieve preset ends, and all of them ignore or minimize the perturbations and opportunities posed by connections to a wider environment. Thompson (1967: 5–6) stresses the closed system assumptions of these theorists. Speaking of Taylor's contributions, he says,

> Scientific management achieves conceptual closure of the organization by assuming that goals are known, tasks are repetitive, output of the production process somehow disappears, and resources in uniform qualities are available.

And of the work of Fayol, Gulick, and Urwick,

> Administrative management achieves closure by assuming that ultimately a master plan is known, against which specialization, departmentalization, and control are determined.

And of Weber's model of bureaucracy,

> Bureaucratic theory also employs the closed system of logic. Weber saw three holes through which empirical reality might penetrate the logic, but in outlining his "pure type" he quickly plugged these holes. Policymakers, somewhere above the bureaucracy, could alter the goals, but the implications of this are set aside. Human components—the expert officeholders—might be more complicated than the model describes, but bureaucratic theory handles this by divorcing the individual's private life from his life as an officeholder through the use of rules, salary, and career. Finally, bureaucratic theory takes note of outsiders—clientele—but nullifies their effects by depersonalizing and categorizing clients.

**TABLE 5–1  Dominant Theoretical Models and Representative Theorists for Four Time Periods and Three Levels of Analysis**

| LEVELS OF ANALYSIS | CLOSED SYSTEM MODELS | | OPEN SYSTEM MODELS | |
| --- | --- | --- | --- | --- |
| | 1900–1930 Rational Models Type I | 1930–1960 Natural Models Type II | 1960–1970 Rational Models Type III | 1970– Natural Models Type IV |
| SOCIAL PSYCHOLOGICAL | Scientific Management Taylor (1911)<br><br>Decision Making Simon (1945) | Human Relations Roy (1952) Whyte (1959) | Bounded Rationality March & Simon (1958) | Organizing Weick (1969)<br><br>Negotiated Order Strauss et al. (1963)<br><br>Ambiguity and Choice March and Olsen (1976) |

**STRUCTURAL**

| Bureaucratic Theory<br>Weber (1904–5)<br><br>Administrative Theory<br>Fayol (1919) | Cooperative Systems<br>Barnard (1938)<br><br>Human Relations<br>Mayo (1945)<br>Dalton (1959) | Contingency Theory<br>Lawrence & Lorsch (1967)<br><br>Comparative Structure<br>Udy (1959)<br>Blau (1970)<br>Pugh et al. (1969) | Socio-technical Systems<br>Miller & Rice (1967)<br><br>Strategic Contingencies<br>Hickson et al. (1971)<br>Pfeffer (1978) |
|---|---|---|---|

**ECOLOGICAL**

| | | Transactions Costs<br>Williamson (1975)<br>Ouchi (1980) | Population Ecology<br>Hannan & Freeman (1977)<br>Aldrich (1979)<br><br>Resource Dependence<br>Pfeffer and Salancik (1978)<br><br>Marxist Theory<br>Braverman (1974)<br>Edwards (1979)<br><br>Institutionalist Theory<br>Selznick (1949)<br>Meyer & Rowan (1977)<br>DiMaggio & Powell (1983) |
|---|---|---|---|

Thus, in all of these models, the variety and uncertainty associated with an organization's openness to its environment is stifled, curtailed, or denied.

### Type II: Closed Natural System Models

Our prime candidates for natural system theorists working predominantly with a closed system conception are the human relations theorists. As described in Chapter 3, this conception originated with the empirical research of Roethlisberger and Dickson (1939) and the theoretical work of Mayo (1945) but expanded throughout the 1940s and 1950s to encompass a great deal of the sociological research on organizations (for example, Whyte, 1946; Whyte, 1948; Katz et al., 1951; Roy, 1952; Dalton, 1959). Although this work caused our view of organizational structure to become more complex and flexible, as diffuse and conflicting goals were recognized and participants were endowed with multiple interests and motives, most of the work within this tradition restricted attention to the inside of the organization. We learn a great deal about the emergence of informal structures—interpersonal systems of power, status, communication, and friendship—and their impact on formal systems, but whether the concern was with formal or informal systems or the relations between them, the focus was primarily on the organization's internal arrangements.

This criticism does not, however, apply to Selznick's (1948) institutional model or to Parsons's (1960) social system model, which we reviewed in Chapter 3. As noted, Selznick's view of the environment is a rather jaundiced one, whereas Parsons's is more balanced, but both of these versions of natural systems models represent more open system conceptions and, hence, are important precursors to type IV models.

### Type III: Open Rational System Models

Beginning in the late 1950s and continuing to the present, a new generation of theories have again focused on the organization as a rational system, but with a difference: now the organization is also viewed as an open system. An important figure in this transformation was Simon, whose major early contributions have already been described. His more recent work with March illustrates the joining of rational and open systems concerns at the social psychological level of analysis. The contingency theorists, whose work we discussed to illustrate open system approaches, also combine rational with open system concerns. We briefly review this work before describing two other types of theories combining these perspectives. Indeed, all of the discussions will be brief since the intent here is merely to introduce important contemporary theories that will be considered at length in Parts Three and Four.

*Bounded rationality revisited*    Important changes are apparent in Simon's view of administrative behavior as developed with March in the late 1950s (March and Simon, 1958, especially chaps. 6 and 7). While there is still a concern with the cognitive limits of individual decision makers and with how structures can help to support improved decisions, there is more recognition of the variable nature of the challenges posed by tasks and environments. The organization is viewed as more open to its environment. March and Simon identify "performance programs" that guide the decisions of individuals, but whereas some of these programs can be routinized others must be problem-solving responses, requiring the decision maker to exercise more discretion in the face of greater uncertainty (p. 139). Moreover, it is recognized that some organizations face such volatile environments that they must institutionalize innovation, devising programs for "routinely" changing existing performance programs, often rapidly (p. 186).

March and Simon suggest a number of additional ways in which decision making is simplified within organizations. Organizations encourage participants to "satisfice"—to settle for acceptable as opposed to optimal solutions, to attend to problems sequentially rather than simultaneously, and to utilize existing repertories of performance programs whenever possible rather than developing novel responses for each situaiton. There is a stronger sense in this later work that organizations face environments of varying complexity, that they must adjust their internal decision-making apparatus to take these variations into account, and that some environments pose levels of complexity that organizations cannot manage unless they impose simplifying restrictions on the information processed.

**Contingency theory reviewed**   We have already described the central ideas of contingency theory as introduced by Lawrence and Lorsch (1967). Their realization that organizations—indeed, divisions within organizations—confront varying environments that pose differing challenges for them is a clear recognition of the open system character of organizations. Their further assumption that organizations will, or should in the interests of effectiveness, adapt their structures to these environmental requirements incorporates the rational system argument.

The combination of open and rational system assumptions also figures strongly in Thompson's (1967) approach. Thompson was among the first organization theorists to recognize the importance of the environment for the structure and performance of organizations, and, as noted, he argued that different locations or levels within structures were differentially open to environmental influences. More so than most theorists, Thompson is quite explicit about the rationalist assumptions that undergird his approach. He prefaces virtually all of his empirical predictions with the phrase "Under norms of rationality, organizations seek to . . ."

Thus, the problem that Thompson and the contingency theorists set for themselves may be stated like this: Given that an organization is open to the uncertainties of its environment, how can it function as a rational system? As hinted at in our review of Thompson's levels model, his principal answer to this question is this: It can do so by creating some closed system compartments in critical parts of its structure. How this is done, by what sealing mechanisms and buffering strategies, will be described in detail in Chapter 8. For now, we simply note the juxtaposition of rational and open systems perspectives that underlie this form of analysis.

**Comparative structural analysis**   Parallel to but somewhat distinct from the efforts of systems design and contingency theorists is the work conducted during the same period by analysts attempting to account for variations in organization structures. Whereas the efforts of the former group tend to be more qualitative and prescriptive, the work of the latter is more quantitative and descriptive. Among the leading figures in comparative structural analysis are Udy (1959*b*), Woodward (1965), Pugh and associates (1969), and Blau (1970) and his colleagues. These were the first analysts to collect systematic data on large samples of organizations rather than on individual participants or organizational subunits. In this work, formal structure is viewed as the dependent variable, its characteristics to be measured and explained. A large variety of explanatory (independent) variables have been examined—with most attention concentrated on size, technology, and uncertainty—but most studies have focused on characteristics of the environment in which the organization is located. In short, organizations are viewed as open systems.

At the same time, organizations are presumed to design their structures rationally. An assumption underlying most of these studies is that organizations are striving to develop effective and efficient structures. Environmental demand and organizational response are mediated by designers or managers who are concerned with cutting cost, developing adequate arrangements to cope with environmental complexity, and creating coordinative mechanisms to manage the requirements of information processing. These are the assumptions of a rational system model, and they dominate much of the empirical and theoretical work on organizations during the 1960s. The findings of these theorists are reviewed in Chapter 10.

**Transactions costs analysis**    An important new perspective combining open and rational systems assumptions was introduced in the mid 1970s by Oliver Williamson (1975; 1981). Based on the work of earlier institutional economists (such as Commons, 1924; Coase, 1937), Williamson has proposed that analysts focus on the costs of entering into transactions—exchanges of goods or services between persons or across boundaries of any sort.

> With a well-working interface, as with a well-working machine, these transfers occur smoothly. In mechanical systems we look for frictions: do the gears mesh, are the parts lubricated, is there needless slippage or other loss of energy? The economic counterpart of friction is transaction cost: do the parties to the exchange operate harmoniously, or are there frequent misunderstandings and conflicts that lead to delays, breakdowns, and other malfunctions? (Williamson, 1981: 552)

To focus on transactions rather than on commodities or services is to shift attention away from technical production concerns to governance structures. For individuals to be willing to enter into exchanges, they must feel certain that their interests are safeguarded. Simple economic transactions that take place "on the spot" as one good or service is exchanged for another of equal value pose no problems and can be safely conducted in the free marketplace. However, as exchanges become more complex and uncertain—because the environment is not stable or predictable and because others cannot always be trusted to abide by the terms of the agreement—various kinds of external controls and supports must be devised to aid the exchanges—that is, to reduce the transactions costs. Organizational structures are viewed as one important arrangement for establishing and safeguarding transactions.

Williamson and his colleagues argue not only that organizations develop in order to reduce transactions costs, but that organizational forms may be expected to vary with the types of exchanges to be governed. We reserve for Chapter 7 a fuller description of this approach to explaining organizations and their structural variety. Here we merely underscore yet another approach that assumes that organizations are both open—responding to the differential demands of their environments—and rational—doing so in such a manner as to economize on the costs of engaging in transactions.

### Type IV: Open Natural System Models

It appears that we are currently in the midst of a major shift in the types of theoretical models that guide our investigations of the structure and operation of organizations. The open rational models that have dominated theory and research since the early 1960s are being challenged by a wide variety of approaches stressing the open but natural character of organizations. The open rational models have not been replaced but they are being joined—and at least for the time being, outnumbered—by open natural approaches. These new models place great emphasis on the importance of the environment in determining the structure, behavior, and life chances of organizations: they are clearly open system models. The assumption that organizations behave as rational systems is strongly challenged in this work. In this section, we will do no more than provide a quick sketch of the more important of these new models. We will begin with a review of Weick's model and then introducing two others developed at the social psychological level, continue with two located at the structural level, and end with several oriented to the ecological level.

***Weick's social organizing again***    Just as it was necessary, armed with our more complex schema, to reclassify contingency theories as not only open but also rational, so it is necessary to re-view Weick's model as combining open with natural systems assumptions. As noted in Chapter 4, Weick gives great attention to the cognitive processes entailed in creating and sustaining organizations, but his view of these processes, unlike those of Simon, for example, is that they operate in an evolutionary fashion: they involve trial and error, chance, superstitious learning, and retrospective sense-making. Also, Weick rejects the notion that evolution necessarily entails improvements in the surviving forms. He points out that successful interlocking of behaviors (that is, organized patterns of action) "can occur without any necessary increase in the productivity or viability of the system" (1979: 179) and insists that we must "free ourselves from the notion that selection is for environmental advantage" (p. 127). In these and many other respects, Weick's model is that of a natural, not a rational, system. And, he combines it with his open system perspective already described to create a view that is both open and natural.

***Negotiated order***   Continuing the tradition begun by the human relations group, a number of more recent social psychologists have emphasized the extent to which social structure—including organizational structure—grows out of interaction processes among participants. What distinguishes some of the more recent contributions is the joining of these earlier natural system interests with an open system model. This connection is developed only haltingly and gradually and is still not firmly established, but its outlines are becoming clear.

Their roots stemming from both Weber (1947 trans.), with his concern that social action can be understood only by taking into account its meaning for those involved, and from the social philosopher George Herbert Mead (1934), who insisted that meanings arise only in the process of social interaction, a large and varied number of researchers have focused minutely on how meanings are created and maintained in organizational settings. This work has been carried on by analysts in the U.S. working in the "symbolic interaction" tradition (for example, Roy, 1952; Goffman, 1961) and by those in England who have been developing an "action approach" to the analysis of ongoing organization (such as, Silverman, 1971; Salaman and Thompson, 1980). In these accounts, such structural features as roles and rules dissolve into a much more fragile set of understandings, misunderstandings, negotiations, and gambits as individual actors struggle for control and meaning.

Especially in the work of Strauss and colleagues (Bucher and Strauss, 1961; Strauss et al., 1963), however, these negotiations are seen as transcending the boundaries of organizations. In their work on medical organizations, for example, these analysts examine the negotiations occurring both among the various segments of the medical profession—such as surgeons and internists—as well as between the profession and other societal groups in order to demonstrate that the division of labor and the control structures within this profession are subject to continuing change and negotiation. Moreover, the results of these wider contests help to shape and constrain the negotiation of order within specific organizational units such as hospitals.

A related approach is suggested by Goffman's (1974) concept of *frames*—a set of background rules that actors impose on specific situations in order to define their meaning and suggest what kinds of interaction are appropriate. (See Gonos, 1977). "Playing a game," "dining," "going to the movies"—all are examples of well-known frames that we impose on everyday situations. As Goffman (1974: 1–2) notes,

> presumably, a "definition of the situation" is almost always to be found, but those who are in the situation ordinarily do not *create* this definition, even though their society can be said to do so; ordinarily, all they do is to assess correctly what the situation ought to be for them and act accordingly.

In short, students concerned with capturing "the rich texture of everyday social life" (Gonos, 1977: 856) that is to be found in great variety within organizations and that has long been of interest to natural system theorists, increasingly recognize that these interactions are framed by meanings and structures external to these situations and organizations.

This concern with negotiated order bears a close relation at the micro (social psychological) level to the work conducted by ethnomethodologists such as Garfinkel (1967), and at the macro (ecological) level to the interests of the institutional theorists discussed later in this section.[5]

***Choice under ambiguity*** James March collaborated with Simon in the work that pushed decision theory toward incorporating more of the concerns of open system analysts, as we have noted. (See March and Simon, 1958). In the years since, March and a number of associates have continued to challenge one after another of the simplifying assumptions associated with the rational system model. At the level of the individual decision maker, March agrees with Weick that actions often precede rather than follow goals, that our preferences are neither very precise nor stable, and that they often need to be discovered. Indeed, one of the more important kinds of learning that occurs is that which changes our ideas about what it is we want. (See March, 1978). Another important feature of many decision situations is that the decision process is often more important than the outcome. "Decision making is, in part, a performance designed to reassure decision makers and others that things are being done appropriately" (March, 1981: 232). Further, many decision situations are fraught with ambiguity. We act and, at least sometimes, elicit a response from the environment, but whether the response is to our actions or completely independent of them is often difficult to determine. Thus, our "learning" is often superstitious.

More important for our purposes than these modifications of the model of individual decision making, however, are March's ideas about decision making in organizations. Thus, March early set aside the assumption of a single or unified decision maker, developing instead the concept of a loose and shifting "coalition" that selects organizational goals (Cyert and March, 1963). The implications of this change are quite profound:

> As long as we assume that organizations have goals and that those goals have some classical properties of stability, precision and consistency, we can treat an organization as some kind of rational actor. But organizations do not have simple, consistent preference functions. They exhibit internal conflict over preferences. Once such conflict is noted, it is natural to shift from a metaphor of problem solving to a more political vision. (March, 1981: 215)

Processes of exchange, of combat, and of compromise and alliance supplant images of a hierarchy of goals or of means-ends chains linking participants throughout the organization. And decision outcomes are seen to be strongly influenced by their contexts as it becomes important to know how the decision has been defined, who is participating, what interests—both problems and solutions—are brought to the occasion, and by what "rules" individual choices are aggregated to produce an organizational decision. (See March and Olsen, 1976.)

We shift now to the structural level of analysis, briefly describing two approaches that emphasize the open natural system perspective.

[5]Ethnomethodologists place primary emphasis on how people "go about the task of seeing, describing and explaining order in the world in which they live" (Zimmerman and Wieder, 1970: 289). Differences in focus and approach distinguishing ethnomethodological and symbolic interaction are reviewed in Maines (1977) and in Burrell and Morgan (1979).

**Socio-technical systems**    At the end of World War II, the Tavistock Clinic, a voluntary outpatient center for psychotherapy in England, reconstituted itself as the Tavistock Institute of Human Relations. Influenced by the human relations research in the U.S., the Tavistock team of researchers began to conduct a series of studies in differing work organizations on ways to improve productivity and morale. From the beginning, the preferred approach was one of "action" research, the investigators working with management and labor to introduce change into a work setting and then attempting to learn from its results (Jaques, 1951). In addition to this somewhat distinctive research style, the group also developed a rather particular problem focus. They proposed that the distinguishing feature of organizations is that they are both social and technical systems: "Their core interface consists of the relation between a nonhuman system and a human system" (Trist, 1981: 25).

Rather than insisting that individual and social units must conform to technical requirements, the socio-technical system approach emphasizes that the needs of both should be served. Rather than obtaining the best "match" between technical and social components, the goal should be one of the "joint optimization" of the needs of both, since the two systems follow different "laws" and their relationship represents a "coupling of dissimilars" (Emery, 1959). The "grain of the fifties" was the celebration of top-down, manager-controlled, technical bureaucracies, but the Tavistock group attempted to go against this grain by designing systems that emphasized discretionary behavior, internalized regulation, and work-group autonomy (Trist, 1981).

Although their early empirical efforts were concentrated at the individual and work-group level, the Tavistock researchers discovered that changes made at these levels did not long survive unless there were compatible changes in larger structures. Further they became increasingly aware that the organizations themselves were open to the wider environment. As Trist (1981: 50) recalls,

> In our action research projects at that time, we and our organizational clients were baffled by the extent to which the wider societal environment was moving in on their more immediate concerns, upsetting plans, preventing the achievement of operational goals, and causing additional stress and severe internal conflict.

In addition to developing a widely influential typology of organizational environments and speculating on their effects on organizational forms (see Emery and Trist, 1965), to be described in the next chapter, the research group attempted to discover ways in which the larger enterprise is shaped by its needs to survive in a specific social and economic environment. (See Rice, 1958; Miller and Rice, 1967.) The most resilient building blocks available to organizations as they respond to these demands are the sets of semiautonomous groups, capable of self-regulation as cybernetic systems, and the larger networks of groups organized into "primary work systems," that are functionally interdependent. Interest in the creation of these units is a common thread throughout many specific studies describing the history of change attempts in particular industrial settings, and it is this emphasis that locates the perspective at the structural level of analysis. Throughout their work, the Tavistock group has remained strongly committed to creating organizational forms that serve the values of human community as well as the interests of technical efficiency.[6]

***Strategic contingency***  This approach starts from the same set of assumptions that guide the contingency theorists, such as Lawrence and Lorsch and Thompson, but by introducing a intermediate, strategic process, it arrives at a very different explanation for the structural features of organizations.

Following contingency theory, the strategic approach assumes organizations to be open systems that confront and respond to variable challenges and opportunities in their environment. Different parts of the environment pose varying challenges, and it is argued that organizations become structurally differentiated—develop specialized subunits—in order to better respond. Up to this point, the arguments are parallel. However, the strategic version, unlike the rational approach, emphasizes that participants in organizations vary in their interests: organizations are coalitions, not monolithic actors. Workers in the production unit may prefer longer, stable runs while the sales units insist on more customized products. Further, organizational subunits differ not only in their interests but in their power.

Power has many sources, but the strategic contingency approach emphasizes that a primary source is the uncertainty posed by the environment. Following Crozier's (1964) observation that mechanics in tobacco manufacturing plants were unexpectedly powerful because they confronted one of the few sources of uncertainty in the plant—machine breakdown—Hickson and colleagues (1971) argued more generally that subgroups in organizations obtain power vis-à-vis one another depending on the amount and significance of the uncertainty to which they relate—and on the extent of their success in coping with it and thereby reducing uncertainty for their co-workers. Those able to control—successfully cope with—more, and more important, strategic contingencies garner power within the organization.

The larger implication of this argument is that "organizational structures are the outcomes of political contests within organizations" (Pfeffer, 1978: 38). Different groups of participants come together, and because some are able to make greater contributions to the stability and survival of the organization than others, these advantaged groups achieve power. And power is not only the outcome but also a determinant in later contests, providing "participants further advantages in the political struggle because of their structural position" (Pfeffer, 1981: 266).

Thus, strategic contingency theorists such as Hickson and Pfeffer have proposed a framework for the political explanation of organizational structure. In Chapter 9 we will consider in more detail this important alternative to the rational system "efficiency" arguments.

Finally, four quite different approaches to analyzing organizations have developed at the ecological level of analysis.

---

[6]This general approach to the "design" of natural systems has been more influential and more often emulated in Europe than in the U.S. Related research has been carried on, for example, by Thorsrud in Norway and Sweden (Emery and Thorsrud, 1969; 1976). In the U.S., some socio-technical themes are to be found in research on the quality of working life (see O'Toole, 1972), and socio-technical action research strategies have been adopted by the organizational development (OD) group.

**Population ecology**   The population ecology or natural selection model of organizations originated in biology with the work of Darwin. Although the application of these ideas to social systems has a long and checkered history (see Hofstadter, 1945), more recent and promising efforts have been stimulated by the work of Hawley (1950) and Campbell (1969). Applications of these general ideas to organizations by Hannan and Freeman (1977) and by Aldrich (1979) have led to a rapidly growing body of research and theory.

The population ecology model differs from other approaches to organizations in that it applies primarily to *populations* of organizations rather than to individual units.[7] It is designed to explain why certain forms or types (or species) of organizations survive and multiply whereas other types languish and die. For example, the model might be employed to examine the decline of teacher's colleges and the growth in the numbers of general colleges over recent decades in the U.S.

It is central to the natural selection thesis that environments differentially select organizations for survival on the basis of fit between organizational forms and environmental characteristics. Three processes are emphasized in evolutionary analysis: the creation of variety, the selection of some forms over others, and the retention of those forms (Campbell, 1969). In the first stage, variety is created by some process, planned or unplanned. In the second, a process occurs by which some forms of organization are differentially selected for survival. And in stage three, the selected forms are preserved in some fashion, by reproduction or duplication. Positively selected variations survive and reproduce similar others, which then form the starting point for a new round of selection as mutants appear (Aldrich and Pfeffer, 1976). Emphasis is placed on *selection* as the prime process by which change occurs in organizations. Hannan and Freeman (1977) have given primary attention to organizational morality as the major force driving natural selection, but as Carroll (1984: 75) points out, natural selection is also determined by birth rates. That is, "population ecology predicts net mortality (deaths over births)."

This approach has created much interest among students of organizations. This is partly because it employs a well-known and highly regarded intellectual framework and has been able to adapt for use quite sophisticated concepts and measures from the work of population biologists. Also, by emphasizing the population level of analysis, it has focused on a new set of issues largely ignored by earlier theorists.

This conception is firmly grounded in an open system model: the importance of the environment can hardly be more strongly underlined than in the population ecology framework. The conception is also clearly a natural system approach. The bottom line is survival. And although based on an evolutionary framework, in its contemporary usage, "evolution is no longer equated with progress, but simply with change over time" (Carroll, 1984: 72). The ability to perpetuate one's form is the hallmark of successful adaptation.

---

[7]Carroll (1984) argues that the underlying evolutionary arguments can be applied to individual organizations and to organizational communities as well as to populations of organizations. (See also, Aldrich, 1979) We discuss these other applications in Chapter 8.

***Resource dependency*** Whereas the population ecology approach stresses selection—attributing observed patterns in the distribution of organizational forms to the action of environmental selection, both in terms of what kinds of organizations are created and which survive—the resource dependence model emphasizes *adaptation*. It is assumed that individual organizations can act to improve their chances of survival.

The resource dependency approach shares many features with the strategic contingency perspective, but has as its primary focus the organization itself—its behavior and its relations with other organizations—rather than its component units. The approach has been developed by a number of investigators and has received a variety of labels. Zald and his colleagues refer to their version as a political economy model (Zald, 1970; Wamsley and Zald, 1973). Thompson (1967), some of whose work employs this model, describes the approach as an exchange, or as a power-dependency model. The most comprehensive development to date of the resource dependence approach is found in the work of Pfeffer and Salancik (1978).

This perspective is strongly rooted in an open system framework: it is argued that one cannot understand the structure or behavior of an organization without understanding the context within which it operates. No organization is self-sufficient; all must engage in exchanges with the environment as a condition of their survival. The need to acquire resources creates dependences between organizations and outside units. How important and how scarce these resources are determine the nature and the extent of organizational dependency. Dependency is the obverse of power. (Emerson, 1962) Economic dependencies give rise to political problems and may succumb to political solutions.

Much more so than in the population ecology approach, organizations are viewed as active, not passive, in determining their own fate. Organizational participants, particularly managers, scan the relevant environment, searching for opportunities and threats, attempting to strike favorable bargains and to avoid costly entanglements. All organizations are dependent on suppliers of inputs and consumers of outputs, but which specific suppliers and consumers are selected as exchange partners and what the terms of exchange are are partly determined by the organization itself. Astute managers are those who not only acquire the necessary resources but do so without creating crippling dependencies. Thus, the resource dependence model views organizations as

> capable of changing, as well as responding to, the environment. Administrators manage their environments as well as their organizations, and the former activity may be as important, or even more important, than the latter. (Aldrich and Pfeffer, 1976: 83)

One of the major contributions of the resource dependency perspective is to discern and describe the strategies—ranging from buffering to diversification and merger—employed by organizations to change and adapt to the environment. We review these strategies in Chapter 8.

***Marxist theory*** Of the influence of the two giants of German, or rather, European social thought, that of Max Weber was apparent from the beginning—indeed, constituted the beginning. The effect of the second, Karl Marx, though widely felt in many areas of inquiry, did not seriously begin to make waves in work on organizations until the 1970s. That decade witnessed a resurgence of interest in Marxist approaches among social scientists in the U.S. (see Burawoy, 1982), although European scholars had long been strongly influenced by this tradition. There is a tortuous trail of social thought leading from Marx's later writings (e.g., 1954 trans.: 1973 trans.) through the contributions of Lukacs (1971 trans.) and Gramsci (1971 trans.) to the contemporary work of Habermas (1971 trans.) and Althusser (1969 trans.).[8] We relate only the more recent developments of particular relevance to organizations.

Consistent with the origins of the natural system perspective, the Marxist approach began essentially as a critique of the dominant rationalist views, and of the earlier natural system models as well, particularly those developed by Barnard and the human relations school. Marxists argue that organizational structures are not rational systems for performing work in the most efficient manner; they are power systems designed to maximize control and profits more than they are technical systems designed to insure effectiveness. Work is divided and subdivided not to improve efficiency but to "deskill" workers, to displace discretion from workers to managers, and to create artificial divisions among the work force. (Braverman, 1974) Hierarchy develops not as a rational means of coordination but as an instrument of control and a means of accumulating capital through the appropriation of surplus value (Edwards, 1979; Marglin, 1974). Human relations and cooperative systems reforms are inadequate because they do not challenge the fundamental exploitative nature of organizations; indeed, they help to shore it up by assuming a congruence of goals and by providing managers with new psychological and social tools for controlling workers and with new arguments justifying this control (Bendix, 1956; Braverman, 1974).

To assume that organizations are rational instruments for the pursuit of goals ignores the question of whose goals are being served. It assumes that there is consensus rather than conflict over goals. From the Marxist perspective, rationality is an ideology—the use of ideas to legitimate existing arrangements and to deflect criticism of those with excessive power by depersonalizing the system of relations. (See Zey-Ferrell and Aiken, 1981.)

In addition to challenging these rational system assumptions,[9] the

---

[8]For a lucid review of the work of these and other theorists who link Marx's writings to contemporary Marxist approaches to organizations, see Burrell and Morgan (1979: 279–392). These two analysts distinguish the early writings of Marx, which inspired the more humanistic approaches of Lukacs, Gransci, Habermas, and others, from the more materialist later writings, which led to the work of Althusser, Dahrendorf, and Miliband. It is the latter emphasis that has stimulated the most interest among contemporary students of organizations.

[9]In his alternative schema for classifying theories of organization, Pfeffer (1982: 13, 162–70) categorizes Marxist theory as a "purposive" or "rational" approach to organizational analysis. This conclusion rests on Pfeffer's belief that to the extent that managers seek control and not efficiency, then the structures they design are effective means to these ends. Although this is a logically defensible position, we prefer to see Marxist approaches as more similar to natural system models with their emphasis on goal complexity conflict, hidden agendas and shifting interests, and more organic, historically shaped, evolutionary structures.

Marxist approach strongly eschews a closed system conception of organizations. Not only do Marxist theorists insist that organizations are strongly affected by their wider political and economic context, they vigorously urge organizational analysts to embrace a more historical perspective. As Benson (1982: 139) comments, Marxists call for "a contextualizing theory that locates observations within a comprehensive mapping of the social world and along an historical trajectory of social change."

Because of their sensitivity to the close interdependence of economic and political structures, Marxist theorists were among the first to call attention to the central role of the state in both public and private organizations (Burrell and Morgan, 1979: 371–77; Burawoy, 1982). Theorists such as Miliband (1969) and O'Connor (1973) emphasize the strong connections between the structure and functions of the modern state and those of the large corporations (the monopoly-capital sectors). These claims have prompted much disputation and have led to a flurry of empirical studies probing the relations between corporate elites and state structures. We review some of this work in Chapter 8.

With their strong emphasis on historical context, Marxist theorists have turned the attention of organizational theorists back to the more neglected aspects of Weber's legacy. As noted in Chapter 2, much of Weber's attention was devoted to describing the characteristics of prebureaucratic forms and the conditions giving rise to the new administrative systems. Marxists have newly underscored the value of a historical perspective for sociological analysis:

> By taking the particular experiences of capitalist society and shaping them into universal experiences, sociology becomes incapable of conceiving of a fundamentally different type of society in the future. . . . In order to conceive of, to anticipate, something "new," one must begin with different premises, which regard history as discontinuous and capitalist societies as fundamentally different from precapitalist and postcapitalist societies. (Burawoy, 1979; 13)

Finally, like the socio-technical school, Marxist theorists stress the importance of *praxis:* combining ideas and action (Benson, 1977). However, the Marxist conception is broader than the socio-technical version. Marxist theorists insist that investigators cannot choose whether to be involved with their subjects: they are inevitably involved. Theories grow out of existing social structures and either serve to "reproduce" them—legitimate and support them—or to transform them. Needless to say, Marxists view the great bulk of theory and research on organizations as, perhaps unconsciously but nevertheless effectively, serving to maintain existing organizational forms.

**Institutional theory**     The last group of ideas to be introduced, like Marxist theories, has developed quite rapidly during the 1970s and up to the present. While sharing the same label as Selznick's early work, discussed in Chapter 3, and having some features in common with it, contemporary versions of institutional theory are more directly related to work originating in the area of the sociology of knowledge. Based on philosophical underpinnings established by German idealists and phenomenologists such as Dilthey and Husserl, and strongly shaped by the work of Alfred Schutz (1962 trans.), most current efforts rest on the foundation built by sociologist Peter Berger.[10]

The most complete and influential statement of Berger's ideas on institutionalization is to be found in his work with Luckmann (Berger and Luckmann, 1967). They argue that social reality is a human construction, being created in social interaction. The process by which actions are repeated and given similar meaning by self and others is defined as *institutionalization.*

These ideas concerning the social construction of reality were first introduced into organizational analysis at the micro or social psychology level by researchers working in the symbolic interactionist and ethnomethodological traditions. Earlier in this chapter we reviewed the former as an attempt to negotiate social order. The latter may be viewed as an attempt to negotiate social reality:

> The ethnomethodologists are interested in the way in which actors make evident and persuade each other that the events and activities in which they are involved are coherent and consistent (Burrell and Morgan, 1979: 250).

In reviewing the empirical work of this group, one is struck by how much of it has been conducted within organizational settings (see, for example, Bittner, 1967; Cicourel, 1968; Zimmerman, 1970).[11]

At a more macro level, Berger and colleagues (Berger, Berger, and Kellner, 1973: 41–62) have argued that the very conception of bureaucracy is a meta-institution, which depicts in a generalized manner a portrait of orderliness, predictability, and, in its emphasis on formalization of relations, "moralized anonymity." Zucker (1983: 1) has pursued and elaborated this theme, arguing that "organizations are the preeminent institutional form in modern society."

Perhaps the most influential application of institutional ideas to the analysis of organizations is that of Meyer and Rowan (1977), who argue that modern societies contain many complexes of institutionalized rules and patterns—products of professional groups, the state, public opinion. These social realities provide a framework for the creation and elaboration of formal organizations. According to Meyer and Rowan, in modern societies, these institutions are likely to take the form of *rationalized myths.* They are *myths* because they are widely held beliefs that cannot be objectively tested: they are true because they are believed. They are *rationalized* because they take the form of rules specifying procedures necessary to accomplish a given end. Law provides a good example. How can property legitimately change hands? How can an organization become a corporation? Legal systems—as complexes of rationalized myths—provide solutions to such problems. Meyer and Rowan (1977: 343) argue that these institutional belief systems powerfully shape organizational forms:

---

[10]A useful summary of Berger's views will be found in Wuthnow et al. (1984: 21–76).

[11]Burrell and Morgan (1979: 225–78) provide a thorough review of the philosophical origins of the ethnomethodological approach as well as the more recent empirical applications to organizations.

Many of the positions, policies, programs, and procedures of modern organizations are enforced by public opinion, by the views of important constituents, by knowledge legitimated through the educational system, by social prestige, by the laws, and by the definitions of negligence and prudence used by the courts. Such elements of formal structure are manifestations of powerful institutional rules which function as highly rationalized myths that are binding on particular organizations.

Institutional theory emphasizes that organizations are open systems—strongly influenced by their environments—but that many of the most fateful forces are the result not of rational pressures for more effective performance but of social and cultural pressures to conform to conventional beliefs.

## SUMMARY

The rational, natural, and open system perspectives for analyzing organizations provide contrasting paradigms. Because of the differing assumptions underlying these paradigms, one may replace another but cannot disprove it.

Nevertheless, several analysts have attempted to reconcile the three perspectives by combining them into more complex models of organizations. Etzioni suggests that the rational and natural system models are complementary, focusing on conflicting tendencies present in all organizations. Lawrence and Lorsch propose that all organizations are open systems, and that rational and natural forms emerge as varying adaptive structures in response to different environmental forces. And Thompson suggests that the three perspectives are differentially applicable to various levels of an organization's structure, the open system being most suited to analyzing the institutional level, the natural system applying best to the managerial level, and the rational system, to the technical level.

An alternative basis for combining the perspectives is to suggest that they have appeared in varying combinations over time and that they are applicable to differing levels of analysis. This framework suggests that the earliest models, dominant between 1900 and 1930, were closed rational system models. Some of these were developed at the social psychological level—for example, Taylor's scientific management approach—while others were advanced at the structural level—for instance, Weber's model of bureaucracy and Fayol's administrative theory. From the 1930s through the 1950s, a new set of perspectives developed that combined closed with natural system assumptions. Again, some of these approaches were developed primarily at the social psychological level—such as the human relations models of Roy and Katz—and others at the structural level—for example, Barnard's theory of cooperative systems and Mayo's version of human relations.

Beginning in the early 1960s, open system models largely replaced closed system assumptions, and analyses at the ecological level began to appear. At the same time, rational and natural system models persisted, providing competing theoretical explanations for organizational structure and behavior. During the 1960s, open rational system models were dominant, represented by the work of March and Simon at the social psychological level and by contingency theory and comparative analyses at the structural level. To these approaches was added, in the 1970s, the transactions costs framework. The open rational system models were joined and challenged by the open natural system models that became dominant in the 1970s and continue into the 1980s. These rapidly proliferating approaches range from the work of Weick and Strauss and March at the social psychological level, through the socio-technical and strategic contingencies models developed at the structural level, to the population ecology, resource dependence, Marxist, and institutional theories at the ecological level.

Our classification emphasizes the historical evolution of organization theory. The types of theories guiding work today differ from those in use ten or forty years ago. A question to be pondered is why this is the case. Does it represent changes in the nature of organizations or changes in the interest of theorists or both?

A great many new and competing theories concerning organizations now occupy the landscape. We have reviewed some of the most influential of these, and will consider them in more detail in later chapters.[12]

[12]See Burrell and Morgan (1979) and Pfeffer (1982) for alternative schemas for classifying organization theories; and see Scott (1986) for a discussion and comparison of the three systems.

# ENVIRONMENTS, STRATEGIES, AND STRUCTURES

## PART THREE

Three general perspectives on the nature of organizations have been described, along with several attempts to combine or integrate them. If these perspectives are as useful as we have claimed, they will enable us not simply to comprehend past efforts to dissect organizations but to better fathom current work and perhaps even to discern future analytic directions.

Part Three combines topics that are often separated in contemporary treatments of organizations. It deals both with the ways in which organizations relate to their environments as well as with the determinants of organizational structure. With the help of the open systems perspective, we see these topics as inseparable: how an organization relates to its environment— indeed, what its environment is—is generally influenced by the organization's structural features, and the characteristics of the organization's structure are strongly affected by the organization's environment. External forces shape internal arrangements, and vice versa.

We learn from the open systems perspective that organizations are not fortresses, impervious to the buffeting or the blessing of their environments. On the other hand, we learn from the rational and natural system perspectives that organizations are not wind tunnels, completely open and responsive to every perturbation of their context. Organizations construct and reconstruct boundaries across which they relate to the outside world. Between the organization and those outside there is not one barrier but many, and for most kinds of organizatons these barriers become higher and more impenetrable as we come closer to the organization's technical core.

Part Three begins with an examination of organizational environments. Having been persuaded that the open system perspective is critically important, we attempt to distinguish among various levels at which environments may be analyzed and to differentiate their technical from their institutional elements. The multiple ways in which organizations interact with their environments are stressed in Chapter 6.

Chapter 7 addresses the fundamental but difficult questions of why organizations exist and how they are created. These questions are pursued from both a historical and a comparative perspective. Rational system explanations stressing efficiency and reduction in transactions costs are contrasted with natural system accounts emphasizing power and conformity to external rules.

Organizations must both distinguish their systems from and connect themselves with their environment. Boundary-defining mechanisms as well as the strategies used by organizations to buffer their technical core and to build bridges to other organizations—both competitors and exchange partners—are examined in Chapter 8. Connections to both technical and institutional environments are considered.

Chapters 9 and 10 describe sources of structural complexity, Chapter 9 focusing on complexity within the technical core and Chapter 10 examining influences on the form of the pheripheral sectors: the wider, encompassing structures. Characteristics of the type of work being performed—the technology—and of the technical and institutional environment pose opportunities and challenges to which organizations respond. These responses have significant consequences for the structure of the organization. The extent to which organizations change by adaptation—the modification of an existing organization—or by selection—the elimination of one form of organization and the generation of new forms—is currently under debate.

Environmental factors are also argued, in Chapter 11, to be critical in determining the size and composition of the dominant coalition: that set of an organization's participants who have sufficient power to set the goals to be pursued by the organization.

Environments shape organizations, but organizations also shape environments. Organizations in part choose which environments to enter and to exit, and they seek, individually and in coalition with others, to influence the contexts within which they function. Organizations relate strategically to environments.

In all of these ways, we challenge the sharp dichotomy between inside and outside, between organization and environment. The structures and processes of organizations and environments penetrate one another in interesting and unexpected ways that are revealed when we combine the open system perspective with the rational and natural system viewpoints.

# 6 conceptions of environments

For a given system, the environment is the set of all objects a change in whose attributes affect the system and also those objects whose attributes are changed by the behavior of the system.

The statement above invites the natural question of when an object belongs to a system and when it belongs to the environment; for if an object reacts with a system in the way described above should it not be considered a part of the system? The answer is by no means definite. In a sense, a system together with its environment makes up the universe of all things of interest in a given context. Subdivision of this universe into two sets, system and environment, can be done in many ways which are in fact quite arbitrary. Ultimately it depends on the intentions of the one who is studying the particular universe as to which of the possible configurations of objects is to be taken as the system.

A. D. Hall and R. E. Fagen, (1956)

Since the emergence and increasing prominence of open systems models, investigators are no longer able to comfortably ignore the effects of environments on organizations. To examine these causal connections, it is necessary to develop some working conceptions of environments themselves: ideas as to how to circumscribe them and how to identify and assess their relevant features. This chapter describes the major conceptions that have arisen and that currently guide investigations in this area.

## THE ANALYSIS OF ENVIRONMENTS

### Levels of Environments

A basic source of variation among conceptions of environments stems from the level of analysis selected. In Chapter 1 we identified the social psychological, structural, and ecological levels, and we have made ample use of these distinctions in our examination of various theories of organizations. Since our current concern is with conceptions of organizational environments—the ecological level—all of the analyses to be developed in this chapter are within this level.[1] It is helpful to identify four sublevels within the ecological level.

**Organizational sets**    The first level of analysis is that of the organization *set* (see Blau and Scott, 1962: 195–99; Evan, 1966). Both Blau and I and Evan acknowledge that the concept of organization set was developed by analogy from Merton's (1957: 368–80) concept of role-set. Merton noted that a single social position such as "mother" is associated with not one but a cluster of different roles depending on the identity of the counterpositions. Thus, a mother has a number of specific role obligations toward her children; other obligations toward the father; still other obligations toward the child's teachers; and so on. Similarly, a given organization participates in a variety of relations depending on the identity of its specific partners. For example, a small grocery store will relate in one manner with its suppliers, another with its customers, yet another with its neighbors, and so on. The fundamental idea is a simple one, but its implications are quite rich. One is led to ask questions about the relative size of the organization set, the extent to which one group of role partners is aware of the demands made by another, the extent to which expectations held by partners coincide, and so on.

One of the more useful concepts to emerge at the analytical level of the organization set is that of organizational *domain* (Levine and White, 1961; Thompson, 1967). An organization's domain consists of the claims it makes with respect to products or services provided and populations served. These claims immediately relate it to a number of other organizations—suppliers, customers, competitors—that affect its behavior and outcomes. An important consideration for any organization is the degree of consensus among members of its set regarding its proper domain.

A crucial, defining characteristic of the concept of organization set is that it views the environment from the standpoint of a specific (*focal*) organization. Relations or connections between other (*counter*) members of the set are of no concern unless they affect the activities or interests of the focal organization. Analysts employing the resource dependence approach, as described in Chapter 5, typically work at the level of the organization set. It is from this level that the interests, the resources, the dependencies of a given organization are best examined and its survival tactics probed. It is also at this level that most discussions of strategic decision making occur (Porter, 1980). Indeed, the great majority of studies of organization-environment connections have been conducted at the organization-set level of analysis.

While the organization-set level of analysis has proved extremely

---

[1]This does not mean the other levels of analysis are not relevant to examining the relation between organizations and environments. Thus, when boundary roles are considered (see Chapter 8) the level of analysis often employed is the social psychological, and when organizational strategies and structural modifications are examined as modes of organizational adaptation to environments (see Chapters 9 and 10), the level of analysis is the structural. The concern at this point, however, is to determine variations in the way in which environments of organizations are circumscribed. In this sense, the four approaches we consider here are at the ecological level.

useful in directing attention to the impact of information and resource flows and relations on a select organization, it does so at the expense of detracting attention from the nature of the larger system of relations in which the focal organization is but one prarticipant among many.

**Organizational populations** A second level identified by analysts is that of the *population* of organizations. This concept is used to identify aggregates of organizations that are alike in some respects—for example, institutions of higher education or newspapers. This is the level at which most natural selection theories have been applied, such as the population ecology model, introduced in Chapter 5.

Those concerned with studying populations have had to wrestle with the question of what it means to be "alike in some respects." How are populations identified? When one studies "colleges," for example, what organizations are included—private as well as public schools? Universities? Community or junior colleges? Technical institutes? Organizational ecologists borrow or adapt biological language and ideas in working on this problem. Hannan and Freeman (1977: 935) remind us that biologic species are defined in terms of genetic structure and propose that the appropriate analogue for organizations might be to define them in terms of their "blueprint for organizational action, for transforming inputs into outputs." McKelvey (1982) adopts a similar stance, suggesting that all organizations in the same population contain "elements of dominant competence," or *comps*, drawn from the same *compool*, or collection of elements. By *dominant competence* McKelvey means essentially the technical core of the organization—that is, the activities—both technical and managerial, that transform "inputs into those outputs critical to a population's survival" (p. 174). Both of these definition of the boundaries of populations are conceptually clear, but neither is easy to apply. Blueprints and comps are hard to measure.

Population ecologists do not agree on the value of devising general classifications of organizations.[2] Some, such as McKelvey and Aldrich (1983: 125), argue that they are of great value:

> A theoretically grounded empirical taxonomy would provide a conceptual framework for describing and understanding the diversity of organizational populations, and would identify populations useful for research of other substantive concerns about organizations.

McKelvey and Aldrich also note that a classification would help prevent overly enthusiastic researchers from recklessly generalizing their findings in one class of organization to classes they have not yet studied. But other ecologists, such as Hannan and Freeman, suggest that a more fruitful approach is to allow the defining criteria to change depending on the analyst's focus. For some studies, universities and research institutes would be considered members of the same population while colleges would be excluded. For other purposes, universities and colleges would be regarded as similar and research institutes excluded. Up to now, most

---

[2]For an extended discussion of typologies of organizations, their uses and limitations, see the first edition of this text. (Scott, 1981: 27–54)

of the empirical studies of organizational populations have relied on fairly common sense definitions of the population and have employed geographical criteria for bounding it. For example, Freeman and Brittain (1977) have studied mergers among national labor unions in the U.S., and Carroll and Delacroix (1982) have studied mortality rates of Irish and Argentine newspapers.

In a population ecology approach, primary attention is given to the analysis of competing forms, to varying strategies of competition, and to the selective effects of changes in environments. Although this level of analysis clearly identifies an important set of questions and has attracted great interest, its emphases direct attention away from connections among organizations, in particular those organizations whose relations are more symbiotic and cooperative than commensalistic and competitive. To examine these connections, we need other models that perhaps change not so much the level as the focus of analysis.

**Areal organization fields**   This level of analysis is employed when the investigator focuses on the relations among a collection of organizations (and perhaps other types of social units) within a geographical area. Also labeled the *ecological community* model (Hawley, 1950), the *interorganizational field* model (Warren, 1967), and the *collective-action* model (Astley and Van de Ven, 1983), this approach emphasizes not the individual organizational units or even their characteristics as an aggregate, but rather the network of relations among them.

Of course, the extent of such networks among organizations varies from time to time and place to place. In a highly theoretical fashion, the influential paper by Emery and Trist (1965) attempts to classify environments by the extent to which organizations sharing the same field have developed such interlocking relations. They distinguish among four types of fields:

> *placid, randomized environments,* in which resources required by organizations in the field are unchanging and randomly distributed over the area;
>
> *placid, clustered environments,* in which resources are unchanging but clustered, so that field location becomes an important factor in survival;
>
> *disturbed, reactive environments,* in which the availability of resources is partially determined by the actions of the organizations themselves, so that a given organization's survival is dependent on the use of strategies that take into account the behavior of competitors;
>
> *turbulent environments,* in which all organizational actors are interconnected, so that the organizational field or network itself becomes a force that each organization must attempt to take into account.

A related but more concrete typology based on the extent to which an "inclusive decision making structure" has come into existence has been proposed by Warren (1967). Four types of organizational fields are identified:

> *Social-choice context:* no formal or informal inclusive structure exists within which the participating organizations make their decisions. All decisions are made at the level of the individual units. An example is the relations among

diverse organizations that happen to reside in the same community.

*Coalitional context:* each organizational unit has its own decision-making apparatus and set of goals but collaborates informally and on an ad hoc basis when some of its goals are similar to those of other member units. An example is a group of independent child-care agencies collaborating to obtain a federal grant.

*Federative context:* Organizational units have individual goals but also participate in a structure in order to set more inclusive goals, which must be ratified by member units. An example is social agencies participating in a community council of agencies that has only delegated powers.

*Unitary context:* Decision making on policies and programs takes place at the top of a hierarchy of organizations, where final authority rests. An example is a center for emergency services established by a collection of community hospitals that coordinates and controls a decentralized network of emergency-service units.

The central message of both typologies—Emery and Trist's and Warren's—is that organizational fields vary greatly in the extent and nature of the relational and normative structures that develop among organizations. It is argued that these structures are important systems in their own right, and it is implied that they will have strong effects on their constituent organizations.

Organizational fields also vary in longevity. Aldrich and Whetten (1981: 387) have identified as an *action-set* a group of organizations "that have formed a temporary alliance for a limited purpose." Action-sets contrast with more permanent and stable organizational fields, although all fields are expected to evolve over time.

The most commonly employed areal unit within which organizational fields have been investigated is the community. There has been a regular and growing stream of research on the nature of the linkages that develop among similar or diverse organizations located within the same community or metropolitan area. (see Litwak and Hylton, 1962; Warren, 1963; Turk, 1977; Lincoln, 1979; Galaskiewicz, 1979; and Fennell, 1980).[2]

From an ecological perspective, the networks developing among organizations sharing the same field are adaptive mechanisms. As Astley and Van de Ven (1983: 250–51) point out,

> Rather than view organizations as pitched in a competitive battle for survival through a direct confrontation with the natural, or exogenous, environment, [areal field theorists] emphasize collective survival, which is achieved by collaboration between organizations through the construction of a regulated and controlled social environment that mediates the effects of the natural environment.

The areal organization field represents a significant shift in focus from that of the individual organization or the organization set. Organizations are treated as components of larger, overarching systems. However, two restrictions characterize this approach, one by definition and the other by usage. First and obviously, attention is restricted by definition to connections among organizations sharing the same territorial area. For many kinds of biological and social units, such a limitation would pose no problem, but for organizations, it is a serious and potentially biasing restriction. Modern transportation and communication systems are such that areal boundaries are for many purposes meaningless. A large number of types of organizations are influenced by distant as well as proximate connections, and for many organizations, the former are more fateful. Numerous organizations are linked to national and even international corporate systems, and many buy from and distribute to national and international markets. Second, by convention, most of the studies at this level give primary attention to "horizontal" relations among organizations—that is, to connections among competing or cooperating organizations lacking formal rights over one another. Neglected are the "vertical" connections that relate organizations in hierarchical systems—regulatory systems linking public and private organizations, formal authority connecting headquarters and branch offices, informal power channels relating dominant and subdominate organizations.

The fourth and final level of analysis to be considered was developed by theorists who wished to focus on the extralocal and vertical connections among organizations.[3]

**Functional organization fields**    A number of analysts have begun to isolate organizational systems for analysis on the basis of functional rather than geographic criteria.[4] As always, there are some differences in detail and terminology among the investigators working at this level. Thus, Hirsch (1972) employs the concept of *industry system* in his study of cultural production systems such as publishing houses, movie studios, and recording companies. (See also, Hirsch, 1985) He defines an industry system as

> all organizations engaged in the process of filtering new products and ideas as they flow from "creative" personnel in the technical subsystem to the managerial, institutional, and societal levels of organization (Parsons 1960). Each industry system is seen as a single, concrete, and stable network of identifiable and interacting components. (1972: 642)

Meyer and I have proposed the related concept of a *societal sector* —a domain in which organizations provide similar or substitutable services. This concept is very similar to that of industries or industrial groups, as studied by economists, but also includes those support, funding, and regulatory groups whose operation affects the central set of providers. (See Scott and Meyer, 1983: 137–39.) And DiMaggio and Powell (1983: 148) have suggested the concept of *organizational field*, which they define as

> those organizations that, in the aggregate, constitute a recognized area of institutional life: key suppliers, resource and product consumers, regulatory agencies, and other organizations that produce similar services or products.

[3]A discussion of previous work leading to a more functional definition of organization fields will be found in Scott and Meyer (1983: 130–36).

[4]Sometimes, of course, areal and functional criteria coincide. It is useful to distinguish them, however, because often they do not.

A number of empirical studies of functional organization fields have been conducted. For example, there have been several studies of new federal programs that were initiated and funded in Washington but created an elaborate set of relations among layers of public and private organizations from the national to the local level. (See, for example, Derthick's [1972] study of the "new towns" program; Aldrich's [1976] study of the Comprehensive Employment and Training Act [CETA]; and Pressman and Wildavsky's [1973] study of the Economic Development Administration's effort to create jobs in Oakland.) Other studies have examined the emergence of self-regulation among organizations lacking formal authority over one another. For example, Stern (1979) has examined the origin and evolution of the National Collegiate Athletic Association, the "voluntary" control system devised to regulate athletic competition among colleges. And there have been a number of attempts to examine the informal connections among organizational elites and between organizations and state structures to determine whether there exists a dominant capitalist class structure in contemporary societies. (See, for example, Herman, 1981; Mizruchi, 1982; and Mintz and Schwartz, 1983.)

Studies at the functional organization field level have been directed primarily at testing hypotheses stemming from the resource dependence, institutionalist, and Marxist perspectives. In later chapters in this volume, we will review some of the findings from these studies.

Organization sets, populations, areal fields, and functional fields are systems that may themselves be the primary object of study. Recall from Chapter 1 that levels of analysis are defined in terms of the dependent variables on which they focus. Much of the research conducted during the past decade has centered on these new units of analysis, examining how sets or populations or fields of organizations come into existence, vary over time, grow, and decline. Viewed in another way, however, these same distinctions among levels can be used as ways of depicting the environment of organizations. The characteristics of the counterorganizations constitute an important environment for the focal organization. Similarly, the distribution of organizational forms in a population may be viewed as a salient aspect of the environment for any particular organization in that distribution, and the characteristics of organizational fields—their degree of centralization or formalization—are of obvious significance for their component organizations.[5] Thus, the levels of analysis just described serve to define both wider systems of organizations and alternative conceptions of environments, depending on how they are employed.

### Characteristics of Environments: Technical and Institutional Aspects

Establishing the level at which organizations and systems of organizations are to be defined is an important step in determining how environments are to be conceived: the environment of a population of hospi-

---

[5]This is not to say that organizations and their interrelations are the only environmental element of importance, but we do insist that other organizations and systems of organizations are of great importance as environmental actors.

**TABLE 6–1    Technical and Institutional Environments with Illustrative Organizations**

|                         |          | Institutional Environments Stronger                        | Institutional Environments Weaker           |
|-------------------------|----------|-----------------------------------------------------------|---------------------------------------------|
|                         | Stronger | utilities<br>banks                pharmaceuticals<br>general hospitals | general manufacturing                       |
| Technical Environments  | Weaker   | mental health clinics<br>schools; legal agencies<br>churches | restaurants<br>health clubs                 |

tals is assuredly different from the environment of a single hospital and its set of related organizations. But once the level of analysis is established, many choices remain. Meyer and I (Meyer and Scott, 1983) have proposed that it is useful to distinguish broadly between two types of organizational environments: technical and institutional. *Technical environments* are those in which organizations produce a product or service that is exchanged in a market such that they are rewarded for effective and efficient performance. These are environments that foster the development of rationalized structures that efficiently coordinate technical work. In the purest case, such environments are identical to the competitive markets so dear to the hearts of classical economists. Most types of manufacturing and service organizations operate in technical environments. By contrast, *institutional environments* are characterized by the elaboration of rules and requirements to which individual organizations must conform in order to receive legitimacy and support. Again in the extreme case, in institutional environments organizations are rewarded for the institution of correct structures and processes, not for the quantity and quality of their outputs. Organizations operating in institutional environments include schools and mental hospitals, whose resources do not depend primarily on evaluations of their outputs in a competitive market. Note that both types of environments place pressures on organizations to which they must be responsive if they are to survive. But the types of pressures and the types of responses required vary between the two.

To make these distinctions more useful, it is better to treat them as dimensions along which environments vary, not as dichotomies. That is, some types of environments pose stronger technical demands than others, but most types of organizations are exposed to some extent to such pressures. Similarly, the extent to which organizations are confronted with rules and procedural requirements varies across environments and over time. Technical and institutional environments are negatively associated, but not strongly so, such that various combinations and mixed cases exist. Table 6–1 cross-classifies the two dimensions and illustrates the types of organizations found in each. Thus, organizations such as utilities and banks are viewed as being subject to strong institutional and technical pressures. On the one hand, there are requirements that utilities produce energy, water, and other basic commodities effectively and reliably; on the other, there are equally strong demands that they conform to regulations governing safety, distribution, pricing, pollution control, employment practices, and so on. In general, organizations in this cell carry out tasks that combine complex technical requirements with a strong "public good" component. Moving to the right, we see most manufacturing organizations operate in environments characterized by strong technical and weaker institutional pressures. The major exceptions are those firms whose operation raises serious issues of health and safety for its employees or the public—for example pharmaceutical firms.

Many types of organizations, particularly professional service organizations such as schools, churches and welfare agencies, law firms, and stockbrokerages, are subject to stronger institutional but weaker technical pressures. Finally, some types of organizations operate in environments in which there are neither strong technical nor institutional pressures. Examples include organizations providing many types of personal services, such as restaurants and health clubs.

In the 1970s, when open rational system models were dominant, the environment was viewed primarily in technical terms. In the 1980s, increasing attention is being given to the institutional aspects of environments. Both conceptions are necessarily abstract, since our attempt is to develop concepts and dimensions applicable to many kinds of organizations. However, it is possible to describe more specific variables or dimensions associated with each type of environment.

**Technical environments.** Perhaps the most commonly held conception of the environment of organizations is that of the *task environment* as first proposed by Dill (1958: 410). This concept is broadly defined as all aspects of the environment "potentially relevant to goal setting and goal attainment," but is typically narrowed in use to refer to sources of inputs, markets for outputs, competitors, and regulators. The conception of a task environment emphasizes that most organizations are created to achieve goals, to perform some type of work. It also emphasizes that no organization is self-sufficient; all must enter into exchanges with the environment. Managers are viewed as ensuring adequate supplies of resources and markets, designing efficient work arrangements, and coordinating and controlling technical activities. Organization structure is viewed as being closely linked to external technical requirements and to internal work systems.

Broadly speaking, there are two types of language for describing what organizations exchange with their environments: some formulations emphasize environments as stocks of resources while others view them as sources of information (Aldrich and Mindlin, 1978). Those stressing the former are apt to focus on the degree to which the organization becomes dependent on others for vital resources. Investigators emphasizing the informational aspects of environments focus primarily on the degree of uncertainty confronting the organization. Both uncertainty and dependency are viewed as problematic situations confronting organizations, and much attention has been devoted to examining the types of strategies and mechanisms organizations use to cope with them. But before turning to attempted "solutions," we need to inquire into the general conditions that give rise to these states.

Several general dimensions have been proposed by investigators as affecting either organizational uncertainty or dependence. Without attempting an exhaustive summary, we will present here the major variables and their expected effects.

### DIMENSIONS AFFECTING UNCERTAINTY

1. *Degree of homogeneity–heterogeneity:* the extent to which the environmental entities to which the organization must relate are similar to one another—for example, the number of different types of clients of a service organization. Other labels: *complexity, diversity* (see Dill, 1958; Thompson, 1967).

2. *Degree of stability–variability:* the extent to which the entities are undergoing change—for example, the rate of product innovation within the industry category to which a given firm belongs. It is possible to differentiate between the rate of change and its evenness or fluctuation (see Lawrence and Lorsch, 1967; Thompson, 1967).

3. *Degree of threat–security:* the extent to which an organization is vulnerable to its environment, or the degree to which "inefficiencies and errors by an organization result in its demise" (McKelvey, 1982: 185). An example is the nuclear energy program, where one mistake can endanger the lives of many and threaten support and funding for the program.

4. *Degree of interconnectedness–isolation:* the extent to which the organization is linked to many other environmental entities whose actions may impinge on it—for example, the number of different suppliers from whom a manufacturing company must buy its inputs (see Pfeffer and Salancik, 1978).

5. *Degree of coordination–noncoordination:* the extent to which the organization confronts a set of environmental entities whose actions are orchestrated or structured. For example, does a seller face a set of independent grocery stores or a chain of supermarkets? (See Jurkovich, 1974.)

In general, we would expect that the greater the heterogeneity, the higher the rate of instability, the greater the threat, the greater the interconnectedness, and the lower the coordination within the environment, the higher the uncertainty facing the organization.

### DIMENSIONS AFFECTING DEPENDENCE

1. *Degree of munificence–scarcity:* the extent to which the resources required by the organization are available in its environment—for example, the availability of petroleum to a chemical company. Other label: *environmental capacity* (See Pfeffer and Salancik, 1978; Aldrich, 1979).

2. *Degree of concentration–dispersion:* the extent to which the resources required are evenly spread throughout the environment. For example, economic concentration has been defined as the proportion of an industry's sales controlled by the largest four or eight firms (see Nutter, 1968; Pfeffer and Salancik, 1978).

3. *Degree of coordination–noncoordination:* the extent to which the organization confronts a set of environmental entities whose actions are orchestrated or structured. For example, does a seller face a set of independent grocery stores or a chain of supermarkets?

The scarcer the resources, the higher the concentration, and the greater the coordination exhibited by entities within the environment, the greater the dependence of the organization.

Note that the two dependent variables, uncertainty and dependence, do not necessarily co-vary in response to a given environmental state. Thus, a higher degree of environmental coordination is expected simultanteously to decrease the organization's uncertainty but to increase its dependence. A similar prediction might well be made for level of concentration.

We belicve that the identification of a number of environmental dimensions at this level of generality represents a significant advance in organization theory, although much work continues to be done on determining which are the primary dimensions. (See Dess and Beard, 1984.) The application of the variables has proved to be a difficult and often frustrating business. This is due partly to the abstract nature of the concepts and to the great variability in the types of organizations and, hence, in the kinds of environments to which they relate. The task of application is rendered particularly difficult by the differentiated nature of organizations: different components or subunits of an organization may confront quite different environmental sectors. For example, Lawrence and Lorsch (1967) investigated variation in the characteristics of some of the environmental sectors confronted by different departments within plastics manufacturing organizations. Their measures revealed that the scientific environment to which the applied research departments related was more uncertain than the marketing environment the sales department confronted. Of course, other specialized units—departments—relate to still other environmental sectors. To state the problem as succinctly as possible: every organization relates to a number of different environments, and these environments may exhibit differing characteristics. And any attempt to determine *the* characteristics of *the* environment requires respondents or investigators to arrive at a summary judgment that may conceal a great deal of variance.

The dimensions of uncertainty and dependence just reviewed are the product of energetic theoretical work and have given rise to an extensive number of empirical investigations testing and elaborating propositions relating environmental conditions and organizational characteristics and actions. We review this work in later chapters. A number of these dimensions can also be used to assess the institutional aspects of organizations, which we consider next.

**Institutional environments**   To the economic and related political aspects emphasized by technical conceptions of environments, institutional analysts have added additional dimensions. The development of interest in institutional environments is more recent, and hence the ideas are less clearly formulated than in the case of technical environments. However, all efforts in this area tend to stress the larger arrangements—network, culture, and history—in which organizations are embedded. A central common message of the institutional view is that the environments of organizations are themselves organized, and increasingly so.

Briefly, network elements consist of the connections among organizations, whether expressed as flows or linkages, such as shared participants. Cultural elements comprise both cognitive and normative systems on which organizations or fields of organizations draw and to which they are subject. And historical elements call attention to the relevance of past conditions for understanding the present and future prospects of organizations. Each set of elements will now be described.[6]

The examination of organizational *networks* is now well under way, with mathematical and graph techniques often employed in depicting and analyzing these complex systems (Burt, 1980). Network approaches differ from conventional social-science methodologies in that they attend to relational and structural connections among units, such as organizations, rather than simply to the attributes of the units. Of course, a variety of types of connections are possible. Some involve flows or exchanges (of services, resources, information); others entail structural linkages. Indeed, an important attribute of a connection is whether it is *multiplex*—whether it has multiple rather than single content (Barnes, 1972). Approaches more relevant to institutional concerns focus on the form taken by a set of linkages; numerous analytic techniques have been developed to measure such network properties as *connectivity*—the degree to which units are linked directly or indirectly—the extent of *clustering* of ties among units the *density* of ties, and so on. (See Laumann, Galaskiewicz, and Marsden, 1978; and Lincoln, 1982.) And since we have argued that the linkages developing within organizational fields are themselves increasingly organized, we can add other, more conventional variables for assessing network structure, such as the extent to which the linkages are *centralized, formalized, loosely coupled,* and so on. (See Aldrich and Whetten, 1981.)

As Burt (1980) has noted, there are two varying approaches to assessing network properties. Most network analysts have measured the *relational* properties of a network—examining the extent and nature of the direct and indirect linkages that exist, using concepts similar to those just described. But White, Boorman, and Breiger (1976) have developed a *positional* approach that assesses the extent to which patterns of relations within a network are similar. Using these techniques, one can assess the degree to which two or more portions of a network (or two or more networks) are *structurally equivalent.* Two networks may be very similar in structure—for example, two systems of prisons in two different U.S. states—although they are not, or are only very indirectly, connected to each other.

Shifting from form to content of organizational networks, we can focus on what types of *resources* are exchanged—such as money, use of staff, clients, technical assistance, or goodwill (see Van de Ven and Ferry, 1980: 325)—or what types of *interpenetrations* are present. As Laumann and colleagues note, some of the important types of connections among organizations are based on "interpenetration of organizational boundaries"—for instance, common membership in a coalition or federation, the undertaking of joint programs, and interlocking directorates (Laumann, Galaskiewicz, and Marsden, 1978: 463–64). In research on organizational sectors, Meyer and I have distinguished among the types of *decisions*—funding, programmatic, instrumental—that are made by higher units in a field that constrain the behavior of subordinate units, and among the types of *interlevel controls*— structural, process, outcome—that are exercised (Scott and Meyer, 1983). Although form has to date received more attention than content in research on linkages, content seems of equal importance, and, indeed, the form that linkages take often varies by content.

[6]This discussion of networks, culture, and history draws on my 1983 paper.

Network analysis has become more popular as levels of analysis have shifted from sets to fields. Its imagery and methods are useful for analyzing both technical and institutional environments. Dimensions such as degree of interconnectedness and extent of coordination obviously lend themselves to network approaches. The connections themselves may involve not organizations or their subunits but various types of interpersonal associations. For example, Powell (1985: 193), in analyzing the organization of book publishing, underscores the importance of "trust, personal networks, norms of reciprocity, reputational effects, and tacit collusion" in relations between editors and authors.

While institutional conceptions of the environment include these more immediate environments, they also emphasize the importance of larger systems of interdependence. For example, organization theorists have not given as much attention as desirable to larger corporate systems—both national and international—that include many specific companies and establishments within a single complex framework. (See Evans, 1981.) And we have not attended as carefully as necessary to the varying structure of different industries or sectors, although economists have long noted the diversity of their concentration and degree of connectedness. We are just beginning to become aware of the importance of state structures and activities—not only as complex interorganizational systems in themselves but as powerful forces shaping the environment of all types of organizations, through tax and regulatory policies, labor and antitrust law, subsidies and contracts, and numerous other ways.

Emphasis on institutional environments also calls attention to the importance of more general *cultural* features shaping organizations and organizational fields, in particular cognitive and normative systems. Of course, major cultural differences exist across societies or nation-states, and there is growing interest in and attention to the ways in which general cultural differences may influence the shape and operation of organizations. (See Crozier, 1964; Landsberger, 1970; Dore, 1973; Lammers and Hickson, 1979*b;* and Child, 1981) For example, Lammers and Hickson (1979*a*), summarizing several studies aimed at detecting cross-cultural differences in organizational types, conclude that current evidence points to at least three distinctive cultural forms. A *Latin* type, exemplified by French, Italian, and Spanish organizations, is characterized by relatively high centralization, rigid stratification and sharp inequalities among levels, and conflicts around areas of uncertainty. An *Anglo-Saxon* type, exemplified by British, United States, and Scandinavian organization, is marked by more decentralization, less rigid stratification, and more flexible approaches to the application of rules. And a *traditional* type, found in third-world, developing countries, is characterized by paternalistic leadership patterns, implicit rather than explicit rules, and lack of clear boundaries separating organizational from nonorganizational roles. And of late there has been a great deal of attention focused on ascertaining the distinctive cultural features that characterize Japanese society and organizations (Cole, 1979; Ouchi, 1981). However, the complexity of wider cultures and their multiple connections with other societal elements—demographic, economic, political—makes interpretations of these associations hazardous.

An ambitious attempt to systematically assess variations across societies in value patterns relevant to the functioning of organizations has been carried out by Hofstede (1984). He identifies four value dimensions— power distance, uncertainty avoidance, individualism, and masculinity— that in combination constitute a generalized framework that can be used to compare and contrast the varying cultural profiles of different societies. Using as data survey responses from over 120,000 respondents in the marketing and service departments of a multinational corporation, Hofstede gathered information in forty societies and at two time periods, 1968 and 1972. Hofstede finds substantial differences among societies on the four value dimensions. A society's position on most of the value profiles can be predicted with considerable accuracy from its geographical latitude, population size, and per capita wealth. And the value differences are strongly associated with the characteristics of organizational structures and practices. For example, cultures with larger power differences (inequalities in power) are likely to contain organizations that are more highly centralized, have higher ratios of supervisory and managerial personnel, and have larger disparities in qualifications and wages among personnel.

Hofstede suggests that not only organizaiton practice but organization theory is culturally based. Thus, Weber, the German, stresses authority of office; Fayol, the Frenchman, power of persons; and Follett, the American, the situational nature of power. More generally, Hofstede (1984: 218) points out that

> what is available as organization theory today is mostly written by Americans, and as such reflects the cultural context of one specific society. A collection of 15 contributions by leading Europeans (Hofstede and Kassem, 1976) shows remarkable differences in focus by culture area. Authors from Latin Europe focus on power; from Central Europe, including Germany, on truth; from Eastern Europe, on efficiency; from Northern Europe, on change; while the Western Europeans, in this case British and Dutch, have a bit of all of these but show more than the others a concern with data collection which we also find in the United States.

Of course, cultural beliefs vary not only between but within societies, and a highly developed and differentiated society such as that of the United States contains multiple, diverse value and meaning systems— cultures associated with regions, ethnic groups, classes, occupational communities, and generations. Similarly, cultural beliefs vary among organizational fields and sectors, both in content and in degree of consensus. Particularly important are those belief systems that define the collective goals or values governing the field, values that provide the basis for domain definition. In some arenas, such as the postal or domestic airlines services, the goals may be relatively noncontroversial; in others, such as criminal justice, there may be deep-seated controversies as to the nature of the mission. Also important are conceptions of the means available to pursue objectives. Theories of practice, as well as actual instrumentalities, are involved. In some fields, we observe the presence of technically defined procedures; in others, actions are based on and guided by rational myths, as noted by Meyer and Rowan (1977).

Closely related to these cognitive aspects of cultures, are the normative structures—collective norms governing behavior in organizational fields. Laumann and colleagues describe the normative contexts of these fields as varying from *competitive* to *cooperative* modalities (Laumann, Galaskiewicz, and Marsden, 1978). They further distinguish cooperation that is *contingent*—in that "organizations are expected to balance their commitments to collective purposes with their more specialized goals"—from cooperation that is *mandated*—a mode that "implies the existence of a centralized control agency, which has the power to structure and restructure the total network" (pp. 466, 468). Clearly, types of behavior that are encouraged in some fields would be condemned in others. For example, mutual cooperation and coordination of services is encouraged among community service agencies but condemned as "collusion" among computer software companies.

Finally, emphasis on institutional environments stresses the importance of a *historical* perspective in examining organizations and organizational fields. We accept Tilly's (1981: 6) straightforward definition that "an analysis is historical to the extent that the place and time of the action enter into its explanations." To call for a historical perspective is not to insist on longitudinal studies—studies collecting data over more than a single time period—although more such studies are needed, but to recognize that even when we observe an organization or a system of organizations at one point in time, we are seeing a cross-section of elements that are the residues of diverse past processes.

Each organization and organization field has its own history, its own sequence of development. Social systems tend to progress through certain developmental phases, a "life cycle" that, while not as definite in its stages or progression as biological systems, nevertheless exhibits a recognizable pattern. (See Kimberly, Miles, et al., 1980.) And where a system is in its own developmental sequence will influence its characteristics and its responses.

Just as significant as a system's own history is the larger historical frame within which it develops and operates. Many of these larger contexts are themselves structured and may be usefully viewed as systems with their own developmental history. Thus Marxist theorists call attention to the capitalist economic system and the relevance for present organizations of operating within the framework of "late capitalism" (Benson, 1982; Burawoy, 1985).

All system elements—units, relations, beliefs—should be thought of as having a time subscript. And knowing *when* some element developed may provide important clues as to its characteristics and behavior. Obviously, technologies and belief systems change over time. For example, our ideas about military defense or about mental illness and how to manage it are quite different today than they were 50 to 100 years ago. Because of differences in technologies, beliefs, and other founding conditions, we would expect the organizations that develop at a given time to differ from those that develop earlier or later. (See Stinchcombe, 1965.)

Also, various system elements may be expected to change at differing rates. Some aspects of organizations, such as technical features, are more easily and quickly changed than others, such as participant's skills or work routines. Both because different organizations and fields are founded at differing times and under varying circumstances and because they may change in differing ways and at varying rates, it is important to attend to time dimensions in examining the structure and composition of organizations and the fields in which they operate.

Both technical and institutional environments shape organizational forms and influence organizational behavior. To this point, we have attempted to review some of the more important environmental dimensions and distinctions used by analysts who are attempting to capture salient features of organizational environments. In later chapters, we review specific predictions and empirical studies attempting to explain how these features of the environment influence organizational structure and performance.

## THE INTERDEPENDENCE OF ORGANIZATIONS AND ENVIRONMENTS

### Enactment, Attention, and Outcomes

In research on organizational environments, a healthy controversy has developed about the relative merits of employing subjective or perceptual versus objective measures of environmental characteristics. This is not simply a measurement issue, but raises important theoretical issues concerning how organizations relate to their environments. A number of analysts (Dill, 1958; Lawrence and Lorsch, 1967; Duncan, 1972) argue that it makes sense to measure the environment in terms of the perceptions of participants, since only factors that they perceive can enter into their decision-making behavior. Weick's formulation is even stronger. He argues, as discussed in Chapter 4, that participants do not merely perceive and react but actively construct, "enact" their environments. Weick (1979: 164) insists that "the concept of an *enacted environment* is not synonymous with the concept of a *perceived environment*." Rather, the label *enactment* is meant "to emphasize that managers construct, rearrange, single out, and demolish many 'objective' features of their surroundings." Whereas symbolic interactionists emphasize the extent to which reality is interpersonally negotiated, Weick stresses the individual, cognitive aspects of the process by which "people, often alone, actively *put* things out there that they then perceive and negotiate about perceiving" (1979: 165).

March and colleagues build on this work by introducing the concept of *attention structure* to describe the distribution of connections among people, the types of information they send and receive, the distribution of problems, and the rules concerning who is entitled to make choices about what is known (Cohen and March, 1974; March and Olsen, 1976). This concept reminds us that although individuals may be the agents who enact their environment, they do so within an organizational structure that influences what types of stimuli reach them and sets some constraints on their decisions and actions. Much of the empirical research on the structuring of attention involves case studies of particular decisions (see for example, March and Olsen, 1976), but Sproull (1981) points out that studies of time allocation by managers are also quite germane. For example, in a very influential study, Mintzberg (1971; 1973) observed and systematically recorded the activities and interactions of the chief executive officer in five diverse organizations for one week each in order to answer the question "What do managers do?" Among the relevant findings, which have been replicated in similar studies, were that managers engage in multiple activities characterized by brevity, such that the manager "is forced to treat issues in an abrupt and superficial way" (1971: B100). Managers were also observed to rely primarily on verbal rather than written communications. Meetings, scheduled and unscheduled, consumed most of their time. Such findings reinforce the importance of attention structures in understanding how organizational participants enact their environments.

Pfeffer and Salancik (1978: 74) embrace these arguments regarding the importance of organizational arrangements for structuring attention and extend them by stressing the significance of the development of specialized units and routines for collecting and processing information.

> The *information system* is conceptualized as the reports, statistics, facts, or information that are regularly collected and their pattern of transmission through the organization. The fact that certain information is regularly collected focuses the organization's attention on it. The collection of certain information occupies the time and attention of the organization, which necessarily restricts the time and attention devoted elsewhere.

Some information is important because it is collected and, hence, available as an input to decision making. In this manner, information systems help to determine attention structures.

We must take care not to overstate the subtlety and complexity of the information systems devised by organizations. Recall in this connection Boulding's (1956) typology of system levels described in Chapter 4 of this volume. Organizations and their participants are capable of responding to their environments at levels 7 and 8 by creating complex consensual images of environmental processes as a basis for doing so. At the other end of the spectrum, organizations also devise and employ simple, tightly coupled mechanisms to track specific environmental variables.

Ashby (1952) stresses the adaptive behavior of which simple systems are capable as they monitor one or a few particular variables linked to one or a few response rules: witness the "intelligence" of the thermostat. Simon (1962) suggests two terms to distinguish between these lower- and higher-level responses. He proposes that a cybernetic response works on the principle of the *recipe:* feedback variables trigger the performance of a specified sequence of activities. Steinbruner (1974: 57) amplifies:

> The simplest cybernetic mechanisms do not confront the issue of variety at all, for they make no calculations of the environment. The mechanisms merely track a few feedback variables and beyond that are perfectly blind to the environment.

Organizational systems relying on recipes can perform effectively as long as the signals they track are reliable indicators of the true state of the variables of concern. However, such is often not the case, because of random error, changed circumstances, or deception. Under any of these circumstances, "smart" systems suddenly act quite stupidly. By contrast, higher-level responses entail the construction of what Simon terms a *blueprint*—an image of the environment that attempts to capture and reflect its salient complexity. Thus, some information systems create vastly simplified pictures of environments whereas others attempt to more fully capture and codify its complexity.

But whether the system is relying on recipes or blueprints, these theorists conclude that the environment of an organization is as much as, if not more then, a function of the organization, the cognitive work of its participants and their structure of attention, and its information system as it is of the external situation.

It is not necessary to embrace fully these phenomenological arguments to accept a related, but different point. Even if we prefer objective measures of an organization's environment, we must still take into account the characteristics and goals of the organization in order to evaluate what aspects of the external world are likely to be salient. If a church replaces a factory on the corner lot of a small town, the environments of the two types of organizations will not be very similar: each defines and functions in a different *domain*. The demands a specific organization makes on its environment, as well as the demands made by the environment on the organization, will vary with each type of organization. Hence, one cannot describe "objectively" the environment of an organization without knowledge of the organization and the domain in which it functions.

Still, we do not want to conclude that all is perception and enactment. The environment of a given organization does vary in its stability, its complexity, its threat—and such matters can be assessed apart from ascertaining what participants believe to be the case. For example, one can examine the density of competing organizations, or count the number of hostile takeovers in an industry, or examine fluctuations in profit margins over time. Participants may or may not attend to these matters, but this does not mean that what they don't know can't hurt (or help) them. Pfeffer and Salancik (1978: 62–63) correctly observe that although environments must be perceived in order to influence actions taken by organizational participants, they can influence organizational *outcomes* whether or not they have been perceived. Outcomes are results. Organizations produce *outputs*—goods and services—but *outcomes* represent the joint product of organizational performance and environment response. The surgeon may perform flawlessly, but the patient may die; the automobile may be well built but fail to sell. In this sense, environments directly influence outcomes. (See Chapter 13.)

Thus, one's measurement strategy should depend on what is being predicted: perceptual measures are necessary if we hope to predict the choices of organizational participants, but they are not sufficient if we wish to predict the outcomes of these choices, since outcomes are a product of many forces, many of which are outside the control of the organization. For example, perceptions of the market held by recording-studio executives can better predict what types of artists are given contracts than how well their records sell.

In Figure 6–1 we collect some of the distinctions we have described and attempt to depict their relations to one another. The result is a cycle of interdependence of organizations and environments. Beginning, arbitrarily, with the organizational structure, we argue that its decision makers determine a domain of operation, selecting what goods and services are to be produced for what types of consumers. Domain selection will strongly affect what types of information will be required. An infor-

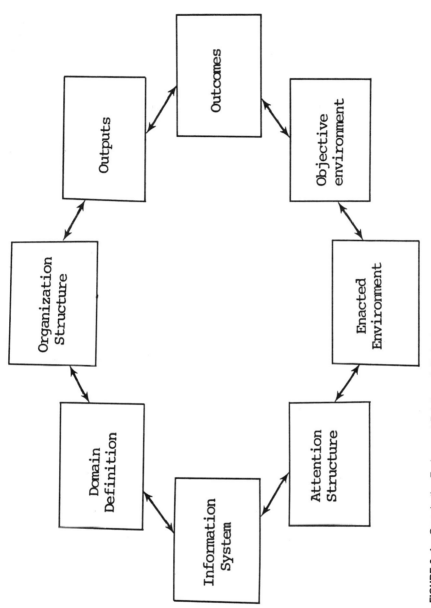

**FIGURE 6–1**  Organization-Environment Relations: A Cycle of Interdependence

137

mation system is designed that, in turn, gives rise to an attention structure that will help to determine what participants in varying locations attend to and what importance is assigned to their concerns. The attention structure contributes to the creation of the enacted environment—the constructed (and reconstructed) picture that participants have of the environment to which they relate.

But these organizational processes do not take place in a vacuum. Starting at the opposite point in the cycle, the "objective" environment directly influences the enacted environment. Environmental factors can also be expected to command attention, and will shape the information system of the organization. The objective environment will also affect the domain definition. An organization may claim to be a day-care center or an automobile-repair shop, but others—clients, distributors, regulators—must acknowledge and endorse these claims for them to have "reality."

Finally, as we have described, the environment can perform an "end run," influencing the structure of the organization indirection by affecting its outcomes. Outcomes are joint products of organizational performance and environmental response.

### Influence

To this point we have suggested that organizations and environments are interdependent in terms of information systems and cognitive processes, and in terms of environmental effects on organizational outcomes. They are also interdependent in more direct ways: organizations attempt to directly influence environments, and vice versa. There is little doubt that environments profoundly shape organizations—their structures, their performances, their outcomes. How this occurs is subject to dispute. For example, resource dependency theorists argue that organizations take steps to adapt to their environment, changing their structural features as required to better match its requirements. By contrast, population ecologists emphasize the structural inertia of organizations; they assume that the more pervasive environmental effects occur through selection rather than adaptation. (See Chapter 8) Organizations are also recognized by many theorists to directly shape their environments. Such actions are obvious in the case of large and powerful organizations, such as monopolies, but they can be observed in other situations as well. Many of the strategies that organizations employ, to be discussed in detail in Chapter 8, involve direct attempts to alter the environment: to change demand by advertising, to absorb uncertainty by contracting, or to change environments by diversifying. Organizations can and do directly affect their environments. Influences are reciprocal.

### Absorption and Interpenetration

We have previously noted the open system assertion that the boundary separating the organization from its environment is somewhat arbitrarily drawn and varies with the flows or activities being examined. For example, if we wish to examine the authority system regulating faculty members at a university, we will want to include professional colleagues from other universities who serve as significant evaluators, helping to determine promotion and tenure decisions for the host school. (See Hind, Dornbusch, and Scott, 1974.) Thus, elements that for some purposes are usefully analyzed as parts of a system's environment are for other purposes included within the system itself.

Also, even arbitrary boundaries change over time. What today is a functioning system operating outside the framework of a given organization may tomorrow be incorporated as a subsystem by the organization. As discussed in Chapter 8, one of the most effective strategies employed by organizations in relating to some aspect of their environment is to absorb it. With increasing frequency, organizations acquire—and disaffiliate from—other systems. In this sense, organizational executives, like researchers, take a pragmatic view of the boundary separating their organization and its environment.

Even without "official" redefinitions, organizations constantly incorporate environmental elements into their own structures. In a fully developed open system conception, all of the "materials" used to create organizations—resources and equipment, but also personnel and procedures—are obtained from the environment. If we add to this the institutionalist ingredients—beliefs, meanings, conceptual categories—then it is no longer possible to think of the environment as something "out there"; its elements are part of the organization, not absorbed by it so that they become separated from the environment but interpentrating it, infusing it with value, and connecting it with larger systems. Like most other ideas, however, these insights are better treated as variables: organizations are open systems, but some are more open than others. Similarly, organizations vary in the extent to which they relate to institutional environments.

The nested nature of organizational environments as well as the penetration of organizations by their environments raises serious problems for investigators who are trying to decide where to draw boundaries for analytical purposes. (See Chapter 8) In studying educational systems, for example, is the proper unit of analysis the individual classroom, the individual school, the school district, or the state educational system? Clearly, there is no way to answer this question without knowing what processes or relations within the system are to be examined. There is always the danger that we will select the wrong unit of analysis for a given topic. We may elect to study the influence of teachers on curriculum and select a sample of classrooms, only to discover that the major curriculum choices are made at the district or state office. Such *specification* errors become more likely when the boundaries of systems are indefinite. The boundaries of many organizations are diffuse with respect to many processes and are variable with respect to space and time. (See Freeman, 1978.)

## THE EVOLUTION OF ENVIRONMENTS

After generating so many distinctions—dimensions, levels, types of measures—we are hesitant to conclude this chapter by commenting on the general direction of environmental change. Since commentators increasingly disagree on this subject, however, we feel somewhat protected from the dangers of overgeneralization.

The prevalent view is that first enunciated by Emery and Trist: "The environmental contexts in which organizations exist are themselves changing, at an increasing rate, and toward increasing complexity" (1965: 21). Except for noting that these conditions are occurring "under the impact of technological change" (p. 30), Emery and Trist are content to describe these developments rather than to explain them. Terreberry cites a considerable number of empirical studies on organizations that, in her opinion support Emery and Trist's thesis that

> these systems are increasingly finding themselves in environments where the complexity and rapidity of change in external interconnectedness gives rise to increasingly unpredictable change in their transactional interdependencies. This seems to be good evidence for the emergence of turbulence in the environments of many formal organizations. (Terreberry, 1968: 598)

However, Terreberry's major argument supporting Emery and Trist's thesis is a conceptual rather than an empirical one. Her reasoning is as follows: Organizations are, by definition, open systems. All open systems tend to evolve from less to more complex states. The environment of any given organization is increasingly composed of other organizations. Hence, it follows that organizational environments are evolving from less to more complex states. Two corollaries are developed: for any given focal organization (1) "these trends mean a gross increase in their area of relevant uncertainty" (Emery and Trist, 1965: 26); and (2) "the evolution of environments is characterized by an increase in the ratio of externally induced change over internally induced change" (Terreberry, 1968: 599).

   We are not convinced by these arguments that all environments of organizations are moving toward greater turbulence—increased uncertainty and interdependency. Although Terreberry is correct that open systems evolve from more to less complex states, increased complexity need not be synonymous with increased uncertainty. Indeed, as Galbraith (1967) and others have noted, differentiation permits specialization of function, and specialization, in turn, permits the application of scientific or engineering knowledge to the problem at hand. Thus, differentiation contributes to rationalization and routinization of a field of action and, in this manner, to increased certainty. Similarly, the spread of organizations into more arenas of activity often results in increased standardization and predictability. Why trust the uncertainty of small-town cuisine when you can count on a Big Mac?

> On the modern McDonald's grills, winking lights tell countermen when to flip over the hamburger. . . . A small group of equipment makers furnished McDonald's with a stream of such continually updated gadgets designed to automate the serving and cooking of food to the ultimate degree: premeasured scoops, ketchup and mustard dispensers, computer-run fryers, infrared warning lights, instruments for testing the solidity of raw potatoes and the fluffiness of shakes. Nothing—as Hamburger Central proudly boasts—was left to chance. (Boas and Chain, 1977: 40–41)

An increase in the connections among organizations in the environment also does not always lead to increased uncertainty: it can lead to the creation of unitary or federative contexts (Warren, 1967), in which coordination and common goals supplant competition.

Not only are there important factors creating certainty among technical organizations, but organizations often confront relatively certain or predictable institutional environments. Thus, Meyer argues that "in post-industrial societies, rationalized states expand their dominance over more and more aspects of social life, increasing centralization and homogeneity in these domains." He insists that through the creation of rationalized myths, modern societies produce "vast new forms of certainty, which organizations may obtain by the mere process of conformity to environmental specifications" (1978: 361, 363).[7] Although Meyer stresses increased certainty in institutionalized environments, we will strike the opposing note. Although new laws, administrative agencies, and professional occupations are continually created, giving rise to new rationalized myths that provide a basis for organized action where none existed before, we should not overemphasize the amount of certainty that results. Laws are often ambiguous and variously interpreted; state and federal bureaus represent an increasingly vast and diverse collection of interests and programs that are often contradictory or competing; and professional occupations challenge one another's visions of truth.

While some arenas of organizational action are probably moving toward increasing certainty—whether because of the routinization of technical operations or the widespread acceptance of institutional rules—we also see evidence of increased uncertainty in many areas of social life. Given these contradictory processes—of standardization and rationalization on the one hand, and uncertainty and turbulence of the other—it seems inappropriate to make any assumption about the general direction of change in the environments within which organizations function. Empirical investigations, not *a priori* assumptions, should determine the rate and direction of environmental change.

## SUMMARY

Determining how the environments of organizations can be usefully characterized and circumscribed is an issue that confronts, analysts embracing the open system perspective. Conceptions of environments vary by level of analysis as well as by substantive focus. Analysis levels—include the organizational set, organizational population, areal organizational field, and functional organizational field. Each focuses on a somewhat different aspect of organization-environment relations, and each is associated with varying theoretical perspectives.

[7]It is of interest to note that Emery and Trist, the authors who see the future of organizations as increasingly turbulent, simultaneously espouse a different view that, although little recognized, bears a striking resemblance to Meyer's conception. They argue that a possible solution for organizations in turbulent fields is represented by "the emergence of values that have overriding significance for all members of the field." These values "can be rational as well as irrational" and are likely to become more rational as "the scientific ethos takes greater hold in a society." The emergence of these commonly accepted values creates a field "which is no longer richly joined and turbulent but simplified and relatively static." (Emery and Trist, 1965: 28) In short, their vision of future organizational fields includes some circumstances—including the emergence of rationalized values—that result in more rather than less certainty for organizations.

Analysts examining environments also vary in substantive interests. A great deal of research has been devoted to the technical aspects of environments—the ways in which stocks of resources and sources of information are distributed and arranged. More recently, investigators have pursued institutional features of environments, studying how relational networks and cultural and historical contexts shape organizational structure and activities.

Organizations are viewed as interdependent with environments in a number of senses. Participants' perceptions of their environments together with the attention structures of organizations result in enacted environments that are products of both environmental features and organizational information systems. Environments directly affect organizational outcomes, which in turn affect subsequent perceptions and decisions. Environments influence organizations, but organizations also modify and select their environments. And environments supply the materials and ingredients of which organizations are composed.

Most observers argue that the environments of organizations are becoming more complex and uncertain over time. The increasing differentiation and interconnectedness of organizations cause increased uncertainty and interdependency for them. But other processes—routinization, standardization, the creation of rationalized myths—create new islands of certainty. We conclude that the extent and the direction of change in the environments of organizations is a matter to be settled not by assumption but by empirical investigation. a

# 7 creating organizations

The distinctive features of modern life derive from the fact that a large share of social activity is governed by bodies of systematic abstract doctrine. . . . The government of activities by doctrines is the primary function of bureaucracy. The foundation of the dominance of professions in modern society is competence in a specialized body of abstract knowledge, systematized and taught by scholars in professional schools. Science, education, bureaucratic administration, the professions—these distinctive features of modern life are primarily concerned with developing, transmitting, and governing activities by bodies of systematized intelligence. The study of modernization is, therefore, in large measure the study of the social role of systematized intelligence and its application to daily affairs.

Arthur L. Stinchcombe (1974)

In this chapter we attempt to explain how and why organizations come into existence. It is helpful to separate this broad question into two categories of more specific questions. The first deals with the emergence of organizations as a distinctive type of collectivity. This category subsumes such questions as these: Have organizations always existed? If not, when did they first emerge? What are the social conditions under which organizations develop? What alternatives to organizations exist for carrying out complex tasks? It will quickly become apparent that "authorities differ" in the answers they give to these and related questions. In particular, we contrast the views of rational system with natural system theorists.

The second set of questions assumes the existence of organizations as one general type of social arrangement and asks how specific organizations obtain resources that support their structures and activities. Questions include the following: What means do organizations use to induce participants to contribute resources to them? What effects are associated with the use of particular types of incentives or with the recruitment of particular types of participants? How do the resource needs of organizations vary by type of organization and by time and place? Although all such questions cannot be definitively answered, they serve to focus the discussion and point to areas of needed work.

## THE EMERGENCE OF ORGANIZATIONS

It is only in modern, industrialized societies that organizations dominate the landscape. Their emergence, proliferation, and consolidation as a ubiquitous and significant building block of society is one of the great social transformations that distinguishes the modern from the premodern world. In a quite literal sense, the history of the development of modern society is also a history of the development of special purpose organizations: organizations were both created by and helped to produce these changes. We shall not attempt to recount here this vast and complex history but will only note some of the changes scholars have identified as among the most fateful for the development of organizations.

### The Changing Relations of Individual and Corporate Actors

When we speak of the emergence of organizations, we are not implying that previous societal arrangements exhibited disorganization. Indeed, in important ways some of the preexisting social systems exhibited higher degrees of order! The correct contrast, then, is between different types of ordered social arrangements. The principal ways in which modern social structures differ from earlier, traditional forms are (1) in the relation of individual actors to corporate actors, and (2) in the relation of corporate actors to one another.

Coleman's (1974) analysis of these differences is most illuminating. Examining the corporate bodies of the Middle Ages, he observes that the basic units—the manor, the guild, the village—wholly contained their members and possessed full authority over them. What rights and interests individuals possessed, they acquired from their membership in these units. (Note that these bodies are the patrimonial systems dissected by Weber, as described in Chapter 2.) Moreover, the corporate actors were themselves organized in a strict hierarchicy, the subordinate units being responsible to and contained within superordinate systems in a concentric pattern (see Simmel, 1955 trans.).

Gradually and fitfully, over several centuries, these relations were altered. Individuals were able to acquire rights and were recognized to have interests, and corporate actors were allowed to acquire rights and to pursue interests that were not simply aggregates of the interests of their members. Coleman summarizes these developments:

> Two things happened. First, men themselves began to break out of their fixed estates, began to have rights to appear before the king's court, rights to make contracts on their own; became, in effect, persons before the law with a certain set of rights (elevated by seventeenth-century philosophers to the status of "natural rights") to engage in a variety of activities at their own pleasure. But second, and as a direct consequence of this fragmentation of

the feudal structure, a different kind of intermediate organization arose in society: a corporate actor which had, under charter from the king, a variety of rights to free and expansive action. This new corporate actor became the instrument through which men could jointly exercise their new-found rights. (Coleman, 1974: 28)

Under these altered conditions, corporate actors no longer contained their individual members but only the specific resources invested in them by persons acting as owners or investors; and they no longer fully controlled their members but only the specific behaviors contracted for by persons who agreed to function as their participants or agents. Individuals were only partially involved in these new organizations. Also, these organizations were no longer arranged in a concentric, hierarchical pattern, but were allowed to function somewhat independently of one another, competing for the loyalties and resources of individuals.

Coleman emphasizes the impact of individualism on the development of special-purpose organizations. Simmel (1955 trans.) in his brilliant essay "The Web of Group-Affiliations" stresses the reverse effect. When social arrangements consist of layers of concentrically related systems, the social spaces created tend to produce homogeneous individuals: batches of individuals are likely to share the same social location and perceive themselves as holding the same social identity. However, as social arrangements shift to contain overlapping and intersecting systems, a vastly increased variety of social spaces is created, and no two individuals are as likely to share the same social location or to hold the same social identity. As Simmel explains,

> The groups with which the individual is affiliated constitute a system of coordinates, as it were, such that each new group with which he becomes affiliated circumscribes him more exactly and more unambiguously. To belong to any one of these groups leaves the individual considerable leeway. But the larger the number of groups to which an individual belongs, the more improbable is it that other persons will exhibit the same combination of group-affiliations, that these particular groups will "intersect" once again in a second individual.
> . . . As individuals, we form the personality out of particular elements of life, each of which has arisen from, or is interwoven with, society. This personality is subjectivity par excellence in the sense that it combines the elements of culture in an individual manner. . . . As the person becomes affiliated with a social group, he surrenders himself to it. A synthesis of such subjective affiliations creates a group in an objective sense. But the person also regains his individuality, because his pattern of participation is unique; hence the fact of multiple group-participation creates in turn a new subjective element. (Simmel, 1955 trans.: 140–41)

Combining the insights of Coleman and Simmel, we conclude that there was an intimate, reciprocal, supportive relation between the emergence of individualism and the development of special-purpose organizations. Given this historical association, it is somewhat ironic that numerous commentators in our own time perceive organizations as the enemy of individualism. (We will explore this paradox in Chapter 12.)

## Societal Conditions Favoring the Development of Organizations

Thus far we have described some quite basic changes in societal arrangements without attempting to determine what brought these changes about. Drawing on the insights of Weber, Durkheim (1949 trans.), and other social theorists, Stinchcombe (1965) suggests that the capacity of a population to develop and support special-purpose organizations is determined by such general factors as widespread literacy and specialized advanced schooling, urbanization, a money economy, and political revolution. To these primarily economic and political factors, theorists such as Eisenstadt (1958) and Parsons (1966) add institutional and normative variables such as increased role and institutional differentiation, allocation of roles by universalistic and achievement rather than particularistic and ascriptive criteria, and increased dissensus among societal groups concerning the priority of goals, together with competition among them for resources. Eisenstadt concludes, "The most important characteristics of the environment conducive to the development of bureaucracies are first, the availability of various 'free-floating' resources, and second, the development of several centres of power which compete over such resources" (1958: 111). To these characteristics, Parsons (1960: 20–21) adds that societal environments support the emergence of organizations by legitimating their specialized functions and independent existence.

These arguments are all at a very general level: most of them describe conditions that are conducive to rationalization of the social structure in general and do not point specifically to conditions favoring the creation of organizations. Stinchcombe (1965: 146–50) recognizes this problem and has attempted to construct more specific arguments that relate these general conditions to the creation of organizations through intermediate variables. He suggests that such general societal factors influence the development of organizations (1) by motivating individuals to form and join such social units, and (2) by improving the chances that these units, once formed, will survive. Thus, individuals are motivated to join organizations by increased literacy, which facilitates the learning of new roles and the keeping of rules and records; by urbanization, which increases social differentiation and encourages the formation of mechanisms for regularizing relations among strangers; by a money economy, which liberates resources, depersonalizes economic relations, and simplifies the calculation of benefits and future conditions; and by political revolutions, which dislodge vested interests and loosen resources for new uses. These same social conditions also improve the likelihood of survival of newly formed organizations. Stinchcombe asserts that organizations suffer the *liability of newness:* new organizations and in particular new forms of organization are likely to fail. New organizations require the creation and learning of new roles, reliance on strangers, and the generation of new markets and customer ties. The same general factors—literacy, urbanization, monetarized exchange, and political upheavals—contribute to the creation of these conditions.

Although somewhat more specific, these arguments can still be sharpened. However, in doing so, we encounter once again the contrasting assumptions and arguments associated with the rational and the natural system views of the nature of organizations.

### Rational System Explanations of the Origin of Organizations

*Division of labor*    Certainly the most widely accepted and one of the most compelling arguments concerning the origins of organizations ties their emergence to the division of labor. The classic statement of this argument was provided by Adam Smith in 1776 in his celebrated account of the manufacture of pins. Smith observed that whereas an untrained worker without the proper machinery could "scarce, perhaps, with his utmost industry, make one pin in a day," vastly different results obtain when the work is properly divided into a number of branches.

> One man draws out the wire, another straights it, a third cuts it, a fourth points it, a fifth grinds it at the top for receiving the head; to make the head requires two or three distinct operations; to put it on is a peculiar business, to whiten the pins is another; it is even a trade by itself to put them into the paper; and the important business of making a pin is, in this manner, divided into about eighteen distinct operations. . . (Smith, 1957 ed.: 2).

So arranged, ten persons "could make among them upwards of forty-eight thousand pins a day."

This miracle of productivity is accomplished primarily by the application of technology to the work process. As Galbraith explains, "technology means the systematic application of scientific or other organized knowledge to practical tasks." This is possible only when the tasks are divided into their components in such a manner that they become "coterminous with some established area of scientific or engineering knowledge." (1967: 24) In addition to this prime benefit, specialization within the work force allows the organization to take advantage of particular skills possessed by a member and also fosters the development of such skills through repetition and learning. And to the extent that the various skills required are of differential complexity, variable pay scales may be introduced, so that further economies are realized through task subdivision. (Braverman, 1974: 79)

The division of labor also tends to encourage its concentration in specified work settings. In order to minimize costs of handling and storage, to take advantage of central energy sources, and to improve surveillance and control, workers are often gathered into a common location.

These types of changes—the division of labor, advances in technology, concentration of the work force in factories—are all associated with the general process of industrialization. In an influential volume, Kerr and his colleagues (1964) attempt to identify a set of developments that are generic to the process of industrialization as well as to examine specific variants of the process that occur under differing societal and cultural conditions. Among the universal consequences, they include the creation of organizations. "The technology and specialization of the industrial society," they assert, "are necessarily and distinctively associated with large-scale organizations." (p. 21).

However, it is not only production organizations that are associated with work division and specialization. As we already know, Weber advanced similar arguments for systems of political administration. His ideal-type conception of bureaucracy places great emphasis on technical expertise and a fixed division of labor among officials. And he was quite explicit that this form replaced earlier, more traditional social structures because of its greater efficiency.

> Experience tends universally to show that the purely bureaucratic type of administrative organization . . . is, from a purely technical point of view, capable of attaining the highest degree of efficiency and is in this sense formally the most rational known means of exercising authority over human beings. It is superior to any other form in precision, in stability, in the stringency of its discipline, and in its reliability. (Weber, 1947 trans.: 337)

Giddens (1983: 202) correctly notes the extent to which Weber's conception draws on technical and mechanical imagery:

> Weber's talk of "precision," "stability" and "reliability" points to the direct connection between bureaucracy and mechanisation that he sometimes makes quite explicit. Bureaucracy, he says, is a "human machine": the formal rationality of technique applies with equal relevance to human social organisation as to the control of the material world.

On the other hand, work division entails overhead costs. Someone must design the work segments and someone must control and coordinate the divided work. A horizontal division of labor is usually accompanied by a vertical hierarchy providing oversight—over those engaged in either tasks of production or administration.

According to these well-known arguments, the division of labor supports the application of technology or rationalized procedures to work, increases the scale of work organizations, and gives rise to a managerial hierarchy. These developments occur because they are associated with increasing productivity and with heightened efficiency of operations. Rational system analysts assume that they are fundamental to the appearance and growth of organizations. As the administrative theorist Luther Gulick concludes, "work division is the foundation of organization; indeed, the reason for organization" (Gulick and Urwick, 1937: 3).

**Transactions costs**    As noted in Chapter 5, a newer rational (and open) system perspective, provides an alternative explanation for the emergence of organizations. This approach, developed by Williamson (1975) and others, shifts attention from technology and the production of commodities to *transactions*—the exchange of goods and services between persons or across boundaries. The typical neoclassical economic model conceived of firms as systems for managing production functions, with the primary decisions focused on the optimal mix of production factors—resources, labor, capital. In this model, variations in organizational structure are largely irrelevant. By contrast, the transactions costs perspective assumes that not the production but the exchange of goods and services is critical, and it emphasizes the importance of the structures that govern these exchanges. Two broad types of governance regimes are contrasted: the market and the organization (hierarchy).

In a market system, exchanges occur between buyers and sellers based on negotiated contractual agreements. These transactions are governed by the price system, which, in aggregate, provides a set of signals concerning what goods and services in what quantity are desired and hence will be profitable to produce. It is presumed that all parties are governed by self-interest. Several advantages are associated with a market arrangement as a basis for organizing transactions. Adam Smith (1957 ed.) was among the first to note that relatively little knowledge is required of the participants in such transactions. Assuming that individuals know their own preferences, price signals provide a comparatively simple basis on which to make decisions. And, as symbolized by Smith's famous simile of the invisible hand, market and pricing mechanisms do provide an overall basis for coordinating individual actions. Hence, it is not necessary to expend resources specifically to achieve coordination; no administrative overhead is required for planning, collective decision making, or control.

Recent analyses suggest that market transactions work well as a framework for *spot contracts*—contracts in which all obligations are fulfilled on the spot, such as the exchange of money for a commodity in hand. They fare less well when the transactions involve future values. When goods or services are not to be delivered on the spot, but at some future time, it is often possible to draw up a *contingent claims contract.* Such a document specifies the obligations of each party to the exchange, contingent upon possible future developments. For example, a farmer may agree to sell his grain to a warehouse if the price does not drop below a specified amount per ton. But as the future becomes more complex or uncertain, it becomes increasingly difficult and costly to draw up contracts that take into account all possible contingencies. In such circumstances, organizations are likely to be viewed as attractive alternatives to market-mediated transactions.

Arrow asserts that "organizations are a means of achieving the benefits of collective action in situations in which the price system fails" (1974: 33). The price system, viewed as a mechanism for the efficient allocation of personnel and resources to production tasks, fails when confronted with very complex relations among these factors or with uncertainty concerning future conditions. As such complexity and uncertainty increases, more information needs to be processed in order for contracts to be negotiated and transactions conducted. Both Arrow and Williamson conclude that the specific way in which organizations are superior to markets in managing complex and uncertain economic transactions is that organizations reduce the costs of such transactions.

Williamson (1975) elaborates the argument by developing an elegant and simple model of the conditions under which markets tend to give way to organizations.[1] The basic elements of the model appear in Figure 7–1.

---

[1]Williamson's terminology differs from our own and can cause confusion on first reading. He employs the term *organization* to refer to any social arrangement within which transactions are conducted. Thus, markets as well as organizations in our sense are regarded as organizations. This is why Williamson's discussion of the limitations of markets is presented in terms of an *organizational failures framework.* Williamson's terms for organizations in our sense are, variously, *internal organizations, hierarchies,* and *firms.*

**FIGURE 7-1**    The Market Failures Framework. *Source:* Williamson (1975), Figure 3, p. 40.

Williamson uses the concept of bounded rationality simply to refer to the limitations of individuals as information processors. The cognitive limitations of individuals are emphasized by Simon (1957) and have already been described in Chapter 2. As environments become more complex or uncertain, these limitations are quickly reached. Hence, it is only when individuals are confronted with excessive environmental demands that their information-processing capacities become insufficient and alternative arrangements are required. Incorporating individual decision makers into organizational arrangements is one such alternative.

We have already described, in Chapter 2, how organizational structures facilitate and support individual decision making. The rational system perspective is the relevant one: the organization permits problem subdivision, simplifies choices, channels information, and restricts alternatives. Goal specificity and formalization overcome the cognitive limitations of individual actors. As Simon (1979: 501) asserts,

> it is now clear that the elaborate organizations that human beings have constructed in the modern world to carry out the work of production and government can only be understood as machinery for coping with the limits of man's abilities to comprehend and compute in the face of complexity and uncertainty.

Williamson uses the second pair of concepts in Figure 7-1—opportunism and small numbers—to develop a different argument regarding the relative advantages of markets and organizations. Opportunism is revealed in individual actors who are capable of "self-interest seeking with guile" and of making "self-disbelieved threats and promises" (Williamson, 1975: 26). In short, some people lie, cheat, and steal! Those of us who are honest will try to avoid entering into transactions with these disreputable types, but we may have no choice if we are faced with a small-numbers condition—that is, few alternative partners. Williamson cogently notes that many situations not characterized in the beginning by a small number of alternative partners may become so as transactions progress, because early exchange partners ("first-movers") gain decided advantages over their competitors.

The creation of organizations helps to solve the problem of opportunism among exchange partners. By bringing economic exchanges under a hierarchical structure, organizations can construct better auditing and surveillance systems. Also, incentive systems within an organization can be arranged so that individual participants are discouraged from behaving opportunistically. Further, arrangements by which individual performance can be more closely monitored are especially helpful when the work involves *nonseparabilities*—products of highly interdependent teams such that it is difficult to determine who has made what contributions. When outputs involve nonseparabilities it is useful to be able to inspect inputs (see Alchian and Demsetz, 1972).

Yet another difference between the market and the organization is the nature of the transactions that take place between exchange partners. In the case of organizations, a new type of contract comes into existence: the employment contract. The institutional economist John Commons first called attention to the special nature of this contract, noting that what the worker sells "when he sells his labor is his willingness to use his faculties according to a purpose that has been pointed out to him. He sells his promise to obey commands." (1924: 284) Under conditions of uncertainty, the advantages of this open-ended or "incomplete" contract are obvious: obedience is promised to a general range of commands,[2] the specific command being determined by the variable and unpredictable requirements of the changing situation.

The transactions costs framework provides a general explanation for the origins of organizations as mechanisms for supporting decisions under conditions of uncertainty and suppressing opportunism under conditions of restricted exchange. It is also useful for explaining how specific organizations determine their boundaries and design their governance systems, but these matters are reserved for later chapters. The transactions costs approach, like other economic explanations, focuses primarily on efficiency. Governance structures, among which organizations and markets are the leading alternatives, are compared and assessed "in terms of their capacities to economize on transaction costs" (Williamson, 1981: 549). Such arguments are well within the rational system perspective.[3]

**Information processing**     Yet another explanation for the emergence of the organization is its superior capacity to manage flows of information. A hierarchical structure incorporates several features—including status distinctions and power differences among positions—but among its most significant components is a centralized communications system. What, if any, are the advantages of carrying on work within a hierarchical structure—specifically, a centralized communications structure—compared with a more informal and equalitarian arrangement? Experiments on communication structures conducted during the 1950s and 1960s examined the effects of centralized versus decentralized communication

[2]The range of commands that will be obeyed automatically in any organizational situation is, of course, restricted. Ordinarily a supervisor does not have the right to tell an employee to perform personal services or to carry out activities beyond those specified in the job description. These boundaries are also influenced by generalized social beliefs. For example, some contemporary secretaries have decided that making coffee is outside their appropriate job definition. Barnard refers to the arena within which employees will unquestioningly comply with directives as the *zone of indifference* (1938: 168–69); Simon refers to the same concept as the *zone of acceptance* (1957: 12).

[3]Williamson's arguments are also functionalist in that they attempt to explain the origins of a structure in terms of its consequences (functions) rather than in terms of the processes or mechanisms that bring it about. (See Granovetter, 1985.)

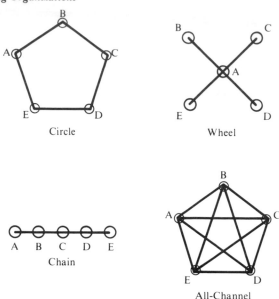

B

A       C

E       D

Circle

B       C

A

E       D

Wheel

A   B   C   D   E

Chain

B

A       C

E       D

All-Channel

**FIGURE 7–2**   Examples of Communication Networks (five-person groups)

networks on the task performance of groups.[4] In a technique developed by Bavelas (1951), a small number of individuals are placed in cubicles and allowed to communicate only by means of written messages passed through slots in the cubicle walls. The slots connecting each cubicle can be opened or closed by the experimenter, so that differing communication patterns can be imposed on the interacting subjects. The most frequently studied communication networks are diagramed in Figure 7–2. The circle and all-channel networks are relatively decentralized communication structures; the chain and particularly the wheel are more highly centralized. A typical task presented to groups placed in these networks is to provide each individual with a card containing several symbols, only one of which is present on the cards of all subjects, and ask all participants to identify the common symbol. Most researchers using this type of task have reported that groups working in the more centralized structures are more efficient in their performance, as measured by the speed of attaining a solution or the number of messages transmitted to arrive at a solution, than groups in more decentralized structures (see Leavitt, 1951; Guetzkow and Simon, 1955).

Vroom accounts for these findings as follows:

[4]Some analysts are reluctant to generalize from findings based on "artificial" experiments to behavior in real-world organizations. However, we believe that, interpreted with caution, results from experimental studies can aid our understanding of natural phenomena. The great advantage of experimental settings is that they permit investigators to isolate certain variables from others whose presence may influence the effects being observed (see Zelditch, 1969). We just noted that hierarchies in organizations contain a number of elements only one of which defines the formal structuring of communication flows. Experiments allow us to examine the effects of these structured flows independently of those produced by formal status and power differences.

The centralized structures more rapidly organize to solve the problems. Participants in peripheral positions send information to the center of the network, where a decision is made and sent out to the periphery. Furthermore, this pattern of organization tends to be highly stable once developed. In less centralized structures the organization problem is more difficult and observed interaction patterns are less stable, as well as less efficient. (Vroom, 1969: 242)

Vroom stresses the functions of formalization, as discussed in Chapter 2. Arrow embraces the same conclusion, but his arguments concerning the superiority of centralized networks are based on efficiency of information processing:

since transmission of information is costly, in the sense of using resources, especially the time of individuals, it is cheaper and more efficient to transmit all the pieces of information once to a central place than to disseminate each of them to everyone. (Arrow, 1974: 68)

Noting that the gathering of information is also essential to arriving at a decision, Arrow applies the same arguments to this process, concluding, "Thus, authority, the centralization of decision-making, serves to economize on the transmission and handling of information" (Arrow, 1974: 69).

Williamson (1975: 41–54) agrees that hierarchies are superior to peer groups or other types of decentralized communication networks in the economies of information flows effected. In addition, he asserts that the use of hierarchies reduces the likelihood of opportunistic behavior by improving surveillance of individual performance.

It would be incorrect, however, to conclude that hierarchies are superior to more decentralized or equalitarian arrangements under all conditions. Other studies employing the Bavelas networks have introduced more complex tasks—for example, mathematical problems—or provided subjects with more ambiguous information to process—for example, asking them to identify similar colors when the samples provided include unusual colors for which there are no common names (Shaw, 1954; Christie, Luce, and Macy, 1952). Such studies show that as tasks become more complex or ambiguous, decentralized nets are usually superior to centralized structures (Shaw, 1964).

Reviewing these communication-network studies, Blau and I (Blau and Scott, 1962: 116–28) concluded that formal hierarchies aid the performance of tasks requiring the efficient coordination of information and routine decision making, but they interfere with tasks presenting very complex or ambiguous problems. Specifically, we argued that hierarchies impede work on the latter by stifling free interactions that can result in error correction, by undermining the social support necessary to encourage *all* participants to propose solutions, and by reducing incentives for participants to search for solutions.

More generally, there appears to be a curvilinear relation between information-processing requirements and the utility of hierarchy. When little information is to be processed, there are no particular advantages to hierarchy and some clear disadvantages (for example, the administrative overhead). As information-processing needs increase up to a certain point, hierarchies can be of benefit, reducing transmission costs and ensuring coordination. But as information-processing needs continue to increase, hierarchies become overloaded and the intellectual resources of peripheral participants underutilized. Such increased demands do not require a return to informal systems, but they do encourage the creation of more decentralized structures. (Specific types of decentralization strategies are described in Chapter 9.)

The same type of argument can be made with respect to the relation between surveillance requirements and hierarchies. The creation of hierarchies can result in improved surveillance and control of participants up to a point, but if extraordinary demands are required for secrecy or loyalty, formal hierarchical surveillance may have to be supplemented or replaced by clan systems relying on more diffuse, internalized controls (see Ouchi, 1980). For example, organizations confronting hostile environments, such as the FBI or the Mafia, are likely to rely heavily on procedures that induce a strong personal commitment (see Wilson, 1978) or on the creation of diffuse interpersonal ties (see Ianni, 1972) to effect tight controls (see Chapter 11).

But we must return to the main theme. To summarize, from Smith and Weber to Arrow and Williamson, there is general agreement that organizations are called into existence by the increasing need to coordinate and control complex administrative and technical tasks and transactions. Enlarged political states, expanding markets, and improved technologies both require and are made possible by the development of organizations that can manage complex exchanges and coordinate diverse, interrelated activities.

### Natural System Explanations of the Origins of Organizations

*Institutional explanations*    As described in Chapter 5, institutional theorists emphasize the extent to which the world is a product of our ideas and conceptions—the socially created and validated meanings that define reality. Associated with the rise of the modern world is not only a set of production technologies and administrative structures for coordinating complex activities but also the growth of certain beliefs and cognitions about the nature of the world and the way in which things happen (Ellul, 1964 trans.). Technology and bureaucracy are more than hardware and filing cabinets filled with papers: they are new states of consciousness. The concomitants of technological production at the level of consciousness include the belief that the work process has a machinelike functionality, that all actions within the process are reproducible, that productive activity entails participation in a large organization and in a sequence of production, that the work being performed is measurable, and so on. Similarly, bureaucracy connotes distinctive spheres of competence, the importance of proper procedures, orderliness, predictability, and an attitude of "moralized anonymity" (Berger, Berger, and Kellner, 1973: 23–62).

It is important to emphasize that such beliefs are widely held by people in modern society and are continually being created and reinforced by a wide range of corporate actors and forces: universities, professional groups, public opinion, the mass media, the state, law. Thus, these beliefs do not exist merely as general values that support organizations, but take on very specific and powerful forms in a variety of guises—as professional expertise, as procedural rules, and as legal requirements.

In short, as we argued in the previous chapter, the environments of organizations are not only technical, providing resources and information in support of the production of goods and services and rewarding efficient performance; they are also increasingly institutional, specifying rules and procedures and containing rationalized myths and roles that organizations are rewarded for incorporating.

> Thus organizational success depends on factors other than efficient coordination and control of productive activities. Independent of their productive efficiency, organizations that exist in highly elaborated institutional environments and succeed in becoming isomorphic with these environments gain the legitimacy and resources needed to survive. (Meyer and Rowan, 1977: 352)

DiMaggio and Powell (1983) have distinguished three mechanisms that are conducive to *isomorphism*—increasing structural homogeneity—among organizations in institutional environments. First of all, *coercive* isomorphism results from formal or informal pressures exerted by one organization on another as a condition for its support or approval. In modern societies, the nation-state, as a vital source of resources and as a major locus of coercive power, imposes uniform structures and/or procedures on many types of organizations. For example, DiMaggio (1983) reports how the National Endowment for the Arts, a federal program established to support artistic endeavors, followed a grants policy that encouraged states and then individual communities to establish arts councils that played a substantial role in determining what groups would receive funds. In this manner, a relatively disorganized organizational field has become rather highly structured around "the creation of a vertical network of public and private arts agencies from Washington to local communities" (p. 151).

The second mechanism identified by DiMaggio and Powell is *mimetic* or imitative isomorphism. They argue that this mode of isomorphism is especially prevalent among organizations confronting uncertainty.

> When organizational technologies are poorly understood, when goals are ambiguous, or when the environment creates symbolic uncertainty, organizations may model themselves on other organizations (DiMaggio and Powell, 1983: 151).

Organizations are quick to embrace "modern" management devices such as MBO (management by objective) or to adopt a multi-divisional structure so as to appear up to date. (See Chapter 10.) A study of the adoption of municipal reforms by the 267 largest American cities during the period 1900–1942 by Knoke (1982) found that the best basis for predicting the adoption, prior to the First World War, of the commission form of government or, prior to the Second World War, of the city manager form was the percentage of other municipalities in the same region that had adopted each administrative reform.

A third source of isomorphic pressure is *normative* isomorphism, which is carried primarily by professionals. The authority of professionals rests primarily on their claims to specialized knowledge and skills. This competence is based in university centers and spread through professional networks that span organizations. (See Clark, 1983.) Professionals seek to impose their own normative standards on the organizations in which they operate—encouraging them to embrace their definitions of the problems, their standards, and their solutions. It is no accident that most colleges contain the same assortment of disciplines or that most hospitals contain the same set of services.

Meyer and Rowan and DiMaggio and Powell emphasize the extent to which rationalized elements in the modern social environments encourage the development of organizations:

> The growth of rationalized institutional structures in society makes formal organizations more common and more elaborate. Such institutions are myths which make formal organizations both easier to create and more necessary. After all, the building blocks for organizations come to be littered around the societal landscape; it takes only a little entrepreneurial energy to assemble them into a structure. (Meyer and Rowan, 1977: 345)

Zucker (1983) argues that the increase in organizations is due to more than just the profusion of rationalized institutional elements that, like prefabricated forms, can be assembled into new structures. In addition, the organizational form itself has become "the focal defining institution in modern society." (p. 13) In order to demonstrate that we are serious about achieving some goal or protecting some value, we must create an organization to symbolize our commitment.

Both Zucker and DiMaggio and Powell suggest that whereas the early impetus for creating organizations was their technical benefits, their more recent growth largely reflects an institutional process. Zucker (1983: 13) argues that

> the rush to create organizations cannot be explained either by the need to counterbalance the power of existing organizations *or* by any distinct advantage inherent in organizational form (such as increased production efficiency). Rather, the rapid rise and continued spread of the organizational form is best interpreted as an instance of institutionalization: early in the process of diffusion, the organizational form is adopted because it has unequivocal effects on productivity, while later it becomes seen as legitimate to organize formally, regardless of any net benefit.

In a similar vein, DiMaggio and Powell (1983: 147) assert that "the causes of bureaucratization and rationalization have changed," in that "structural change in organizations seems less and less driven by competition or by the need for efficiency" and is more likely to reflect institutional processes.

Although we agree that both technical and institutional processes give rise to organizations, it does not seem obvious that technical forces were dominant in earlier periods and have now given way to institutional forces. New technologies are constantly being created, and institutional forms that were once strong—such as religion—are no longer as robust. Moreover, professions such as medicine that earlier could make few supportable claims to a scientific base are in a far stronger position to do so today. Technical and institutional systems both compete with and complement each other. Both appear vigorous across varying contemporary organizational environments.

**Marxist explanations**    We have already discussed, in Chapter 5, the crux of the Marxist explanation for the origin and growth of organizations: they exist to exercise control. While recognizing that all social structures involve role differentiation, most Marxists argue that the minute division of labor that developed in the early days of industrialization was aimed more at maximizing managerial control than at achieving productive efficiency. In their famous tract, Marx and Engels (1955 trans.: 65) described how in the factories of capitalist systems, the worker "becomes an appendage of the machine, and it is only the most simple, most monotonous and most easily acquired knack, that is required of him." Marx argued that the type of work division developed in these organizations destroyed the craft skills of workers:

> Hence, in the place of the hierarchy of specialized workmen that characterizes manufacture, there steps, in the automatic factory, a tendency to equalise and reduce to one and the same level every kind of work that has to be done by the minders of the machines (Marx, 1954 trans.: 420).

Braverman and Marglin have amplified Marx's position. The dissection of work separates workers from their products; deskills workers, turning artisans into operatives; increases the potential pool of workers, thereby weakening the job security of each; and segments workers, fragmenting their common experience and undermining their class consciousness (Braverman, 1974).

Not only does the division of labor reduce the power of workers, it increases and legitimates the power of managers. Returning to Adam Smith's pin factory, Marglin (1974: 38) insists that

> without specialization, the capitalist had no essential role to play in the production process. . . . Separating the tasks assigned to each workman was the sole means by which the capitalist could, in the days preceding costly machinery, ensure that he would remain essential to the production process as integrator of these separate operations into a product for which a wide market existed.

Indeed, dividing work provides many managerial and technical roles: not only that of integrator but those of designer of the work process, hirer, trainer, inspector, troubleshooter, procurer of supplies, securer of markets, and so forth.

In addition to arguing that discretion was removed from workers and transferred to managers (and their growing technical staff), Marx insisted that the surplus value created by productive labor was stripped from workers and grasped by manager-capitalists. Although Marx and many other social analysts have condemned this practice, Marglin (1974: 34) acknowledges that this form of "enforced savings" created the surplus capital that led to the subsequent technological revolution. He argues that "the social function of hierarchical work organization is not technical efficiency, but accumulation."

Both Stark and Burawoy suggest that Marx and Braverman have overstated the cohesion and unity of managers under capitalism and understated those of workers. Stark emphasizes the resourcefulness of workers who have found ways to counteract and undermine the effectiveness of the new control systems. Some changes introduced to improve managerial control have actually increased the power of workers:

> Assembly line production, for example, decreases the degree of direct cooperation among workers, but the objective interdependence of workers also increases their ability to disrupt production either through individual acts of sabotage, collective activity, or the more passive form of simply not showing up for work (Stark, 1980: 93).

And, as we noted in our introductory discussion of scientific management in Chapter 2, these attempts to rationalize the work process were resisted not only by workers but also by managers, who did not want to see their powers usurped by engineers. As Burawoy (1985: 46) notes, control over the labor process emerges as a result, "not only of struggle between capital and labour, but also of struggle among the different agents of capital. . . . one cannot *assume* the existence of a cohesive managerial and capitalist class that automatically recognizes its true interests."

Power contests are not restricted to factories. In his illuminating history of the rise of the Prussian bureaucracy, Rosenberg (1958) argues that many of the Prussian bureaucratic reforms were imposed by the newly emerging administrative elite on the Crown, restricting his arbitrary powers of appointment and promotion, rather than the reverse. (See also Chs. 10 and 11.)

In short, while it is important to recognize the power aspects of changes in the division of labor or in the structuring of work processes, it is an oversimplification to view all of the power advantages as being on any one side, or to presume that there are only two sides. The work setting is indeed a "contested terrain," as Edwards (1979) has argued, with various parties vying for control and for a greater share of the value created there; the outcomes to date do not support the conclusion that any single party has been either omniscient or all-powerful.

But, as might be expected, there is even disagreement about what outcomes have occurred. Marx predicted that the forces inherent in capitalist systems, unchecked, would lead inevitably to the proletarianization of the work force. Kerr and his colleagues insist that Marx's dark descriptions and dire predictions have not been borne out by the actual course of industrialization. They note that

> industrialization in fact develops and depends upon a concentrated, disciplined industrial work force—a work force with new skills, and a wide variety of skills, with high skill levels and constantly changing skill requirements. . . . The industrialization process utilizes a level of technology far in

advance of that of earlier societies. . . . The industrial system requires a wide range of skills and professional competency broadly distributed throughout the work force. (Kerr et al., 1964: 17)

But Braverman (1974) challenges this picture as misleading, insisting that the net effect of industrialization as it has progressed in the twentieth century has been the deskilling of a large segment of the population. He reviews considerable data bearing on job requirements at varying levels and concludes,

> Clearly the "average" scientific, technical, and in that sense "skill" content of these labor processes is much greater than in the past. But . . . the question is precisely whether the scientific and "educated" content of labor tends toward *averaging*, or, on the contrary, toward *polarization*. . . . The mass of workers gain nothing from the fact that the decline in their command over the labor process is more than compensated for by the increasing command on the part of managers and engineers. (Braverman, 1974: 425)

Moreover, Braverman argues that much of the upgrading of occupational groups does not reflect real changes in skill level but is an artifact of distinctions made by census categories that, for example, label workers who have any type of contact with a machine as *operatives* or *semiskilled* workers and that regard any type of office or clerical employment as superior to blue-collar work. Braverman also observes that the fastest-growing occupational sectors are those involved in service work, sales, and clerical positions. These positions are less affected by industrialization, require lower skills, and are generally associated with lower pay. And these are the positions into which women—a vast new labor pool—are primarily drawn.

Thus, the controversy over both the causes and the consequences of industrialization continues. All parties, however, seem to agree that an important by-product of the process has been the rapid growth of large-scale organizations.

We have reviewed a variety of rational and natural open system explanations for the emergence of organizations as distinctive forms of social structure. Accounting for the origins of organizational forms is, however, not the same as explaining how any particular organization is created and maintained. We view the latter process as a matter of mobilizing resources.

## THE MOBILIZATION OF RESOURCES

Oberschall provides a useful definition of *mobilization*—"the process of forming crowds, groups, associations, and organizations for the pursuit of collective goals" (1973: 102). Organizations do not spontaneously emerge but require the gathering and harnessing of resources—materials, energy, information, and personnel. The availability of such resources varies from place to place and from time to time. In traditional societies, material resources are locked into landholdings and individuals into caste and kinship systems; in modern societies, to repeat the observation of Eisenstadt (1958), resources are more "free-floating" and easier to mobilize into the service of specialized goals. We have already reviewed, in the first section of this chapter, the general societal factors that facilitate the creation of these conditions.

Many factors affect the mobilization process, as we will see. The conditions present at the time of the founding of the organization have significant and enduring effects on an organization; what types of incentives are employed to induce contributions will affect the structure of the organization as will the characteristics of the members recruited; and the competitive environment confronting an organization will help to shape its distinctive strategies and structures.

### Initial Resource Mix

Each specific type of organization presents a particular combination of resource requirements—economic and technical as well as social. The technological base on which the organization rests must be in place; labor, trained and movable, must be available; capital is required from individuals willing to risk it; and an appropriate organizational form must have been invented. Larger cultural norms must support the venture: the goals of the enterprise together with the means employed in their pursuit must be regarded as legitimate.[5] A given combination of requirements cannot always be met. Appropriate conditions come together at certain periods, creating new possibilities for the support of organizations that could not exist under different circumstances. This accounts for the pattern of organizational founding noted by Stinchcombe (1965: 154), who points out that

> an examination of the history of almost any type of organization shows that there are great spurts of foundation of organizations of the type, followed by periods of relatively slower growth, perhaps to be followed by new spurts, generally of a fundamentally different kind of organization in the same field.

Stinchcombe cites numerous United States examples: the founding of savings banks and the first factory industry, textiles, in the 1830s; the development of railroads and steel companies in the 1850s and 1870s; the founding of universities and labor unions from the 1870s to the 1900s; the development of department stores in the 1850s and mail-order houses in the 1870s; the growth of the oil, rubber, and automobile industries in the 1920s; the emergence of the airline manufacturing and transportation companies during and after World War II; and the development of data-processing and electronic equipment since the 1960s (1965: 154–55).

Given the similar resource requirements confronting each of these types of organizations, it should come as no surprise that each cohort of organizations of the same type is quite similar in its occupational composition and structural features. As Stinchcombe observes, "organizations

---

[5]Weber's (1958 trans.) most famous essay, "The Protestant Ethic and the Spirit of Capitalism," deals with the role of religious values and belief systems, particularly Christian asceticism such as Calvinism, in legitimating the accumulation and investment of capital and effort in economic enterprise.

which are founded at a particular time must construct their social systems with the social resources available (1965: 168). What is remarkable is that once established, an organization of a given type tends to retain the basic characteristics present at its founding. Organizational forms are *imprinted:* they are likely to retain the features acquired at their origin. Stinchcombe (pp. 155–69) cites a variety of evidence to support this conclusion: for example, industries composed of small firms at the outset tend to retain this characteristic; industries relying heavily on unpaid family workers tend to continue to do so. And only those firms established during the last few decades use professional staffs extensively.

Both rational and natural system explanations may account for this association between organizational characteristics and time of founding. The characteristics may provide a competitive advantage over alternative arrangements (a rational system argument); they may be preserved by a set of "traditionalizing forces," including vested interests; or the organizations that exhibit the characteristics may not be confronted by competitive forces and may therefore live on without major changes or technical improvements (a natural system explanation). Whatever the case, it is instructive to realize that the form organizations acquire at their founding are likely to affect the structure they retain over their life. The mix of initial resources out of which an organizational structure is created has lasting effects on the attributes of that structure.

### Balance of Contributions and Inducements

Of all the many resources required by organizations, the most vital are the contributions of its human participants. Not only are these contributions themselves of infinite variety, they are also the ultimate means by which all other resources are acquired. More than other early theorists, Barnard (1938) stressed the importance of an organization's ability to motivate participants to continue to make contributions—of time, resources, effort—to it rather than to some competing system. Barnard's concerns were pursued by Simon (1957), the result being the Barnard-Simon theory of *organizational equilibrium.*[6] *Equilibrium* refers to the organization's ability to attract sufficient contributions to ensure its survival. The basic postulates of the theory are as follows:

1. An organization is a system of interrelated social behaviors of a number of persons whom we shall call *participants* in the organization.
2. Each participant and each group of participants receives *from* the organization *inducements* in return for which he makes to the organization *contributions.*
3. Each participant will continue his participation in an organization only so long as the inducements offered him are as great or greater (measured in terms of *his* values and in terms of the alternatives open to him) than the contributions he is asked to make.
4. The contributions provided by the various groups of participants are

[6]Recall from Chapter 2 that Barnard and Simon distinguish between the decisions a participant makes to join and continue to participate in an organization and those that he or she makes *as* a participant in the organization. The current discussion deals with the first category of decisions.

the source from which the organization manufactures the inducements offered to participants.

5. Hence, an organization is "solvent"—and will continue in existence—only so long as the contributions are sufficient to provide inducements in large enough measure to draw forth these contributions. (Simon, Smithberg, and Thompson, 1950: 381–82)

Although it points to an essential truth about the survival of organizations, the theory "verges on the tautological," as Simon himself observes (March and Simon, 1958: 84). It is difficult to measure the balance of inducements and contributions independently of the individual's decision to stay with or leave the organization. Also, as noted by Krupp, since the concept of organizational inducement includes techniques for changing an individual's values or needs, it is difficult to distinguish between inducements that "win participation because they create satisfactions at a given level of willingness and inducements that shift the level of willingness" (1961: 107). Further, it is difficult to determine what utilities or values are attached by individual participants to the contributions they are asked to make and the inducements they are offered. Indeed, one of the major contributions of the human relations school in attempting to counteract the myth of the economic person is its demonstration of the diversity of factors to which individuals attach importance—working conditions, tools, skills, personal relations, office furnishings, and raw materials—for example—whether they are processing fish or preparing desserts in a restaurant (see Whyte, 1948; Whyte et al., 1955). And related work emphasizes that level of satisfaction is not assessed on an absolute scale but depends on choice of reference of comparison group. That is, how one worker assesses his or her own benefits depends on those received by others regarded as comparable (see Adams, 1965; Homans, 1961; Patchen, 1961; Martin, 1981).

One of the most useful approaches to understanding how organizations attract and reward participants for their contributions is based on a simple typology developed by Clark and Wilson (1961: 134–36; see also Wilson, 1973). Clark and Wilson differentiate among three types of incentives:

*material incentives:* tangible rewards; rewards with a monetary value—for example, wages, interest, fringe benefits, patronage;
*solidary incentives:* intangible rewards derived from the act of association—for example, sociability, status, identification;
*purposive incentives:* intangible rewards related to the goals of the organization—for example, satisfaction obtained from working on the election of a candidate whose position on issues is similar to one's own, or the rewards perceived by a pacifist who contributes money and time to antiwar groups.

Like Etzioni (1961), whose similar typology was developed at the same time, Clark and Wilson (1961: 137–49) suggest that although all organizations use all three types of incentives, it is usually possible to identify a predominant type for each. And associated with each type are important structural and operational differences.

Organizations that rely primarily on material incentives are labeled *utilitarian organizations;* examples are business firms, trade unions, and political machines. Clark and Wilson predict that such organizations will explicitly seek material rewards for their members and develop fairly precise cost-accounting machinery. Executives will devote their energies first and foremost to obtaining the material resources needed to provide incentives; central conflicts within the organization will center on their equitable distribution. The substantive goals pursued by the organization will be of only secondary importance. Such organizations can be flexible about their goal-related activities: these "activities may change without disrupting member participation as long as material incentives continue to be available" (Clark and Wilson, 1961: 140).

*Solidary organizations* include most service-oriented voluntary associations and social clubs. Members make contributions in return for sociability and status. Executive efforts must therefore be devoted to obtaining additional organizational prestige, publicity, or good fellowship. The goals of such organizations need to be noncontroversial and socially desirable. Solidary organizations are tactically less flexible than utilitarian organizations: the means utilized must be acceptable to powerful participants, and projects must often be carried on publicly to stimulate the flow of approvals and publicity.

In many ways, *purposive organizations* represent the most interesting case. These organizations "rely almost exclusively on their stated purposes as incentives to attract and hold contributors" (Clark and Wilson, 1961: 146). This would appear to be the ideal organizational arrangement: members join because they wish to help achieve the goals espoused by the organization, and the organization, in achieving its goals, supplies inducements to its members to secure their continuing contributions. Wilson's (1962: 1973) analyses, however, suggest that this "ideal" is very difficult to realize. Executives in these organizations—like their counterparts in other organizations—must secure a continuing flow of inducements to sustain the interests of members, but many of the types of goals sought by purposive organizations are difficult to achieve. Political parties do not always succeed in electing their candidates; religious organizations do not always succeed in transforming the world or converting the heathen; and social movements may not succeed in achieving their specific goals—which range from achieving equality for minority racial groups to banning nuclear warheads. Sometimes the goals of such organizations may be only vaguely stated—so that the organization can appeal to a large number of potential adherents—but when the time comes for action and goals are more specifically defined, many participants may feel betrayed or at least sense that their interests are not being served. Alternatively, specific goals can serve as a guide to action but may only appeal to a narrow minority and prevent the organization from growing by attracting new recruits. Most purposive organizations are forced to set up intermediate objectives—for example, political clubs hold meetings in which their members debate and "endorse" specific positions in order to "manufacture" inducements for participants. Such contrived inducements can undermine the attainment of the organization's original goals. Thus, the club's endorsements of controversial political positions often embarrass, unduly constrain, or help to defeat candidates in the general election (Wilson, 1962).

Olson (1965) suggests yet another reason why purposive organizations are difficult to sustain. Under the classical economic assumption that individuals attempt to behave rationally and to pursue their self-interest, Olson points out that no individual should be expected to join an organization in order to achieve common or public interests. Rational persons will realize that their own act of joining, except under very special conditions, will not appreciably affect the chances of the organization to succeed in its mission. These individuals will also observe that because the goals served represent a collective good—one that cannot be unequally distributed but is available to all—they will share in the benefits of the organization's success whether or not they have contributed to its attainment.

Thus, both the analysis by Clark and Wilson and that by Olson conclude that purposive organizations—those attempting to equate organizational goals with individual motives—are difficult to manage and to maintain. Except for the most ideologically pure or the most extreme redemptive varieties (see Wilson, 1973: 45–51), purposive organizations typically supplement their primary incentives with material inducements—to retain a core staff—and solidary incentives—to help sustain the rank and file through the dry spells.

### Membership Demographics

We have seen that there are a variety of ways in which organizations induce participants to contribute their time and resources to them, and that the mix of inducements employed has important consequences for the organization. The mix of participants also has important consequences. Considering only those participants who are identified as members of the organization, who are recruited and how long they stay has a wide range of implications for the structure and performance of the organization. The *demography* of the organization—the aggregated characteristics of its members, including their age, sex, education, ethnicity, and length of service—is increasingly recognized as a major determinant of organizational structure and performance. (See McNeil and Thompson, 1971; Pfeffer, 1983.)

The demographic composition of organizations is determined by such factors as the growth rate of the organization and the industry in which it is located, the rapidity with which the organization's technology is changing (the more rapid, the more likely the organization will be hiring new and better-educated workers), the personnel practices that are followed (for example, some types of organizations promote only from within their own ranks), and unionization (which is likely to promote longer tenure for workers) (Pfeffer, 1983).

The effects of demographic composition are wide-ranging and have yet to be fully explored. Their variety can be indicated by a few illustrations. Kanter (1977*a*) has examined the consequences of widely varying proportions of group members having one or another attribute—for example, the ratio of men to women, whites to blacks, or younger to older participants—on the attitudes and performance of the group. Focusing on a collection of women who occupied less than 10 percent of the exempt (salaried) jobs in a corporation, Kanter observed that the few women reaching the upper levels of management were treated as tokens: because they were "different" they were highly visible, the ways in which they varied from the majority took on exaggerated importance, and performance pressures were heightened by their "life in the limelight." Kanter (1977a: 241–42) explains how tokenism can shape the behavior and expectations of those involved:

> Tokens of Type O who are successful in their professional roles face pressures and inducements to dissociate themselves from other O's, and thus they may fail to promote, or even actively block, the entry of more O's. At the same time, tokens who are less than successful and appear less than fully competent confirm the organization's decision not to recruit more O's, unless they are extraordinarily competent and not like most O's. And since just a few O's can make the X-majority people feel uncomfortable, X's will certainly not go out of their way to include more O's.

In this manner, tokenism can become a self-perpetuating system.

Another example of the importance of membership composition is provided by Reed's (1978) analysis of the effects of cohort composition on the operation of the American Foreign Service bureaucracy. A *cohort* is simply a population of individuals who have experienced the same events at the same periods of their life. Thus an organizational cohort would be composed of those individuals who are recruited at the same time and whose careers develop in a parallel manner. Cohorts can significantly influence individual careers. Obviously, an individual's chances for promotion are going to be greatly affected by the size of one's own and preceding cohorts, especially in a system like that of the Foreign Service, where all promotions are made from within and few persons voluntarily transfer into some other system. But Reed also suggests that cohort composition can have organization-level effects. He argues that the slowness with which the Foreign Service adapted to its rapidly changing environment during the period surrounding World War II was significantly influenced by the characteristics of the cohort in charge—a collection of officers recruited many years earlier and under very different political and social conditions. A closed-career service bureaucracy is not well suited to changed demands that require rapid response.

A final example of the import of demography is suggested by the work of Ouchi (1980; 1981) on varying systems of organizational control. Ouchi argues that the Japanese-style model of the employment relation, which is based on the presumption of a lifetime commitment of organization to employee and vice versa, provides the basis for the creation of much more diffuse and informal control systems that rely greatly on the socialization of employees and their internalization of company norms and values than can be developed when there is a more rapid turnover of personnel. More generally, Pfeffer (1983) argues that the fewer the average years of service of the employees of an organization, the larger and more elaborate the bureaucratic control apparatus.

Thus, it is not only the initial resource mix and the assortment of incentives that shape the structure and performance of organizations. The creation of an organization is not a one-time event but a continuing process, and particularly fateful for the later stages of this process are the numbers and types of participants recruited earlier.

### Acquisition of Resources

How difficult it is to garner the necessary resources to support an organization depends greatly on the nature of the organization and its goals. Much recent work has been devoted to describing protest or social-movement organizations that pursue controversial or change-oriented programs. Such organizations face a decidedly uphill struggle in their search for resources—including adherents and constitutents—and, more often than not, fail to survive (see Oberschall, 1973; Gamson, 1975).

Earlier theory and research on collective behavior—studies of crowds, mobs, riots, rebellions—stressed the importance of a common sense of grievance and discontent in motivating individuals to take collective action in behalf of their interests. More recent views emphasize that collective action is more a function of resource availability and mobilization, including organizational skills and connections, than of shared discontent (Zald and Ash, 1966; Tilly, 1978). Jenkins (1979: 224) summarizes this approach:

> The main thrust of "resource mobilization" theory has been to argue that discontent is at best secondary in accounting for the emergence of insurgency, that organizational resources and the changing power position of the aggrieved, not sudden increases in their grievances, are the major factors leading to the outbreak of disorders.

Thus, research by Snyder and Tilly (1972) demonstrates that industrial strikes in France were not associated with fluctuations in the discontent of workers but were affected by the size and strength of union organization. Such studies underline the significance of resource availability and acquisition in the creation of organizations.

Research also shows that some types of resources exact costs on their acquiring organizations. If the interests undergoing mobilization are resource-deprived and disorganized—as was the case with the National Welfare Rights Organization, an organization representing black welfare mothers that emerged in the 1960s—they may become dependent on more mainstream groups, such as foundations, for support. The latter are unlikely to subsidize radical attempts to change the system, so that in the case of the NWRO its goals were turned in more conservative and less activist directions. (Piven and Cloward, 1977)

All organizations must compete for resources, but various types of organizations face quite different circumstances affecting their survival. An important determinant of the competitive environment of any organization is the type of industry structure in which it is located. Porter (1980) has classified the many factors influencing industry competition into five major categories: rivalry among existing firms, the bargaining power of suppliers and of buyers, the threat of new entrants, and the threat of substitute products or services.

Population ecologists have reminded us of the difficult time faced by many types of organizations in acquiring sufficient resources to survive. While the birth rate of new organizations in a developed society such as the United States is high, so is the failure rate. Although data on organizational births and deaths are difficult to acquire and are limited largely to the business sectors, Aldrich (1979: 36) cites data from a discontinued census on the numbers of new businesses, businesses transferred to a new owner, and businesses discontinued for nine selected years between 1940 and 1962. During these years, roughly 3.4 million new businesses were started, 3.1 million were transferred, and 2.5 million ceased to exist. As would be expected, the likelihood of failure is considerably higher among newer and smaller organizations. Records collected by Dun and Bradstreet reveal that over half (54 percent) of the businesses that failed in the United States during 1980 were five years old or less (see Bedeian, 1984: 333). The "liability of newness" is often lethal. But it is not only the newer and smaller firms that fail or cease to exist as independent entities. If longer periods are used, then there is a surprising amount of turnover in the populations of all types of organizations. (See Carroll, 1984.)

If we shift the level of analysis from the population of organizations to that of the individual organization, it is useful to think of each organization as undergoing an evolutionary process from birth to maturity to old age and death. Although the organizational *life cycle* is not as distinct and regular as the life cycle of plants or animals or humans, it is nevertheless instructive to identify general phases of development and decline. (See Kimberly, Miles, et al., 1980.) Theorists have developed a variety of schemata for distinguishing stages of development (see Bedeian, 1984, for a review).

As an example of one such model, after examining a number of case studies of corporate development, Greiner (1972) identified five general evolutionary stages. He proposed that each stage ends in a predictable crisis calling for some type of appropriate adjustment by management if the organization is to survive and proceed to the next stage. For example, the first crisis typically encountered is that of leadership: the founding members of the organization—often technical experts or entrepreneurial types—give way to managers who are more skilled at consolidation and routine administration. The next crisis occurs because controls become too centralized; the solution is more delegation, decentralizing of decision making. But decentralization in turn raises problems of integration that call for additional coordinating devices—planning procedures, reports, formal reviews. But these mechanisms multiply, causing a crisis of red tape, which in turn is solved by greater emphasis on trust and informal collaboration. And so development is accompanied by a series of more or less predictable crises.

Greiner's model is instructive in that each solution at one stage becomes the problem at the next. A leadership style or a structural arrangement that is adaptive at one level of size and complexity is unsuitable for another. Similarly, one would expect to observe changes over time in the relevance and utility of different types of personnel and resources. The problems encountered and hence the types of resources required vary with the stage of development. Obtaining sufficient capital resources to expand operations may be critical at the earlier stages of growth—and may represent a much greater challenge, since the risks to investors are higher—but less important in later stages, when capital will be easier to raise and may be available through internalized savings mechanisms. Resource acquisition is a necessary, but variable, process that continues throughout the life of the organization.

The ecologists in particular stress the difficulties confronting all organizations as they attempt to acquire and maintain a flow of resources adequate to perpetuate themselves. By contrast, institutional theorists such as Meyer and Rowan emphasize the ease with which some types of resources can be assembled to constitute an organization. To repeat their summary of the situation: in developed societies, "the building blocks for organizations come to be littered around the societal landscape; it takes only a little entrepreneurial energy to assemble them into a structure" (Meyer and Rowan, 1977: 345). That is, the more institutionalized the environment—the more it contains rules, accepted procedures, licensed actors, and taken-for-granted frameworks for carrying out specified actions—the less difficult it is to create and sustain organizations. However, although organizations in these circumstances may be able to more readily assemble various elements and actors, whether these resources can be fully mobilized by their managers is open to question. We will pursue these matters in Chapter 10.

## SUMMARY

Organizations, as we know them, have not always existed. They evolved during the past few centuries as part of a dual-level process. The same social changes that brought about the development of individualism—the freeing of resources (including the individual) from all-absorbing social structures—are responsible for the growth of organizations. Both developments celebrate the legitimation of specialized, particularized goals and the freedom to own and mobilize resources in their pursuit.

From a rational system perspective, organizations arise to take advantage of the production economies offered by an elaborate division of labor and to meet the cognitive and control challenges posed by a complex and uncertain environment. From a natural system perspective, institutionalists propose that organizations emerge as an embodiment of rationalized belief systems that proliferate in the wider social structure; Marxists argue that organizations arise as structures created by capitalists to expropriate surplus value from productive labor. All of these explanations can be correct, but for different times and places and types of organizations.

The costs and benefits of creating organizations are more easily evaluated if organizations are compared with alternative social forms for carrying on complex work. Organizations are viewed as having advantages over market mechanisms when the tasks to be carried out are sufficiently complex and uncertain as to exceed the information-processing capacities of individuals, and when so few potential buyers or sellers exist that they may attempt to take advantage of one another. Under these conditions, organizations offer mechanisms for reducing transactions costs and for constraining opportunistic behavior. Organizations are viewed as superior to informal peer groups as mechanisms for overseeing and coordinating complex work. However, conventional hierarchies in organizations may function poorly on ambiguous or highly complex tasks that require the exercise of individual discretion and the exchange of large amounts of information.

All organizations must secure a continuing supply of resources—including participants—from their environment. The initial mix of resources that are mobilized at the creation of a particular organization are critical in that they constitute a structural pattern that tends to persist—imprinting the organization with characteristics that are preserved across succeeding generations of it. The types of incentives for participants to contribute and the mix of participants have important consequences for the structural features and flexibility of the organization. All organizations compete for resources, but the consequences and costs of obtaining them vary with the type of organization and environment as well as with the stage of development an organization has reached.

# boundary setting and boundary spanning

# 8

The organizational world bubbles and seethes. Observed for a lengthy interval, the configuration of organizations within it changes like the patterns of a kaleidoscope. Organizations expand, contract, break up, fuse. Some surfaces become thick and opaque, reducing exchanges between their interior contents and the external environment, while others etherealize and permit heavier traffic in one or both directions. Shapes are altered. Some processes are depressed, some intensified. Levels of activity rise and fall. Organizations disintegrate and vanish as others form in droves, and the birth and death rates vary over time and space. Nothing stays constant.*

Herbert Kaufman (1975)

The central insight emerging from the open system model is that all organizations are incomplete: all depend on exchanges with other systems. All are open to environmental influences as a condition of their survival. By contrast, both the rational and natural system perspectives insist that organizatons, as a condition of their existence, must maintain boundaries that separate them from their environments. In the absence of distinguishable boundaries, there can be no organizations as we understand that term. In this chapter we explore the interdependence and the independence of organizations, and we examine the types of mechanisms used to set (and reset) and to span their boundaries.

## THE SOCIAL BOUNDARIES OF ORGANIZATIONS

The problems confronting organizations in setting and policing their boundaries are complex and subtle. Given the essence of organizations as open systems, their boundaries must necessarily be sieves, not shells, ad-

*Excerpt from The natural history of human organizations, by Herbert Kaufman is reprinted from *Administration and Society* Vol. 7, No. 2 (August 1975) p. 143 by permission of the Publisher, Sage Publications, Inc.

mitting the desirable flows and excluding the inappropriate or deleterious elements. Determining what is desirable or harmful can be a difficult decision, in part because the criteria can vary from time to time and from location to location in the organization. To explicate these issues, we will first concentrate on the social boundaries of organizations, examining the various indicators used to mark those boundaries and the criteria employed by organizations in determining whom to admit or reject.

For the sake of simplicity, we focus on the organization as the principal unit of analysis. Other units—including individuals, groups, and coalitions within organizations; occupations and labor markets that crosscut organizations; and industries, sectors and fields incorporating organizations—provide important alternative systems around which to frame organizational analyses.

## Determining Organizational Boundaries

Early in Chapter 1, after laboring over the concepts of normative and behavioral structure, we quietly slipped in the concept of *collectivity*. This concept serves to bring together the two components of structure but also adds a new element: the notion of boundary. A collectivity is a specific instance of social organization—an indentifiable "chunk" of the social order. As noted, the criteria for the existence of a collectivity are (1) a *delimited* social structure—that is, a *bounded* network of social relations—and (2) a normative order *applicable to the participants* linked by the network. All collectivities—including informal groups, communities, organizations, and entire societies—possess, by definition, boundaries that distinguish them from other systems.

Accepting the view that organizations, as a type of collectivity, possess boundaries is one thing, but deciding what and where they are is another. Establishing the boundaries of an organization is a difficult business, raising both theoretical and empirical problems.

To embrace the notion of organizations as open systems is to acknowledge that organizations are penetrated by their environments in ways that blur and confound any simple criterion for distinguishing the one from the other. How are we to regard customers? Clients? Stockholders? A second difficulty is the growing number of organizations that are subsumed under broader structures—for example, schools within districts, local banks that are branches of larger financial enterprises, and firms or establishments that are parts of multi-divisional corporations. Such connections may strongly influence many aspects of the structure and performance of the local units, so that treating them as independent units may create serious errors. Third, because more of our studies are including measures at more than one point in time, we need to realize that organizational boundaries are very likely to change. (See Freeman, 1978.)

Laumann, Marsden, and Prensky (1983) have noted that two approaches and, within each, three substantive focuses are used in attempts to define boundaries. The two approaches are the realist and the nominalist. In the *realist* approach, the investigator adopts the "vantage point of the actors themselves in defining the boundaries" of the system, assuming that this view will importantly influence their behavior. Under the *nominalist* strategy, the "analyst self-consciously imposes a conceptual framework constructed to serve his own analytic purposes." (p. 21) Regardless of the approach selected, the investigator must also determine what features of the situation to examine. Laumann and associates distinguish among three alternatives—the characteristics of the actors (or nodes), their relations, and their activities. Many investigators define the boundaries of an organization by focusing on its actors—for example, attempting to determine who is and who is not regarded as a member.

A second approach—favored by network analysts—is to establish the boundaries of the system by noting which actors are involved in social relations of a specified type. A widely used behavioral indicator of relatedness is frequency of interaction. Although no social unit is completely separated from its environment on the basis of this criterion, Homans (1950: 85) suggests that it is possible to locate the system boundaries where the web of interaction shows "certain thin places."[1]

The third possibility is to focus on the nature of the activities. We would expect to observe a change in the activities performed by individuals as they cross a system boundary.[2] Pfeffer and Salancik (1978: 32) favor this criterion, arguing that organizational boundaries are coterminous with activity control:

> When it is recognized that it is behaviors, rather than individuals, that are included in structures of coordinated behavior, then it is possible to define the extent to which any given person is or is not a member of the organization. . . . The organization is the total set of interstructured activities in which it is engaged at any one time and over which it has discretion to initiate, maintain, or end behaviors. . . . The organization ends where its discretion ends and another's begins.

A focus on relationships or activities emphasizes behavioral criteria for defining the limits of organizations. Since both interactions and activities require time and space, two useful indicators of significant boundaries are an organization's spatial barriers and their guardians (for example, fences, walls, doors, guards, receptionists) and the temporal systems (for example, working hours and activity schedules) it creates to contain them. By contrast, a focus on the characteristics of actors emphasizes normative criteria for defining the significant characteristics of membership.

Most groups, and particularly organizations, carefully differentiate members and nonmembers, developing explicit normative criteria for determining who is to participate in them. Why is this true? What is the importance of membership boundaries for the functioning of organizations?

---

[1] It is not only social scientists who wrestle with the question of how to bound a system under study. Other social analysts, such as novelists, confront a similar problem. The strategy proposed by Henry James (1907: vii) is not dissimilar to that adopted by scientific investigators:

> Really, universally, relations stop nowhere, and the exquisite problem of the artist is eternally but to draw, by a geometry of his own, the circle within which they shall happily *appear* to do so.

[2] Barnard (1938) took the position that activities, not participants, are the basis elements of organizations. Thus, he defined an organization as "a *system of coöperative activities* of two or more persons." (p. 75)

**Recruitment Criteria**

Rational system theorists are quite certain that they understand the functions of organizational boundaries: boundaries contribute to organizational rationality. Several of the characteristics Weber (1947 trans.: 334–35) identified as defining rational-legal systems may be viewed as bounding or insulating the organization from its social context. For example, his stipulation that officials be appointed by free contract according to their technical qualifications is intended to ensure that selection criteria are organizationally relevant and that the selection process will be relatively free from the influence of other social affiliations, whether religious, economic, political, or familial.

Udy's (1962) study of thirty-four production organizations in thirty-four different nonindustrialized societies lends strong credence to Weber's concerns. Udy sought to determine how the internal features of an organization's structure are related to the type of recruitment criteria used by the organization. His measures of structure are rather crude because the data are drawn from a systematic file of secondary data sources—the Human Relations Area File—based primarily on anthropological field studies. However, because the sample of organizations is drawn from nonindustrialized societies, it contains much greater variation in environmental and organizational characteristics than would be present in a comparable sample of organizations in industrialized societies. Udy differentiated five types of recruitment, ranging from participation in a production organization because of "voluntary self-commitment and self-defined interest" (high *social insulation*) to participation that was "required by compulsory political ascription" (high *social involvement*). To assess the structural characteristics of the thirty-four organizations, Udy developed a scale that measured the extent to which they reflected rational principles of organization. The presence or absence of seven indicators—including the organizational pursuit of limited objectives, rewards based on performance criteria, specialization, and rewards controlled by superiors—determined the degree of structural rationality within each organization. Analysis of the data revealed that the higher the degree of social insulation the organization achieved, the more likely it was to exhibit a rational structure.

Udy's findings do not seem surprising. Consider the case of a family that decides to run a retail store. The father might feel obliged to pay the older son a higher wage, in recognition of his superior status in the family structure, even if he does not contribute as much as others toward achieving the goals of the organization. The more an organization is insulated from its social environment—in this case an externally defined kinship structure—the more it can select, deploy, and reward its participants according to organizationally relevant criteria.

Organizationally controlled recruitment criteria are but one important mechanism fostering insulation of the organization from its social environment; Weber (1947 trans.) pointed to the need for others. His insistence that officials, once recruited, should regard their office as their sole, or at least their primary, occupation indicates his recognition that other occupational affiliations of members may affect their performance within organizations. And it is not only other occupational demands that may create claims on participants that may conflict with those of the focal organization. As the kinship example emphasizes, any social identity may become the basis of conflicting expectations and behavior patterns. Externally reinforced status characteristics such as age, sex, ethnicity, and social class are one important source of these expectations and obligations (see Hughes, 1958: 102–15; Dalton, 1959; Kanter, 1977*a*). And as the number and variety of other special-purpose organizations grow, membership in them supplies new identities and sources of power that may impinge on the participant's role performance in the organization. Salient identities can also develop as the result of interactions and exchange processes among participants in the organization, and these give rise to informal status distinctions (see Homans, 1961; Blau, 1964).

The external identities of individual participants play a relatively small role in rational system views of organization: they are viewed primarily as a problem to be managed by appropriate recruitment criteria and control mechanisms. By contrast, the many faces of participants are of great interest to natural system analysts. To begin, from a natural system perspective, it is impossible for any organization to eliminate completely these sources of "disturbance": social identities—externally validated roles, qualities, interests—are among the most portable of baggage. Some extreme types of organizations do attempt to eliminate the external status connections of a subset of their participants. This is the case for such "total institutions" as prisons, mental hospitals, monasteries, and army barracks. As Goffman (1961: 14) explains,

> the barrier that total institutions place between the inmate and the wider world marks the first curtailment of self. In civil life, the sequential scheduling of the individual's roles, both in the life cycle and in the repeated daily round, ensures that no one role he plays will block his performance and ties in another. In total institutions, in contrast, membership automatically disrupts role scheduling, since the inmate's separation from the wider world lasts around the clock and may continue for years. Role dispossession therefore occurs.

In addition to imposing these time and physical barriers, many such institutions forbid all contact with outsiders, strip the inmate of personal possessions, segregate sex or age groups, issue institutional garb, and restrict interaction among inmates. (see McEwen, 1980.) It is possible to view these measures as a set of mechanisms for ensuring that organizations will be buffered from the disturbing effects of the external roles occupied by participants. However, in our view they are sufficiently rare and extreme that they serve better to remind us how difficult it is for any organization to eliminate the influence on its participants of their nonorganizational roles and relationships. Total institutions are best viewed as a limiting case—as defining one extreme on a continuum. Most organizations do not erect excessive barriers or engage in elaborate stripping tactics; hence, we should expect most organizations to be composed of participants who possess multiple identities and behave accordingly. Certainly, natural system analysts embrace this view. We have already noted (in Chapter 3) the interest of human relations investigators in the effects of sex, class, and ethnicity on the allocation of workers to roles and on worker behavior.

And Selznick's analysis of individual "commitments" and the constraints they place on the rational deployment of personnel (also reviewed in Chapter 3) is highly germane to these issues.

Most natural system theorists do not emphasize the disruptive and constraining effects of participants' other roles; indeed, they insist that these characteristics are a vital resource for the organization. Even within a rational-system, performance-oriented context, natural system analysts point out that most organizations do not themselves train their members to talk, to think, or to use specialized tools: these fundamental skills are typically acquired in different settings and imported into the organization. But, from the natural system perspective, goal-attainment considerations are secondary to survival, and many participants are recruited precisely because they possess extraorganizational characteristics viewed as valuable to this end. For most organizations—and especially for those operating in more institutionalized environments—it is important to recruit the "right" participants, for symbolic as well as for technical considerations. Schools need to hire certificated instructors; nursing homes, licensed administrators; universities, instructing staffs with Ph.D.'s; and financial organizations, certified public accountants. Such environmental connections insure legitimacy and increased confidence in the organization.

Organizations also conform to the expectations of their social environments by maintaining some consistency between their own status systems and the stratification criteria used in the larger society (Anderson et al., 1966). For example, until recently women were not often promoted to high managerial positions in most United States corporations, partly because their special social identities were viewed by their male colleagues as introducing additional sources of uncertainty into transactions requiring high trust (Kanter, 1977a), but also because organizations wish to inspire confidence in outsiders with whom they conduct business, and so try not to violate widely shared community norms. Further, for certain types of boundary-spanning roles, such as being a member of a board of directors, an individual's selection may depend entirely on his or her external roles and connections. Thus, a banker may be asked to serve on the board of directors of a hospital because of ties with the financial community. The general point is that the external identities and connections of participants—far from being disruptive and restrictive—are, under many conditions, a primary resource for the organization, providing skills, legitimacy, and valued connections with the larger social environment.

### Social Insulation and Social Engulfment

The strategic question facing all organizations is how to recruit participants and harness their roles and resources in the service of organizational goals (whether goal attainment or survival), while avoiding or minimizing the danger of becoming captive to participants' external interests or personal agendas. Once pipelines are established, resources may flow in either direction! Katz and Eisenstadt (1960) discuss this issue from a less organization-centered point of view. They note that problems can occur from either of two types of imbalance—when an organization imposes too many or too few restrictions on the types (and imputed relevance) of other roles held by its participants. When nonorganizational roles impinge on organization roles inappropriately, then we have the problem of *de-bureaucratization.* The simplest examples are those of nepotism or corruption. The reverse problem occurs when organizational roles improperly assume priority over nonorganizational roles, leading to *over-bureaucratization.* Examples of this process are provided by Whyte's (1956) best seller, *The Organization Man,* which describes the unreasonable requirements placed by some corporations on the personal lives of upwardly mobile managers and their wives. It is by no means always a simple or noncontroversial matter to determine when external roles are or are not properly impinging on organizational roles, and vice versa. Clearly, value judgments are involved, and depending on which normative system provides the standard, different judgments are likely to be made. Courts of law and regulatory agencies often are asked to resolve these controversies. (Other problems associated with overbureaucratization are discussed in Chapter 12.)

The extreme case of de-bureaucratization involves the disappearance of the organization. An organization no longer exists when it does not maintain a delimited network of social relations to which a distinctive normative order is applicable. Diamond (1958) provides an interesting case study of a disappearing organization: the famous Virginia Company associated with the founding of the Jamestown colony.[3] This company was established in 1607 to exploit the riches of a new continent and the labors of its native peoples. Virginia proved to be different from previous English colonial sites in that native labor refused to be mobilized and mineral wealth was not to be found. It became necessary to establish an agricultural community based on voluntary labor imported from England. Over time, the company was forced to supply more and more inducements to its colonists: land became easier to acquire, women were recruited to become the wives of settlers, and company discipline was limited as representatives of the settlers acquired some voice in government. Diamond (1958: 471) summarizes these changes:

> At one time in Virginia, the single relationship that existed between persons rested upon the position they occupied in the Company's table of organization. As a result of the efforts made by the Company to get persons to accept that relationship, however, each person in Virginia had become the occupant of several statuses, for now there were rich and poor in Virginia, landowners and renters, masters and servants, old residents and newcomers, married and single, men and women; and the simultaneous possession of these statuses involved the holder in a network of relationships, some congruent and some incompatible, with his organizational relationship.

Gradually, settlers came to regard their roles outside the company as more important and were no longer willing to accept their organizational position as the primary basis of legitimate order. Thus, a society emerged where before there had been only an organization.

Note that we have now located both ends of the continuum of organizational control over the relevant properties of participants. At one

---

[3]This account is paraphrased from an earlier summary written with Blau (see Blau and Scott, 1962: 234).

end of this continuum of *social involvement,* to use Udy's phrase, the organization is highly insulated from its social environment, the limiting case being that of the *total institution* as defined by Goffman. At the other end, the organization is highly involved in its social environment, the extreme case being the *engulfed organization,* exemplified by the Virginia Company as described by Diamond.[4] Of course, the majority of organizations are somewhere between these two extremes, able to exert some control over the multiple roles participants bring into the organization or informally develop within its confines, but rarely in a position to eradicate or dominate them. In most cases organizations do not wish to eliminate these external roles but to mobilize them in their service.

### Labor Markets
### and Organizational Boundaries

The emergence of internal labor markets provides an especially pertinent example of how modern organizations manage their social boundaries. The classical economic assumption that workers move freely from job to job and firm to firm, governed by pressures to maximize the fit between their skills and the requirements of their job, and hence between their productivity and their earnings, has been severely challenged by labor and institutional economists such as Kerr (1954) and Doeringer and Piore (1971). The latter analysts have emphasized the extent to which information, opportunities, mobility, and rewards are differentially structured and shaped by varying occupational, industry, and organizational arrangements. Among the more important distinctions they introduce is that between internal and external labor markets. Doeringer and Piore (1971: 1) define *internal labor markets* as those within "an administrative unit, such as a manufacturing plant, within which the pricing and allocation of labor is governed by a set of administrative rules and procedures." The key features of internal labor markets are (1) a cluster of jobs that (2) are hierarchically structured into one or more job ladders representing a progression in knowledge or skills, and that (3) include a few "entry ports" at the lower levels connecting them with wider, external labor markets (Althauser and Kalleberg, 1981). The more internal labor markets that exist, the more that mobility processes within a society are shaped by organizational job structures and their hiring and promotional processes rather than by market processes, and the more control organizations have over their membership boundaries.[5]

And what are the factors that lead to the creation of internal labor markets? As might be expected, rational and natural system theorists have posed alternative explanations. Working within the transactions costs

---

[4]Note that Katz and Eisenstadt have in mind a different continuum. One end point, de-bureaucratization, is the same as Udy's high social involvement, but the other end point, over-bureaucratization, extends beyond the point where the organization insulates itself from the environment (as a total institution) to include situations in which the organization imposes its normative system on formerly autonomous systems.

[5]Althauser and Kalleberg (1981) also point out that internal labor markets can exist within and under the control of occupations. Occupations provide an alternative to organizations in the structuring of jobs and work activities, as discussed in the first edition of this text. (See Scott, 1981: 153–156)

framework—a rational open system model—Williamson (1981) argues that the most important influence on what type of labor market is created is the specificity of the human assets. The human assets of an organization are, of course, the skills and knowledge of its personnel. Specificity refers not simply to the extent of specialization of knowledge and skills, but to the degree to which these skills are transferable across employers. The deeper and more specialized one's skills are in the view of a specific employer, the more dependent is that employer on that employee, and vice versa, so that it is in the interests of both to create a "protective governance structure, lest productive values be sacrificed if the employment relation is unwittingly severed" (1981: 563). An internal labor market serves the employee's interests by providing the prospects of upward mobility through a regularized career of advancement, with increased earnings accompanying progression in skills. And the employer's interests are served because valuable workers in whom investments in training have been made are less likely to desert to a competitor.

In a related discussion, Williamson and Ouchi (1981: 361) distinguish between *hard* and *soft* contracting.

> Under hard contracting, the parties remain relatively autonomous, each is expected to press his or her interests vigorously, and contracting is relatively complete. Soft contracting, by contrast, presumes much closer identity of interests between the parties, and formal contracts are much less complete.

Soft contracting is characteristic of internal labor markets. It assumes a more elaborate governance structure (job ladders, grievance procedures, pay scales) and a higher level of investment and trust on the part of both employers and employees. In this sense, internal labor markets may be viewed as mechanisms for bringing employees more fully and firmly within the boundaries of an organization than is the case with external labor markets, in which the "hard" bargaining between employers and employees more closely resembles that occurring between two independent contractors.

The existence of internal labor markets is explained in a rather different manner by natural open system theorists. Marxist theorists such as Edwards (1979) argue that internal labor markets are more likely to arise in "core" segments of the economy—in large and powerful firms that have obtained an oligopoly, or near monopoly, in their industries. (See Averitt, 1968.) As these firms grow in size and complexity, they shift from simple hierarchical to technical to bureaucratic control systems. Edwards (1979: 131) explains:

> *Bureaucratic* control, like technical control, differs from the simple forms of control in that it grows out of the formal structure of the firm, rather than simply emanating from the personal relationships between workers and bosses. But while *technical* control is embedded in the physical and technological aspects of production and is built into the design of machines and the industrial architecture of the plant, *bureaucratic* control is embedded in the social and organizational structure of the firm and is built into job categories, work rules, promotion procedures, discipline, wage scales, definitions of responsibilities, and the like. Bureaucratic control establishes the impersonal force of "company rules" or "company policy" as the basis for control. (Emphasis added)

Because they rely on social definitions rather than technical distinctions, bureaucratic control structures can be elaborated with ease: the number of offices, levels, titles, and salary levels can be multiplied without limit. Moreover, incentives can be added to reward not simply effort and productivity but also such qualities as dependability, loyalty, and commitment to the organization.

Labor economists such as Averitt (1968) and Doeringer and Piore (1971) distinguish between core and peripheral economic sectors, arguing that large, highly differentiated, technically advanced firms are clustered in key manufacturing industries and provide employment for workers who are likely to be male, white, highly skilled, and educated; smaller, simpler organizations are to be found in more competitive, marginal industries, and employ workers who are likely to be female or minority, semiskilled, and less educated. However, empirical research by a number of sociologists has found only limited and mixed support for these generalizations linking economic sectors, organizational features, and labor market characteristics. (See, for example, Berg, 1971; Tolbert, Horan, and Beck, 1980; Zucker and Rosenstein, 1981.) Baron and Bielby (1984) point out that these economic theories imply—but do not explicate or empirically test—the proposition, familiar to organization theorists, "that organizational forms and environments cohere, yielding groups of enterprises with distinctive structures of work and opportunity" (p. 445) or, more specifically, that "key industries are the most complex organizational environments and accordingly are composed of firms that are the most internally complex" (p. 456). Although environmental location and organizational form are surely related, they are not the same. Baron and Bielby separated these two dimensions, developing a measure of environmental locus—occupation of a crucial location within key segments of the economy—and a measure of organizational form—size and technical complexity. Based on a study of 415 companies in California during the period 1959–1979, these analysts reported a correlation of .67 between their measures of location and form, suggesting that external location and internal features are associated, but not identical. Internal labor market features were more likely to be found in firms that were both centrally located and organizationally complex.

Jobs are locations within organizational structures, and so if we wish to understand how individuals are matched with jobs, we need to know what positions exist, how they are connected, and what rules are employed for sorting workers among them. This kind of research can be conducted only at the organizational level. (Baron and Bielby, 1980; Baron, 1984; Hodson and Kaufman, 1982) Not only are workers with differing characteristics employed, but workers with similar characteristics are treated differently depending on the organizational setting. For example, Stolzenberg (1978), using data from a national employment survey, has shown that size of the employer strongly affects the relation between a worker's education and his or her occupational status. Specifically, the larger the organization, the stronger the impact of education on position and earnings.

Talbert and Bose (1977), examining survey data on retail clerks in a single metropolitan area, observed that in addition to the characteristics of individual workers, such organizational features as the degree of work routinization, type of clientele served, and status of merchandise handled affect employees' wages. Since women and men are differentially located in organizations, much of the disparity in their earnings is attributable to sex segregation among store types, departments within stores, and jobs within departments. Although state and federal rules prohibit overt job discrimination by race or gender, we know far too little about the intraorganizational processes by which employees, once hired, are routed to different organizational locations that, independent of individuals' abilities, have a major impact on potential earnings and career opportunities. Kanter's (1977*a*) description of the maze of traps, dead ends, escalators, and fast tracks associated with different positions and departments in the large corporation she studied suggests how intricate and subtle are the mobility processes at work in contemporary organizations. Much detailed research remains to be done on how job structuring and mobility rules within specific organizations affect the returns to employees for their efforts.

Let us return to the more specific matter of internal labor markets. Marxists see the benefits to workers associated with these structures as reflecting their greater power vis-à-vis their employers, but they also view the structures as

> graded hierarchies that foster a docile "status" orientation and dissuade workers from utilizing the power implicit in their skills. Internal labor markets also institutionalize cleavages among workers along racial, sexual, and ethnic lines, thereby reducing the likelihood of working-class cohesion. (Baron, 1984: 40)

Pfeffer and Cohen (1984) employed data from a sample of about 300 large organizations in the San Francisco Bay area to test alternative explanations of internal labor markets. Degree of specificity of skills, as measured by extensiveness of employer training, somewhat predicted internal markets, providing support for the transactions cost arguments. But so did extent of unionization and being located in the core industries, providing support for a Marxist interpretation. In addition, Pfeffer and Cohen report that the development of internal labor markets was associated with the existence of a personnel department, a finding that supports an institutional interpretation of the spread of this structural form. Once such structures have been created in the more advanced organizations, they are apt to be picked up and promoted by professional personnel officers as being consistent with the principles of modern human-resources management. (See Dobbin et. al., in press.)

Although there remain differences in the explanations of internal labor markets, there is agreement that their existence within an organization constitutes a significant social boundary: would-be participants encounter barriers to entry and are restricted to a limited number of low-level positions from which they must work their way up; current employees enjoy job security and anticipate future advancement, reducing the probability of turnover and increasing their commitment to the organization.

From a broader historical perspective, there is no doubt that organizations have helped to bring about basic changes in societal stratification systems. (See Eisenstadt, 1981.) In our simple example of the family-run retail store, to the extent that the father does not honor the expectations generated by the kinship system in his distribution of rewards among family members, the kinship structure has lost power over the economic system. One of the "great transformations" of the last few centuries has been the increasing autonomy enjoyed by economic organizations in relation to other institutional sectors (Polanyi, 1944). Many excellent historical accounts describe the gradual, halting process by which ascriptive, hereditary stratification systems have given way to more competitive, open-class systems, and this change is attributable partially to the increasing use of organizationally relevant recruitment criteria (see Tout, 1916; Barker, 1944; Rosenberg, 1958). Individually, and in the short run, most organizations adapt to the demands of their social environments; collectively, and in a longer view, organizations gradually transform their environments.

## MANAGING TASK ENVIRONMENTS

In Chapter 6, following Dill (1958), we defined the task environment as those features of the environment relevant to the organization viewed as a production system—in particular, the sources of inputs, markets for outputs, competitors, and regulators. Since no organization generates all the resources necessary for its goal attainment or survival, organizations are forced to enter into exchanges, becoming interdependent with other environmental groups, typically other organizations. Unequal exchange relations can generate power and dependency differences among organizations, which are therefore expected to enter into exchange relations cautiously and to pursue strategies that will enhance their own bargaining position. This general perspective, labeled the resource dependence approach (see Chapter 5), has given rise to considerable theoretical and empirical work since the early 1970's on these strategies. The level of analysis most often associated with this approach is that of the organization set: the environment is viewed as it relates to and impinges on some particular organization, which serves as the primary focus of the analysis. Using a different set of assumptions, transactions costs theorists and population ecologists have also examined the relation of task environments to organizational forms.

As discussed in Chapter 6, determining the nature and scope of its domain is a critical concern for any organization. We noted that in arriving at their domain definition, organizations must negotiate and bargain with members of their organization set so that their claims to be in a given business are recognized as legitimate by others to whom they must relate. The higher the consensus on an organization's domain, the easier it will be for its members to conduct routine transactions.

Domain definition concerns not simply the general arena of activity, but what particular roles or functions the organization will perform. The manufacturer decides not simply to produce toys, but particular types or lines of toys targeted to particular types of customers—distributors and consumers. Porter (1980) regards decisions concerning product differentiation—the creation of relatively distinctive products and services—and focus—the identification of a selected buyer group or segment of a product line—to be among the most significant made by organizations in determining their competitive strategies. Among other effects, these decisions determine the identity of the organization's most significant competitors and partners—its strategic location within the broader industry or sector.

In addition, organizations must determine what subset of all the stages involved in producing a particular product or service they are going to embrace. The toy company does not ordinarily produce its own steel or plastic, but purchases these inputs, in varying stages of completion, from other firms. All organizations are confronted by basic decisions concerning which items or services they will make and which they will purchase from others. As Williamson (1975; 1981) points out, these "make or buy" decisions are tantamount to defining the technical boundaries of the organization. To "make" goods or services is to bring these activities within your own boundaries; to "buy" them is to relinquish them to the environment. As we would expect, Williamson predicts that firms will set their boundaries in such a manner as to minimize their transactions costs. Even if we do not accept this account as the only or even the most important basis for setting boundaries, it is clear that these are critical boundary-defining decisions. And it is important to see that organizations can and do regularly review and revise these decisions, eliminating former departments (for example, by contracting out the services they handle) and adding new units (for example, through vertical integration). They can also decide to change domains (for example, by merging with a company in a different business.)

We continue our discussion of managing task environments by reviewing the main concerns and contributions of the resource dependency theorists. In general, two lines of argument may be distinguished. The first focuses on the central work processes of the organization and asks how they may be protected from disturbances arising from the task environment. The strategies considered are those designed to *buffer* the organization's technical core—to amplify its protective boundaries. This argument emphasizes the need to close the system artificially to enhance the possibilities of rational action.[6] The second line of argument recognizes that among the most important actions organizations can take is the modification of their boundaries, more or less drastically and more or less formally. These actions include boundary-spanning and boundary-shifting strategies that *bridge* organizations and their exchange partners, competitors, or regulators.

### Buffering Strategies

Organizations may be viewed as technological systems—as mechanisms for transforming inputs into outputs. It is almost always possible to identify one or more central sets of tasks around which the organization is built. Teaching in schools, surgery and patient care in hospitals, laboratory work in research organizations, line work in assembly plants, legislating in Congress—these are examples of central tasks in varying types of organizations. Following Thompson (1967), we will refer to the arrangements developed to perform these central tasks—including the skills of personnel employed to carry them out—as the *core technology* of the organization.

---

[6]Some kinds of task demands make it impossible to exclude uncertainty from the technical core. Structural accommodations for dealing with these situations are examined in Chapter 9.

A key proposition formulated by Thompson is that "under norms of rationality, organizations seek to seal off their core technologies from environmental influences" (1967: 19). This proposition follows from Thompson's attempt to reconcile the rational, natural, and open system perspectives, as described in Chapter 5. He argues that the rational system perspective is most applicable at the technical level of the organization. Here, if anywhere, there is expected to be a concern with the careful selection of means to pursue ends and an attempt to reduce to a minimum the extraneous forces that can upset these connections. The purest example of these tendencies, which are expected to be present to some degree in all organizations, is the organization that is able to develop a *long-linked technology,* a series of sequential, interdependent production activities, exemplified by the assembly line in a manufacturing company (Thompson, 1967: 15–16).

Long-linked technologies can be created only when certain conditions are met. They require (1) a clear understanding of the cause-effect relations linking inputs with outputs, so that by carrying out the proper activities it is possible to produce the desired effect regularly; (2) a stable supply of appropriate inputs; and (3) a continuing demand for the standardized outputs. The last two conditions require the organization to deal with its environment. The long-linked technology, while effective and efficient for achieving limited objectives, is quite inflexible and, hence, vulnerable to change or uncertainty.

All organizations, but especially those with long-linked technologies, are highly motivated to secure enough stability, determinateness, and certainty to be able to function efficiently and effectively in environments that contain unknowns and uncertainties. Organizations seeking to buffer their technical flows from environmental perturbations may pursue a number of strategies.

Buffering strategies come in many forms and guises, but they all may be regarded as intraorganizational techniques aimed at reducing uncertainty for the technical core. As with all strategies, there are potential costs as well as gains for the organization, and in our brief review we will touch on both.

**Coding** Organizations can classify inputs before inserting them into the technical core. Preprocessing of inputs aids their proper routing and, if necessary, their exclusion. If inappropriate or inadequately processed inputs inadvertently gain entry, they can cause delays, create machinery problems, or require special attention, often from supervisory personnel. For example, on an automobile assembly line, the parts are carefully inspected and rejects are culled before they are placed on the conveyor belt. Coding is not restricted to long-linked technologies or even to industrial concerns; for example, human-service agencies classify clients as a means of determining their eligibility for service and facilitating their routing to the appropriate service units.

The costs of coding should not be overlooked. The coding process itself consumes resources and is always imperfect. No set of codes can capture all of the relevant properties of the raw materials; codes always simplify, sometimes in useful, but sometimes in distorting or biasing ways. Also, we should recall Weick's (1979) admonition: organizations need to reduce equivocality (by coding) in order to ensure some stability, but they also need to retain some equivocality in order to learn how their environment is changing and to retain flexibility (see Chapter 4).

*Stockpiling*    Organizations can stockpile raw materials or products and thereby control the rate at which inputs are inserted into the technical core or outputs released to the environment. Organizations are likely to stockpile critical resources, those whose supply is uncertain or whose price fluctuates greatly over time. The hope is that regardless of vicissitudes on the supply side, the organization will be assured of a continuous flow of resources. Similarly, on the output side, products may be held in warehouses in order to be released on the market at the most propitious time. But the capital tied up in reserves is not productive, and the costs of stockpiling include storage costs and possible loss through spoilage, damage, deterioration, or obsolescence. The problem confronting all organizations is to ensure that inventories are sufficient to meet all needs—both on the supply and demand sides—while defending against the possibility of obsolescence as production needs or customer demands change.

*Leveling*    Leveling, or smoothing, is an attempt by the organization to reduce fluctuations in its input or output environments. Whereas stockpiling is a relatively passive technique, leveling entails a more active attempt to reach out into the environment to motivate suppliers of inputs or to stimulate demand for outputs. Organizations may use advertising to stimulate demand for their products; retail stores may schedule sales during slack periods, utilities may stimulate or discourage use of their power supplies by variable time-of-day rates, and colleges may hold conferences in the summer to use idle facilities. Even hospitals may smooth their work flow by scheduling elective surgery during slack periods. The costs associated with such efforts are self-evident: seeking out suppliers or customers consumes energy and resources, and many of the techniques used, such as advertising, tend to combine high costs and high risks.

*Forecasting*    If environmental fluctuations cannot be handled by stockpiling or by leveling, organizations may have to settle for forecasting: anticipating changes in supply or demand conditions and attempting to adapt to them. Environmental changes are often patterned, exhibiting a weekly or a seasonal trend. Organizations taking account of such regularities can often accommodate them. For example, taxi companies can anticipate changes in demand for their services over a twenty-four-hour period and arrange drivers' schedules accordingly; beaches or amusement parks can make educated guesses about crowd size based on school and holiday schedules. Costs associated with forecasting, in addition to those entailed in guessing wrong, include the difficulties of expanding and contracting capacity, in particular the problems and inefficiencies of using part-time or short-term help.

*Growth*    One of the most general strategies employed by organizations is to change the scale of operations, to expand the technical core. (We postpone to the following section a discussion of growth by merger with other organizations.) Technological factors may encourage growth:

there are favorable economies of scale for virtually every kind of technical process, and Thompson argues that organizations will tend to expand "until the least-reducible component is approximately fully occupied" (1967: 46). Other, probably more compelling factors encourage growth as well. Distinct advantages accrue to the firm that is large, particularly in relation to its market. Large organizations are better able to engage in *planning,* in Galbraith's sense of that term: "much of what the firm regards as planning consists in minimizing or getting rid of market influences" (1967: 25). Thus, large firms are better able to set prices, control how much they produce, and influence the decisions of related organizations. Pfeffer and Salancik (1978: 139) summarize the advantages of size:

> Organizations that are large have more power and leverage over their environments. They are more able to resist immediate pressures for change and, moreover, have more time in which to recognize external threats and adapt to meet them. Growth enhances the organization's survival value, then, by providing a cushion, or slack, against organizational failure.

We have argued that buffering strategies are employed to help seal off or cushion the technical core from disturbances in the environment. The strategies described are particularly useful for organizations employing long-linked technologies, but as we have noted, other organizations often use some variant of them. Organizations also use bridging strategies, some of which buffer the technical core. More often, however, bridging strategies are oriented toward enhancing the security of the organization in relation to its environment. Safety, survival, and an improved bargaining position are the prizes that motivate bridge building, rather than simply increased certainty for the organization's technical operations.

### Bridging Strategies

Virtually all of the formulations of power and exchange relations among organizations build on the conception of power developed by Emerson (1962). Emerson emphasizes that one actor's power over another is rooted in the latter's dependency on resources controlled by the former. As expressed by Emerson, "the power of A over B is equal to, and based upon, the dependence of B upon A" (1962: 33). Further, the dependence of one actor on another varies as a function of two factors: B's dependence on A (1) is directly proportional to the importance B places on the goals mediated by A, and (2) is inversely proportional to the availability of these goals to B outside the A–B relationship. Obviously, the actors involved may be individuals, groups, or organizations. (See also Chapter 11.)

Emerson's formulation is useful for several reasons when applied to a given organization and the set of organizations to which it relates (see Thompson, 1967). Power is not viewed as some generalized capacity but as a function of specific needs and resources that can vary from one exchange partner to another. Thus, it is possible for an organization to have relatively little power in relation to its suppliers, but considerable power in relation to its buyers. Further, we would expect each supplier's power to vary with the importance of the resources it supplies and the extent to which alternative suppliers are available. This approach avoids a *zero-sum* view of power, in which it is assumed that when one actor gains power another must lose it. Rather, it becomes possible for two actors to both gain in power over each other—through an increase in the extent of their interdependence.

Bridging strategies may be viewed as a response to increasing organizational interdependence. Interdependence can occur when two or more organizations that are differentiated from one another exchange resources. This is known as *symbiotic* interdependence and can give rise, as noted, to power differences if the resources exchanged are not of equal importance. Interdependence also occurs when two or more similar organizations compete for the resources of another party. This is known as *competitive* or commensalistic interdependence. Competitive interdependence is often resolved by differentiation, former competitors becoming exchange partners (Blau and Scott, 1962: 217–21). For example, an automobile manufacturer may be unable to compete successfully by selling automobiles but may survive by supplying parts to other automobile companies.

The most complete analysis of bridging strategies to date is that provided by Pfeffer and Salancik (1978: 43); our summary draws heavily on their work. Their general thesis is simply stated: "The typical solution to problems of interdependence and uncertainty involves increasing coordination, which means increasing the mutual control over each other's activities. . . ." Although all bridging strategies share this feature, they are quite varied in the strength and the nature of the connections forged. We shall discuss some of the more common types of bridging strategies.

***Bargaining***  We use the term *bargaining* to refer not to one but to a large family of strategies by which the focal organization attempts to ward off dependence. To be compulsively precise, bargaining is not really a bridging but a prebridging strategy: it consists of things to do before calling in the bridge builders or while waiting for them to arrive. Much of the bargaining to be done, of course, is concerned with the defining and defending of the organization's domain. Other types of bargaining are aimed at helping the organization increase its independence. Examples of bargaining strategies include (1) attempts by the focal organization to develop alternative suppliers of critical resources, and (2) selective disclosure of conflicting demands by two or more members of the organization set—for example, a company may call the attention of its regulators to a union's wage demands in the hope of enlisting their support in resisting the union. Pfeffer and Salancik (1978: 92–111) provide an excellent guide to these types of bargaining strategies, including such subtle tactics as organizations "helping" the various members of their set to define their demands on the focal organization and gaining control over the determination of when a demand made on them has been met.

***Contracting***  According to Thompson (1967: 35), contracting is "the negotiation of an agreement for the exchange of performances in the future." For present purposes, contracts may be more or less formally drawn up and more or less legally binding. The critical point is that they represent attempts by organizations to reduce uncertainty by coordinating their future behavior, in limited and specific ways, with other units. As we have learned from Williamson (1975), there is a limit to how much uncertainty can be hedged or handled by contracts (see Chapter 7), but Williamson himself notes (pp. 90–95) that contracts can be modified to handle considerable uncertainty; contingent claims contracts, incomplete long-term contracts, and sequential spot contracts are examples. The negotiation of contracts with labor unions and principal suppliers and buyers is one of the chief ways in which organizations assure themselves of some degree of certainty in a changing future.

Stinchcombe (1985) has observed, apparently in contradiction to the predictions of transactions costs theory, that contracts are sometimes employed as the principal control mechanism, even under conditions of extraordinary complexity and uncertainty—for example, in relations between defense agencies and supplier firms, or between nation-states and oil-construction and -production companies. We would ordinarily expect such transactions to be brought inside an organizational framework, where "softer" bargaining and greater controls are possible. But Stinchcombe usefully suggests that it is important to see "hierarchies" (organizations) and markets not as dichotomies but as a continuum, and that it is possible to build many hierarchical features into contracts. For example, defense contracts often allow the purchaser to inspect compliance to requirements and progress toward objectives as necessary; to change requirements or specifications as the work proceeds; and to renegotiate the allocation of costs and benefits depending on what outcomes occur. Such hierarchical rights undermine the autonomy of the independent contractors and constitute a step in the direction of creating a joint venture between the contracting parties—except that the "venture" is a specific project rather than a continuing organization. Such admittedly complex contracting arrangements seem to be widely employed in high-cost-high-gain (high-risk) situations, such as large-scale construction and defense and space technology.

***Co-optation***    As defined in Chapter 3, co-optation is the incorporation of representatives of external groups into the decision-making or advisory structure of an organization. The significance of this practice in linking organizations with their environments was first described by Selznick (1949), who also noted its possible costs. Selznick argued that by co-opting representatives of external groups, organizations are, in effect, trading sovereignty for support.

Most studies of co-optation have focused on boards of directors, investigating the extent of interlocking ties among various types of organizations.[7] It is argued that allowing representatives of other orga-

---

[7]There are two different, but related, perspectives from which interlocking directorates have been examined. The first is an interorganizational approach that assumes organizations are entities pursuing interests, during which they establish connections with other organizations. The resource dependence approach embraces this perspective. The second is an intraclass approach that assumes that individual actors, such as members of the business elite, have interests and that organizations are the agents they use to establish relations with other individuals sharing their class interests. (See Palmer, 1983; Mizruchi, 1982.) These two perspectives take basically similar views of the functions of interlocks—they secure resources, information, and support, for example—but differ as to what set of interests is being promoted—organizational versus class.

nizations to participate in decision making in the focal organization is an important indication of interdependence and an effort by all the organizations to coordinate their activities. Such representatives may range from strong, controlling directors imposed by one organization on another to common messengers transmitting information of mutual interest. (Pennings, 1981) Not all board members are environmental representatives: some are there to provide specialized expertise, to oversee and augment the administrative skills of management.

To the extent that directorate ties function as a co-optative strategy for dealing with the interdependence of organizations, we would expect board appointments to vary with the amount and type of resource needs and flows confronting the focal organization. Although it is often difficult to measure needs and flows, and although co-optation is only one possible means of managing interdependence, there is considerable evidence to support this interpretation. For example, studies by Pfeffer of eighty randomly selected nonfinancial corporations (1972*a*) and fifty-seven hospitals in Illinois (1973) provide empirical support for the expectation that board appointments are used by organizations to establish linkages with important segments of the environment on which they are dependent. Thus, the corporations that exhibited a high debt/equity ratio were observed to have a higher proportion of representatives from financial institutions on their boards. And hospitals having larger budgets, and those receiving a higher proportion of their capital budgets from private donations and lacking federal or religious affiliations, were more likely to stress fund-raising ability as a criterion for selecting board members.

More convincing evidence is provided by Burt and his colleagues (Burt, Christman, and Kilburn, 1980; Burt, 1983), who examined the extent of interlocking directorates among a sample of the largest manufacturing firms from each of twenty industries in the United States for 1967. In their approach, the economy is viewed as a network of industrial sectors, differing in degree of concentration and extent of interconnections as measured by empirical studies of interindustry sales (input-output ratios). The analysts propose that firms in more highly concentrated sectors that buy and sell to many other sectors that are less highly concentrated are likely to be more profitable and to have less need to establish interlocks. Interlocks are more common among firms in less highly concentrated industries and among firms having to deal with buyers and sellers in more highly concentrated sectors. These predictions were confirmed for profitability and for three types of directorate ties: firms owned by the same corporation (and thus having the same directors); firms owned by two corporations sharing one or more directors; and firms owned by two corporations sharing a director with the same financial institution. Burt and associates (1980: 821) conclude that

> each of the three types of directorate ties tends to occur where there is market constraint and tends not to occur in the absence of constraint. Further, the three types of ties are coordinated as multiplex directorate ties. Where establishments in one sector constrain those in another, there is a strong tendency for all three types of directorate ties to exist between the two sectors. . . . Whatever the cooptive intent of the directorate ties described, they are patterned as if they were intended to coopt market constraints on corporate pricing discretion.

Finally, Burt and associates note that the use of interlocks to manage dependence is much more common between firms in different industries than between firms in the same industry, probably because of antitrust regulations that prohibit such visible techniques of cooperation (collusion?) among competitors. High interdependence within industries is more likely to be resolved by merger.

Co-optation is also widely employed as a coordinating strategy among public agencies and nonprofit associations. From the mid 1960s, the era of the Great Society programs, to the late 1970s, a great many federally sponsored organizations were created whose hallmark was decentralized decision making combined with mandated participation of representatives from the areas affected. Such programs included community action agencies, model cities programs, community mental health programs, area agencies for the aged, and health systems agencies (See Piven and Cloward, 1971; Sundquist, 1969.) There is considerable controversy concerning the merits of this federal strategy and its outcomes, in part because the programs themselves were diverse and the effects of any single program were not uniform across sites. Some studies suggest that federal bureaucrats and reformers used the local participation ideology as a smoke screen simply to legitimate federal intervention (see Krause, 1968). Others suggest that influence ran in the reverse direction: local interests captured and subverted the reform-oriented goals of the designers of the programs (see Moynihan, 1970). The truth of the matter is probably that both processes were occurring: each of the parties was to some extent using the others to achieve its own objectives, and all were somewhat constrained by the need to take into account the interests of others. Co-optation as a bridging mechanism provides a two-way street, with both influence and support flowing sometimes in one direction, sometimes in the other, but more often in both.

With the coming of more conservative policies in the 1980s, including the reduction in the federal role and in funding for community services, co-optation has shifted from being a primarily vertical strategy to being a horizontal strategy. Community agencies employ numerous co-optation mechanisms—joint board memberships, liaison roles, interorganizational brokers—as a way to increase resources, reduce uncertainty, and increase legitimacy. (See Galaskiewicz, 1985.) Indeed, federal and state programs currently place great emphasis on coordination among community agencies, often as a condition of being eligible for funding. Whereas federal regulations proscribe co-optation among competing organizations in the for-profit sector, they mandate it as a means of coordination among public and nonprofit agencies.

***Joint ventures***  A joint venture occurs when two or more firms create a new organization to pursue some common purpose. Joint ventures differ from mergers, to be discussed next, in that they entail only a limited pooling of resources by the participating organizations. For example, several wholesale companies may combine resources to purchase a trucking operation, or a wholesale company may combine assets with a farmers' cooperative to build a canning company. As these examples suggest, joint ventures may occur among either competitors or exchange partners. Testing the hypothesis that joint ventures tend to reflect resource interdependencies, Pfeffer and Nowak (1976) examined data from 166 joint ventures occurring over a decade. In support of the hypothesis, they found that the more exchanges there were between different industry groups, as measured by interindustry sales figures, the more likely firms from these industries were to enter into joint ventures. Pfeffer and Nowak also tested the prediction that firms within industry groups facing higher competition would be more likely to develop joint ventures as a means of reducing competitive pressures. Again, the data supported the prediction: joint ventures were found to be more frequent within industries exhibiting an intermediate level of concentration, a situation of maximum competitive pressure.[8]

**Mergers**    One of the most drastic strategies used by organizations in relating to critical units of their environment is to absorb these units: two or more independent organizations become a single collective actor. Three major types of mergers have been identified.

1. *Vertical integration,* in which organizations engaged in related functions but at different stages in the production process merge, backward or forward, with one another. Vertical integration, of course, takes place between exchange partners, organizations that are symbiotically related. For example, furniture manufacturers may merge (backward) with lumber companies or (forward) with furniture distributors or showrooms.
2. *Horizontal merger,* in which organizations performing similar functions merge to increase the scale of their operation. For example, two car dealerships that formerly handled only one line of automobiles may merge into one dealership handling two or more brands.
3. *Diversification,* in which one organization acquires one or more other organizations that are neither exchange partners nor similar organizations competing with each other, but organizations operating in different domains. For example, in the 1960s International Telegraph and Telephone, an electronics-manufacturing company, acquired a rent-a-car company, a major hotel chain, a home-building company, a baking company, a producer of glass and sand, a consumer-lending firm, and a data-processing organization. The extreme form of diversification is the *conglomerate.*

This country has experienced several waves of mergers, each of a differing type. Drucker (1970) argues that most mergers at the turn of the century involved horizontal or vertical integration as a dominant industrialist or financier attempted to gain control within a single industry. Mergers occurring in the 1920s represented a "defensive" reaction to these earlier developments as smaller companies jockeyed for position in the second tier. Most recent mergers involve the creation of conglomerates, either as a result of organizations attempting to diversify or as a result of their being "taken over" by aggressive asset managers who promise stockholders a better return on capital.

[8]Industry groups with high concentration ratios are those dominated by a relatively small group of firms. These firms are likely to have developed an "understanding" with one another, and together they control the conditions of survival for the smaller firms within the industry. On the other hand, industry groups with low concentration ratios are, by definition, composed of a great many small firms, no one of which is able to generate great competitive pressures on its neighbors.

Research by Pfeffer (1972*b*) supports the expectation that mergers involving vertical integration are more likely to occur among companies in industries engaged in frequent transactions. His study of 854 large mergers of companies in manufacturing and mining shows that mergers tended to occur more often among types of firms highly interdependent in their resource flows. Further, his findings on the effects of competitive interdependence replicated those reported for joint ventures: horizontal mergers were more likely to occur among firms located in industries exhibiting intermediate levels of concentration—situations of maximum intraindustry competition. Finally, Pfeffer and Salancik argue that mergers involving diversification are most likely to occur "when exchanges are very concentrated and when capital or statutory constraints" limit the use of other options for managing interorganizational interdependence (1978: 127).

As we have seen, the resource dependence approach emphasizes the extent of interorganizational resource flows and the degree of market concentration as the basis for generating predictions about mergers in general and vertical integration in particular. And as noted earlier, Williamson (1975; 1981) suggests that decisions concerning vertical integration can also be explained as attempts to reduce transactions costs. It is expected that as the assets required by an organization become more specific, firms will elect to produce them internally to avoid becoming overly dependent on a small number of external suppliers. This prediction was tested by Monteverde and Teece (1982) in a study of decisions made by General Motors and by Ford for a list of 133 automotive components. Measuring asset specificity by the amount of development effort required to produce a given component, they reported that, as expected, specificity was positively associated with the decision to integrate-in the manufacture of the component. Walker and Weber (1984) studied sixty decisions made in a component division of a large U.S. automobile manufacturer, decisions both to integrate (make rather than buy) and to de-integrate (buy rather than make) components. Consistent with transactions costs predictions, the division was more likely to manufacture components itself if there were few competing suppliers and if the volume of parts needed was uncertain. Unexpectedly, however, the strongest predictors were comparative manufacturing costs. Production costs appeared to be more significant in this situation than transactions costs.

Resource dependency and transactions costs explanations of mergers are not necessarily in conflict, although the former place greater stress on the organization's interest in reducing uncertainty and dependence while the latter stress its interest in increasing economic efficiency.

**Associations** Associations are arrangements that allow similar (and sometimes diverse) organizations to work in concert to pursue mutually desired objectives. They operate under many names, including trade associations, cartels, coordinating councils, and coalitions.

Both similar and dissimilar organizations enter into associations at the community or local level. We find many associations of similar organizations—for example, hospital councils and associations of retail merchants—as well as examples of associations of diverse organizations—the community chest and chambers of commerce. Individual organizations join associations in order, variously, to garner resources, secure information, exercise influence, or obtain legitimacy and acceptance. The structure and strength of associations vary greatly: some are informal and weak, others are formally structured and exercise great power over their members. (See Warren, 1967.) Although these structures have been increasingly examined as areal organizational fields, they have received little help from resource dependency theorists, since, as Laumann, Galaskiewicz, and Marsden (1978: 470) comment,

> little insight into how the totality of interorganizational linkages is organized can be attained using a perspective centered on atomistically conceived, bilateral transactions.

The trade association is an important type of association operating at a national and even international level. It is "a coalition of firms or businesspersons who come together in a formal organization to cope with forces and demands to which they are similarly exposed" (Staber and Aldrich, 1983: 163; see also, Staber, 1985). There is some evidence that trade associations are more likely to form in less highly concentrated sectors where too many firms are present to permit more tacit coordination (Pfeffer and Salancik, 1978: 179).

The power of trade associations varies markedly from society to society. Trade associations in the United States are more numerous, more specialized, and much less influential than those in most Western European countries, Japan, and Korea. Trade associations in the United States are not sufficiently strong or organized to serve as vehicles for centralizing and representing the interests of industries, as do trade associations in the more corporatist states. (See Berger, 1981; Okimoto, 1984. Corporatism is discussed later in this chapter.) By the same token, only relatively recently has the United States government been sufficiently strong and active in economic matters to serve as a target for associations' influence attempts. Since not only associations but individual organizations can try to influence governmental policies, we treat these efforts as a separate bridging strategy.

***Government connections***     Governments at all levels—local, state, and national—affect the resource transactions of organizations in two general capacities: (1) as sources of authority specifying what types of negotiations and exchanges can legally occur among organizations, and (2) as parties that directly engage in transactions with organizations, exacting resources from some and providing them to others.

The first function is, broadly speaking, an institutional one: governments help to shape and play a central role in enforcing the general rules under which technical environments operate. However, because the rules concern the exchange of resources, we describe them here rather than in the following section on institutional environments.

Lindblom (1977: 21) has pointed out that "an easy way to acknowledge the special character of government as an organization is simply to say that governments exercise authority over other organizations." Although Lindblom goes on to caution that governmental authority is sometimes contested, it is nevertheless essential to take account of governments' special powers and of the unique role a government plays as an organization among organizations. Some requirements apply to all types of organizations—for example, those specifying general property rights, rules of fair trade, and employee benefits such as workmen's compensation and social security. Although the overall policies are generally applicable, their impact is determined by the specific wording of the statues, regulations, and court interpretations by which they are implemented. Individual organizations and associations of organizations are therefore motivated to influence these policies. Thus, when laws are being formulated or revised, organizations will see to it that their concerns and interests are expressed in testimony before legislative committees, in lobbying efforts directed at individual legislators, and in commentaries on the "feasibility" and fairness of proposed administrative regulations; when the laws are being enforced, organizations will court the favor of administrative officials and seek expert legal counsel to help themselves define and defend their interests through litigation.

Governments also place special constraints on the transactions conducted by certain categories of organizations. Many types of organizations confront governmental regulatory bodies that monitor closely the quality of their products or services or their transactions with exchange partners or competitors. Utilities, railroads, banks, and pharmaceutical companies, for example, have long operated under the close scrutiny of public regulatory bodies. Numerous observers have pointed out that although such surveillance may, as intended, help to protect the public interest, it also has had the unintended effect of protecting the interests of the organizations being regulated—by restraining competitive pressures, restricting the entry of new firms, and managing prices. (See Stigler, 1971; Wilson 1980; Noll, 1985). Thus, government regulation of economic transactions often reduces uncertainties in the environments of organizations and so is likely to be cultivated by them.

In addition to regulating economic transactions, public organizations also participate in them. Governments are able to impose both general and specific taxes on organizations, and for many organizations they are a major provider of resources. Some resource flows are indirect, coming in the form of tax breaks or exemptions; others are more direct, involving outright transfers of funds in the form of subsidies or grants; and still others involve the government's acting not as an interested third party but as a direct participant in the transaction—as a buyer of products or a client of services. Some departments of the federal government, such as the Pentagon, are the primary purchasers of the products of a vast complex of organizations—in its case, defense-oriented manufacturers. And some families of organizations—for example, applied research organizations such as RAND and SRI—exist largely on contracts to conduct studies and provide services for a large range of governmental agencies. Although it is often argued that organizations selling services to government are part of a highly concentrated market, in fact the operations of the government are becoming increasingly differentiated, so that sellers often find several governmental units of the same kind bidding for their services.[9]

[9]Competition among governmental units has long existed at the level of state and local governments, as individual jurisdictions compete with one another—using tax incentives, land grants, tax-exempt bonds, and labor policies—to attract business to their area. In recent years, as indicated above, the federal government has become large and fragmented enough so that a similar competition has developed among its several branches and departments.

The tactics organizations employ to influence governmental organizations are not the same ones they use with private organizations. In particular, as Pfeffer and Salancik (1978: 192) have noted, private organizations requesting special treatment from governmental agencies must justify their private claims on the grounds that they serve the public interest. Thus, universities seek to preserve academic freedom not primarily because professors and university administrators prefer unconstrained decision making but because academic freedom must be preserved "for society's good." And the Chrysler Corporation's successful pursuit of $1.5 billion in loan guarantees from the federal government was justified in the name of preserving competition in the automobile industry and safeguarding the jobs of American workers.

## MANAGING INSTITUTIONAL ENVIRONMENTS

As discussed in earlier chapters, our ideas concerning institutional environments are more recent and less developed than those concerning technical environments, and we know less about how organizations relate to them. But there are at least two clear differences between organizational responses to technical and institutional aspects of their environments. First, most connections with technical environments involve flows or exchanges—of information, resources, personnel. Although some connections with institutional environments also involve flows—particularly of information—a more important linkage process is absorption or incorporation. Whereas organizations *exchange* elements with their technical environments, they are *constituted* by elements drawn from their institutional environments. Technical elements are secured, combined, and transformed by organizational processes so that they commonly are no longer visible in their original state. By contrast, institutional elements are secured and utilized without being transformed. Great efforts are made to insure their visibility to outsiders, and it is essential that their distinctive features remain intact.

Second, although organizations necessarily will attempt to screen out undesirable or inappropriate elements from their institutional environments, and in this sense engage in buffering processes, most of the arguments to date stress that bridging processes are central to these connections. Both Meyer and Rowan (1977) and DiMaggio and Powell (1983) propose that institutional *isomorphism* is the master bridging process pursued by organizations in their institutional environments: by incorporating institutional rules within their own structures, organizations become more homogeneous, more similar in structure, over time. It is important to emphasize, however, that the processes producing isomorphism are assumed to operate within a given institutional sphere or sector, so that to the extent that sectors vary in their rules, organizational forms would also be expected to diverge. (See Scott, 1983: 61.) While recognizing that it is not easy to develop a precise typology of isomorphic strategies, we can identify four somewhat distinctive institutional bridging mechanisms.

### Institutional Bridging Strategies

*Categorical conformity*    This is the broadest and most general strategy, and can easily be extended to include as special cases the other three types. Categorical conformity is the process whereby institutional rules in the form of typifications, or taken-for-granted distinctions, provide guidelines to organizations on the basis of which they can pattern their structures. These distinctions are the aspects of institutionalization emphasized by Berger and Luckmann (1967) and by Meyer and Rowan (1977) (see Chapter 5). General distinctions such as those between research and development, production and distribution functions, blue- and white-collar workers, or professionals and administrators are widely accepted and often become the basis of structural differentiation within organizations. Organizations also incorporate and build their structures around widely institutionalized general roles such as students and teachers, managers, stockholders, and board members.

These types of distinctions are fundamental examples of more or less widely shared cognitive structures. They are built into our language. Meyer and Rowan (1977: 349) refer to them as "vocabularies of structure." All of them are aspects of a reality that is socially constructed but widely believed, so that, as Zucker (1983: 2) notes, "certain social relationships and actions come to be taken for granted, that is, part of the 'objective situation.' " Zucker also emphasizes that categorical conformity is not produced or reinforced by sanctions, but occurs because it seems the natural or "obvious" way to proceed.

Organizations incorporate these cognitive belief systems because doing so enhances their legitimacy and hence increases their resources and survival capacities. As Meyer and Rowan (1977: 349) argue,

> vocabularies of structure that are isomorphic with institutional rules provide prudent, rational, and legitimate accounts. Organizations described in legitimated vocabularies are assumed to be oriented to collectively defined, and often collectively mandated, ends. . . . On the other hand, organizations that omit environmentally legitimated elements of structure or create unique structures lack acceptable legitimated accounts of their activities. Such organizations are more vulnerable to claims that they are negligent, irrational, or unnecessary.

**Structural conformity**   Sometimes environmental actors impose very specific structural requirements on organizations as a condition for acceptance and support. Organizations are required to adopt specific structural elements—tables of organization, departments, roles—in order to merit approval. DiMaggio and Powell (1983: 152) point out that organizations confronting high levels of uncertainty often borrow structural forms, sometimes by consciously modeling a successful form, sometimes by bringing in personnel from other organizations who are known to be capable of importing innovative forms, and sometimes by seeking assistance from consulting firms, "which, like Johnny Appleseeds, spread a few organizational forms throughout the land."

The nation-state is an important source of structural isomorphism, creating fields of organizations with virtually identical forms or requiring existing organizations to adopt particular structural units as a condition of eligibility for funding. During the past three decades, the federal government has imposed considerable structural unity on many types of regional, state, and local agencies. In arenas ranging from mental health and community cancer control to museums and arts councils, many federal programs specify in considerable detail the structures and components to be established. (See Foley and Sharfstein, 1983; DiMaggio, 1983.) Also, governmental statutes frequently require that particular offices or units be added to existing structures—for example affirmative-action officers or safety units.

But it is not only governmental organizations that impose structural uniformity on numerous other types of organizations. Many quasi-public bodies, such as foundations and professional associations, have similar effects. Thus, the Joint Commission on Hospital Accreditation—a "private" joint venture involving the American College of Physicians and Surgeons and the American Hospital Association—requires as a condition of accreditation that hospitals have specific structural features, such as a medical staff organization with specific subcommittees to review staff admissions, quality assurance, medical records, and so forth. Although no hospital is compelled to conform to these requirements, there are strong normative pressures to do so, which are reinforced by financial policies that often restrict reimbursement to care received in accredited institutions.

Thus, both by choice and by coercion, organizations frequently exhibit structural isomorphism as a mechanism for adapting to their institutional environment.

**Procedural conformity**    Organizations are often placed under pressure from their institutional environments to carry out activities in specified ways. As with structural conformity, such pressures are sometimes the result of uncertainty—the procedures being adopted or copied by organizational choice—and sometimes the result of explicit normative or coercive pressures that require their adoption under threat of informal or formal sanctions.

Many of the rational myths described by Meyer and Rowan (1977) define procedures, spelling out in greater or lesser specificity the steps to be followed in carrying out certain types of activities. In a sense, rational myths are institutionally defined technologies specifying means—ends chains an organization is to follow in order to realize desired objectives. A vast range of procedural rules—from committing mental patients, to incorporating organizations, to baptizing new church members, to implementing PERT (planning, evaluation, and review techniques)—are devised in institutional environments and incorporated into organizations as part of their standard operating procedures.

In modern societies, the two major types of collective actors generating procedural requirements are governmental units and professional groups. DiMaggio and Powell (1983: 147) assert that

> bureaucratization and other forms of homogenization [are] effected largely by the state and the professions, which have become the great rationalizers of the second half of the twentieth century.

In some situations, particularly when professional groups are strong, the nation-state will collaborate with professionals in attempting to rationalize an arena of activity. For example, in the quality-assurance programs mandated by the federal government in the 1970s, such as the Professional Standard Review Organizations, dominant decision-making roles were reserved for physicians. (See Goran et al., 1975; Scott, 1982.) In other areas, such as social welfare, recent legislation has reduced the discretion of social workers, lowered the qualifications they must meet for employment, and in general substantially deprofessionalized the public welfare program in the United States (Simon, 1983). Rationalization can take many forms and can locate discretion at more or less centralized nodes in the organizational structures created. The state is more likely to prefer more centralized structures, and the professions, more decentralized systems of procedures.

Lawyers, particularly in the United States, operate under the mantle of both state power and professional authority. They occupy most of the positions in our legislative bodies and our courts, as well as a large proportion of the positions in public administrative agencies. They are the acknowledged experts in devising procedural approaches to dispute resolution and problem solving. Even when the demands being enforced are primarily technical, the requirements are often couched in procedural language—the language of lawyers—rather than in language that attempts to specify outcomes. (See Majone, 1980.) Regulatory units as varied as the Health Systems Agencies, the Food and Drug Administration, and the Environmental Protection Agency operate primarily by specifying elaborate procedures—certificates of need, clinical trials, environmental impact reports—to be followed in justifying the introduction of new products or constructions. Critics have noted that these procedures readily become disconnected from outcomes, creating legalistic mazes and bureaucratic rituals rather than providing a framework to support rational decision making (see Bardach and Kagan, 1982). But institutionalists would emphasize that adherence to procedural specifications is one way in which stable organizational forms can be created and legitimated to work in conflict-ridden arenas. That the decisions are technical is irrelevant in these arenas since the decisions involve value conflicts: how or in whose interests is the technology to be used? Since any outcome will be controversial, the resolution of the matter must rest on the legitimacy of the decision process.

***Personnel conformity***   One of the primary building blocks of complex, differentiated, formal organizations is the large number of educated, often certified workers who assume specialized roles within them. As Meyer (1978: 354; 1985) points out, cultures vary considerably in where in the social structure rationality is institutionalized, but in contemporary Western societies, there is heavy emphasis on the individual as the prime locus. The Western cultural conception is one of

> the competent, achieving individual, whose productive action brings rewards to the self and corresponding gains to the collectivity (in such conceptions as the gross national product). This individual is institutionally located and managed primarily in the system of education. . . . (Meyer, 1985: 593)

Institutional environments often specify what types of actors—in terms of their (primarily educational) qualifications—are to be allocated to particular functions or roles. Conformity to institutional rules often entails the hiring of specific types of personnel. The most obvious examples involve certification and licensure. To be licensed as a "skilled nursing facility" an institution must include on its staff a specified proportion of registered nurses; governmentally mandated audits must be performed by certified public accountants; and accreditation bodies require that university faculties contain sufficient numbers of Ph.D's. In a great many arenas, organizational designers and managers have no or little control over the definition of jobs or the types of personnel recruited to fill them: these decisions have been made by external certification, licensure, and accreditation agencies. For example, once a hospital decides to offer a particular service, it is highly constrained by licensing rules in its decisions on what types of personnel are to be hired and how work is to be allocated among them. (See Somers, 1969; Freidson, 1970*a*.) Even when licensure is not required as a condition of operation or of funding, it is often used by occupations and organizations as a means of assuring the public that employees are qualified to perform their duties. From aerobics instructors and bartenders to tree surgeons and television repairmen, certification is looked to as an important source of legitimation.

More generally, a number of analysts have argued that education provides an important base for most personnel systems within organizations. Modern employment and promotion structures are heavily interlaced with educational requirements, which are justified in terms of technical skills and specialized knowledge required by the job. Yet, a number of other analysts have assembled evidence that challenges the presumed association between education and job qualifications or between education and productivity. (See Berg, 1971; Collins, 1979.) It has been proposed that the connection between education and occupational attainment is better viewed as having an institutional rather (or more) than a technical basis. Hiring certified or educated employees signals to the environment that the employer is a modern, responsible firm employing rational criteria of personnel selection and promotion. Without insisting that education and certification have no relation to performance, it is possible to embrace the institutional insight that, independent of performance, the hiring of individuals with appropriate educational credentials enhances the legitimacy of the employing organization and secures for it additional support and resources.

## COMBINING INSTITUTIONAL AND TECHNICAL ARGUMENTS

Zucker and Tolbert have argued that there is an important temporal dimension to environmental effects: earlier developments are dominated by technical processes but later phases are better explained by institutional processes. Tolbert has also suggested that once institutional linkages are in place, the kinds of adaptive linkages predicted by resource dependency theory may not be necessary. These arguments have been pursued both as a broad historical account of the growth of organizational forms and the variable timing of their penetration of differing sectors, and as an explanation of the diffusion of particular structural patterns in a delimited organizational field.

As discussed in Chapter 7, Zucker (1983: 13) formulates the broader version, suggesting that although the creation of organizational forms may have been encouraged by their superior production efficiency, "the rapid rise and continued spread of the organizational form is best interpreted as an instance of institutionalization: . . . it becomes seen as legitimate to organize formally, regardless of any net benefit." Emerging first in the manufacturing sector, organizations spread over time to become the dominant form for structuring local government, social services, and even social movements. Zucker (1983: 20) concludes,

> Initially, organizational form was adopted rationally to handle large-scale production and to create predictable conditions of work. . . . However, as the organizational form gained legitimacy and diffused outward to organize most economic, political, and (later) collective activities, it became a taken-for-granted element, so that it was unthinkable for a new business or political activity to take place *not* located in an organizational structure.

As discussed, we do not find these arguments convincing. Zucker's data are too sparse to support this broad a conclusion, and one can cite many instances of political and even religious systems being formally structured long before large-scale production systems developed. Nevertheless, it is apparent that organizational forms have spread over time into rather unlikely social arenas, with, for example, romantic pairings increasingly arranged by dating services and child care provided by licensed facilities.

The narrower arguments are better supported. Tolbert and Zucker (1983) examined the introduction of civil service procedures into a sample of ninety-three American municipal governments in states that did not mandate adoption of the reform, during the period 1880 to 1935. They report that early in this period, adoption of the reforms was associated with city characteristics such as number of immigrants, proportion of white-collar versus blue-collar inhabitants, and size. These are the types of associations that would be predicted by resource dependency theory: local governments were adopting changes that would buffer them from "undesirable elements" and link them to better segments of the community. However, after 1885 municipal characteristics no longer predicted adoption. The explanation offered is that the reforms had become institutionalized: after being adopted by a sufficient number of cities, they came to signify a modern community with a "rational" city administration, and so their adoption became widespread. (See also, Knoke, 1982)

Tolbert (1985) elaborates this argument in her study of administrative structures in a random sample of public and private colleges and universities. Resource dependency theory would predict that organizations depending on particular financial resources would be likely to develop offices that manage and protect those sources. Thus, private colleges were more likely to report the presence of a development officer and a director of admissions, whereas public colleges were more likely to have positions for managing sources of public funding, such as directors of planning and information. However, contrary to the predictions of resource dependency, among those institutions that were more heavily dependent on public funding, only the private and not the public schools showed a more differentiated structure; the reverse was true for institutions that were more heavily dependent on private gifts: only the public institutions added new officials to manage these flows. To account for these findings, Tolbert argues that specialized roles for managing interorganizational exchanges are necessary only when these exchanges are not institutionalized.

> Thus, increasing dependence does not necessarily produce administrative differentiation. It is only when dependency relations are not institutionalized that increasing dependency is strongly associated with the development of separate administrative offices to manage them. (1985: 11)

These studies are of interest because they are among the first to seek to determine how competing explanations of organizational structure can be combined. It is apparent that although some of these explanations are inconsistent, others may not be once we have better specified the conditions under which they are applicable. Also, it is likely that under some conditions the operation of some types of structures or relations will obviate the need for others.

## ADAPTATION VERSUS SELECTION

### Change in Organizations

Our discussion of the buffering and bridging strategies employed by organizations has been conducted primarily within the frameworks of resource dependence and institutional theory. We have emphasized that this approach works at the level of the organization set: we examined how the world appears from the windows of a specific focal organization and asked what strategies are available to that organization as it seeks at least to survive and, if possible, to thrive in its environment. Thus far we have not emphasized a second important characteristic of this approach: it assumes that organizational structures can be modified, that they are subject to manipulation by participants who are attempting to improve their adaptation. The strategies we have reviewed presume the presence of decision makers who survey the situation, confront alternatives as well as constraints, and select a course of action. They presume, in short, that organizational structures can be changed by modifications of existing structures.

This assumption is challenged by ecologists studying organizations at the population level of analysis. They argue that much of the variation in structural forms is due to environmental *selection* rather than adaptation (see Aldrich and Pfeffer, 1976). It is not necessary to insist that organizations do not exhibit structural change as a means of adapting to their environments, but only that many organizations do not learn about their environments and fail to modify their structures as quickly as their environments change (Hannan and Freeman, 1984).

In an earlier discussion, Hannan and Freeman (1977: 931–32) cite a large number of constraints upon change in organizations. Their list includes such internal limitations as the organization's investment in capital equipment and trained personnel, constraints on the transfer and processing of information, the costs of upsetting the internal political equilibrium, and the conservative forces of history and tradition. Equally important are the external constraints, including legal and fiscal barriers to entry and exit from markets, environmental limitations on the flow of information, and the difficulty of securing the external political and social support needed to legitimate any change. Evidence regarding the stability of organizational structures over time is provided by Stinchcombe's (1965) analysis, described in Chapter 7, of the link between time of founding and current structural characteristics of organizations. Stinchcombe's thesis of organizational imprinting is consistent with the view that organizations do not easily or quickly change their structural features. Thus, structural *inertia* is an important cause of environmental selection: structural forms are unable to keep pace with environmental change.

More recently, Hannan and Freeman (1984: 149) have suggested that the inertial properties of organizations may also be a *consequence* of selection: "high levels of structural inertia in organizational populations can be explained as an outcome of an ecological-evolutionary process." Both technical and institutional explanations are utilized. On the technical side, organizations are seen as being highly valued for their *reliability*—their capacity to "produce collective products of a given quality repeatedly." Such reliable performances are possible only in relatively stable structures. On the institutional side, organizations are prized for their *accountability*—their adherence "to norms of procedural rationality." (1984: 153) Organizations that exhibit either high reliability and/or high accountability are more likely to survive, given a reasonable degree of environmental stability. However, under conditions of higher environmental uncertainty, inertia becomes a liability rather than an asset, preventing the organization from changing enough, or quickly enough, to survive.

In the research to date, much attention has been devoted to states of the environment that give rise to particular adaptive forms. An environmental dimension of considerable importance is that of environmental *variability*—the extent of change observed (in resources, the level of competition, and so on) over a specific period. A related dimension is that of *grain*—the frequency with which changes occur over the period. An environment characterized by very rapid changes is said to be *fine-grained* and one with less frequent changes, *coarse-grained*. Following general ecological arguments, Freeman and Hannan (1983) predicted that generalist organizations—those organizations performing a greater diversity of tasks and having higher levels of excess or "slack" resources—would be more likely to survive in coarse-grained environments. Specialist organizations were expected to flourish in stable environments but also in those with rapid change—fine-grained environments. Specialist firms were expected to be able to ride out environmental changes in which a given state was rapidly replaced by an alternative state. But only the generalists were expected to survive wide fluctuations of longer duration.

These predictions were tested and generally confirmed in a study of restaurants in eighteen California cities (Freeman and Hannan, 1983). The variability of the environment was measured in terms of the variation in gross restaurant sales over the three-year period of the study; frequency of change, or grain, was based on the extent of seasonal variation experienced by each restaurant. Generalists were distinguished from specialist restaurants by the range of items on the menu, the differentiation of staff, and whether or not seating was provided to customers. During the three years, 13 percent of the 788 restaurants studied "died" and another 13 percent were sold. Modest and mixed empirical support was obtained for the prediction that specialist firms were more likely to survive in stable, and in fine-grained environments. The prediction that generalists survive better in coarse-grained environments received strong support. The results were observed only for restaurant deaths; sale rates were not responsive to these measures of environmental variation. Finally, as in most studies of organizational populations (see Carroll, 1984), newer restaurants exhibited a much higher death rate than older restaurants, a finding consistent with the alleged liability of newness.

The adaptation arguments of the resource dependence school and the selection arguments of the population ecologists are not completely incompatible and in fact can be viewed as complementary. Specifically, the population ecology approach seems to us to be particularly useful in focusing on the core features of organizations, explaining the life chances of smaller and more numerous organizations, and accounting for changes in organizational forms over longer periods. By contrast, the resource dependency approach emphasizes the more peripheral features of organizations, is better applied to larger and more powerful organizations, and stresses changes occurring over shorter periods. Let us briefly amplify each of these sources of divergence.

The population ecology approach usefully emphasizes that there are important constraints on the variability and adaptability of organizational structures. This argument applies particularly to those characteristics that are closely associated with the core technology:[10] it is here that we find the major investments in capital equipment and skilled personnel, investments not readily changed. On the other hand, the resource dependency advocates are correct in pointing out the many possibilities open to organizations in modifying their peripheral structures—their buffers and bridges. To label these structures as *peripheral* is not to regard them as superficial or of little adaptive consequence. As we have tried to argue throughout this chapter, the strategies employed by organizations to buffer and bridge can have profound effects on their chances for survival and their level of functioning. (See Chapter 10.)

The population ecology approach is more readily applied to relatively small and numerous organizations that are not individually in a position to exert much effect on their environments. (But such organizations can and do exert collective pressures through associations.) The approach has been usefully applied to the study of such organizations as newspapers, restaurants,[11] and semiconductor firms (see, for example, Carroll and Delacroix, 1982; Brittain and Freeman, 1980). Larger and more powerful organizations can be studied—for example, labor unions and trade associations (see Freeman and Brittain, 1977; Staber and Aldrich, 1983)—but this requires longer periods so that enough of the events of interest—births and deaths—can be observed. Further, the larger and more powerful the class of organizations under investigation,

---

[10]The emphasis placed by natural selection models on the core production processes of organizations is discussed in Chapter 6.

[11]Freeman and Hannan (1983) regard restaurants as the "fruit flies" of the organizational world. Since their expected life span is so brief, it is easier to observe changes in this species of organization over several "generations."

the more likely it is that they will be able to alter their environments significantly, and hence the more difficult it will be to sustain and test the argument that environments select organizational forms.

Finally, the population ecology approach is best suited to explain changes in the distribution of organizational forms over the long run—over a period of decades or centuries. For example, it is better used for explaining changes over time in the number of junior colleges in relation to other organizational forms in higher education than for explaining structural changes made by one college in reaction to some environmental challenge. The resource dependence approach is best employed to account for adaptive responses of specific organizations over a relatively short period.

Thus, we regard both points of view as valuable. However, we do take sides in the controversy to this extent: we believe that a single organization is capable of extensive structural change and elaboration over both shorter and longer periods. In our opinion, some population ecologists have overemphasized the structural rigidity or inertia of organizations. Perhaps this is because many of their general ideas and models are adapted from the work of biological ecologists. Although there are important analogies between biological and social forms, we side with the open system theorists in insisting that an important hallmark of the latter is their unusual capacity for structural modification and elaboration. Substantial portions of Chapters 9 and 10 are devoted to these significant and distinctive organizational processes.

### Adaptation of Organizational Fields

Adaptation is not the exclusive province of the individual organization, but also occurs in important ways at the level of the organizational field. Biological ecologists observe that adaptation processes may involve the behavior of isolated organisms, the behavior of populations, or more elaborate, interspecies communal responses. Similarly, human ecologists have long insisted that human communities are usefully analyzed as collective adaptative responses of differing but interdependent populations to the constraints and opportunities posed by specific environments. (See Hawley, 1950.) Ecological perspectives emphasize the more "natural" and unwitting aspects of such adaptive behavior, but network theory and related approaches stress that such collective mechanisms are also created by purposeful actors joining forces to improve the circumstances for all their constituents. Although resource dependence ideas are typically applied at the organization-set level in examinations of the adaptive capabilities of individual organizations, many of the specific strategies employed—for example, contracts, co-optation, joint ventures, and associations—involve the creation of interorganizational systems that are themselves vehicles of collective action and adaptation operating at a different level of analysis. (See Astley and Van de Ven, 1983; Astley, 1985.)

These conceptions of communal or collective adaptation have been applied most frequently to examinations of the adaptive functions of interorganizational systems in areal organizational fields, but they are also applicable to the analysis of functional organizational fields. Applications at each of these levels can be briefly reviewed.

***Areal fields***    As noted in Chapter 6, a large literature has developed on community structures as interorganizational systems. (See Laumann, Galaskiewicz, and Marsden, 1978, for a review.) An important axis around which community interests may turn is local versus extralocal dependence. Some organizational interests—local businesses, financial institutions, local media, realtors, and lawyers—are highly dependent on and greatly advantaged by community growth and have strong incentives to combine forces to forge their community into a "growth machine." (Molotch, 1976) These are the groups that are most likely to be active in and centrally connected with local interorganizational networks. (Galaskiewicz, 1979) By contrast, local plants or branch offices of national corporations headquartered elsewhere are less likely to be involved in such communal systems.

Even though non-local organizations are not strongly connected to areal systems, they can exercise great influence when and if their interests are affected. (Freidland, 1980) The power of such organizations is based not only on their economic dominance, but also on their capacity to "exit": to move out of a specific community. While "dominant and mobile actors participate less than nondominant, immobile ones" (Friedland and Palmer, 1984: 410), their influence may be exerted in less direct ways. They can apply, informal pressure on political leaders or their business associates, and they influence what is put on the agenda for decision making more than they determine what decisions are made on those matters that do reach the agenda.[12] (See Chapter 11.)

Thus, which collective interests are mobilized in areal fields such as communities will be greatly influenced by how those interests are affected by a given decision matter. Moreover, some interests may be sufficiently powerful that little or no visible mobilization or active participation is required for their influence to be felt by the other parties to the decision.

***Functional fields***    One of the most complete and persuasive studies conducted to date at this level of analysis is that of Miles (1982), who studied the response of the "Big Six" corporations in the United States tobacco industry to the threat posed by the demonstration of a causal link between smoking and impaired health. Although there was some early warning, the publication of the surgeon general's report linking smoking and cancer and subsequent actions taken by various federal agencies constituted a major environmental crisis for these organizations. Although each corporation adopted a variety of strategies ranging from product innovation to diversification, they also engaged in collective action. For example, during the first signs of trouble, they created the Tobacco Industry Research Committee to conduct their own studies of the effects of tobacco use. Following the surgeon general's report, they collectively engaged in a wide variety of lobbying efforts, providing cancer-research grants to the American Medical Association and various universities and

---

[12]Preventing issues or questions from being raised and shaping the agenda of decision making have been identified as important, albeit difficult-to-investigate, modes of power. These types of power have been variously labeled *structural* and *systemic*, and this area of inquiry has been termed the study of *nondecisions*. (See Bachrach and Baratz, 1962; Alford and Friedland, 1975.)

monitoring closely and attempting to influence legislative and administrative actions affecting their interests.

Numerous studies have been conducted of the extent to which organizational fields within particular industries or societal sectors have developed networks or structures to support collective action. For example, Hirsch (1975) has contrasted the relatively successful efforts of companies within the pharmaceutical industry to organize to protect their interests with the much less successful activities of firms within the record industry. Although the two industries are somewhat similar in their level of technical development, reliance on batch processing, and dependence on external gatekeepers (physicians and disc jockeys) to mediate between themselves and their customers, pharmaceutical firms have been much more successful in obtaining legislation protecting brand-name drugs, in securing patent protections, and in co-opting physician groups in support of their interests. By contrast, record companies have been unable to obtain much collective control over pricing or distribution, have not secured exclusive copyright protections, and have not been able to co-opt disc jockeys to represent their interests. (The payola scandals of the 1950s and mid 1980s—attempts by record companies to bribe the staffs of radio stations—represent a notably crass and unsuccessful attempt to secure disc jockeys' loyalties.) It is not clear why pharmaceutical firms have been more successful in their collective efforts than record companies, but it is obvious that the degree of success associated with collective action by organizations within the same field can greatly affect the environment confronting each firm.

Although the results remain inconclusive, there have been a large number of studies of the extent to which private organizations are linked into networks of collective assistance that span industries or sectors. As we have already noted many of these connections are intraorganizational, involving the acquisition of many formerly independent firms and/or merger with these firms into vertically integrated or functionally diversified corporations. (We will consider these connections further in Chapter 10.) But other connections entail varying types of bridges among formally independent units that join forces to secure mutual benefits. There is disagreement over what interests are being served by such arrangements. Marxist theorists tend to emphasize class-based interests, focusing on connections among the elite families controlling major corporations, who utilize a variety of social networks—connections developed in elite colleges, corporate boards, and social clubs—to orchestrate and facilitate the safeguarding of their class advantages. (See Domhoff, 1983; Useem, 1980.) Other analysts point out that with the increasing separation of ownership from control rights in corporations, managerial interests—which emphasize the importance of organizational growth and security, rather than profits—are more likely to serve as the criteria by which interorganizational alliances are formed. Whether ownership has effectively been disconnected from control is, however, much in dispute (see Zeitlin, 1974), and whether managers pursue interests different from those of owners has not been established (see Pfeffer, 1982).

Although there is little doubt that complex adaptive patterns that connect corporate organizations into complex networks or systems have developed in more advanced economic systems—Marxists would describe these patterns as being characteristic of "late," or monopoly capitalist, systems—the specific features and functions of these arrangements remain in dispute. For example, whereas Scott (1979) has emphasized the ways in which interlocking directorates support information exchanges necessary for coordinating action, Palmer (1983) has noted that a high proportion (85 percent) of interlocks that accidentally broke—due to the death, retirement, or transfer of the incumbent—were not reconstituted, suggesting that such ties were not crucial to the corporation so linked. And there is controversy over whether banks and other financial institutions play a special role in connecting and controlling other types of organizations. Although the ownership by these institutions of large blocks of corporate stock is patent, their exercise of control over the firms whose stock they purchase has not been established. (See Mintz and Schwartz, 1983.) In this area, the hypotheses and questions seem to multiply more rapidly than the facts and findings. (See Glasberg and Schwartz, 1983; Mizruchi and Schwartz, 1986.)

Other analysts have examined the changing nature of functional fields in public service arenas. A number of observers have argued that there has been a growing trend toward "sectoralization," with services being defined in limited, functionally differentiated terms—for example, housing, employment, child care, and mental health (see Wildavsky, 1979). Employing network-analysis techniques, Laumann and colleagues (Knoke and Laumann, 1982; Laumann, Knoke, and Kim, 1985) have examined the ways in which shifting populations of public and private organizations become active in the setting of national policy in the sectors of health and energy. The boundaries of such interorganizational policymaking systems are vague, with participation being determined by interest in the issue (domain), capacity to mobilize relevant resources—such as staff, funds, and expertise—and centrality of location in the system.

Once policies are formulated, a different network of organizations—again spanning both the public and private sectors—is often constructed to link federal, state, and local agencies into a complex decision-making and implementation system. Meyer and I (Meyer and Scott, 1983) have argued that such networks in this country are likely to exhibit relatively high centralization of financial or funding decisions combined with more decentralized programmatic decision making. This is particularly the case for the more professionalized service sectors, such as health care and education. In such organizational fields, vertical controls among organizations are likely to be exercised primarily by financial officers and accountants.

> Rather than the development of a centralized hierarchical structure stretching from local delivery systems through regional and state agencies to a central federal agency, we have the burgeoning of accounting departments and fiscal units responsible for mediating the funding and reporting relations between delivery systems and funding sources. The controls exercised are indirect rather than direct, specifying what services will be reimbursed— not what services will be offered. (Meyer and Scott, 1983: 104)

Sectoral structuring of organizational services represents an attempt to create a coherent, rational system for implementing public policies in a specialized arena. In the case of the United States, two problems in the operation of these organizational fields have received considerable attention. First, it is argued that the interorganizational systems that are created for the purposes of policy making and implementation operate too independently from one another—that although policies are devised as though they will be implemented in insulated areas, there are inevitably important interdependencies in outcomes. Programs devised to subsidize rapid transit in cities interact with programs for renewing neighborhoods and improving housing. The current call by governmental reformers is for greater attention to the coordination of programs across sectors. (See Sundquist, 1969; Rogers and Whetten, 1982.) Although this may be partly a matter of simply designing better incentives for interagency cooperation and developing better ˙mechanisms to bridge organizations, it is also partly an issue of how to reconcile the two somewhat competing bases of structuring organizational fields that we have identified. Some actors are attempting to rationalize a functional field, to design an interorganizational system that will support the implementation of a specific program in many different areas; other actors are struggling to articulate many different functional programs that converge in complex and unexpected ways to affect a single territory. The two attempts at rationalization may conflict, since what is viewed as rational will depend on how the boundaries of the system are defined. (See Scott, 1985a.) On the other hand, we should not be too quick to assume that rational design is the name of the game.

Benson (1982: 170) suggests that a different game is being played. He regards the problem of inadequate coordination as signifying the more general problem of "interorganizational feudalism" and suggests that its basis is to be found in the historic weakness of central governmental structures in the United States, which are largely incapable of overcoming the vested private interests that tend to dominate outcomes in most societal sectors. This is the second major criticism leveled at organizational systems created to implement public programs. Benson argues that these organizational fields are shaped by existing structures of interest and power that importantly influence and constrain policy goals and programs. Similar to the analyses of Lowi (1969), Lindblom (1977), and Wolfe (1977), Benson asserts that in a large number of arenas in this country, public authorities have been willing to collaborate with private interests, not only by giving them access to public resources and allowing them to exert influence on public decision makers but also by bestowing on them varying degrees of public authority. Private interests are alleged to dominate and undermine attention to the public good.

The examination of the bases around which organizational fields or sectors are organized thus leads us directly to the organization of the nation-state. One does not have to be a Marxist—although Marxist theorists have been at the forefront of this work—to recognize the important role played by the nation-state. (See Bright and Harding, 1984; Krasner, 1984; Skowronek, 1982.) While the power of the state is general and affects the structure of all organizational fields, its influence varies from sector to sector, and differing societies vary in their capacity to exercise influence in one or another domain.

A number of modern nation-states have moved far in the direction

of articulating the connections between public agencies and private interests into a relatively tight and consciously directed system known as
*corporatism.*

> Corporatism can be defined as a system of interest representation in which
> the constituent units are organized into a limited number of singular, com-
> pulsory, noncompetitive, hierarchically ordered and functionally differenti-
> ated categories, recognized or licensed (if not created) by the state and
> granted a deliberate representational monopoly within their respective cate-
> gories in exchange for observing certain controls on their selection of
> leaders and articulation of demands and supports (Schmitter, 1974: 93–94).

Two types are identified. The first, *societal* corporatism, is one in which
private interests in a given sector have gradually become more singular,
noncompetitive, and hierarchically organized so that specific, centrally
located organizations gain the legitimacy to represent the interests of their
"constituency" in negotiations with the state. Trade associations often perform this function. (See Staber, 1985) The societal type of corporatism is
best exemplified in Sweden, Switzerland, the Netherlands, Norway and
Denmark, and, to a lesser extent, Great Britain, West Germany, France,
Canada, and the United States. (See Berger, 1981.) The second type, *state*
corporatism, involves a much more active role on the part of the state:
sectors are defined and representatives created or selected by state decree. This pattern is currently to be found primarily in "Iberian" countries such as Portugal, Spain, Brazil, Chile, Peru, Mexico, and Greece,
and, in the past, in such totalitarian regimes as fascist Italy and Nazi
Germany. (Schmitter, 1974: 102–4)

Although the U.S. state is widely acknowledged to be relatively
"weak" as a formal, administrative system of rights and powers (see Huntington, 1966), it is important to insist that this weak state resides within a
strong and active *polity.* There has long existed a larger set of political and
cultural institutions that locates a substantial portion of legitimate public
authority in bodies formally outside of the state. The weakness of the
state is offset by the strength of the society. (See Thomas and Meyer,
1984.) And it is this rich institutional environment that has given rise to
much of the variety and complexity of the organizational fields that have
arisen in United States society.

Thus, a rapid and fruitful convergence is occurring between the
long-standing but recently reinvigorated interests of political scientists in
the structure of the nation-state and the interests of organizational theorists in the structure of organizational fields. (See DiMaggio and Powell,
1983; Meyer and Scott, 1983; Olsen, 1983; Evans, Rueschemeyer, and
Skocpol, 1986.) While from one point of the view the two subjects are
causally interdependent, from another they are but two sides of the same
complex societal system.

## SUMMARY

At one and the same time, organizations must be open to their environments and attentive to their boundaries. This poses an intricate problem

with respect to the recruitment of participants. Organizations require some control over the criteria by which individuals are admitted and rewarded, and in some extreme cases organizations hold sufficient power to eliminate participant characteristics or identities that are based on their involvement in other social systems. In the more usual case, however, an organization has neither the power nor the desire to eliminate such identities, which can be put to use by the organization. How to mobilize these characteristics in the service of organizational goals while preventing participants from using organizational resources in the service of other goals is a continuing challenge for managers of all organizations.

To varying degrees, organizations try to internalize labor market processes exerting a major effect on individuals' mobility chances—determining what positions are to be filled, what positions are open to entry from outside, what linkages exist among positions, and how individuals are selected or positions.

Two broad classes of strategies have been identified by which organizations relate to their task environments. Organizations employ buffering techniques—coding, stockpiling, leveling, forecasting, and growth—to seal off their technical core from environmental disturbances. They use bridging techniques—bargaining, contracting, co-optation, joint ventures, mergers, associations, and governmental connections—to increase the number and variety of their linkages with competitors and exchange partners and thereby enhance their security in technical environments. Other types of bridging strategies—categorical, structural, procedural, and personnel conformity—are employed in securing legitimacy and support in institutional environments. Analysis of such strategies is most readily conducted at the level of the organization set and presumes that the managers of an organization can fashion its activities so as to enhance its security or effectiveness. This assumption is challenged by analysts working at the population level, who emphasize the inertia of organizational behavior and insist that most change occurs because of natural selection—the differential survival of different organizational types—rather than rational selection—conscious design by organizational managers.

Adaptation occurs not only at the level of the individual organization but also at the communal level: within areal and functional fields. Both adaptation and selection approaches—which are addressed to different levels, time periods, and types of organizations—appear useful for examining organization-environment interdependencies.

# sources of structural complexity: the technical core

9

> Every organized human activity—from the making of pots to the placing of a man on the moon—gives rise to two fundamental and opposing requirements: the *division of labor* into various tasks to be performed, and the *coordination* of these tasks to accomplish the activity. The structure of an organization can be defined simply as the sum total of the ways in which it divides its labor into distinct tasks and then achieves coordination among them.
>
> Henry Mintzberg (1979)

Whether by natural or rational selection—by evolution or learning—organizations tend to move toward higher levels of complexity. This thesis will be amplified at two levels. First, in this chapter we examine the sources of structural complexity that develop within the technical core of an organization. The prime source of core complexity is the nature of the work being carried out—the demands made by the technology on the structure. Second, in Chapter 10 we consider the sources of structural complexity that occur outside the technical core, in the peripheral sectors of the organization, including the managerial and institutional levels. These structures respond in particular to demands posed by the size or scale of the organization and to the task and institutional environments. At the conclusion of Chapter 10 we examine the relation between the core and peripheral structures.

The structural features of organizations that are of primary interest are those defining the division of labor—structural differentiation, including occupational and role specialization, departmentalization, and multi-divisional forms—and those relating to coordination and control of work—formalization, hierarchy, centralization, and various structures for facilitating lateral information flows.

Contingency theory provides the primary orienting framework for the topics addressed in this chapter. As described in Chapter 4, this approach insists that there is no single best way in which to design the structure of an organization. Rather, what is the best or most appropriate structure depends—is contingent—on what type of work is being performed and on what environmental demands or conditions confront the organization. Lawrence and Lorsch and Jay Galbraith utilize a rational open perspective and stress formalized responses to task complexity. Other theorists, such as the Tavistock group, Burns and Stalker, Cole, and Ouchi, assume a natural open system perspective and emphasize the value of more diffuse and informal control systems. Both groups will inform our attempts to account for the complexity of the technical core.

To the extent possible, organizations attempt to seal off their technical core from environmental disturbances. This central proposition developed by Thompson (1967) helps to account for the defensive behavior of many types of organizations. The specific strategies devised by organizations to buffer their technical core were reviewed in the previous chapter. But what if the buffers are inadequate and uncertainty penetrates the technical core? As organizations take on more complex and unpredictable tasks, we cannot assume that all traces of uncertainty will be buffered out of the core. How can the structure of the technical core be modified so as to accommodate more demanding tasks? To address this question, we need to develop a clearer conception of how to define and measure the work performed in the technical core.

## DEFINING AND MEASURING TECHNOLOGY

As we pointed out in Chapter 1, *technology* is the term that has come to refer to the work performed by an organization.[1] This concept is broadly defined by organization theorists and includes not only the hardware used in performing work but also the skills and knowledge of workers, and even the characteristics of the objects on which work is performed. We must acknowledge at the outset that there is considerable overlap between *technology, task environment,* and *environment* as these terms are employed by organizational analysts. *Environment* is the more inclusive term and incorporates political, technological, and institutional aspects of the organizational context. *Task environment* emphasizes those features of the environment relevant to its supply of inputs and its disposition of outputs but also includes the power-dependence relations within which the organization must make its exchanges. *Technology,* as defined above, is the more restricted term. However, it is important to emphasize the extent to which an organization's technology—although an "internal" element—links the organization to its environment: the environment not only is the source of inputs and the recipient of outputs but also is the major source of the work techniques and tools employed by the organization. Most organizations do not themselves invent their technologies but import them from the environment. Also, given the degree of overlap between the concepts of technology and environment, it should not surprise us to find many of the same analytical dimensions being used by analysts to identify their relevant features.

Earlier students of industrial and organizational sociology have noted the impact of technical and production features of the work process on worker behavior and work group structure (for example, Sayles, 1958;

---

[1]The following discussion draws on my description (Scott, 1975) of the characteristics of technology and the relation between technology and structure.

Trist and Bamforth, 1951; Walker and Guest, 1952; Whyte, 1948). But it was the empirical research of Woodward (1958; 1965) and a theoretical article by Thompson and Bates (1957) that first called attention to technology as a general determinant of organizational structure. Woodward's conception of technology as applied to industrial organizations was broadened and generalized by Thompson (Thompson and Bates, 1957; Thompson, 1967), by Litwak (1961), and by Perrow (1967; 1970) so as to be applicable to all types of organizations.

An examination of the many recent attempts to define and measure technology indicates that the concept has been viewed very broadly to include (1) the characteristics of the *inputs* utilized by the organization; (2) the characteristics of the *transformation processes* employed by the organization; and (3) the characteristics of the *outputs* of the organization.[2] Alongside this view of technologies varying by stage of processing, Hickson, Pugh, and Pheysey (1969) point out that approaches to technology vary by whether analysts emphasize (1) the *materials* on which work is performed, (2) the *operations* or techniques used to perform the work, or (3) the state of *knowledge* that underlies the transformation process. If these two sets of distinctions are cross-classified, they allow us to both categorize and summarize many of the specific measures that have been employed to assess organizational technologies. The classification together with illustrative measures appears in Table 9–1.

Although a great many specific measures of technology have been generated, we believe that it is possible to identify three general underlying dimensions that encompass most of the more specific measures and, more to the point, isolate the most critical variables needed to predict structural features of organizations.[3] These three dimensions are complexity or diversity, uncertainty or unpredictability, and interdependence. We will discuss each briefly.

**Complexity or diversity**   This dimension refers to the number of different items or elements that must be dealt with simultaneously by the organization. Specific measures such as multiplicity and customization of outputs and variety of inputs tap this dimension.

**Uncertainty or unpredictability**   This dimension refers to the variability of the items or elements upon which work is performed or to the extent to which it is possible to predict their behavior in advance. Some of the general factors affecting the degree of uncertainty of the organiza-

[2]A large number of output measures have been developed by the Aston group—a team of researchers working at the University of Aston in Birmingham, England (see Pugh et al., 1969: 99–102). These researchers regard their measures as relating to the concept of *charter*—the social function or goals of an organization—rather than to an organization's technology. In fact, though, many of the measures relate to the characteristics of outputs—for example, multiplicity of products and degree of customization—and so from our point of view are appropriate measures of technology.

[3]The stage-of-processing distinction illustrated in Table 9–1 is also useful for predicting structural features since it indicates *where* in the technical core work-processing demands are likely to be heavier. Input units that must deal with a large amount of uncertainty will be structured differently than input units that handle only a small amount of uncertainty.

**TABLE 9–1.  Classification of Technology Measures.** *Source:* Scott (1975), pp. 5–6.

| FACETS OF TECHNOLOGY | STAGE OF PROCESSING | | |
| --- | --- | --- | --- |
| | *Inputs* | *Throughputs* | *Outputs* |
| *Materials* | Uniformity of inputs (Litwak, 1961) Hardness of materials (Rushing, 1968) Variability of stimuli (Perrow, 1970) | Number of exceptions (Perrow, 1970; Lynch, 1974) Interchangeability of components (Rackham and Woodward, 1970) | Major project changes (Harvey, 1968) Multiplicity of outputs (Pugh et al.1969) Customization of outputs (Pugh et al., 1969) |
| *Operations* | Preprocessing, coding, smoothing of inputs (Thompson, 1967) | Complexity of technical processes (Udy, 1959b; Woodward, 1965) Work-flow integration (Pugh et al., 1969) Routiness of work (Hage and Aiken, 1969) Automaticity of machinery (Amber and Amber, 1962) Interdependence of work units (Thompson, 1967; Lynch, 1974) | Control of outputs through stockpiling, rationing (Thompson, 1967) Value added in manufacture |
| *Knowledge* | Predictability (Dornbusch and Scott, 1975) Anticipation of fluctuations in supplies (Thompson, 1967) | Knowledge of cause-effect relations (Thompson, 1967) Analyzability of search processes (Perrow, 1970; Van de Ven and Delbecq, 1974) Information required to perform task compared with information possessed (Galbraith, 1973) | Time span of definitive feedback (Lawrence and Lorsch, 1967) Anticipation of fluctuations in demand (Thompson, 1967) |

tion's task environment described in Chapter 6 are also relevant here. Specific measures of uncertainty include uniformity or variability of inputs, the number of exceptions encountered in the work process, and the number of major product changes experienced.

**Interdependence**   This dimension refers to the extent to which the items or elements upon which work is performed or the work processes themselves are interrelated so that changes in the state of one element affect the state of the others. Thompson (1967: 54–55) has proposed a useful typology for assessing degree of interdependence. Three levels are identified: (1) *pooled* interdependence, in which the work performed is interrelated only in that each element or process contributes to the overall goal (for example, selecting fabrics and color schemes for the inside decor of a jet airplane is related to the plane's aerodynamic design only in that both contribute to the overall objective or final product); (2) *sequential* interdependence, which exists when some activities must be performed before others (for example, component parts of a jet engine must be produced before they all can be assembled into a single functioning unit); and (3) *reciprocal* interdependence, which is present to the degree that elements or activities relate to each other as both inputs and outputs (for example, design decisions regarding the weight and thrust of a jet engine and the aerodynamic design of the fuselage and wings must take each other into account). Thompson points out that these three levels of interdependence form a Guttman-type scale, in that elements or processes that are reciprocally interdependent also exhibit sequential and pooled interdependence, and processes that are sequentially interdependent also exhibit pooled interdependence.

As indicated, these dimensions are of interest because they can be employed to predict the structural features of organizations.


## TECHNOLOGY AND FORMAL STRUCTURE

Since matters can rapidly become complicated, we will state at the outset the major linkages that are expected to exist between an organization's technology and its structure. In noting these main effects, we recognize that the interaction effects—the effects produced by two or more of the variables in combination—are more powerful and frequently of greater interest. The predictions are as follows:

1.  The greater the technical complexity, the greater the structural complexity. The structural response to technical diversity is organizational differentiation.

2.  The greater the technical uncertainty, the less formalization and centralization.

3.  The greater the technical interdependence, the more resources must be devoted to coordination. More specifically, Thompson (1967: 55–56) argues that pooled interdependence can be managed by *standardization*, the development of rules or routines; sequential interdependence requires the development of *plans* or *schedules*, which specify timing and order in the work processes; and reciprocal interdependence requires the use of *mutual adjust-*

*ment* or coordination by feedback, in which the interrelated parties must communicate their own requirements and respond to the needs of each other. Each coordination strategy is increasingly costly in terms of resources.

## Coordination Mechanisms

Galbraith (1973; 1977) has usefully argued that one way in which the varying demands of technologies on structures can be summarized is to ask how much information must be processed during the execution of a task sequence. He argues that information requirements increase as a function of increasing diversity, uncertainty, and interdependence of work flows. Using this simple formula to gauge information-processing demands, Galbraith then outlines a series of structural modifications organizations can make in their technical core as a means of adapting to increased demands for the processing of information. The following formal structures, discussed in order of increasing complexity, may be employed to manage the work flow.

***Rules and programs*** Organizations performing the simplest and most routine tasks rely primarily on rules and performance programs to secure acceptable outcomes. And, of course, organizations carrying on even the most complex types of work perform many activities that can be regulated by rules and programs. These structural devices represent agreements about how decisions are to be made or work is to be processed that predate the work performance itself. They can be made to handle considerable complexity and some uncertainty, particularly as regards the sequence of events. For example, it is possible to develop rules for carrying out specific task activities and to add "switching rules" that signal which of several clusters of activities is to be performed or the order of their performance (see March and Simon, 1958: 142–50).

***Schedules*** Schedules are necessary when different kinds of activities are to be carried on in the same location or when sequential interdependence is present. To information concerning the what and how of task performance, schedules add the dimension of when. Schedules also specify the period they are in force, and so are subject to modification. Galbraith suggests that increasing uncertainty can be handled by shortening the *plan-replan cycle*—that is, the period during which a given set of rules and schedules is in force.

***Departmentalization*** One of the most difficult and critical of all decisions facing organization is how work is to be divided: what tasks are to be assigned to what roles and what roles to departments. As described in Chapter 2, early administrative theorists suggested that homogeneous activities be placed in the same organizational units, but critics noted that there are often several, competing bases for determining homogeneity (see March and Simon, 1958: 22–32). Thompson (1967: 57) has proposed that organizations will seek to group tasks according to their degree of interdependence, with reciprocally related tasks placed in the same or closely adjacent units, sequentially related tasks placed in less closely adjacent units, and tasks exhibiting pooled interdependence placed in the least closely adjacent units. Organizations are expected to behave in this manner because the type of coordination mechanism needed to cope with reciprocal tasks—mutual adjustment—is the most costly in terms of organizational resources; schedules, which are used to cope with sequential tasks, are the next most costly; and rules are the least costly. In short, Thompson argues that organizations attempt to group tasks so as to minimize coordination costs. It is instructive to note that Thompson's principle of minimizing coordination costs as an explanation for the location of departmental boundaries can be viewed as a special case of Williamson's (1975) principle of minimizing transactions costs as an explanation for the location of organizational boundaries (see Chapter 7).[4]

**Hierarchy**    Hierarchy can be used to respond to increased information flows in two ways. First, as Fayol and other administrative theorists emphasized early in this century (see Chapter 2), officials can be used to deal with unexpected or irregular occurrences on an "exception" basis. Of course, this practice can provide a satisfactory solution only if the exceptions do not arise too frequently. Second, as suggested by open system theorists (see Chapter 4), hierarchies can be used to group tasks (Simon, 1962). According to Thompson (1967: 59);

> it is unfortunate that [hierarchy] has come to stand almost exclusively for degrees of highness or lowness, for this tends to hide the basic significance of hierarchy for complex organizations. Each level is not simply higher than the one below, but is a more inclusive clustering, or combination of interdependent groups, to handle those aspects of coordination which are beyond the scope of any of its components.

As the amount of interdependence among organizational tasks increases, it becomes more difficult to handle it by departmentalization—to contain, for example, all of the instances of reciprocal interdependence within an organizational unit. As interdependence overflows departmental units, a heavier burden of information processing is placed on hierarchical officers who are expected to provide links across units. For example, consider a manufacturing firm that begins to perform more customized work, fitting the product to the customer's particular requirements. We would expect the interdependence between the sales and the production departments to increase and to be reflected in higher levels of information to be processed during task performance: for example, specifications of desired products, information about cost and feasibility, and requirements for and predictions concerning delivery date. Under these circumstances, we would expect the sales and production units to be clustered under a common superior, who would facilitate the flow of information between the two as a means of coordinating their work.

---

[4]Williamson's concept of transactions costs is broader than Thompson's concept of coordination costs because it includes the costs of negotiations between prospective exchange partners as well as the negotiations needed to coordinate exchanges once an agreement has been established. Within most organizations the former negotiations do not occur: one department is not allowed to determine whether or not to enter into exchanges with another unit in the same organization. However, in some very large organizations an attempt is made to simulate a market situation, and departments are allowed to decide whether to enter into exchange agreements with other internal units or to seek more favorable exchange rates externally.

*Delegation*   Rather than attempting to program and regulate closely the work of all participants and requiring that all decisions be made above the level of the performers, organizations confronting increased complexity and uncertainty can delegate some autonomy to workers. Galbraith (1973) refers to this arrangement as *targeting* or *goal setting*, indicating that coordination is secured not by minute descriptions of work procedures but by specification of the desired outcomes. In the example of the manufacturing firm performing more customized work, a manager could provide the production department with a detailed specification of the desired product together with cost and time constraints but allow participants to exercise their own judgment and skills in arriving at a product that would satisfy these requirements. Delegation is present to some extent and for some positions in most organizations. However, it reaches its most highly developed form in professional organizations, a form to be discussed more fully later in this chapter.

## Reducing Information versus Increasing Capacity

Rules and programs, schedules, departmentalization, hierarchy, and some delegation: these are the ubiquitous features of complex formal organizations. By means of these conventional structural mechanisms, organizations are able to respond to task demands posing moderate information-processing requirements. But what if the levels of diversity, uncertainty, and interdependence are higher still so that conventional solutions prove inadequate? Galbraith argues that an organization confronting excessive levels of task complexity and uncertainty can choose one of two general responses: it may elect to (1) "reduce the amount of information that is processed," or (2) "increase its capacity to handle more information" (1973: 15). Although these two responses push in different directions, they are not necessarily incompatible. Moreover, each response may be made through one of several strategies, and an organization may pursue more than one strategy at the same time. Strategies designed to reduce information processing are described first.

*Slack resources*   An organization can reduce its information-processing demands simply by reducing the required level of performance (see Galbraith, 1973). Higher performance standards increase the need for coordination; lowered standards create slack—unused resources—which provides some ease in the system. For example, if delivery deadlines are not set so as to challenge the production units, then the need for information processing is reduced. If there are few constraints on inventory levels, then rapid response to changes in supply and demand messages is less essential. And, to use a nonmanufacturing example, if every third-grade teacher uses the first several weeks to reteach the basic lessons and skills of the second grade, then the sequential interdependence between second- and third-grade teachers is reduced, and there is less need for coordination of their efforts.

In addition to storing extra components and introducing redundancy into task performances, an organization can store surplus task or work-flow information. In his study of the complex structures that supply repair services for the electronic equipment required to support the

U.S. Naval Air Systems Command, Kmetz (1984: 272) details the use of *information buffers*—"pools or collections of information formed to support decision making or monitoring of workflow variables." At critical junctures in the repair process, varying types of information—samples of data, knowledge of legitimate and unsanctioned routines, backup guides and records—develop as alternatives to or supports for the official communications and data packages. For example, "a relatively formalized buffer, such as a workaround notebook, supports repair of a WRA [weapon replaceable assembly] independently of the accuracy of the test program" (1984: 273). Such slack resources allow looser coupling of interdependent work systems.

Some slack in the handling of resources, including information, is not only inevitable but essential to smooth operations. All operations require a margin of error—an allowance for mistakes, waste, spoilage, and similar unavoidable accompaniments of work. The question is not whether there is to be slack but how much slack is to be permitted. Excessive slack resources increase costs for the organization that are likely to be passed on to the consumer. Since creating slack resources is a relatively easy and painless solution available to organizations, whether or not it is employed is likely to be determined by the amount of competition confronting the organization in its task environment.

**Product versus process organization**   We have noted that information-processing costs can be reduced by placing highly interdependent tasks in the same or adjacent work units. This principle underlies the creation of product-based departments. For example, a publishing organization may begin with a departmental structure based on function or process criteria: editorial, production, and marketing divisions. Suppose that two product lines develop: college texts and *trade* (commercial bookstore) publications. At some point, the costs of attempting to handle the information that must accompany these quite different types of products across the three divisions may become sufficiently high that the company decides to reorganize on a product basis. Now we have two divisions: text and trade, each with its own departments of design, production, and marketing. The diversity of information processing required by the former structure has been substantially reduced by a shift from process to product organization.

The costs accompanying the use of product departments are primarily those associated with the loss of economies of scale. The scale of each unit has been reduced, and this may prevent the use of specialized personnel or machinery that can be supported only by a large volume of work. Product-based organization also reduces the likelihood that the benefits of variety—stimulation, transfer of learning, overlap of domains—will be available to enrich the organization or its participants.

The remaining strategies are intended to increase the information-processing capacity of the organization. We describe here only the more formalized strategies—those that rely on the explicit design of new roles and relations to process heightened information flows.

**Augmented hierarchies**   Many analysts have observed that although hierarchies can assist the coordination of work by imposing patterns and constraints on the flow of information, if the messages sent become too numerous or the content too rich, a hierarchical system can quickly become overloaded (see Chapter 7; see also Guetzkow, 1965; Rogers and Agarwala-Rogers, 1976). The capacity of the hierarchical system can be increased in two ways. The first is to improve the methods by which information is gathered and transmitted to the decision-making centers. In earlier times, and at the present time for many functions, this is accomplished by adding specialized administrative and clerical personnel— inspectors, accountants, secretaries—charged with gathering and summarizing the information needed for decision making. More recently, some of these functions have been taken over by increasingly sophisticated electronic monitoring, transmission, and data-reduction systems. The design of systems that will permit the rapid transmission of relevant, "on-line" information through feedback loops to appropriate decision centers is one of the major aims and achievements of the modern systems-design movement (see Simon, 1960; Myers, 1967; House, 1971).

The second method for increasing a hierarchical system's capacity to process information is to work not on the receptors or the transmitters but on the decision centers, the nodes of the system. One of the earliest and most widely used structural modifications of the simple hierarchy—the creation of the staff-line distinction—may be viewed as a means of increasing the information-processing and problem-solving capacity of the system without formally decentralizing or sacrificing the unity-of-command principle. Staff "experts" give technical assistance and specialized advice to the generalist managers who are empowered to make the final decision. However, we know from a large number of studies that although the staff-line distinction may preserve the appearance of a unified command system, much actual power passes from the hands of line officers to staff associates (see Dalton, 1959; Goldner, 1970). In addition to these staff-line arrangements, the modern executive is likely to be supported not only by technical specialists but also by a variety of "assistants," "assistants-to," and "associates" who perform stable or shifting duties but always act on behalf of and subject to the approval of their superiors. All, however, contribute to the capacity of the system to process information.

The new generation of microcomputers can affect both the collection of information and the transmission, processing, and analysis of it. There are conflicting predictions and evidence regarding the impact of this new technology on the centralization of decision making and on participant skill levels. (See Whisler, 1970; Zimbalist, 1979; Giuliano, 1982)

**Lateral connections**  Consider the following situation. An aircraft company has reorganized, grouping workers within divisions by product, and one of the divisions is responsible for the development and testing of new types of jet engines. The departments have been created on a functional basis: there is a department housing the scientists and engineers responsible for design, a production department composed of the mechanical engineers and technicians responsible for building prototype engines, and a department of scientists and engineers responsible for evaluating and testing the models. Clearly this situation involves high levels of task complexity, uncertainty, and interdependence and will require the exchange of large amounts of information as the work is carried on. In a normal hierarchical structure, the communications required to coordinate performance among departments would be expected to flow up the chain of command from workers through supervisors to departmental managers. The managers would be expected to exchange information among themselves and with the division manager, arrive at a comon definition of how the work was to proceed, and then communicate detailed instructions back down the hierarchies within each department. Given the extent of interdependence and the amount of information to be processed, such a process would entail long delays and great inefficiencies.

In situations of such heavy information flow, the development of more direct, lateral connections across work groups and departments is an obvious response. That is, lateral connections allow information to flow more directly among participants in interdependent departments or work groups, rather than up and over through hierarchical channels. Although the opening of such channels may seem both simple and obvious, it represents an organizational revolution! Informal communications and arrangements among interdependent workers exist in virtually all organizations and undoubtedly often save them from floundering because of inadequacies of the vertical channels. But we are dealing here not with informal but formal structures: we are discussing the official legitimation of connections among workers across departmental boundaries. To permit such developments is to undermine the hierarchical structure: department heads are no longer fully in control of, and so cannot be held fully accountable for, the behavior of their subordinates. This is why organizations—even organizations facing fairly high degrees of uncertainty and interdependence—are reluctant to develop formal lateral connections. But if they decide to do so, they may choose among several mechanisms (see Galbraith, 1973; 1977), including the following.

## •LIAISON ROLES

Liaison roles are specialized positions or units created to facilitate interchange between two or more interdependent departments. The responsibilities of such integrating roles may include troubleshooting, conflict resolution, and anticipation of problems. These positions are similar to staff roles except that they relate to two or more managers rather than to one. Lawrence and Lorsch (1967) examine the functions of such positions in organizations and discuss the characteristics of those individuals who fill them successfully. Their work is discussed more fully in Chapter 10. Note that the creation of liaison roles makes for a more complex management structure but does not undermine the hierarchical principle.

## •TASK FORCES

A task force is by definition a temporary group that is given a delimited problem to solve. The expectation is that the group will be dissolved once its work is completed. The task force may involve its members full or part time. Participants are drawn from several departments, and frequently from several levels, and are selected not only because of their interest or ability with respect to the work of the task force but also because of their stature in their own departments. In the case of the jet engine division, a task force involving representatives from all three departments might be created to codify the technical terms and symbols used by members of that division. The strength of the task force is that it allows multiple representatives to interact intensively over a short period to achieve a specific objective. Status distinctions that hinder free interaction are typically suspended during the group's existence. That such distinctions are present but ignored contributes to the special atmosphere of a task force (see Miles, 1964).[5] Because the task force is defined as temporary, its existence is compatible with the maintenance of the hierarchy. Indeed, task forces may function as safety valves, reducing tensions and solving problems generated by the continuation of the hierarchy.

### •PROJECT TEAMS

Whereas task forces are temporary systems created to solve nonrecurring problems, project teams are groupings of personnel across departmental lines that carry on some portion of the regular work of the organization. In the jet engine example, a team comprising several members from each department could be built around the design and testing of a highly experimental prototype engine. Members would be released from their regular duties over an extended period in order to better contribute to this effort. The typical project team would have a leader or manager responsible for planning and coordinating the work of the team as long as it performed as a unit. Departmental officers would, in effect, delegate authority to the project manager to act on their behalf during the project but would see to it that their own personnel were being used and treated appropriately.

### •MATRIX STRUCTURES

The hallmark of the matrix is its multiple command structure: vertical and lateral channels of information and authority operate simultaneously. The ancient and sacred principle of unity of command is set aside, and competing bases of authority are allowed to jointly govern the work flow. The vertical lines are typically those of functional departments that operate as "home bases" for all participants; the lateral lines represent project groups or geographical arenas where managers combine and coordinate the services of the functional specialists around particular projects or areas. (See Davis and Lawrence, 1977; Hill and White, 1979.) This type of structure is illustrated in Figure 9–1, which depicts the formal structure of the rocket division of a space agency.

---

[5]A particularly interesting and dramatic example is provided by President Kennedy's creation of a task force—the Excom, composed of trusted advisers and associates—to make recommendations to him on the course of action to be pursued during the Cuban missile crisis of 1962. The best account of this group's structure and deliberations is provided by the president's brother, Robert Kennedy (1969).

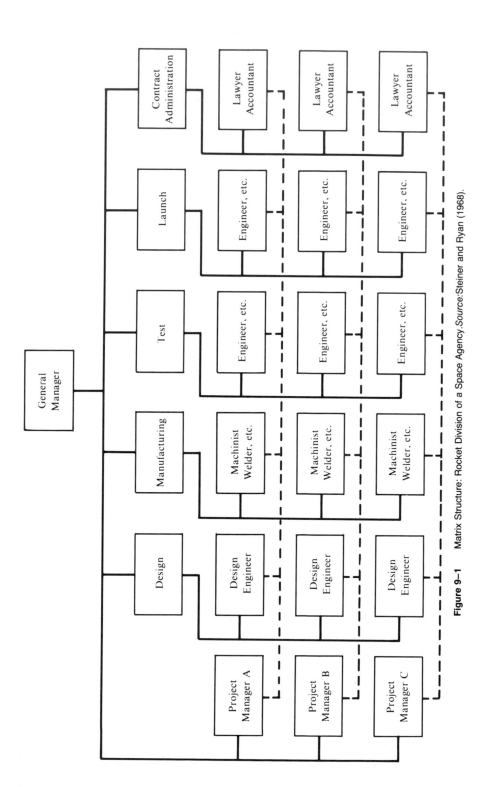

**Figure 9—1**   Matrix Structure: Rocket Division of a Space Agency. *Source:* Steiner and Ryan (1968).

The constituent units of matrix structures may be relatively permanent or shifting (Sayles, 1976). The permanent matrix structure is illustrated by a multi-location department store that organizes functionally around merchandise lines but also geographically around stores. Examples of organizations employing a shifting matrix structure are those who carry on most of their work within various project teams. These organizations also rely on a functionally based structure, often focused on occupational or disciplinary specialization, for one side of the matrix, but allocate varying combinations of specialists to a shifting set of project teams as the second basis of control. Such organizations include aerospace firms and research centers. All participants are responsible both to their functional superior and to one or more project leaders.

The conflicts between function and product that exist in at least a latent form in most organizations are elevated by the matrix organization into two competing structural principles. Although such institutionalization of conflict does not resolve it, it does ensure that both the functional and the product (or areal) interests are viewed as legitimate and have managerial representatives who will continually define and defend them. Moreover, assigning specific roles the responsibility for defending particular values gives them higher visibility and makes trade-offs or compromises more evident: conflicts between decision makers are more visible than conflicts within a single decision maker.

Some of the overt interrole conflicts built into the matrix structure are managed by sequential attention to one or another set of priorities. In what has been called the *matrix swing*, functional priorities may receive more attention at the beginning and ending of a project cycle as personnel are hired or released and as budgets are negotiated, but once a project is under way, attention and authority swing to the project leader. Still, much ambiguity must be tolerated and competing claims accommodated for the matrix to function. For many participants, matrix structures are high-demand, high-stress work environments. (See Davis and Lawrence, 1977.)

Matrix structures suffer some of the same diseconomies of scale as other types of product-based systems. For one, each project group tends to duplicate some of the capacities of the others. Also, these structures presume enormous flexibility of resources and personnel, for project teams are continually being initiated, discontinued, and reconstituted.

## PROBLEMS IN RELATING
## TECHNOLOGY AND STRUCTURE

In the previous sections, we argued that characteristics of the work being performed—in particular, its complexity, uncertainty, and interdependence—are associated with the characteristics of the structure devised to organize the work—for example, the extent of its differentiation, decentralization, and modes of coordination. With the help of Thompson, Galbraith, and others, we attempted to illustrate ways in which formal structural arrangements can be adjusted to accommodate differences in task demands. But although we have argued and illustrated, we have presented little in the way of evidence. When we turn to the empirical studies relating technology and structure, we find that the evidence is, at best, mixed. Although some studies do support the arguments (for example, Woodward, 1965; Hage and Aiken, 1969; Khandwalla, 1974; Van de Ven, Delbecq, and Koenig, 1976), others report at best weak and often conflicting evidence (for example, Hickson, Pugh, and Pheysey, 1969; Mohr, 1971; Child and Mansfield, 1972).

### Measurement Problems

Some of the confusion in research findings is due to the variety of measures employed for assessing both technology (see Table 9–1) and structure: there is not much consensus on what variables to measure or how to measure them. Another source of difficulty is differences in the types of data gathered and in the level at which information is collected (see Scott, 1977b). The data employed may be obtained from documents and records, informant reports, or individual responses to surveys, and, in Lazarsfeld and Menzel's (1961) terms, defined in Chapter 1, the measures developed on the basis of these data may be analytical, structural, or global. Substantial problems of reliability and validity attend each of these data sources, and in the case of collective measures based on the aggregated response of individual participants, it is difficult to determine how weights should be assigned to each response.[6] Moreover, there is sometimes little agreement among different types of measures of the same variables. For example, Pennings (1973) used a variety of types of measures of structural variables, such as centralization and formalization, in a study of ten organizations. When measures of these variables based on the judgments of officials acting as informants were compared with measures of the same variables based on aggregated survey data from rank-and-file participants, correlations among them proved to be very low, and in some cases were negative, indicating their low convergent validity.

### Theoretical Issues

In addition to these important methodological problems, several unresolved theoretical issues generate disagreement among investigators and militate against the cumulation of consistent empirical findings. We will review three of these issues: inconsistencies in the organizational levels at which the predictions relating technology to structure are formulated and tested; disagreements over the conception of technology; and differences in hidden or implicit assumptions that underlie research on the relation between technology and structure.

*Varying organizational levels*    The relation between technology and structure has been studied at differing organizational levels, including

---

[6]For example, as an indicator of centralization, participants may be asked to describe where decisions of various types are made in the organization. A common procedure in organizational studies is to combine all responses to the question and calculate a mean, which in effect gives the same weight to each response. However, as I note elsewhere,

> equal weighting flies in the face of everything we know about social structure—both formal and informal—the most important characteristic of which is differentiation: differentiation of knowledge, of competence, of influence, of commitment, of power, etc. (Scott, 1972: 141).

those of (1) the organization as a whole (for example, Woodward, 1965; Hickson, Pugh, and Pheysey, 1969; Khandwalla, 1974); (2) the work group or department (Bell, 1967; Lawrence and Lorsch, 1967; Grimes and Klein, 1973; Hrebiniak, 1974; Van de Ven and Delbecq, 1974); and (3) the individual participant (Hrebiniak, 1974; Dornbusch and Scott, 1975).

Efforts to relate technical and structural measures at the organizational level are extremely hazardous because organizations tend to employ a variety of technologies and to be structurally complex. Some analysts have attempted to resolve the difficulty by what might be termed a "mix-master" method: data on technology and structure are gathered from various participants and work units and then combined to produce overall scores for the two subsystems. Thus, the Aston group (Hickson, Pugh, and Pheysey, 1969) aggregated data gathered by interviews with chief executives and a number of department heads into a single measure, work-flow integration, to characterize the technology of the organization as a whole. And Hage and Aiken (1969), while careful to give greater weighting to the reports of the supervisory staff, combined worker and supervisor responses across departments to arrive at a single measure of routineness of work for each organization in a sample of health and welfare agencies. Similarly, structures that are likely to exhibit considerable diversity in centralization or in formalization, for example, are characterized by an average score reported for the organization. A different approach to the problem of technical and structural heterogeneity is exemplified by the work of Woodward (1965) and Khandwalla (1974), who restricted their studies to the "production systems" of the organizations they surveyed. But the structure of one department or division is not likely to be representative of the entire organization.

Analysts studying technology and structure at the departmental level confront less severe, but similar, problems caused by technical and structural heterogeneity. Many work groups and most departments include different types of work, particularly in the case of product-based organizational structures. Further, studies (for example, Bell, 1967; Mohr, 1971) that measure the characteristics of tasks performed by individual workers and aggregate them to form measures of some modal task characteristics may not only cause the analyst to overlook variance across individual workers but fail to capture those characteristics of technology that are distinctive to the group level, such as work variety or complexity at the departmental level (see Comstock and Scott, 1977).

Dornbusch and I (Dornbusch and Scott, 1975), in collaboration with a large number of graduate student colleagues, conducted a series of studies on the relation between technology and structure at the level of the individual participant. We focused on the participants' conception of the nature of the work performed and their perception of the work arrangements governing them. Studies of diverse types of workers in varied settings, including school teachers in public and alternative schools, university faculty members, football players, assembly bench workers, Catholic priests, and members of a hospital house staff, convinced us that most workers perform a variety of tasks and work under a number of structural arrangements. How much uncertainty is confronted, how much interdependence is present, how complex are the demands posed—all vary depending on what tasks or aspects of a given participant's work are singled out.

In summary, given the great diversity and complexity of the types of work and the structures encompassed by most organizations, we should not be surprised to learn that many specific studies report varying and contradictory findings. When the subject of study is variable and complex, findings will be highly susceptible to differences in the variables and indicators employed, the sample drawn, the level of organization studied, and similar research decisions.

The choice of the level of organization at which to conduct a study is particularly critical because organizational levels often relate in a complementary fashion: that is, uncertainty may be relatively low at one level *because* it is high at another. Thus, it is quite possible for individual workers to be confronted by complex and uncertain tasks within a relatively simple administrative system—for example the work of physicians in a small group-practice clinic. Conversely, individual workers may carry out a few simple tasks as part of a technology that is highly complex when viewed at the departmental level, as is the case with workers on an assembly line (see Mohr, 1971). The level of complexity and uncertainty at two adjacent organizational levels may vary dramatically. Indeed, an important aspect of organizational design is to decide where to locate such demands.

Given these conditions, in our opinion, if progress is to be made, researchers must exhibit greater sensitivities to the complexities of organizational systems. Our measures and predictions should allow for differences in the relation between technology and structure at the individual, work-group, and organizational level. Thus, Comstock and I (Comstock and Scott, 1977), in a study of the organization of 142 patient-care wards in a sample of sixteen hospitals showed that the predictability of the tasks confronting individual nurses was more closely associated with the characteristics of the nursing personnel in that unit (for example, level of qualifications and professionalism) than with the characteristics of the control system of the ward itself (for example, degree of formalization and centralization). The latter were more closely associated with measures of complexity and uncertainty at the *ward* level—for example, ward size, the extent of staff differentiation, and the level of work-flow predictability. By analogy, the same type of argument applies when one attempts to characterize the structure of the organization as a whole. Rather than treating the wider organizational structure as some kind of average of the characteristics of its work activities and work units, it would seem more appropriate to treat it as an overarching framework of relations linking subunits of considerable diversity, and to develop measures that capture the distinctive characteristics of this suprastructure.

***Varying task conceptions***    Most investigators assume that organizational participants agree on the characteristics of the technology in use: on the nature of the materials, the operations, and the state of knowledge. Presumably such consensus exists because these technological traits are real and objective, determined by the state of the environment. It appears, though, that the characteristics of technologies are much less solid than they seem at first, that they are often socially determined and can vary from participant to participant or from one set of participants to another. Thus, given the same set of task objects, it is possible for participants to emphasize their uniformity or their diversity, their unpredictability and complexity or their certainty and simplicity. (See Scott, 1972; Dornbusch and Scott, 1975: 76–91.) For example, historical and comparative accounts of treatment of the mentally ill demonstrate that conceptions of the raw materials—in this case, mental patients—have varied enormously over time and place. Under such circumstances, Perrow (1965) has suggested that ideology substitutes for technology. Similarly, conceptions of students' characteristics vary somewhat from one teacher to another, but even more from one type of school to another—for example, traditional public schools versus alternative schools (see Swidler, 1979). In like manner, participants may disagree on the characteristics of the operations performed. Where one sees repetitive activities another sees ingenuity and artful adaptation. Thus, Freidson (1970*b*) has pointed out that physicians are likely to insist on the problematic and unpredictable nature of many aspects of their work that others regard as relatively straightforward and routine. And although the differences might not be as large, we would expect similar disagreements in task conceptions among individuals working with physical or material objects and techniques.[7]

Differing task conceptions may also develop between performers and administrators within a given type of organization. The conceptions of performers are relevant inasmuch as performers must relate directly to the task objects and perform the task operations; the conceptions of administrators are of interest because administrators are responsible for designing the structure within which the work is to be carried out. We would expect that, in general, participants more closely associated with the actual conduct of task activities will be more likely to emphasize the uncertainty and the complexity of the task performed. And as we move from the work location to administrative levels, perceived variability tends to diminish. In addition to variation in task conceptions rooted in distance from the work, performers and administrators often differ in their views of the scope of the task. Performers are more apt to concentrate on individual cases, but administrators will be more concerned with classes of objects or events. For example, a classroom teacher may view the task of teaching as reacting appropriately to the differing needs and problems of individual students. School administrators, however, are more likely to be concerned that all students perform sufficiently well to move smoothly from one class or grade to another.

Variations in conceptions of work are expected to be associated with variations in *preferred* work structures. Performers who view their work as more uncertain and complex will desire more discretion and work autonomy; administrators who view the work of performers under their control as more predictable and routine will prefer work arrangements that are more formalized and centralized. How are these discrepancies between the conceptions of work held by performers and administrators to be resolved?

----

[7]We had presumed that the task of making beds in a hospital was relatively simple and certain, but many nurse's aides informed us that this job was highly variable and often very difficult, depending on the location of the bed in the room, the attitude and the weight of the patient, the quality of the sheets, and so on.

***Hidden assumptions***    To answer this and related questions regarding the relation between technology and structure, it is necessary to expose some hidden or implicit assumptions underlying much of the work in this area. Certainly, one of the most pervasive assumptions made by investigators in this area is that of rationality of decision making. We have already noted that Thompson prefaces all of his propositions relating technology and structure with the phrase "Under norms of rationality." Theorists such as Galbraith presume that structures are designed to match information-processing needs of the tasks performed. And even Perrow, whose work is grounded primarily in the natural system perspective, embraces a rationalist orientation when he focuses on this topic: "We must assume here that, in the interest of efficiency, organizations wittingly or unwittingly attempt to maximize the congruence between their technology and their structure" (1970: 80).

Precisely what is meant by congruence or fit is seldom specified. Schoonhoven (1981) notes that although contingency arguments implicitly assume an interaction effect between two variables—for example, complexity and coordination—and a third, such as effectiveness, the shape or form of the relation—whether it is a simple monotonic relation, a multiplicative relation, or a threshold effect—is rarely considered. Contingency theorists, to their credit, explicitly argue that organizations devise specific structural arrangements in order to be efficient and effective.[8] This suggests that the predicted relations between technology and structure will be observed only, or most strongly, within a subset of organizations—those that are functioning effectively. But only a portion of the empirical studies in this area include measures of organizational effectiveness and employ them as intervening variables to test contingent hypotheses. Among this portion of studies again the evidence is mixed, but findings consistent with the contingency argument are reported in the original Lawrence and Lorsch (1967) investigation and in later studies by Khandwalla (1974), Tushman (1979), and Argote (1982). Contradictory findings or inconsistent support are reported in studies by Mohr (1971) and Pennings (1975).

The assumption of rationality not only implies that those who attempt to design organizational structures will be correct in their analysis of what is required, given the tasks to be performed, and will be effective in implementing these structures; it also assumes that managers and others in a position to design structures are attempting to serve performance goals. As we know, a number of theoretical perspectives challenge this assumption. Marxist theorists assert that the structures devised by managers are primarily designed not to maximize efficiency but to insure control. It is not necessary to review but only to note the relevance of these arguments here (see Chapter 7). It should be pointed out that most of the empirical support for this approach to date consists primarily of detailed, qualitative historical and contemporary case studies of the organization of work (the labor process) in particular situations (see Burawoy, 1985; Zimbalist, 1979).

---

[8]In Chapter 13 we discuss problems and complexities in defining and measuring efficiency and effectiveness.

Another perspective that emphasizes the role of power in shaping organizational structure is the *strategic contingency* approach. As described in Chapter 5, this perspective can be viewed as combining the contingency assumptions about the need of the organization to adust its structural configuration to the demands of its environments with the resource dependence arguments concerning the varying threats and opportunities posed by different segments of the environment. The organization becomes differentiated to deal with these varying environmental contingencies. But whereas the resource dependence approach emphasizes the implications of these processes for boundary setting and spanning, focusing on the use of buffering and bridging strategies, the strategic contingency approach stresses their consequences for the organization's internal structure.

Like interorganizational relations, intraorganizational relations are significantly shaped by power-dependence processes both internal and external to the organization. Complex environments not only give rise to complex, differentiated organizational structures; they also generate varying interests within organizations as well as new sources of power that can be used to pursue these interests. (Hickson et al., 1971) The recognition of multiple interests within organizations has led to the coalitional model of organizations: many organizations are in no sense unified actors but are instead shifting combinations of varying interest groups moving in and out of the organization and up and down in relative power. If a particular group has a corner on some valued resource, such as legal expertise or scientific creativity, and there is no readily available alternative, it is likely to acquire power *within* the organization. And one of the uses to which power is put is to shape the structure of the organization.[9] More powerful actors are likely to attempt to locate more discretion in the positions they occupy and to attempt to reduce that located in other positions. Thus, physicians and hospital administrators are regularly engaged in a contest—both in nationwide forums and in local hospital organizations—over what decisions should be controlled by physicians and which by administrators. Such arguments are invariably accompanied by claims that the nature of the work performed—its complexity, its value— justifies one's own need for discretion.

Thus, it appears that task conceptions are not neutral descriptions of work demands but value-laden claims concerning the "appropriate" conditions of work. If people desire greater autonomy and discretion over their work, they are likely to emphasize the complex and uncertain nature of the tasks for which they are responsible. Alternatively, if managers prefer to retain control over the workplace by centralizing decisions and promulgating rules, they will attempt to define the work as predictable and will respond to complexity with increased differentiation—which reduces the skill level of individual workers. Whose task conceptions prevail will be determined, at least in part, by the power position of the participants. As Benson (1977: 7) argues,

[9]A related use to which power is put is shaping the goals of the organization (see Chapter 11).

the ideas which guide the construction of the organization depend upon the power of various participants, that is, their capacity to control the direction of events. Some parties are in dominant positions permitting the imposition and enforcement of their conceptions of reality. Others are in positions of relative weakness and must act in conformity with the definitions of others.

Power no less than technology is a major determinant of structure.[10]

Conflicts over task definitions occur in all organizations, but are particularly visible in organizations employing professional workers (see Scott, 1972). Such occupational groups are more likely to develop divergent task conceptions, these notions being transmitted by external socializing organizations and reinforced by peer-group processes (see Chapter 7). Because specific alternative task conceptions are collectively held by performers, these shared conceptions and expectations concerning appropriate work arrangements become important unifying forces for occupational groups across varying settings (see Reeves, 1980; Clark, 1983; DiMaggio and Powell, 1983). In addition, a more or less tight monopoly over the performance of some aspects of the work, plus in some cases the ability to regulate the supply of performers, ensures that professional groups will be in a relatively powerful position vis-à-vis organizational managers.

These arguments concerning power also challenge a second major assumption underlying the conventional arguments relating technology and structure: that technology causes structure rather than the reverse. If conceptions of technology are socially determined, then it is clear that one of the most powerful influences on task conceptions are the structural arrangements within which the work is performed. Whoever controls the structure can have a powerful effect on performers' task definitions. Thus as noted in Chapter 8, the combined efforts of administrators and lawyers have succeeded in transforming the definition of the work of the caseworker administering the Aid to Families with Dependent Children (AFDC) public-assistance program. In less than two decades, there have been extensive reductions in worker discretion: the number and detail of the rules governing decisions has increased; the extent and type of hierarchical controls have been intensified; and the professional and educational qualifications for workers have been reduced. The organized power of social workers has not proved sufficient to successfully resist the deprofessionalization of work that had once been defined as requiring considerable expertise and the discretion necessary to apply generalized norms and standards to specific cases. (Simon, 1983)

Structures affect the nature of work in even more direct ways. How uncertain or complex work is at a given point in the system is, in large measure, a question of how the structure is designed. Through differentiation, complex tasks can be divided and made simple; alternatively, through professionalization, complex tasks can be retained and delegated to individual performers. Similarly, how much interdependence is present in a given system is, in part, a matter of structural design. The interdependence of work groups can be reduced by a product-based division of

---

[10]These arguments concerning both the sources and the consequences of power are developed at length in Pfeffer (1981) and Mintzberg (1983).

labor and increased by a functional structure. So does technology determine structure or does structure determine technology? The answer must be that the relation is reciprocal but variable. Presumably technology always exerts some general constraints on the shape of the structure, but within these limits market conditions and power processes may be expected to play an important role (see Chapter 7).

A third assumption that guides studies of technology and structure is that the relation between the two is determined primarily by intraorganizational forces. This assumption is challenged by much of the previous discussion, which argues that market forces and occupational systems external to the organization help to shape both the participants' conceptions of work as well as the outcomes of struggles between performers and administrators for control over work structures. It is also called into question by examples such as the following. The major incentive for many organizations to develop a project-management structure came not from within as a rational response to information processing demands but from outside the organization. The Department of Defense required its contractors to use this structural arrangement in the 1950s as a condition for obtaining financial support! (Wieland and Ullrich, 1976: 39). Government contract officers were tired of getting the runaround from functional department heads, each of whom had only partial control over any given project. The development of a project management format gave these officers someone they could more easily relate to and hold responsible for the successful and timely completion of the project. We should never overlook or underestimate the effect of environmental forces on "internal" structures and processes.

A fourth and final assumption that underlies the structural models described to this point for dealing with technical complexity, uncertainty, and interdependence is that they all embrace the rational system view of the benefits of formalization. The rational system response to increasing task demands is to shorten and strengthen the leash: provide superiors with more and faster information so they can more rapidly change the instructions to performers; increase the ratio of superiors to performers so that more information can be processed more quickly and revised guidelines supplied to performers. Some of these modifications move in the direction of decentralization: power and authority are more widely dispersed as hierarchies are augmented and, particularly, as lateral connections are added. But formalization is, if anything, increased in these systems.[11] New types of roles are created and new linkages specified that increase the complexity, flexibility, and capacity for change in the structure. But the flexibility involved is designed, not spontaneous, and the changes reflect capacity to shift rapidly from one set of formal rules and roles to another.

We know, of course, that this central assumption is challenged by natural system theorists, who stress the advantages of informal structures, particularly as strategies for dealing with task uncertainty. These alternative approaches, which have received much recent attention, rely primarily on enlarged roles, internalized control, and informal structures to confront high levels of uncertainty and complexity. Rather than augment-

---

[11]The relation between formalization and decentralization is discussed in Chapter 10.

ing hierarchies, they minimize vertical distinctions, and rather than creating new, specialized lateral roles and relations, they encourage more direct, face-to-face communications among any or all participants as required. Decision making and the exercise of control become more decentralized, and organizational roles less formalized. In the next section, we review some of the major models stemming from the natural system perspective for dealing with complex technologies.

## TECHNOLOGY AND INFORMAL STRUCTURE

Several discussions of natural open system responses to task complexity and uncertainty will be briefly reviewed. All are alike in stressing the value of informal structures, but each contains somewhat varying emphases, including differences in the level of analysis.

### Socio-Technical Systems and Work Redesign

We have briefly described the socio-technical system approach developed at the Tavistock Institute in London following World War II (see Chapter 5.) One of the guiding premises of this approach is that work involves a combination of social and technical requisites and that the object of design is to "jointly optimize" both components—not sacrifice one for the other. By contrast, rational system approaches are more likely to focus on the demands of the technical system, ignoring the psychological and social needs of workers. Technical systems are designed; then human workers are "fitted in" to their requirements. And to fit human behavior into a prespecified technical system requires that it be highly programmed, that the activities and interactions be specified and predictable—in a word, formalized.

If human as well as technical requirements are to be served, then it is necessary to determine what kinds of work situations motivate and satisfy workers. The Tavistock group emphasizes both individual task features as well as social organizational, particularly work-group, features. At the task level, repetitive, undemanding, isolated jobs undermine commitment and performance motivation. And at the work-group level, competition and close supervision foments stress, petty deceptions, scapegoating, and low morale. These effects were observed when more highly mechanized approaches were introduced in British coal mines—technical approaches that disrupted worker autonomy and work-group cohesion. (Trist and Bamforth, 1951) The solution was to restructure the situation so as to give more attention to its social components. In the restructured situation,

> groups of men are responsible for the whole task, allocate themselves to shifts and to jobs within the shift, and are paid on a group bonus. Thus the problems of overspecialized work roles, segregation of tasks across shifts with consequent scapegoating and lack of group cohesion were overcome. (Pugh, Hickson, and Hinings, 1985: 86)

The rational system assumption that worker performance is enhanced when work demands are routinized and standardized—when complexity is factored into simple tasks and when uncertainty is removed—is strongly challenged by this approach. Organizations may thrive on certainty, but individuals do not! This counterassumption originating in the socio-technical school has given rise to a large body of theory and research pursued primarily at the social psychological level of the individual worker. The most influential of these are *job characteristics* theory and its elaboration in *work design and individual needs* approaches.

Briefly, research on job characteristics pursues the assumption that specific attributes of the job, such as variety, autonomy, and required interaction, are associated with worker motivation and work performance. Turner and Lawrence (1965) developed and tested these predictions by measuring the characteristics of forty-seven industrial jobs, but found the expected relations held only for workers in rural areas, who were presumed to have different needs or expectations for work than urban workers. Later research has pursued this "contingent" assumption that the relation between job characteristics and worker responses is mediated by worker expectations or needs (see Hackman and Oldman, 1980.) The same types of job characteristics—variety, task identity, autonomy—are identified as important, as having "high motivating potential," but whether the potential is recognized depends on the psychological needs of the particular worker. Although a number of empirical tests of this more complex model of task characteristics and performance have been conducted (see, for example, Brief and Aldag, 1975; Stone, Mowday, and Porter, 1977; Steers and Spencer, 1977), the support is at best weak, and the research has been criticized on both methodological and theoretical grounds (see Roberts and Glick, 1981; Salancik and Pfeffer, 1977; Staw, 1984).[12]

The socio-technical approach has placed greater emphasis on the social organization of work groups—together with the necessary support features at higher organizational levels—than on the narrower matter of the design of individual jobs. Work groups, properly structured, can provide workers with an ongoing source of incentives, error correction, assistance, and social support that no amount of attention to individual job design can hope to match. The restructured semiautonomous work groups developed for the British coal mines suggests the type of approach deemed suitable to mechanized organizations with moderate levels of uncertainty and interdependence. A similar solution was developed by Volvo of Sweden when it decided to replace the traditional conveyor line for assembling its automobiles with movable automobile carriers that would permit more task variety and worker discretion embedded within a system empowering work groups as the central work elements (see Gyllenhammar, 1977). And Cole (1979) has described how on the other side of the globe, Toyota Auto Body of Japan reorganized its work process to enrich worker

---

[12]As might be expected, the concerns raised are similar to the problems already discussed involving the relation of technology to structure, including the issues of task conceptions (subjective versus objective views of task characteristics), direction of causation, and levels of analysis. For more detailed, critical reviews of this research, see Pfeffer (1982: 54–63) and Staw (1984).

skills, enlarge worker discretion, and activate work-group incentives and controls in the now-famous "quality circles." These work groups are ordinarily organized around a particular type of job and are granted primary responsibility for such matters as safety and quality control. They become involved with "almost every other kind of problem, including improvement of productivity, the speed and way of stopping the conveyor belt, job procedures, job training, and human relations problems" (Cole, 1979: 161).

When the organizational environment becomes more turbulent and the work demands more uncertain, a socio-technical design suggests that redundancy of function is superior to redundancy of parts (Emery and Trist, 1965). Pugh, Hickson, and Hinings (1985: 89) summarize the critical difference between these two emphases:

> The traditional technocratic bureaucracy is based on *redundancy of parts*. The parts are broken down so that the ultimate elements are as simple as possible; thus an unskilled worker in a narrow job who is cheap to replace and who takes little time to train would be regarded as an ideal job design. But this approach also requires reliable control systems—often cumbersome and costly.
>
> An alternative design, based on the *redundancy of functions*, is appropriate to turbulent environments. In this approach individuals and units have wide repertoires of activities to cope with change, and they are self-regulating. For the individual they create roles rather than mere jobs; for the organization, they bring into being a *variety-increasing* system rather than the traditional control by variety reduction. . . . Autonomous working groups, collaboration rather than competition (between organizations as well as within them) and reduction of hierarchical emphasis, are some of the requirements for operating effectively in modern turbulence.

### Organic Systems and Clans

During the early 1960s, Burns and Stalker studied a rather diverse group of about twenty industrial firms in Great Britain. Their sample included rather traditional textile companies, engineering firms, and a number of firms attempting to move into the rapidly growing market of electronics. Early in their field research, the investigators were struck by the presence of two quite distinct management styles—which they labeled the *mechanistic* and the *organic*. They noted that the two approaches tended to be associated with differing industries, or, more accurately, with differing types of industrial environments. The mechanistic firms were to be found in relatively stable environments, the organic in more rapidly changing environments. Burns and Stalker (1961: 5–6) describe these two organizational systems as follows:

> In mechanistic systems the problems and tasks facing the concern as a whole are broken down into specialisms. Each individual pursues his task as something distinct from the real tasks of the concern as a whole, as if it were the subject of a subcontract. "Somebody at the top" is responsible for seeing to its relevance. The technical methods, duties, and powers attached to each functional role are precisely designed. Interaction within management tends to be vertical . . .
>
> Organic systems are adapted to unstable conditions, when problems and requirements for action arise which cannot be broken down and distributed

among specialist roles within a clearly defined hierarchy. Individuals have to perform their special tasks in the light of their knowledge of the tasks of the firm as a whole. Jobs lose much of their formal definition in terms of methods, duties and powers, which have to be redefined continually by interaction with others participating in a task. Interaction runs laterally as much as vertically. Communication between people of different ranks tends to resemble lateral consultation rather than vertical command.

More recent analyses have added to our understanding of this type of structure. Ouchi (1980; 1981) defines it as a *clan* or *type* Z structure. Building on the distinctions proposed by Williamson, he argues that just as hierarchies replace markets when transactions become moderately uncertain and complex, in a parallel fashion hierarchies fail and are replaced by clan structures when the transactions reach levels of extreme complexity and uncertainty.[13] Ouchi suggests that the costs of monitoring very complex exchanges by conventional or augmented authority systems is prohibitive and will increasingly give rise to "organizational failures" and the search for alternative structures. One viable alternative is the clan—a group that may or may not be linked by kinship ties but is based on common internalized goals and strong feelings of solidarity.[14]

Although clan structures are distinguished from formalized bureaucracies by a number of elements—including nonspecialized roles and career paths, implicit and internalized control mechanisms, holistic rather than segmented concerns, and slow and diffuse evaluation—Ouchi argues that their most important feature is the long-term, often lifetime, employment that they offer their participants. This characteristic was identified quite early as a distinctive feature of Japanese organizations (see Abegglen, 1958; Dore, 1973); Ouchi proposes it as a defining characteristic of all clan organizations—which include not only Japanese organizations but many others including some of the most "modern" and progressive U.S. firms, including Hewlett-Packard, IBM, and Eastman Kodak (see Ouchi, 1981).

The expectation of long-term employment creates the conditions for a different type of control system. The employee sees his or her career prospects as being directly linked to the company's success. And the long-term commitment provides both incentive and opportunity for the organization to "invest" in its employees, not only increasing their specific work skills and knowledge by providing extensive training and varied job experience, but also developing their general understanding of organizational needs and programs and increasing their commitment to its goals and values. In short, we have the conditions for the development of elaborated internal labor markets. (See Chapter 8.)

These discussions that emphasize internalized controls and more

---

[13]Note that whereas the structural mechanism—informal, diffuse ties among participants—is one associated with the natural system perspective, the argument—reduction in transactions costs—is one stemming from the rational system perspective.

[14]Granovetter (1985) argues that Williamson greatly exaggerates the effectiveness of hierarchies in combating opportunism and underestimates the importance of informal, interpersonal controls in building trust and discouraging malfeasance. Thus, from this perspective, Ouchi's concept of clan is only a more highly developed instance of the control processes operating in all organizations.

diffuse, long-term attachments have been supplemented by analyses that stress the importance of creating and sharing a common corporate culture. Cultural symbols and meanings are held to be an important alternative to structural forms. (See Deal and Kennedy, 1982; Peters and Waterman, 1982.) We discuss and evaluate these arguments in Chapter 11.

## PROFESSIONAL ORGANIZATIONS

Certainly the most elaborate and intricate organizational arrangements yet devised for coping with high orders of complexity and uncertainty in production systems are to be found in the *professional organization*. We began the discussion of technology and structure by stating three general principles relating characteristics of technology and of structure: greater technical complexity is associated with greater structural complexity, greater technical uncertainty is related to lower formalization and centralization, and greater interdependence is associated with more elaborate coordination structures. We now call attention to an important exception to the first principle. Technical complexity does not invariably give rise to greater complexity of structure; it may give rise instead to greater "complexity" of the performer. That is, one way to manage greater task complexity is not to divide the work and parcel it out among differentiated work groups or departments, but to confront the complexity with more highly qualified and flexible performers—with professionals. This response is particularly effective when (1) the work is also uncertain, a condition that militates against preplanning and subdivision, and (2) the work does not involve high levels of interdependence among workers. As an example of the latter, the teaching by faculty members in universities, the work of lawyers in law firms, and the work of physicians in clinics as customarily performed tend to involve relatively little interdependence. Whether complexity and uncertainty of work give rise to complex organizations or to complex performers is determined partly by the characteristics of the work itself but is also influenced by the political and social power of the performer group. (See Chapter 9; and Larson, 1977.)

As complexity, uncertainty, and interdependence increase, professionals are more likely to move their work into organizational structures and take advantage of a more explicit division of labor and more formalized coordination mechanisms. Thus, complex performers enter into and are supported by complex organizational structures.

Professionals perform the core tasks of the organization under two general types of arrangements. The first, which we have labeled the *autonomous* professional organization, exists to the extent that "organizational officials delegate to the group of professional employees considerable responsibility for defining and implementing the goals, for setting performance standards, and for seeing to it that standards are maintained" (Scott, 1965b: 66). The professional performers organize themselves—as a "staff" in hospitals, as an "academic council" in universities—to assume these responsibilities. A fairly well demarcated boundary is established between those tasks for which the professional group assumes responsibility and those over which the administrative officials have jurisdiction. Even when professionals occupy the administrative positions, as is often the case, the boundaries tend to remain intact, so that the professional officials exercise authority over administrative procedures but are not granted direct control over professional tasks (see Goss, 1961). Rather, considerable discretion and autonomy are delegated to individual professionals, and they are subject only to collegial review and control systems, some formally mandated but others operating only informally. Examples of types of professional organizations likely to conform to the autonomous pattern include general hospitals, therapeutic psychiatric hospitals, medical clinics, elite colleges and universities, and scientific institutes oriented to basic research (see Stanton and Schwartz, 1954; Clark, 1963; Smigel, 1964; Freidson, 1975).

We have labeled the second type the *heteronomous* professional organization because in this arrangement "professional employees are clearly subordinated to an administrative framework," and the amount of autonomy granted them is relatively small (Scott, 1965b: 67). Employees in these settings are subject to administrative controls, and their discretion is clearly circumscribed. Unlike their autonomous counterparts, they are subject to routine supervision. This type of professional organization is exemplified by many public agencies—libraries, secondary schools, social welfare agencies—as well as some private organizations, such as small religious colleges, engineering companies, applied research firms, and public accounting firms (see Bidwell, 1965; Etzioni, 1969; Kornhauser, 1962; Montagna, 1968). Also, as Hall (1968) has pointed out, the distinction between autonomous and heteronomous structures can be applied to organizational departments as well as to entire organizations. Thus, the research and development department of a manufacturing company is likely to be organized as a heteronomous structure.

The structure of heteronomous professional organizations is in many respects similar to the arrangements already described in which organizations handle somewhat complex and uncertain tasks by *delegation*. The work of the professionals takes place within a structure of general rules and hierarchical supervision, but individual performers are given considerable discretion over task decisions, particularly those concerning means or techniques. Thus, individual teachers make choices regarding instructional techniques, and individual engineers make decisions concerning design or construction strategies.

Given that performers are expected to exercise more autonomy, we might expect to observe savings in supervisory costs: lower ratios of managers to performers or larger spans of control for supervisors. Several empirical studies, however, report just the opposite. In a study of 30 departments within a community hospital, Bell (1967) found that the greater the complexity of work performed by departmental participants, the smaller the spans of supervisory control—the fewer workers a supervisor could manage. Similarly, in a study of 252 public personnel agencies, Blau, Heydebrand, and Stauffer (1966) found that the higher the qualifications of staff members, the higher the manager-worker ratio. (See also Pugh, Hickson, and Hinings, 1969: 118–19). Blau and colleagues interpret these unexpected findings in terms that are now familiar to us: more managers are needed to handle the larger amount of information that must be communicated upward. Blau (1968) also points out that having more supervisors or managers reduces the centralization of decision making.

These analyses suggest that the more complex work carried on in heteronomous professional organizations is managed by both delegation and *augmentation of the hierarchy.* The hierarchy is augmented by the simple expedient of hiring more managers and reducing the span of control. Note, however, that the terms *manager* and *span of control* are misleading in this context, because the managers are themselves professionals and the proportional increase in their numbers signifies not increased closeness of supervision but an attempt to improve the transmission of information and the decision-making capacity of the organization.

The organization of autonomous professionals takes many forms, depending in particular on the degree of interdependence among the individual performers and performer groups. One of the primary strengths of the full-fledged professional is that he or she is deemed capable of independent decision making and performance, and this includes coordinating work with others as required by the situation. Thus, in many kinds of autonomous professional organizations we would expect to see coordination, through *direct contacts,* of the formal organization of the professional staff with its elaborate committee structures—the whole functioning much in the manner of Burns and Stalker's (1961) *organic system.* However, more explicit structural forms for coordinating work are required as professionals themselves become more highly specialized and are expected to coordinate not only their own work but the work of a growing number of paraprofessional workers, and as interdependence among work groups and departments increases. In many cases *project teams* are used. In hospitals such teams may be built around a particular type of surgical procedure—open-heart surgery is a dramatic example— or around the care of a particular group of patients—for example, children with cancer (see Fox, 1959; Beckhard, 1972). And faculty members in universities conduct an increasing amount of their research in project teams, each of which has a coordinator or leader, often designated the principal investigator. These arrangements support collaborative effort across disciplinary or departmental lines. *Matix designs* are common in research organizations such as RAND (Smith, 1966) and are used in some hospital departments (Neuhauser, 1972). In many of these organizations professional participants and administrators exercise roughly equivalent power—an arrangement we have termed the *conjoint* professional organization (see Scott, 1982). Such arrangements attempt to combine the advantages of both professional and bureaucratic forms.

Organizations that in one way or another utilize lateral relationships as legitimate avenues of information and influence flows constitute the new generation of organizational forms. As we have attempted to illustrate, a number of different lateral structural arrangements are in use—including project teams, matrix structures, organic or clan systems, and professional organizations. All move us away from unitary hierarchical arrangements, "beyond bureaucracy," or "from bureaucracy to adhocracy." Futurists and social commentators such as Bennis and Slater (1968), Bell (1973), Toffler (1970; 1980) and Naisbitt (1982) agree that these new organizational forms offer new opportunities and challenges to participants but at the same time impose greater pressures and requirements on them.

## SUMMARY

Most efforts to explain the structural complexity within the technical core of an organization focus on the characteristics of the work being performed—on the technology. A great many specific measures of technology have been proposed, some emphasizing different phases of the work process—inputs, throughputs, or outputs—and some focusing on different facets of the process—materials, operations, or knowledge. Most important for explaining differences in structural characteristics of organizations are three dimensions of technology: complexity, uncertainty, and interdependence. In general, we expect technical complexity to be associated with structural complexity or performer complexity (professionalization); technical uncertainty with lower formalization and decentralization of decision making; and interdependence with higher levels of coordination. Complexity, uncertainty, and interdependence are alike in at least one respect: each increases the amount of information that must be processed during the course of a task performance. Thus, as complexity, uncertainty, and interdependence increase, structural modifications need to be made that will either (1) reduce the need for information processing—for example, by lowering the level of interdependence or by lowering performance standards—or (2) increase the capacity of the information-processing system, by increasing the channel and node capacity of the hierarchy or by legitimating lateral connections among participants.

Empirical studies of the relation between technology and structure show mixed and often conflicting results. Among the factors contributing to this confusion are methodological problems, such as lack of consensus on measures or on measurement strategies, and theoretical problems, including misspecifications of the level of analysis at which the measures apply, disagreements among participants about the nature of the technology employed, and lack of clarity about the causal connections between technology and structure.

Although significant attention has been devoted to the relation between technology and formal structures such as rules, schedules, hierarchies, and coordinating roles, much recent work emphasizes the importance of informal structures, particularly when high levels of uncertainty are confronted. Organic systems or clan structures are viewed as simultaneously fostering reliability and flexibility and as increasing worker motivation and commitment.

Professional organizations combine elements from both formal and informal approaches, stressing internalization of controls and worker autonomy and at the same time utilizing more formalized control systems such as project teams and matrix structures.

# 10

# sources of structural complexity: the peripheral sectors

The device by which an organism maintains itself stationary at a fairly high level of orderliness . . . really consists in continually sucking orderliness from its environment.

Erwin Schrödinger (1945)

The division between the technical core and the peripheral sectors of an organization is admittedly somewhat arbitrary. It is intended to emphasize that organizations are composed of different units that respond to different forces. The previous chapter emphasized those portions of the organization—labeled the technical core—that carry on its primary work. We argued that the characteristics of the work performed are related to the characteristics of the structures created to contain the work. (Whether work characteristics produce structural characteristics or the reverse was discussed but not fully resolved.) Attention was limited to the characteristics of those structures that contain, control, or are close to the organization's central work flow.

In this chapter the focus broadens to include structures less directly tied to the technical core. They are peripheral in this sense and only in this sense: *peripheral* is not synonymous with *marginal*. The peripheral structures, for present purposes, encompass many aspects of the managerial and the institutional levels as defined by Parsons (see Chapter 3). We will examine, in particular, the structural changes at these levels that accompany the organization's attempt to buffer its technical core and construct bridges to other social units. These changes accompany the organization's efforts to adapt to and modify its task environment. We also will examine structural features associated with the size of the organization. As we will learn, the meaning of size is far from clear, but its importance as a determinant of structural characteristics is well established. In the final section, relations between the core and peripheral structures are discussed.

A brief methodological note: Examinations of the structural features of organizations, their determinants, and their interrelations require the collection of data from a large sample of organizations. In these studies, the organizations are themselves the units of analysis. Ideally, what is required is a large sample of organizations randomly drawn from a population of independent organizations. The two major series of comparative studies to date—the research by Blau and his associates and the studies in England conducted by the Aston group—only partially meet these requirements, as will be discussed. Nevertheless, these pioneer projects constitute an important beginning to the systematic comparative study of organizational structure.

## SIZE AND STRUCTURE

### Defining and Measuring Size

What is size? Some analysts treat it as a dimension of organizational structure like formalization or centralization—one of several structural properties of an organization that may be seen to co-vary (see, for example, Hall and Tittle, 1966). Others treat size more as a contextual variable that measures the demand for an organization's services or products and thereby provides opportunities for and imposes constraints on its structure (see, for example, Blau and Schoenherr, 1971; Pugh et al., 1969). Like technology, size appears to be a variable that is on the interface between the organization and its environment: both variables are, on the one hand, internal features interacting with other structural properties and, on the other hand, features strongly shaped by external conditions. And, because it is externally driven like technology, size is more likely to be treated as an independent variable that shapes and determines other structural variables. If technology assesses what type of work is performed by the organization, size measures how much of that work the organization carries on—the scale on which the work is conducted.[1]

As Kimberly (1976) notes, several different indicators of organizational size have been employed by researchers, each measuring a somewhat different aspect of size. Thus, some indicators, such as square footage of floor space in a factory or number of beds in a hospital, measure the physical capacity of an organization to perform work. Others, such as the sales volume or number of clients served during a given period, focus less on potential capacity and more on current scale of performance. And indicators such as net assets provide a measure of discretionary resources available to the organization.

Most studies of the relation between organizational size and structure have used the number of participants (usually employees) as an indicator of size. The advantages of this measure are that it tends to reflect both the capacity of the organization for performing work as well as the current scale of actual performance. Also, most of the dependent variables of interest—formalization, centralization, bureaucratization—are measures of methods for controlling and coordinating people, so that numbers of individuals are of more relevance than other possible indicators of size. However, using the number of participants as an indicator of

[1]Size can also be given an institutional interpretation. Size, particularly relative size, is closely associated with visibility. Larger organizations are more likely to be the targets of institutional actors (for example, state regulatory bodies) and are also more likely to provide the models imitated by other organizations.

size poses some problems. As previously discussed, it is often difficult to determine how to set the boundary between participants and nonparticipants. Also, comparisons of numbers of participants across different types of organizations can be misleading, since some types of organizations are much more labor-intensive than others.[2]

We turn now to consider the major predicted and empirical relations between size and structure.

### Size, Bureaucracy, and Differentiation

Early interest in the effects of size focused on its relation to the degree of bureaucratization, defined as the relative size of the administrative component of an organization. A number of critics—for example, Parkinson (1957)—have asserted that large organizations are overbureaucratized, devoting a disproportionate amount of their staff resources to administration. Empirical investigations of the relation between organization size and bureaucratization conducted during the 1950s reported contradictory results: some researchers found that the administration was disproportionally large in larger organizations (for example, Terrien and Mills, 1955); some, that the proportion of administrators was smaller in large organizations (for example, Melman, 1951; Bendix, 1956); and some, that there was no association (for example, Baker and Davis, 1954). One important reason for the absence of any clear results is noted by Rushing (1966b). He points out that the administrative component of an organization is not a unitary structural element but rather, in his words, a "heterogeneous category" composed of varying participants performing quite different functional roles. Numerous studies have shown that if the administrative component is separated into its occupational categories— for example, managerial, professional and technical, and clerical—then these categories relate differently to size. In general, the proportion of managers tends to decline with increases in size, but the proportion of technical and clerical personnel is positively associated with size (see Rushing, 1966b: Blau and Schoenherr, 1971; Kasarda, 1974). The general point, however, is that the administrative component comprises various occupational groups that may relate differently to size.

A second basic reason for the absence of consistent associations between organizational size and administrative size is that size produces two different effects, which have opposing consequences for the size of the administrative component. On the one hand, organizational size is positively associated with structural differentiation. Studies of a wide variety of organizations show reasonably consistent and positive associations between size of organization and various measures of structural differentiation, including number of occupational categories, number of hierarchical levels, and spatial dispersion of the organization—for example, the number of branch offices (see Blau, 1973; Blau and Schoenherr 1971; Hall, Haas, and Johnson, 1967; Meyer, 1972; 1979b; and Pugh et al., 1969). Larger organizations tend to be structurally more complex. On the other

---

[2]For an extended discussion of conceptual and empirical difficulties associated with current definitions and measures of size, see Kimberly (1976).

hand, size is positively associated with the presence of more activities of the same general type. Size involves an increase in the *scale* of operations, which means not necessarily more kinds of operations (that is, differentiation) but more operations of the same kind.

As noted, these two effects of size have opposing consequences for the size of the administrative component. In a remarkable series of propositions, Blau (1970) attempts to summarize and resolve these conflicts, as follows. Large size is associated with structural differentiation, and differentiation, in turn, creates pressures to increase the size of the administrative component. This occurs because differentiation increases the heterogeneity of work among the various subunits and individuals, creating problems of coordination and integration. The administrative component expands to assume these responsibilities. On the other hand, organizational size is associated with increases in the average size of units, within which the work performed is relatively homogeneous. The larger the number of persons engaged in similar work, the smaller the number of administrative personnel needed to supervise them. In sum, larger organizational size, by increasing structural differentiation—that is, by increasing the number of different types of organizational subunits—increases the size of the administrative component, which must coordinate the work of these units; at the same time, larger organizational size, by increasing the volume of homogenous work within organizational subunits, reduces the size of the administrative component, which must supervise work within these units.

In their analysis of the fifty-three state employment security agencies, Blau and Schoenherr conclude that

> large size, by promoting differentiation, has the indirect effect of enlarging the managerial component, but the savings in managerial manpower resulting from a large scale of operations outweigh these indirect effects, so that the overall effect of large size is a reduction in the managerial component (1971:91).

Such a conclusion may well hold for the type of organization studied, but in our opinion should not be generalized to other types of organizations. Whether the administrative component is, on balance, affected positively or negatively by size would seem to depend primarily on what type of differentiation, is involved. For example, differentiation that merely creates new units of the same type (segmentation) would be expected to have a less positive effect on the administrative component than functional differentiation which creates new types of units. And how much functional differentiation occurs would be determined primarily by the type of work the organization is performing—that is, by its technology—and by the type of environment—both technical and institutional—in which it is operating. We amplify these comments later in this chapter.

### Size, Formalization, and Centralization

We have defined formalization as the extent to which roles and relationships are specified independently of the personal characteristics of the occupants of positions. Most empirical studies of formalization emphasize the extent to which rules such as formal job definitions and procedural specifications govern activities within the organizations. A Weberian model of structure would lead us to expect that the larger the size of the organization, the more formalized its structure would be, and indeed, most empirical studies support this prediction. Hall, Haas, and Johnson (1967) report only moderate but fairly consistent positive correlations between size and six indicators of formalization, including "concreteness" of positional descriptions and formalization of the authority structure. Blau and Schoenherr's (1971) study of state employment security agencies reports a positive association between organizational size and the extent of written personnel regulations in the state's civil service system.[3] And the Aston group (Pugh et al., 1969), in their study of forty-six work organizations, reports a strong positive correlation between size and scales measuring formalization and standardization of procedures for selection and advancement.

The conventional view of the bureaucratic model of organizational structure would also lead to the prediction that large organizations will have more highly centralized systems of decision making (see Hage, 1965). However, the studies by Blau and Schoenherr and the Aston group do not support this expectation. Rather, both research groups found that organization size was negatively correlated with several indicators of centralization. (For example, Blau and Schoenherr used measures of the decentralization of influence to division heads and the delegation of responsibility to local office managers, and Pugh and his colleagues developed scales for determining the level in the hierarchy where executive action could be taken subject only to pro forma review.) Consistent with the positive association between size and formalization, centralization was negatively associated with most of the measures of formalization. This pattern of results was also reported by Child (1972), who applied the scales developed by the Aston group to a national sample of eighty-two business organizations in Britain. And Mansfield (1973) reanalyzes these data to show that although the relationships are not very strong, the negative association between measures of centralization and standardization or formalization persist when the effects of size are controlled.

Blau and Schoenherr explain this unexpected pattern of results by suggesting that centralization and formalization may be viewed as alternative control mechanisms: more formalized arrangements permit more decentralized decision making. They argue that

> formalized standards that restrict the scope of discretion make decentralized decisions less precarious for effective management and coordination, which diminishes the reluctance of executives to delegate responsibilities way down the line to local managers far removed in space as well as in social distance from top managment at the headquarters (1971: 121).

Mansfield, perhaps with the aid of hindsight, scolds his colleagues for expecting a positive relation between formalization and centralization in the first place, arguing that Weber has been misread:

[3]Noting that this relation might better be tested at the state rather than the agency level, Blau and Schoenherr (1971: 58–59) also report a strong positive correlation between the total number of all state employees, as an indicator of the size of the state government, and the extent of formalized personnel regulations in the state's civil service system.

It can be argued, paradoxically, that the only method by which the director-ate in large organizations can retain overall control of the organization's functioning is by decentralizing much of the decision making within the framework of bureaucratic rules. It is reasonable to interpret Weber as implying a moderate negative relationship between the bureaucratic vari-ables and the centralization of decision making. This proposition, however, runs counter to everyday notions of bureaucracy. (1973: 478)

Mansfield's interpretation of Weber's view is supported by our conclusion (in Chapter 2) that Weber's model of rational-legal authority provides a structure of roles that supports the exercise of relatively greater indepen-dence and discretion, within specified constraints, than are found in ear-lier administrative arrangements. The extent of bureaucratization and centralization is also affected by the organization's technology and, espe-cially, by the degree of staff professionalization; we will discuss these relations after we briefly comment on some problems in determining the effects of size on structure.

### Problems in Relating Size and Structure

A number of problems attend studies of the relation between size and structure. Kimberly (1976) has addressed many of the more impor-tant issues. In addition to the fundamental question of the theoretical status of size—what does size measure?—the causal status of this variable is problematic. One reason we know little about the causal relation be-tween size and structure is that virtually all of the studies conducted have relied on cross-sectional data. Several longitudinal studies suggest that inferences based on cross-sectional studies of organizations regarding the effects of organizational growth or decline on structure may prove quite misleading.

Holdaway and Blowers (1971), using data from 41 urban school systems in western Canada, report that when the data are examined cross-sectionally, the relation between organization size and administrative ratio exhibits the expected negative relation, but when they are viewed longitu-dinally, administrative ratios do not decline as a function of increasing size in most of the districts examined over a five-year period. And a study by Freeman and Hannan (1975) based on data from 769 California school districts suggests that different relations obtain between size of organiza-tion and the administrative component, depending on whether the orga-nization is in a period of growth or decline. Their analysis reveals that the size of the administrative component increases along with the size of the organization during periods of growth, but that during periods of decline the size of the administration does not decrease at the same rate as the rest of the organization. This disparity in rates leads Freeman and Hannan to be skeptical about attempts to develop generalizations relating organization size and administration from cross-sectional studies, since these studies will inevitably combine data from both growing and declin-ing organizations.

Meyer (1979*b*) examined changes in the structure of 240 finance agencies located within the public bureaucracy of larger urban communities (greater than 50,000 residents), larger counties (greater than 100,000 residents), and the fifty states. Some data on change were collected as part of a panel study, with surveys being conducted in 1966 and again in 1972, but other change measures involved reports by agency officials describing when specified events occurred. Although Meyer's findings are complex and not easily summarized, they underline the importance of time of founding on structure: agencies established prior to 1900 exhibited lower levels of formalization than those founded between 1900 and 1939, and the latter class of firms was less formalized than those founded after 1940. Unlike the previous studies reported, Meyer found no association between formalization and decentralization, but he did find positive correlations between formalization and number of levels in the hierarchy and between levels and decentralization. Meyer (1979*b*: 179) suggests that his longitudinal data support the conclusion that "hierarchy follows from extensive personnel procedures [formalization] and decentralized decision making from hierarchical differentiation."

Even these few studies make it clear that our present understanding of the interrelations among various structural characteristics of organizations is likely to be improved if not entirely transformed by the inclusion of longitudinal and historical data and analyses.

## TECHNOLOGY, SIZE, AND STRUCTURE

### Professionals and Structure

In Chapter 9 we discussed the relation between the presence of professionals and the structural features of the technical core. We also noted that the presence of professional workers can affect the characteristics of more remote administrative structures. We cited findings from a study of public personnel agencies that those with a greater proportion of highly educated workers were characterized by higher manager-worker ratios (Blau, Heydebrand, and Stauffer, 1966). Similar results are reported in a study of United States hospitals (Heydebrand, 1973). Data from a study of finance departments also indicate that decision making is more decentralized in organizations having more highly qualified workers (Blau, 1968).

Hall's (1968) study of varying occupational groups in twenty-seven different organizations provides more complete information on the relation between professional employees and organizational structure. Hall assessed six structural features of these organizations: hierarchy of authority (defined as the extent to which the locus of decision making is prestructured); the division of labor (extent of functional specialization); presence of rules; extent of procedural specification; impersonality (degree of formalization); and technical competence (extent to which universalistic standards such as qualifications and education are used in selection and promotion). Reasonably strong, positive correlations were found among all of these dimensions with the exception of technical competence. This variable was negatively correlated with all of the other structural attributes! Moreover, dividing the sample of organizations according to our distinction between autonomous and heteronomous types revealed that, as expected, the former organizations were much lower than the latter in their levels of each of the structural variables, with the exception of level of technical competence. The more highly qualified professionals were found in those organizations that exhibited fewer "bureaucratic" attributes, as Weber defined the term: that is, those organizations with lower levels of task specialization, formalization, and standardization.

These results suggest that whether work is simplified and divided among less highly skilled participants or assigned to workers with higher skills who are granted more autonomy of action has implications not only for the immediate structure of the technical core but for the more re- mote, general structural characteristics of organizations. They also should remind us of the criticisms by Parsons, Gouldner, and others that Weber's model of bureaucracy tends to overlook the difference between authority based on office and that based on expertise or technical qualifications (see Chapter 2). Further, the results suggest that Udy (1959a) was correct to insist that Weber's ideal-type model of bureaucratic structure should be subjected to empirical validation. Udy's early study, based on a sample of 150 production organizations in 150 different nonindustrial societies dis- tinguished a highly intercorrelated set of bureaucratic (hierarchical) char- acteristics from a second set of intercorrelated characteristics that mea- sured the presence of limited objectives and a performance emphasis—a cluster of "rational" characteristics. These results suggest that rational organizations may or may not assume a hierarchical form (see Chapter 2; Blau and Scott, 1962: 206–9; and Blau, 1968).

We conclude that one of the great watersheds in the design of or- ganizations is the decision concerning whether work is to be divided and hierarchically coordinated or left intact and delegated to a professional- ized work force. Both are instances of rational organization. But each is associated with a different overall structural form.

### Technology versus Size

With two externally driven factors affecting the structural character- istics of organizations, the question naturally arises as to which is the more powerful. Both Blau and his colleagues and the Aston group argue for the overriding importance of size. Thus, early in the presentation of their findings on the employment security agencies, Blau and Schoenherr sum- marize the conclusion to which their data point: "Size is the most impor- tant condition affecting the structure of organizations" (1971: 57). It is difficult to accept this sweeping generalization because of the design of this and other studies carried out in Blau's program of comparative studies. In each of several studies—of employment security agencies, pub- lic finance departments, colleges and universities, industrial firms—a single type of organization was selected for study. This has the effect of not allowing technology to vary meaningfully across organizations, since organizations of the same type all perform basically the same tasks or functions, while permitting size to vary freely, since both large and small organizations of the same type were included within the sample. Focusing on a single type of organization also reduces variation in other important environmental factors, such as the organization's political and economic context. (The effects of these environmental factors on organizational structure are examined in the following section.) It is not appropriate to make comparative assertions as to the relative power of classes of variables under circumstances in which certain of them—in this case, technology and environment—are arbitrarily restricted in variation or excluded from consideration. (See Beyer and Trice, 1979)

The studies conducted by the Aston group seem better designed in this respect (Pugh et al., 1963; 1968; 1969; Pugh and Hickson, 1976.) Concerned with the limitations of focusing on one or a few selected variables, they defined and measured a large number of structural and contextual variables. These measures were then applied to a heterogeneous, random sample of forty-six organizations in the Birmingham area in the original study and to a similar national sample of eighty-two British organizations in Child's (1972) replication. However, the Aston studies are difficult to interpret and, in particular, to compare with other studies because of the way in which the measures of structure and technology were treated. After carefully developing complex scales and subscales for measuring a number of widely recognized structural dimensions, including specialization, standardization, formalization, centralization, and configuration (the shape of the hierarchy), the analysts examined the interrelations of all of the scales. Rather than retaining the original theoretically based dimensions, they performed a factor analysis to determine what scales were sufficiently highly correlated to suggest the presence of a common underlying dimension or factor. Three major factors emerged from this empirical procedure: the first, labeled *structuring of activities*, emphasized the covariation of those scales measuring specialization, standardization, and formalization; the second, *concentration of authority*, emphasized measures of centralization; and the third, *line of control of work flow*, emphasized control over work by line officials rather than by impersonal mechanisms. The factor analysis used was such that the resulting factors are orthogonal—relatively independent of one another. These factors were then related to such "contextual" variables as size and technology. And, as noted in Chapter 9, technology itself was measured by a complex series of scales combined to measure what the analysts termed *work-flow integration*.

As reported, size was found to exhibit strong and positive associations with the factor structuring of activities but was not correlated with the other two factors (Pugh et al., 1969). Technology, as measured by work-flow integration, showed "modest but distinct" correlations with all three factors, positive with structuring of activities and line control of work-flow, negative with concentration of authority. But after a more detailed analysis of these data, including multiple correlations in which technology was combined with other variables, Hickson, Pugh, and Pheysey (1969: 388–89) conclude,

> Operations technology as defined here is accounting for but a small proportion of the total variance in structural features. Other variables contribute more. On this sample, the broad "technological imperative" hypothesis that operations technology is of primary importance to structure is not sup-

ported. . . . The present data suggest that operations technology has only a limited specific effect compared with size.[4]

Although the Aston group's design appears better suited to comparing the relative effects of size and technology, a number of problems reduce confidence in their conclusions. The use of factor scores disrupts the connection between theoretically defined variables and empirical measures, so that it is often difficult to interpret measures of relations. Also, the measure of technology, work-flow integration, seems both to be narrow and to combine measures of work and work-flow inappropriately across levels, so that it also is difficult to interpret or accept. In addition, there are problems with the samples developed. The first sample was drawn exclusively from the Birmingham area and so can hardly be regarded as a representative sample of independent—that is, unrelated—organizations.[5] Further, as Child (1972) has noted, the sample contained a large number of branches, in contrast with independent companies, and this may have resulted in an inflated score for centralization and affected the observed relation between structuring of activities and centralization. The second sample used in the replication study was drawn from a broader sampling frame—all of Britain—but was restricted by type to business organizations. It seems clear that if investigators hope to conduct convincing studies of the relative impact of varying factors on the structural features of organizations, more care and attention must be devoted to adequacy of measurement and to sample design (see McKelvey and Aldrich, 1983).

Finally, the problems with this research are not only methodological but theoretical. Aldrich (1972) has shown that the specific empirical findings reported by the Aston group may be used to support quite varying interpretations of the relations among size, technology, and structure. The correlational data are consistent with models in which technology is presumed to influence structure directly as well as indirectly through size as well as with models in which size is assumed to have causal priority. Therefore, empirical results from cross-sectional studies alone cannot resolve the issue of the relative importance of size and technology as determinants of organization structure.

[4]Hickson and his colleagues intend this generalization to apply only to the relation between technology and peripheral organizational structure. They did find associations between technology and some aspects of the technical core structures and suggest that the pervasiveness of these effects is a function of organizational size. They argue that

> structural variables will be associated with operations technology only where they are centered on the workflow. The smaller the organization the more its structure will be pervaded by such technological effects: the larger the organization, the more these effects will be confined to variables such as job-counts of employees on activities linked with the workflow itself, and will not be detectable in variables of the more remote administrative and hierarchical structure. (Hickson, Pugh, and Pheysey, 1969: 394–95)

[5]The same criticism can be made of Woodward's (1965) sample of industrial firms, all of which were drawn from the same region of South Essex, and of Hage and Aiken's (1969) sample of sixteen health and welfare organizations, all of which were located in the same metropolitan area (see Scott, 1977b). Thus, each of these studies was limited to a sample of organizations within the same areal field.

## ENVIRONMENT AND STRUCTURE

### Buffering, Bridging, and Structural Complexity

Chapter 8 was devoted in part to describing some of the specific mechanisms used by organizations to buffer their technical cores from disturbing environmental influences and to build bridges to essential exchange partners and allies. Such organizational responses to the technical environment are not a simple matter of utilizing selected techniques or mechanisms. Associated with their use are fundamental changes in the structure of the organization.

*Mapping environmental complexity*   What changes may be expected when organizations employ one or more of the several buffering techniques we have described: coding, stockpiling, leveling, or forecasting? Such activities will require the development or recruitment of personnel with new and different skills from those employed in the technical core itself. These participants will require additional space and special equipment. In short, as the need for such buffering techniques grows, we would expect to observe the development and growth of new specialized roles and departments at either end of the technical core—in other words, buffering units that interface with the input and output environments of the organization.

Consider also the use of the simpler bridging techniques, such as bargaining, contracting, and co-optation. As the task environment becomes more differentiated and active with the development of segmented labor markets, rapid technical and scientific developments, multiple types of buyers and sellers, subcontractors to oversee, and competitors to watch and attempt to outmaneuver, the organization responds by adding new types of occupational groups and specialists to deal with each of these environmental sectors. Organizations hire personnel officers and labor relations experts to deal with more complex labor markets; scientists, engineers, research administrators, and patent lawyers to participate in and keep pace with scientific developments; purchasing agents and marketing specialists to relate to the input and output environments; contract specialists and auditors to negotiate with and police contractors, market analysts, and sometimes even industrial spies to look after competitors. Most of these additions to the organizational structure involve the creation of new staff or support departments attached to the managerial level of the organization.

Structural elaboration may also occur at the institutional level as the size of boards of directors is increased to allow for the addition of new types of board members, who will connect the organization with sectors or units of importance in their environment. Or it may occur as advisory structures are created to broaden the linkage of the organization to its task environment. Thus, the increasing complexity of the task environment is adapted to by increased structural complexity—differentiation—on the part of the organization.

This adaptation occurs not only in response to technical environments but also as a reaction to institutional environments. Organizations in such environments enhance their own chances for survival and resource acquisition by adhering closely to the institutionally defined patterns, by incorporating them in their own structures, by becoming structurally isomorphic with them. (Meyer and Rowan, 1977; DiMaggio and Powell, 1983)

As might be expected, organizations are very sensitive to the nuances of the normative climate in their institutional environments: they take account of the amount of support for and conflict over particular reforms and proposed changes. Rowan (1982) has examined changes in the staffing of a sample of California school districts between 1930 and 1970. He reports that the hiring of district specialists in the areas of health, psychology, and curricular matters was highly responsive to the level of support and attention to these domains that was reflected in broader educational movements and national and state political acts. The higher the consensus—or, in Rowan's words, the more "balanced" the institutional environment—the more widely diffused were officials identified with these movements; the more unbalanced the domain, the more irregular were the patterns traced by the districts in hiring and retaining appropriate specialists.

Whereas the career lines of specialists are subject to disruption because of changing levels of consensus and variations in the power and influence of groups shaping institutional norms, administrative officials in general appear to thrive on conflict. A widely accepted proposition in open systems theory is that organizations located in more complex and uncertain environments will exhibit more complex internal structures. When the environmental units take the form of varied public funding and regulatory bodies whose actions are not coordinated but fragmented—a relatively common pattern in the United States (see Meyer and Scott, 1983)—organizational complexity is likely to develop particularly at the administrative levels where boundary-spanning activities are centered. Thus, Rowan (1981) reports that, controlling for size and internal technical complexity, school districts in California receiving larger amounts of federal and state funding for special programs had a larger complement of administrators than districts not engaged in such programs. Similar results were found in a study of public districts and schools and private schools in the San Francisco Bay area (Scott and Meyer, 1986). Meyer and I found, for both public and private schools, that the larger the number of special state and federal programs in which the schools were participating, the greater the proportion of administrators at both the district and the school level. Administrative structures above the school level—district and state structures—are particularly affected in the public system.

> It is exactly these organizational levels that expanding environmental controls from state and national levels have acted to foster in recent decades: the complex fundings, programs, and requirements in which public schooling is immersed create pressures that generate much administrative expansion (Scott and Meyer, 1984: 39).

Whether differentiation of organizational structure occurs as a rational system response designed to support the buffering and bridging activities of organizations attempting to regulate critical resource flows, or as a natural system response designed to coalign the structure with its institutional environment to ensure its survival, the more general processes at work here are best depicted by the open systems perspective. This approach insists that an organization, as an open system, adapts to more complex environments by itself becoming more complex: it is a type of system "whose persistence and elaboration to higher levels depend upon a successful mapping of some of the environmental variety and constraints into its own organization on at least a semipermanent basis" (Buckley, 1967: 63).

It is important to stress that the organization's "mapping," or incorporating, of portions of the "environmental variety" into its own structure introduces new and different, and sometimes alien and hostile, elements into its own system. For example, the hiring of a labor relations specialist by a personnel department presumably introduces a person with expertise in, and experience with, labor unions. Such persons are hired because of their ability to understand, communicate, and negotiate with unions and their representatives. They may be more similar in background and training and attitudes to their counterparts in the unions than to their colleagues in the personnel department (see Goldner, 1970). The same is true for hundreds of other types of occupational groups whose services are required by the organization but whose value depends on their marginality to the system and on their connections with similar groups in other organizations. These associations among persons in similar occupational groups—accountants, computer specialists, labor lawyers, public relations experts, advertising managers—across different organizations are among the most important bridges linking contemporary organizations. The flow of individuals back and forth across these bridges sometimes creates problems for the larger society (see Chapter 12) but always creates problems for the host organization, which must attempt to control and integrate their activities and resolve their conflicts.[6]

***Integration and loose coupling***    The study by Lawrence and Lorsch (1967) of plastics manufacturing companies, which has been referred to several times in this volume, illustrates many of the major points we wish to emphasize.[7] As will be recalled (see Chapter 4), their research showed that (1) the task environments confronting the plastics manufacturing companies were highly varied, differing for research, production, and marketing functions; (2) this environmental variety was mapped into the structure of the organization, resulting in the creation of separate departments to confront these diverse environments; (3) the more closely aligned were the structural characteristics of each of these departments with the characteristics of the task environments they confronted, the

---

[6]The effect of these connections among similar occupational groups across organizations on the generation of power differences is discussed in Chapter 11.

[7]The results of interest in the present context are based on a study by Lawrence and Lorsch of only six plastics companies. Since the organizations themselves were the units of analysis, this is a very small sample on which to base any firm conclusions. We prefer to treat their research as a stimulating exploratory study valuable chiefly for the ideas generated, not for the hypotheses confirmed.

more effective was the organization;[8] (4) hence, the more differentiated the organization's departments—the more unlike their structural characteristics—the more effective the organization; (5) however, the more differentiated the departments within each organization, the more likely were disagreements and conflicts to develop and the more difficult the problems of coordinating and integrating their work; and (6) therefore, the more differentiated the departments *and* the more successful the organization in integrating their efforts, the more effective the organization.

The primary integrating mechanism used in the plastics companies studies was that of liaison roles: special roles were created to help to integrate the work of the three basic departments and resolve conflicts among them. Lawrence and Lorsch (1967: 54–83) report that the more successful integrators possessed attributes and orientations intermediate to those of the units they bridged, exercised influence based on technical competence, were oriented to the performance of the system as a whole, and enjoyed high influence throughout the organization. Walton and his colleagues (Walton, Dutton, and Fitch, 1966; Walton and Dutton, 1969) have also studied interdepartmental conflict in organizations and strategies for resolving it. They note that such conflicts often develop out of mutual task dependence, task-related asymmetries, conflicting performance criteria, dependence on common resources, communication obstacles, and ambiguity of goals as well as organizational differentiation. Such conflicts can be met with varying responses, from structural redesign to third-party consultation and attempts at reeducation of participants (see Blake, Shephard, and Mouton, 1964; Likert and Likert, 1976; Walton, 1969).

Note, however, that it is a rational system perspective that underlies most of these concerns with the integration of structurally differentiated departments. It is assumed that the organization is primarily a production system and that when conflicts occur among subunits, they must be resolved. Conflict interferes with goal attainment, and its resolution is associated with greater effectiveness of performance. A quite different view of conflict and conflict resolution processes is associated with the natural system perspective, which presumes that interdepartmental conflict is not primarily a product of error, ambiguity, and ignorance but results from quite fundamental divergences in group interests, and that the struggles are concerned not simply with means but with the goals to be served by the organization. These matters will be discussed in Chapter 11.

The assumption that integration is required because differentiation is present is also consistent with the rational system assumption that the various parts of the organization should be tightly coupled, each harnessed in the service of unified objectives. By contrast, the open systems model of organizations envisages a system of more or less loosely coupled elements, each capable of autonomous action (see Chapter 4). Weick (1976) notes a number of ways in which loose coupling of these structural elements may be highly adaptive for the organization, particularly when it

---

[8]To arrive at a composite rating of effectiveness Lawrence and Lorsch (1967: 40) combined objective measures of change in profits, sales volume, and number of new products with subjective ratings by managers of how well their companies were performing. We will examine these and other measures of effectiveness in Chapter 13.

confronts a diverse, segmented environment. To the extent that department units are free to vary independently, they may provide a more
sensitive mechanism for detecting environmental variation. Loose coupling also encourages opportunistic adaptation to local circumstances, and
it allows simultaneous adaptation to conflicting demands. Should problems develop with one department, it can be more easily sealed off or
severed from the rest of the system. Moreover, adjustment by individual
departments to environmental perturbation allows the rest of the system
to function with greater stability. Finally, allowing local units to adapt to
local conditions without requiring changes in the larger system reduces
coordination costs for the system as a whole.

Obviously some organizations effect tighter coupling among their
department than others, and within a given organization we will see variation in the degree of coupling. In general, we would expect to observe
tighter coupling between units within a technical core linked by serial or
reciprocal interdependence than between core units and those operating
on the boundaries. Nevertheless, two words of caution merit emphasis.
First, the extent of the interdependence, coordination, or coupling between any two organizational subunits is a matter for empirical determination, not assumption. Second, whether looser or tighter coordination or
coupling is adaptive for the organization depends on the specific circumstances confronted, and is also a matter for investigation, not prejudgment.

**From unitary to multi-divisional structures**    Before we conclude our
discussion of the structural consequences of buffering and bridging
strategies, two techniques remain to be considered: growth and merger.
Both represent changes in the scale of the organization, and, based on
our discussion in the previous section, we would expect increased size to
be associated with increased structural differentiation. But we can be
more specific than this. Chandler (1962; 1977) and Williamson (1975;
1985) argue that when firms grow beyond a certain point, not just further
differentiation but a structural reorganization is likely to take place. This
shift is described as a change from a unitary to a multi-divisional structure. The *unitary* structure is the conventional organizational form composed of a central office and several functionally organized departments.
The *multi-divisional* structure is depicted in Figure 10–1. It consists of a
general office and several product-based or regional divisions, each of
which contains functionally differentiated departments. These departmental units are subdivided into work units (establishments) that are distributed on a geographical or product basis.

In his classic account of the history of American business enterprise,
Chandler (1962) points out that the multi-divisional form first appeared
in this country shortly after World War I, and that it apparently was
independently developed at about the same time by a number of major
companies, including du Pont, General Motors, Standard Oil of New
Jersey, and Sears, Roebuck. Chandler's arguments are complex and
varied, but in brief, he identifies four phases of growth for American
industrial enterprise. The first period, just after the Civil War, was a time
of rapid expansion and resource accumulation. This was the age of the
larger-than-life entrepreneurs who expanded their organizations, most
often through vertical integration. In the second phase, a new generation

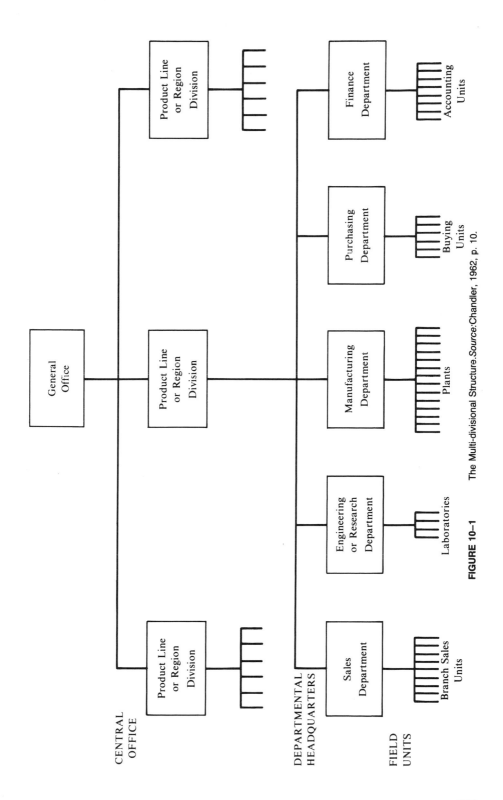

**FIGURE 10–1** The Multi-divisional Structure. *Source:* Chandler, 1962, p. 10.

255

of professional managers developed "methods for managing rationally the larger agglomerations of men, money, and materials" (1962: 388). Attention was concentrated on the reduction of unit costs and the coordination of diverse functional activities. The first two phases are best represented in the United States by the development of the railroads. Chandler (1977: 87) points out that

> the safe, reliable movement of goods and passengers, as well as the continuing maintenance and repair of locomotives, rolling stock, and track, roadbed, stations, roundhouses, and other equipment, required the creation of a sizable administrative organization. It meant the employment of a set of managers to supervise these functional activities over an extensive geographical area; and the appointment of an administrative command of middle and top executives to monitor, evaluate, and coordinate the work of the managers, resonsible for the day-to-day operations. It meant, too, the formulation of brand new types of internal administrative procedures and accounting and statistical controls. Hence, the operational requirements of the railroads demanded the creation of the first administrative hierarchies in American business.

Of course, the expansion of the railroads had a significant impact on the development of all types of businesses, the availability of reliable and inexpensive transportation enabling them to vastly expand their input and output markets.

Thus, phase three, lasting from the turn of the century to the First World War, witnessed the filling out of existing product lines as firms continued to expand. And, in order to ensure the continuing and efficient use of their resources, firms began to diversify, moving into related fields that would capitalize on their technical skills and marketing contacts.

In the fourth phase, following World War I, a few major companies that had diversified and were attempting to manage several related product lines found it necessary to reorganize in order to ensure the efficient employment of their resources. The new form that emerged was the "decentralized" or multi-divisional (M-form) structure, whose chief advantage was that it suported the clear separation of entrepreneurial or strategic from operational decision making. Day-to-day operational and tactical decisions were delegated to managers at the divisional level; longer-range entrepreneurial or strategic decisions were located at the general-office level. (See Figure 10–1.)

Firms can undertake horizontal mergers in order to increase the size of their markets, or vertical mergers in order to incorporate more phases of the production or distribution process and still fit comfortably into a unitary structure. However, as the firm begins to diversify its products and attempts to enter markets related or unrelated to those presently served, it will benefit from moving into a multi-divisional form. This is the sense in which Chandler insists that a firm's structure should be suited to its strategy. He argues that

> unless structure follows strategy, inefficiency results. This certainly appears to be the lesson to be learned from the experience of our four companies [du Pont, General Motors, Standard Oil, and Sears, Roebuck]. Volume expansion, geographical dispersion, vertical integration, product diversification,

and continued growth by any of these basic strategies laid an increasingly heavy load of entrepreneurial decision making on the senior executives. If they failed to reform the lines of authority and communication and to develop information necessary for administration, the executives throughout the organization were drawn deeper and deeper into operational activities and often were working at cross purposes to and in conflict with one another. (Chandler, 1962: 314–15)

Chandler argues that, given a diversified strategy, the new multi-divisional form is superior to the unitary form because it frees some officials from the tyranny of daily operational decisions and allows them to concentrate on positioning the organization in its environment and determining the proper mix of product lines and markets and thereby the allocation of resources among divisions. The M-form is also particularly well suited to supporting a multinational strategy, in which numerous divisions offering the same general product lines are situated to take advantage of multiple national markets (see Vaupel and Curhan, 1969; Tsurumi, 1977).

   Williamson (1975: 132–54) points out that Chandler's historical account of the problems accompanying diversification and the structural solution to these problems is consistent with predictions generated by the transactions cost framework. He argues that the principal problem created by diversification is that it creates increasing complexity and uncertainty—this time *within* the organization rather than in the environment—up to a level that exceeds the information-processing and decision-making capacity of the managers. The structural development that occurs is one that simplifies the informational and decision situations by clearly differentiating between the long-range policy decisions to be handled by the general office and the short-run operational decisions to be determined at the divisional level. Also, since companies within a diversified structure may be expected to buy from each other where possible, a small-numbers situation prevails that may motivate opportunistic behavior at the divisional or departmental levels. To curb these natural tendencies, an elite staff is attached to the general office to perform both advisory and auditing functions and in this manner to secure greater control over the behavior of the operating divisions. Williamson (1985: 283–84) amplifies the advantages of the multi-divisional structure in controlling opportunism:

> The M-form structure removes the general office executives from partisan involvement in the functional parts and assigns operating responsibilities to the divisions. The general office, moreover, is supported by an elite staff and has the capacity to evaluate divisional performance. Not only, therefore, is the goal structure altered in favor of enterprise-wide considerations, but an improved information base permits rewards and penalties to be assigned to divisions on a more discriminating basis, and resources can be reallocated within the firm from less to more productive uses. A concept of the firm as an internal capital market thus emerges.

   Viewing the M-form as an "internal capital market" introduces a fifth phase—one that carries the historical progression beyond the development charted by Chandler. In important respects, the emergence of the *conglomerate* firm represents a further extension of M-form logic. Conglomerate firms are those containing divisions engaged in unrelated businesses: the diversification spans industry groups, not simply product lines. But, as Williamson (1985: 288) notes, its development builds logically on the M-form structure:

> once the merits of the M-form structure for managing separate, albeit related, lines of buiness (e.g., a series of automobile or a series of chemical divisions) were recognized and digested, its extension to manage less closely related activities was natural.

In such firms, divisions are treated primarily as profit centers: the prime criteria for their continuation and support is their current or future profitability, and the general office functions as an (internal) capital market, by which cash flows are directed to high-yield uses. Although capital requests and allocations are formally internalized—a division approaches its own headquarters with its financial requests—in some of the more extreme cases the allocation decisions appear to rest primarily on almost pure market criteria. More often, however, other types of organizational criteria enter into decisions regarding the fate of the divisions. Thus, in important respects, as Eccles and White (1983) have pointed out, markets and hierarchies—come together within the modern corporation, each of these types of control systems helping to determine the disposition of the divisional profit centers.

Several empirical studies have attempted to test the explanations proposed by Chandler and by Williamson, and in general the findings are supportive. For example, Armour and Teece (1978) studied a sample of firms in the petroleum industry and concluded that those adopting the M-form exhibited higher performance, as measured by profitability, than those failing to do so. And in a study based on data from 125 of the largest 500 U.S. corporations in 1964, Palmer and colleagues (Palmer et al., 1986) developed a causal model to test the argument that firms that are industrially diversified and operating in geographically dispersed areas are more likely to adopt the M-form structure. The empirical evidence confirmed both predictions. The analysis also shows that although size contributes to both diversification and dispersion, it does not have a direct effect on structure, confirming Chandler's assertion that large size does not, in itself, cause firms to adopt the M-form structure. Finally, Fligstein (1985a) has assembled a data file containing information on 216 large U.S. firms spanning the period 1919 to 1979. His sample contains the 100 largest nonfinancial corporations in existence during each of three periods: 1919–1939, 1939–1959, and 1959–1979. This data set reveals that whereas less than 2 percent of these major corporations had adopted the multi-divisional structure before 1929, over 84 percent had done so by 1979. And again, Chandler's central predictions are confirmed:

> Industries where product-related strategies dominated, like machine, chemical and transportation industries, adopted the MDF [M-form] in large numbers relatively early; while industries that were more likely to be vertically integrated, like mining, metalmaking, lumber and paper, and petroleum, adopted the MDF later and to a lesser extent (Fligstein, 1985a: 386).

Although these results support Chandler's and Williamson's efficiency-based explanations, other evidence suggests that institutional pressures have also influenced both the extent and timing as well as the specific strategies involved in the adoption of the multi-divisional form. Applying DiMaggio and Powell's (1983) notions of the role of mimetic processes in producing structural isomorphism in organizational fields, Fligstein (1985a: 387) reports that by 1939 and thereafter a mimetic effect is observed "whereby firms in industries with other firms who have already changed to the MDF are more likely to do so," independent of strategy. Giant corporations were observed to embrace the multi-divisional structure not as a solution to internal problems but as a signal to external constituencies. Fligstein also calls attention to the role of the state—a major actor in the institutional environment of large corporations—which responded to increasing concentration in product lines within industries by passage in 1950 of the Celler-Kefauver Act. This act together with subsequent court decisions curtailed corporate efforts to increase market share within the same industry, and in effect forced corporate expansion to occur in product-unrelated areas—that is, through conglomerate strategies. Thus, Fligstein (1985a; 1985b) suggests that what we have characterized above as a fifth phase of corporate development—the shift to conglomerates—was the adaptive response of expansionist-oriented firms to governmental restrictions imposed on earlier, successful product-related strategies.

### Assumptions involved in Explanations of Structure

Just as we did in our examination of the relation between technology and the core structures of the organization, we need to make explicit the assumptions underlying attempts to account for the characteristics of the organization's peripheral structures. Most analysts who have examined the relation between technology and structure, size and structure, or task environment and structure attempt to account for these associations by using rational open system arguments. Blau, Galbraith, Lawrence and Lorsch, Thompson, Chandler, Williamson—all explain their empirical findings or justify their predictions on the basis of improved performance or reduced costs or other language that implies that organizations are fundamentally goal-attainment systems seeking to maximize effectiveness and efficiency. Thus, Thompson argues that to a large extent the variation in organizational structure "can be accounted for as attempts to solve the problems of concerted action under different conditions, especially conditions of technological and environmental constraints and contingencies" (1967: 74). Structure is viewed as a "joint result" of adaptations to technology and environment.

Child criticizes much of the research relating technology, environment, and structure on the grounds that it allows insufficiently for the exercise of choice on the part of those who design the organization. He points out that these studies

> attempt to explain organizational structure at one remove. They draw attention to possible constraints upon the choice of effective structures, but fail to

consider the process of choice itself in which economic and administrative exigencies are weighed by the actors concerned against the opportunities to operate a structure of their own and/or other organizational members' preferences. (Child, 1972: 16)

Certainly, Chandler (1962) insists on the importance of choice. His study, summarized above, of the development of multi-divisional forms by selected United States firms stresses the role of strategy—the setting of goals and objectives—and the uncertain relation between "strategy and structure"—the design of a satisfactory organizational form. He notes that even in the four innovative organizations he studied—du Pont, General Motors, Standard Oil, and Sears, Roebuck—

there was a time lag between the appearance of the administrative needs and their satisfaction. A primary reason for delay was the very fact that responsible executives had become too enmeshed in operational activities. (Chandler, 1962: 315)

His survey of seventy other large industrial companies, some of which adopted the structural changes and others of which did not, revealed that although "expansion did cause administrative problems which led, in time, to organizational change and readjustment," any fundamental "reshaping of administrative structure nearly always had to wait for a change in the top command" (1962: 380). Such comments remind us of the importance of organizational inertia, a feature stressed by the populational ecologists (see Chapter 8). Child and Chandler stress that organizations change—and fail to change—because of choices made by organizational participants.

Contingency theory—which predicts a relation between structure-environment match and performance—is consistent with either the rational selection view that successful managers design their structures to fit environmental contingencies or with the natural selection view that environments select organizations so that only those best matched to their environments survive.

If organizational change or its absence reflects not only external constraints but also internal choices, we may still ask what determines the choices made by organizational participants. Most analysts would embrace the assumption of, at least, intended rationality: members may not always behave rationally, because of misinformation or ignorance or a lapse of attention, but they are believed to be motivated to serve the goals of the organization. However, natural systems analysts, as we already know, would challenge this view.

Early natural system researchers have devoted their efforts to accounting for the departure of behavior from the dictates of formal structure or describing the emergence of the informal structure (see Chapter 3). However, since the early 1960s they have concerned themselves with the determinants of the formal structure itself. As we know, some of these theorists, following Cyert and March (1963), view the organization as a coalition of groups, each pursuing its own interests. Pfeffer (1978: 36) has attempted to spell out the possible implications of this view for explaining organizational structure:

> If we take seriously the conceptualization of organizations as coalitions, then a critical issue is not just what the consequences of various structural arrangements are, but who gains and who loses from such consequences. Structure, it would appear, is not just the outcome of a managerial process in which designs are selected to ensure higher profit. Structure, rather, is itself the outcome of a process in which conflicting interests are mediated so that decisions emerge as to what criteria the organization will seek to satisfy. Organizational structures can be viewed as the outcome of a contest for control and influence occurring within organizations.

Similar to our own discussion in the previous chapter, Pfeffer points out that the relation between technology and structure may result from power processes rather than from rational design decisions: powerful participants defend the definitions of their work as uncertain and hence prevent its routinization. He also suggests that the relation between environmental diversity and structural differentiation may be explained simply by the organization's tendency to incorporate external interest groups into its own structure as a means of co-opting or placating them. And the same argument is used to explain the relation between organizational size and differentiation: size is associated with diversity of interests encountered by the organization, and differentiation is its response to this diversity. While these and related arguments require further refinement and verification, they appear sufficiently plausible to suggest that many features of organizational structure can be explained by nonrational power or conflict models as well as, if not better than, by rational models.

## CONNECTING THE CORE AND PERIPHERAL STRUCTURES

### Tight and Loose Coupling

Much of what passes for organizational structure consists of varying types of mechanisms for controlling the behavior of participants. Hierarchy, formalization, centralization, modes of coordination—are all devices to help ensure that the organizational managers can shape and influence the behavior of other participants charged with carrying on the production activities of the organization. Indeed, a primary justification for the existence of managers is the impact of their ideas and decisions and designs and plans on the behavior of other participants. Many accounts of organizational structure—or, alternatively, many types of organizational structure—emphasize the tight coupling of managers and performers' behavior. Managers decide, performers implement; managers command, performers obey; managers coordinate, performers carry out specialized tasks. Organizations or segments of organizations of this type certainly exist, particularly in situations in which work activities have been divided and routinized. Rational system analysts emphasize this view of organizational structure.

By contrast, early natural system analysts, with their interest in behavioral rather than normative structures, looked more carefully at the operation of these supposedly tightly coupled systems and failed to observe the presence of the taut command systems described by the textbooks in administrative science. Rather, their studies revealed that workers were reluctant to accept close supervision and likely to develop protective work-group mechanisms or understandings with their supervisors that allowed them some leeway and breathing space in defining and meeting requirements (see Roethlisberger and Dickson, 1939; Roy, 1952; Gouldner, 1954; Rushing, 1966*a*). The control systems were less tightly coupled in operation than in theory.

All formal structural devices, however, do not connote tight coupling of activities. Decentralization, delegation, professionalization, even the creation of the staff-line distinction—these are mechanisms for ensuring *some* coordination and control but also for legitimating and supporting the exercise of discretion. They build in flexibility and encourage initiative in the technical core of the organization and so reduce its dependence on and its responsiveness to hierarchical directives. Moreover, as Parsons (1960: 65–66) pointed out when he distinguished among the technical, managerial, and institutional levels of organization, a qualitative break in the line-authority relation exits at the points where the three levels connect (see Chapter 3). Parsons argues that only within a level can a superior directly supervise the work of subordinates and assume responsibility for it, since differences in the nature of the work performed at each level are too great to permit direction of the lower by the higher levels. Thus, board members functioning at the institutional level would not be expected to exercise direct, routine line authority over managers but to grant them considerable freedom in exercising their managerial responsibilities; managers, in turn, would not ordinarily exercise direct line authority over the technical functions of workers. In short, the functions performed at each level are seen to be relatively distinct and not readily linked to one another. Thus, even the relatively conventional views of rational and natural system theorists recognize the presence of considerable loose coupling as an important structural and operational feature of most organizational systems.

Meyer and Rowan (1977) take a more extreme view of the possibilities of loose coupling in organizations. They suggest that organizations in institutional environments will be inclined to selectively *decouple* their formal structures from the activities carried on in their technical core. The rationalized myths that provide meaning and legitimacy to the formal structures often do not provide clear and consistent guidelines for technical activities. The result is that the organization conforms closely to the ritually defined meanings and categories supplied by the environment but does not attempt seriously to implement them at the operational level. For example, Meyer and Rowan argue that educational organizations adhere closely to the ritual categories of education: "There seem to be centralized and enforced agreements about exactly what teachers, students, and topics of instruction constitute a particular school" (1978: 84). But at the operational level, there is little organizational coordination or control over instructional activities. These activities are delegated to teachers, and there is little or no attempt to evaluate and control their performance—either hierarchically or collegially—or to collect and use data on outputs, such as student-performance scores, as a means of improving their performance.[9] The solution of decoupling is particularly effective where environmental rules impose conflicting requirements on organizations. Thus, schools may be simultaneously required to give special treatment to educationally handicapped children but at the same time to *mainstream* them, not segregate them from their fellow students. Organizations can adapt to conflicting demands by creating appropriate programs and offices at the administrative level that can create the required reports, but then decoupling these offices from the operational level.

In a closely related discussion, Marshall Meyer (1979*a*) argues that changes in organizational structure can serve as an important signaling mechanism to the organization's constituencies. For example, the creation of an office for affirmative action can signal to interested parties an organization's commitment to the goals of this program independently of whether or not affirmative action policies are pursued. Meyer points out that such signals are taken seriously by outsiders because changes in structure are highly observable and do cost money (unlike pronouncements of goals or policy statements, which are relatively inexpensive and hence discounted), but are still much less costly than actual changes in rules together with the imposition of inspection and sanctioning procedures to ensure conformity with the new program.

The arguments of these institutional theorists are novel because they suggest that the formal structures of organizations have meaning and importance *regardless of whether they affect the behavior of performers in the technical core.* Formal structures can symbolize meaning and order. And, as Meyer and Rowan (1977: 352) have emphasized, organizations that devise structures that conform closely to institutional requirements "maximize their legitimacy and increase their resources and survival capabilities."

It is important to stress, however, that organizations in both technical and institutional environments engage simultaneously in tight and loose coupling activities, but in different directions. Meyer, Deal, and I (Meyer, Scott, and Deal, 1981: 152–53) summarize the contrasting strategies:

> Organizations arising in connection with technical flows closely control and manage them. Their structures act to regulate the flows, to buffer them from uncertainty, and thus to insulate them in some measure from external forces. . . . The intent is to decouple technical work from environmental conditions so that it can be more tightly managed by the organization.

[9]As Meyer and Rowan note, the problem is not typically the absence of data on student outputs:

> Schools use elaborate tests to evaluate pupils and to shape the course of their present and future lives. But the same data are almost never aggregated and used to evaluate the performance of teachers, schools, or school systems. (Some data of this kind are made available for school and district evaluation in California, but only under the pressure of the state legislature, not the local school system.) (1978: 88–89)

Meyer and Rowan cite numerous benefits associated with these practices, including increased commitments of school participants, both teachers and students; the shielding of ritual classifications from uncertainties arising in the technical core; and the provision of mechanisms allowing schools to adapt to inconsistent and conflicting institutionalized rules.

By contrast, institutionalized organizations closely integrate their own structural arrangements with the frameworks established by the larger institutional structures. In doing so they tend to buffer their structures from the actual technical work activities performed within the organizations. . . .

Thus the technical organization faces in toward its technical core and turns its back on the environment, while the institutional organization turns its back on its technical core in order to concentrate on conforming to its institutional environment.

### Managing Up and Down

It is certainly obvious that over the course of this century, organizational forms have become more and more top-heavy. As Bendix (1956) and others have pointed out, the proportion of administrators to production workers has grown continuously throughout this period (see Chapter 1). A number of factors contributing to this result have been described in previous portions of this volume: the augmentation of the hierarchy to increase the information-processing capacity of the organization as the tasks performed become more complex and uncertain; the elaboration of managerial and staff positions in response to the need to buffer core departments and build connections with other units in the task environment; the incorporation of representatives from external units at the managerial or institutional level in order to relate more adequately to these interests, either as exchange partners or symbolically.[10] All of these developments imply the growth of peripheral roles and structures in relation to the technical core. However, only some of them orient the managerial level in and down toward the activities of the technical core. Many direct their attention up and out to the larger social and political environment. Managers of today's organizations must devote as much time and energy to "managing" their environments as to managing their production system.

Marxist theorists point out the close, interdependent connections between control arrangements within organizations and political systems in the wider society. Economic enterprises always rests on a political base. Whereas the prevailing rhetoric in capitalist societies stresses that enterprise is free and independent from state interference, Burawoy (1985) argues that political regimes within firms and in the wider polity are always linked. Capitalist systems differ from state socialism not in the absence of connections but the directness and visibility of those connections that do exist.

When the environment is heavily institutionalized, managers have their work cut out for them. Although, as we have already noted, Meyer and Rowan (1977: 345) suggest that "it takes only a little entrepreneurial energy to assemble" the relevant components—roles, rules, rituals—which are "littered around the societal landscape," to assemble these components is one thing and to fully mobilize them is another. (See Chapter 7.) Tilly (1978: 69) has proposed that the level of mobilization is a function of

[10]In addition to these changes in the "numerator," important changes in the "denominator" have also transpired. The number of production workers has continuously declined in many industries because of technological developments substituting capital equipment for labor.

the product of two factors: the value of the resources acquired and the probability of "delivering" them when needed. He further suggests that the variables affecting delivery include "the extent of competing claims on the resources involved, the nature of the action to which the resources are to be committed, and how organized the mobilizing group is" (p. 71). It is apparent that many of the resources managers acquire in order to adapt to institutional requirements incorporate elements—whether professional roles or legal rules—that are subject to many competing claims, and are not likely to be readily assimilated or mobilized in the service of organizational objectives.

These conditions help to account for Meyer's (1983) assertion that as the larger societal structures become more "rationalized," individual organizations attempting to operate within them become less "rational."

> Modern rationality has a vastly expanded jurisdiction, and many fewer aspects of society are organized in other ways. All these rationalized perspectives enter into the life of typical formal organizations, which contain and must legitimate the rationalistic perspectives of citizen-members, representatives of various occupational perspectives, carriers of bodies of authoritative knowledge, and organized representatives of a variety of external perspectives that penetrate the organizations and have some sovereign standing. It is exactly this rationalization of so many aspects of society that limits the rationality of formal organizational structure: modern formalized organizations are built up around the acknowledgment of the external legitimation, definition, and control of their internal processes. (Meyer, 1983: 269)

In this fashion, modern organizations "look less like rational organizations than holding companies incorporating various institutionally defined packages" (p. 262). The packages can be acquired and exhibited, but not mobilized in the service of specific goals. The increasingly rationalized institutional structures to be found in modern societies constitute a normative exoskeleton that both supports and constrains its constituent organizations.

## SUMMARY

This chapter has examined some of the factors affecting the larger structure of the organization: the extent of its bureaucratization, centralization, formalization, and differentiation. Although the characteristics of the organization's core technology influence its peripheral features, the latter also respond to other forces, in particular the organization's size and its task environment. A number of empirical studies show that larger organizations are more highly differentiated and more formalized than smaller organizations. However, these studies also reveal that larger organizations tend to be less bureaucratized and centralized in their decision-making structures. It is suggested that reductions in bureaucratization occur because of administrative economies resulting from the managing of more of the same type of work, although these savings are counteracted and may be offset by increased administrative costs associated with greater differentiation—the costs of managing more different kinds of work. Decentralization is both necessary, because of information overload at the top caused by increased size and differentiation, and possible, because formalization promotes consistency of decision making. Technology also affects the characteristics of peripheral structures; in particular, the division and routinization of work are associated with higher levels of differentiation, formalization, and bureaucratization, but the delegation of work to professional personnel is associated with the opposite structural effects. Whether the effects of size or of technology dominate in determining structural features of organizations cannot be determined from existing studies: longitudinal studies designed to test explicit casual models based on better samples of organizations are required.

The peripheral structures of organizations are also affected by the buffering and bridging strategies employed by organizations in relating to their task environment. Associated with all of these specific techniques are structural modifications—additions of new roles and departments and representatives of external interests. Open systems map critical features of their environments into their own structures as a major adaptive strategy. Structural reorganization is also associated with organizational growth. A prime example of such reorganization is the shift during the first half of this century in many major corporations from a unitary to a multi-divisional structure.

The extent to which managerial units control and coordinate work in the technical core varies by type of organization but has probably been overstated. Considerable looseness of coupling has not only been observed in most organizations in the behavior of supervisors and workers but is legitimated by many types of formal arrangements. Recent analysts have called attention to some of the adaptive features of loosely coupled systems—whether the coupling involves boundary units relating to specific environmental segments, connections among boundary units, or connections between boundary and core units. The symbolic importance of structure has also been noted. Changes in structure at the institutional or managerial level are important whether or not they are associated with changes in procedures or behaviors within the technical core.

Managers must expend as much time and energy in relating to environmental demands as in directing the internal affairs of the organization. Balancing and reconciling—as well as buffering and segregating—are the primary administrative tasks in contemporary organizations.

# 11 goals, power, and control

Group decision-making extends deeply into the business enterprise. Effective participation is not closely related to rank in the formal hierarchy of the organization. This takes an effort of mind to grasp. Everyone is influenced by the stereotyped organization chart of the business enterprise. . . . Power is assumed to pass down from the pinnacle. Those at the top give orders; those below relay them on or respond.

This happens, but only in very simple organizations— the peacetime drill of the National Guard or a troop of Boy Scouts moving out on Saturday maneuvers. Elsewhere the decision will require information. Some power will then pass on to the person or persons who have this information. If this knowledge is highly particular to themselves then their power becomes very great.

John Kenneth Galbraith (1967)

The subjects of goals, power, and control have recurred frequently enough throughout the preceding chapters of this volume that their importance must now be established. Although we have touched on these topics in many places—and have skirted them in others—we have not yet confronted them directly. We begin by discussing the concept of organizational goals, indicating some of the reasons it has proved so obstreperous. We will find that it is helpful to change the questions What are goals: and Do organizations have goals? to the question Who set the goals in organizations? It is here that the questions of goals and power come together. It is also instructive to ask whether there are organizations that lack goals and, if so, what effect this has on their structure and functioning.

We also examine control systems in organizations. What are the sources of power, and how does power become authority? Some organizations substitute internal for external control systems, relying heavily on shared cultural beliefs. These types of controls are also described.

## GOAL SETTING IN ORGANIZATIONS

### Problems in Conceptualizing Organizational Goals

*The varying uses of goals*    The concept of organizational goals is among the most slippery and treacherous of all those employed by organizational analysts. Many factors contribute to the confusion in this area. A brief description of some of these factors may not resolve all of the questions but at least will clarify some of them. One source of difficulty is that statements of organizational goals are used in a number of ways by organizations. Thus, rational system analysts emphasize that goals provide criteria for generating and selecting among alternative courses of action (Simon, 1957; 1964). These analysts stress the *cognitive* functions of goals: goals provide directions for and constraints on decision making and action. Natural system analysts, such as Barnard (1938) and Clark and Wilson (1961), emphasize that goals serve as a source of identification and motivation for participants. And Selznick (1949) notes that goals may be employed as ideological weapons with which to overcome opposition and garner resources from the environment. These analysts all emphasize the *cathectic* (emotional) properties of goals: goals serve as bases of attachment for both organizational participants and external publics. Note that a goal statement that is satisfactory for analysts concerned with the cathectic properties of goals may be unsatisfactory for analysts intersted in their cognitive contributions. Vague and general descriptions of goals may suffice for motivational purposes—indeed, they may be especially suited to this function—but be unsatisfactory for cognitive guidance. For example, colleges may be able to attract students or funds with the claim that they are "preparing tomorrow's leaders," but such goal statements will provide little help in designing the curriculum or hiring the faculty.

Institutional analysts stress the *symbolic* functions of goals. Whereas the cognitive and cathectic properties of goals emphasize their effects on organizational participants, the symbolic aspect of goals points to their significance for organizational audiences: publics, clients, taxpayers, regulators. The goals an organization espouses, the goals it appears to be serving, the goals it embodies and is perceived to represent—these symbolic goals have important effects on the organization's ability to acquire legitimacy, allies, resources, and personnel.

Still other analysts have challenged the conventional view of behavior in which goals precede actions. Weick has insisted on the relevance of dissonance theory as formulated by Festinger (1957) and others to decision making in organizations. Weick argues that

> rationality seems better understood as a postdecision rather than a predecision occurrence. Rationality makes sense of what has been, not what will be. It is a process of justification in which past deeds are made to appear sensible to the actor himself and to those other persons to whom he feels accountable. (Weick, 1969: 38)

In short, behavior sometimes precedes goals, and goal statements can serve as a *justification* for the actions taken (Staw, 1980).

Goal statements also serve as a basis for *evaluating* the behavior of participants or of entire organizations (see Scott, 1977*a*). They provide criteria for identifying and appraising selected aspects of organizational functioning. We will examine goals used as evaluation criteria applied to organizational performance in Chapter 13. The criteria used to evaluate performance may or may not be the same as those employed to direct it.

More generally, the various types of goal statements—that goals are used to guide behavior, to motivate it, to symbolize it, to justify it, or to evaluate it—may not coincide closely not only because they serve different functions but because they emanate from different sources. Symbolic goals are likely to be promulgaged at the institutional level of the organization, which seeks to legitimate organizational purposes by stressing their larger social functions. The top managers of a company are likely to stress cathectic goals as a way of developing commitment among their participants. From Barnard (1938) to Selznick (1957) to Peters and Waterman (1982) the "functions of the executive" are said to be articulate and inculcate commitment to corporate values. Middle-level managers, in concert with their technical staff, are expected to translate general aspirations into specific products and services, and so may be expected to emphasize the cognitive aspects of goals. Evaluators at all levels employ goals as a source of criteria for evaluating participants as they carry on the work of the organization, and participants at all levels employ goal statements to help them justify their past actions when asked to give an accounting. In Chapter 13, we pursue further how goals enter into the evaluation of organizational performance.

**Individual and organizational goals**   Simon (1957; 1964) has most forcefully urged the distinction between individual goals that govern the decision to join or remain in an organization, and organizational goals that are expected to govern the decision of individuals as participants (see Chapters 2 and 7). Simon proposes that for the sake of clarity such individual goals be labeled *motives*. This rational system conception of a relatively clear distinction between individual motives and organizational goals is challenged by the natural system perspective, which insists that individuals are not completely contained within their roles but may be expected to impose their own preferences on the choice of opportunities that confront them as participants. Simon (1964) does not deny the operation of such processes but insists that the distinction retains value. He notes, for example, that many requirements organizations impose on their participants are orthogonal to their motives—for example, it is a matter of indifference to individuals who have accepted employment as secretaries whether they type one letter rather than another. More generally, one would need to deny the existence of social roles and their impact on individual behavior in order to maintain that organizational goals are indistinguishable from individual motives. The separation of these concepts is also aided by Clark and Wilson's (1961) discussion of incentive systems (see Chapter 7). Their typology reminds us that in only a limited set of organizations—which they label *purposive*—do individual motives and organizational goals coincide. In most organizations the goals toward which participants direct their behavior are different from the goals that motivate them to participate in the organization.

One implication of these considerations is that we will not want to survey individual participants and then aggregate their individual objectives to arrive at a description of the organization's goals. In escaping from this reductionist fallacy, however, we must be careful not to go to the opposite extreme and posit the existence of some type of metaphysical corporate mind in which collective goals are formulated. To do so is inappropriately to reify the organization, granting it anthropomorphic properties it does not possess. We can avoid both reductionism and reification by reformulating our question. Instead of asking, Do organizations have goals? we will ask, Who sets organizational goals, and How are organizational goals set?

## The Dominant Coalition

The most satisfactory answer to date to the question of who sets organizational goals is provided by Cyert and March (1963). They note that the classic economist's response to this question is to point to the goals of the entrepreneur and to equate the organization's goals with this person's objectives: the firm is seen as the shadow of one powerful actor. A second proposed solution is to presume that goals are consensually defined: all participants share in goal setting. Both of these models of goal setting are rejected as exceptional patterns found only rarely in nature. Cyert and March ((1963: 27–32) propose the alternative conception of organizational goals being set by a negotiation process that occurs among memers of *dominant coalitions*. We will briefly summarize this important conception.

Organizations are viewed as being composed of coalitions—groups of individuals pursuing certain interests. Each group will attempt to impose its preferences (goals) on the larger system, but in the typical case, no single group will be able to determine completely what goals are to be pursued. Group members seek out as allies other groups whose interests are similar, and they negotiate with those groups whose interests are divergent but whose participation is necessary. One group will make a *side payment* to another to secure its cooperation; that is, will accede to that group's demands. For example, a management group, to secure its goal of continued growth, will agree to provide a given level of return on investment to its stockholders and will agree to pay a specified level of wages to its employees. Note, however, that what is a goal for one group is viewed as a side payment by another group, and vice versa. Each group whose interests must be taken into account helps to define the goals of the organization.

All such groups are, by definition, members of the dominant coalition. Each negotiated agreement provides guidance to the organization and places constraints on what may be regarded as an acceptable course of action. And the goals themselves are complex preference statements that summarize the multiple conditions any acceptable choice must satisfy. Simon (1964:7) amplifies this latter point:

> In the decision-making situations of real life, a course of action, to be acceptable, must satisfy a whole set of requirements, or constraints. Sometimes one of these requirements is singled out and referred to as the goal of the

action. But the choice of one of the constraints, from many, is to a large extent arbitrary. For many purposes it is more meaningful to refer to the whole set of requirements as the (complex) goal of the action.

Simon points out that the complexity of these goal statements provides yet another reason why there is often disagreement over whether organizations may be said to have goals. He argues that

> If we use the phrase organization goals broadly to denote the constraint sets, we will conclude that organizations do, indeed, have goals (widely shared constraint sets). If we use the phrase organization goals narrowly to denote the generators [preferences held by individual coalition participants that are proposed as satisfactory alternatives], we will conclude that there is little communality of goals among the several parts of large organizations. (1964: 9)

The conception of the dominant coalition, though certainly not the last word on the subject of who sets organizational goals, does help to avoid many of the problems that have plagued earlier explanations. We embrace this conception because it offers the following features:

> •The problem of reification is avoided: individuals and groups have interests, and the process by which these preferences come to be imposed on the organization is specified.
> •It is recognized that although individuals and groups are allowed to specify the goals of the organization, there is no presumption that they do so on an equal footing, nor is it assumed that they hold common objectives.
> •It is recognized that although individuals and groups impose goals on the organization, in most cases no single individual or group is powerful enough to determine completely the organization's goals; hence, the organization's goals are distinct from those of any of its participants.
> •Allowance is made for differences in interests among participants. Some, but not all, of these differences may be resolved by negotiation, so at any time, conflicting goals may be present.
> •It is recognized that the size and composition of the dominant coalition may vary from one organization to another and within the same organization from time to time.

Coleman (1975) points out that another advantage to this general approach to goal setting in organizations is that it easily permits the analyst to shift the level of analysis from, for example, the individual groups and their interests to the organization as a unit comprising these interests. He asserts that

> if we conceive of this system [the organization] as an actor in the next level (which I shall call a "corporate actor"), then its interests are given by the values of events at the lower level. In such an integrated system, the organization acts as if it were a single actor, and the directions in which it acts are given by the values of events generated at the lower level. . . .
> Thus the shift between levels in this theory is accomplished by conceiving of organizations as continuing systems of action, subject to internal analysis, and also as corporate actors, with interests derivable from that internal analysis. (Coleman, 1975: 86)

Coleman's explication helps to clarify the model, but in so doing calls attention to a major weakness.

With all of its advantages over previous conceptions, the coalition model of goal setting remains basically an aggregative model. Individual actors and even groups are allowed to have genuine interests, but organizations are not: they are viewed simply as collections of interests or, in Pfeffer and Salancik's words, "as settings in which groups and individuals with varying interests and preferences come together and engage in exchanges" (1978: 26). Such a conception may suffice for a coalitional or open systems theorist but cannot be expected to be acceptable to a rational or natural system analyst. Wallace voices the latter's concerns in his critique of Coleman's view that " 'interests' are fixed in individuals" and that "causal dominance" is located at the bottom rather than the top of the hierarchy.

> . . . Coleman appears to deny or ignore the reverse possibility that the values of events at the higher level may "give" the interest of the individual actor; he also appears to overlook the possibility that genuinely new interests may emerge from a new arrangement (especially a hierarchical arrangement) of individual actors.
> Coleman's rejection of corporate determination of individual interest and his apparent choice of interest-aggregation over interest-emergence between the individual and the corporate levels seem clearly to constitute psychological reductionism. (Wallace, 1975: 127)

Although interests are certainly brought to the organization and imposed on it by some powerful participant groups, it seems entirely plausible that interests also are generated within the organization. Managers who stand to profit from economies realized by increased scale or technical innovation may be expected to coalesce around these "new" interests, and others whose power is closely associated with the condition and survival prospects of the larger enterprise may be expected to champion the interests of the organization as a whole.

The natural system theorists are correct in assuming that in most cases a set of participants will perceive that their interests are served by the survival and strengthening of the organization. Thus, we need to allow for the possibility that new interests and new coalitions will emerge over time in response to the opportunities and dangers created by the existence of the organization itself. The dominant coalition model can thereby be modified and interpreted so as to avoid the reductionist fallacy.

As noted, all organizations are not expected to look alike in the size and composition of their dominant coalitions. We need to examine what factors account for these differences.

### Factors Affecting
### the Dominant Coalition

There are many potential sources of power in modern organizations. Those who own property, whether in the form of capital, land, machinery, or disposable goods, have "a socially defensible right to make a decision on how to use" these resources (Stinchcombe, 1983:131). *Ownership* is an important basis of power in most economic systems. However, usually the person or group that has a socially and legally defensible right to make a decision on the use of the resource does not do so directly. . . . Instead, the fund of resources is entrusted to an administrative apparatus, of which the property-owning group (the board of directors) is the formal head. . . . the property rights are . . . used to make the activities of an administrative apparatus controlling the resources legitimate. (Stinchcombe, 1983: 135–36)

Owners delegate control over resources to *managers,* who are expected to act on their behalf—to serve as their agents. But, as numerous analysts from Berle and Means (1932) to Galbraith (1967) to economic agency theorists (such as Alchian and Demsetz, 1972; Jensen and Meckling, 1976; Fama, 1980) have noted, the interests of owners—whether capitalists or widely dispersed middle-class stockholders—and managers may diverge; managers develop their own power base as owners become dependent on their expertise and detailed knowledge of the administration of the enterprise.[1]

Organizations also depend on the energies and skills of workers or *labor* who carry out the work of transforming resources. Although as individuals they may exercise relatively little power, collectively workers are often able to acquire considerable power by engaging in or threatening strikes, slowdowns, or sabotage and expressing their demands through collective bargaining or other forms of negotiation. And, as noted in Chapter 8, the higher the specificity of worker skills in a particular organization, the more power workers will enjoy.

Finally, power accrues to those who occupy critical *boundary roles* in the organization. Individuals and work groups that connect with important resource suppliers, mediate the demands of critical regulatory agencies, or embody the concerns of institutional actors obtain power within the organizations they serve.

Hickson and colleagues (1971) have proposed a useful set of dimensions for explaining power in organizations. Like the resource dependency theorists, they build on Emerson's (1962) formulation of power-dependency relations, but rather than applying these ideas to interorganizational relations, they focus on explaining the distribution of power within organizations a strategic contingency approach.

Hickson and associates offer three general propositions relating to the acquisition of intraorganizational power. First, building on the insights of Crozier, they propose that subunits that cope more effectively with uncertainty are more likely to acquire power. The source of uncertainty may vary from technical to environmental disturbances. Crozier (1964), in an intensive case study of the French tobacco manufacturing industry, observed that mechanics held considerable power—much more than their formal position in the organization would suggest—because they were capable of dealing with machine breakdowns, the major source of uncertainty in the highly mechanized plants. The importance of environmental uncertainty for internal power is further illustrated by Goldner's study of the industrial relations (IR) unit in a manufacturing organization. Goldner writes that

[1]See Chapter 12 for a discussion of the same process in public bureaucracies: the power of administrative officials grows to challenge that of the political rulers.

the major source of IR's power over specific plant-level issues was . . . the use of the union as an outside threat. Recognition that their nominal antagonists were the source of their internal power was even made explicit by one IR manager: "As I told one of the (other IR) guys who was damning the unions—Don't bite the hand that feeds you." (Goldner, 1970: 104–5)

Uncertainty is not a constant but is subject to change over time. For example, improvements in technology can lead to increased routinization of work and hence, to reductions in uncertainty. Thus, in the corporation studies by Goldner,

> the dominant theme in the recent history of the operations unit has been its steady loss of power, which had accompanied the increased rationalization of the organization. Those in operations were subject to the effect or more extensive decision-making by others on matters that directly affected operations. They had lost autonomy and resented it. (1970: 109)

However, the main contribution of this first proposition by Hickson and colleagues is its insistence that it is not the presence of uncertainty alone but the *successful coping with uncertainty* that produces power for the subunit. Only if the subunit can effectively manage the uncertainty confronted, and in doing so protect the other units from its disturbing effects, can the subunit parlay uncertainty into power. In Goldner's example, for the IR unit to profit from the threat posed by the union, it had to be able to cope with that threat, thereby reducing uncertainty for the rest of the organization.

The second proposition is "the lower the *substitutability* of the activities of a subunit, the greater its power within the organization" (Hickson et al., 1971: 221). This prediction is a direct application of Emerson's principle that power is inversely affected by alternative sources. In operational terms, this variable can be measured by the extent to which an organization can obtain alternative services to those provided by the unit or by the extent to which the personnel within the unit are replaceable.

The third proposition relates to the *centrality* of the subunit, which is defined as having two components: pervasiveness—"the degree to which the workflows of a subunit connect with the workflows of other units"— and immediacy—"the speed and severity with which the workflows of a subunit affect the final outputs of the organization" (1971: 221–22). Hickson and colleagues predict that the higher the centrality—pervasiveness and immediacy—of the subunit, the greater its power.[2]

These researchers have tested these propositions in a study of four principal subunits—the engineering, marketing, production, and accounting departments—in each of seven small manufacturing organizations, or twenty-eight subunits in all (Hinings et al., 1974). A sample of organizations was selected so as to vary the uncertainty faced by the subunits, in particular, marketing. Independent variables were measured by scales

---

[2]Those interested in designing more egalitarian organizations must not only be attentive to the design of the formal authority system but must also guard against these sources of differential power. Among the techniques employed are task and worker rotation, demystification of expertise, and de-differentiation of work roles—attempts to insure that coping skills are shared, work is substitutable, and centrality is shared and thus neutralized. (See Rothschild-Whitt, 1979; Rothschild-Whitt and Whitt, 1986.)

based on both questionnaire and interview responses. The dependent variable, power, was measured in several ways: perceived influence attributed to the subunits over a variety of task areas; perceived formal authority over the same task areas; and reported participation in decision making. The several power indicators showed, in general, high and positive intercorrelations. Generally speaking, the data provided support for the three propositions. In terms of relative importance, coping with uncertainty was observed to have the greatest impact on power, followed, in order, by immediacy, nonsubstitutability, and pervasiveness.

But alongside these technical arguments, we need to add the institutionalist perspective. As Meyer (1978: 357) points out,

> organizations and their internal units derive legitimacy, power, and authority from their status in social environments. . . . the social validity of a given unit—a professional group, a technical procedure, or a departmentalized function—is often defined more importantly in the environment than by internal technical efficacy.

Such units have power—based on their external connections and supports—that is *independent* of their contributions to internal operations.

These various arguments suggest that as environmental conditions vary, we may expect power to shift within an organization from one group to another. Thus, Perrow's (1961) case study of a community hospital documents the gradual transition of power from the owners and trustees to the physicians, as a result of the increasing ability of the latter group to effectively cope with medical uncertainties presented by patients, and the more recent shift of power from the physicians to the professional administrators, as a result of the importance of internal coordination and external boundary mangement and the administrators' capacity to deal with these problems. Similarly, Fligstein (1986) has shown that as the environments confronting major corporations have changed over this century, the composition of the dominant coalition has also varied. Using as an indicator of power shifts the type of department from which the CEO is selected, Fligstein examined the departmental background of the top executive in his sample of 216 major corporations and observed how this background changed between 1919 and 1979. He reports that whereas entrepreneurs—the founders and builders of corporations—dominated during the period 1880–1920, CEOs tended to be selected from manufacturing departments between 1920 and 1940, from sales departments between 1940 to 1960, and from finance departments from 1960 into the 1980s. He argues that these shifts mirror the changing challenges confronting corporations: production problems dominated in the 1920s and 1930s, distributional problems in the 1940s and 1950s, and capital problems from the 1960s to the present.

The number of potential power holders and the various sources of power help to explain why the size of the dominant coalition has increased in most organizations in recent years. Rather than highly centralized hierarchies in which one or a few persons exercise most of the power and make most of the decisions, most contemporary organizations exhibit power and decision-making structures that include a substantial number of individuals. Galbraith (1967) argues that one of the most fundamental changes in the organization of the modern corporation is a shift from an entrepreneurial mode in which a single powerful person dominates the enterprise to a *technostructure* in which power is widely diffused. According to Galbraith (1967: 58), the technostructure consists of

> men of diverse technical knowledge, experience or other talent which modern industrial technology and planning require. It extends from the leadership of the modern industrial enterprise down to just short of the labor force and embraces a large number of people and a large variety of talent. [It constitutes the] new locus of power in the business enterprise and in the society.

More so that Galbraith, Thompson (1967: 127–36) makes clear the reason for the increasing size of the organization's power structure. Consistent with the views of Crozier and Hickson, Thompson argues that the number of positions of power within the organization and hence the size of the dominant coalition, is affected both by the nature of the organization's technology and by its task and institutional environments. The more uncertain the technology and the greater the number of sources of uncertainty in the organization's environment, the more bases for power there are within the organization and the larger will be the dominant coalition. When organizations embrace more uncertain technologies, as in the case of professional organizations, and when the sources of uncertainty increase in the environment of the organization, we may expect those who cope with these problems to demand and receive a place in the decision-making councils of the organization.

What difference, if any, does it make when power shifts from one group to another or is shared with a larger proportion of the participants? The difference should be reflected, of course, in the goals pursued by the organization. Admission to the dominant coalition is an empty victory if the new partners cannot affect the definition of the goals to be served. And, on the basis of his case study of the community hospital, Perrow (1961) asserts that as doctors replaced trustees, hospital goals shifted from community welfare concerns to business-professional objectives, including research; and as the administrators gained dominance over the physicians, the hospital's goals shifted to emphasize the role of the hospital as the medical center for the community. And in the case of the coalitions of interests present in the modern corporation, Galbraith argues that although the stockholders must receive their side payment of a satisfactory return on their investment, the maximization of profits associated with the entrepreneurial regime has given way to a new goal prefered by the now-dominant coalition of technical and managerial specialists: "the greatest possible rate of corporate growth as measured in sales." This goal is valued by the technostructure because "expansion of output means expansion of the technosctucture itself ... including more jobs with more responsibility and hence more promotion and more compensation" (1967: 171).

Similarly, Fligstein (1985a; 1985b) asserts that associated with changes in the origins of the types of persons assuming command within the corporations are basic changes in the goals of these organizations—the types of strategies being pursued. Founding entrepreneurs pursued strategies of horizontal merger in attempting to control the market. As the scale of production increased, coordination and resource problems came to the fore and manufacturing officials became dominant, pursuing strategies of vertical integration. Functional (unitary) forms were constructed to support these strategies.

> Once production is routinized, power shifts to sales and marketing personnel as the key issue for the organization becomes growth. . . . A sales and marketing strategy focuses on attempting to broaden the firm's markets by expanding across regions and countries. (Fligstein, 1985*a*: 380)

This strategy is supported by the creation of multi-divisional forms to support production and product-related distribution systems. Finally, governmental actions in the 1950s designed to prevent further concentration forced the development of alternate strategies: corporations were forced to abandon their attempt to increase their market share and began to pursue growth through multiple, unrelated product lines. Financial experts were in the best position to devise these strategies, and the conglomerate form was best suited to their support.

Environmental changes, shifting power-dependency relations, changing goals and strategies, and new structural forms—while the temporal sequence and the causal ordering of these elements are not clear, and will often be difficult to establish, it does appear that there are strong interdependencies among them.

In more differentiated and loosely coupled systems such as universities, power differences among subunits may be reflected not so much in direct attempts to redefine the goals of the larger system but in efforts to lay claim to a disproportionate share of the organization's resources. This process is well illustrated in a study by Pfeffer and Salanick (1974) of the allocation of general university resources among twenty-nine academic departments examined over a thirteen-year period. These researchers convincingly show that the greater power of individual departments, as measured by indicators such as perceived influence and representation on powerful university committees, the greater the proportion of general university funds they received. Although such budgetary decisions may appear remote from the general goals of the university, they are in reality highly relevant: the allocation of scarce resources among diverse university programs is one of the clearest indicators available of the "real" goals of the institution.

### Anarchies and Adhocracies

Both the bureaucratic-administrative model of the rational system perspective and the coalitional-bargaining model of the natural and open system perspectives provide for the development of a set of goals by which organizational decisions can be made. Both allow for the construction of relatively clear criteria or preference orderings in terms of which priorities can be set and selections made among alternative courses of action. But there are classes of organizations—and, more important, classes of decision situations within many organizations—in which no clear preference orderings have been determined. Such organizations are on the fringe if not beyond the pale of those collectivities included within the conventional definitions and theories of organizations (see Chapter 1). Yet they present both interesting and instructive cases.

Thompson and Tuden (1959) focus on these situations by constructing a typology that combines two dimensions: (1) how much agreement there is among participants of the organization about the goals or preferred outcomes of the system, and (2) how much agreement there is about the means or the casual processes by which these outcomes can be realized. The cross-classification of this simple ends-and-means distinction produces four types of decision contexts, each of which is argued to be associated with a different decision strategy:

| BELIEFS ABOUT CAUSATION | PREFERENCES ABOUT OUTCOMES | |
|---|---|---|
| | Agreement | Disagreement |
| Agreement | *Computation* | *Compromise* |
| Disagreement | *Judgment* | *Inspiration* |

We are most interested in the right-hand column—situations in which participants lack consensus on goals—but let us briefly comment on the simpler and more familiar situations in which such agreement is present. Thompson and Tuden use the term *computation* to denote those decisions most suited to the typical bureaucratic decision-making structure, which, as we have often noted, is most appropriate in situations in which goals are clearly defined and the technology relatively certain. The term *judgment* is employed to refer to the strategies required when agreement on goals exists but the means of achieving them is uncertain. This situation is best confronted with a collegium and is well illustrated, in our opinion, by the structure of professional organizations previously described.

As for the column of interest, Thompson and Tuden argue that there are sometimes situations in which participants agree about how to accomplish some objective or about what the expected consequences of available alternatives are, but disagree over which alternative is preferable. A mild version of this situation is provided by the coalitional view of decision making—which, as we have described, is resolved by negotiation, bargaining, and sequential attention to goals. More extreme instances of disagreement and conflict can sometimes be resolved through the creation of representative bodies that allow for the expression of differences and the engineering of compromises. Most such forums—for example, the United Nations and the United States Congress—presume the existence of substantive differences in preferences but rely on procedural agreements—such as Robert's Rules of Order—for resolving them.

The fourth and final decision situation is characterized by the absence of agreement about either ends or means. Thompson and Tuden suggest that these anomic situations are more commonly found among organizations than conventional theories suggest. They propose that such circumstances, if they are not to be followed by complete system disintegration, call for *inspiration*, perhaps of the type suggested by Weber's (1947 trans.) description of the charismatic leader. This is not inconsistent with Weber's own views, described in Chapter 2, in which charismatic leaders are viewed as more likely to emerge in crisis situations—times when conventional goals are being challenged and established procedures are not working. And, like Weber, Thompson and Tuden expect such leadership to give rise over time to a computational (bureaucratic) structure based on a new definition of goals and accepted procedures, as charisma is routinized.

March and his colleagues (March and Olsen, 1976; Cohen, March, and Olsen, 1972, 1976; Cohen and March, 1976; March, 1978) have also examined decision making under conditions of "inconsistent and ill-defined preferences," "unclear technologies," and "fluid participation"—the shifting involvement of members in decision situations (Cohen, March, and Olsen, 1972: 1). They label these conditions *organized anarchies*. But unlike Thompson and Tuden, March and associates do not view these circumstances as crises or as transitory states. Rather, they insist that they have been "identified often in studies of organizations," "are characteristic of any organization in part," and "are particularly conspicuous in public, educational, and illegitimate organizations" (Cohen, March, and Olsen, 1976: 25).

The portrait of organized anarchies is set within a more general framework that stresses the ambiguity in decision making. (See Chapter 5) March and Olsen comment on their approach:

> We remain in the tradition of viewing organizational participants as problem-solvers and decision-makers. However, we assume that individuals find themselves in a more complex, less stable, and less understood world than that described by standard theories of organizational choice; they are placed in a world over which they often have only modest control. (March and Olsen, 1976: 21)

The organizational world depicted here is similar to that described by Weick (1969; see also Chapter 4): individual decision makers have cognitive and attention limits; external conditions constrain alternatives and affect outcomes but often go unnoticed; and choices by individuals in decision-making positions may not eventuate in organizational action. Under such conditions, all choices are somewhat ambiguous.

> Although organizations can often be viewed conveniently as vehicles for solving well-defined problems or structures within which conflict is resolved through bargaining, they also provide sets of procedures through which participants arrive at an interpretation of what they are doing and what they have done while in the process of doing it. From this point of view, an organization is a collection of choices looking for problems, issues and feelings looking for decision situations in which they might be aired, solutions looking for issues to which they might be the answer, and decision makers looking for work. (Cohen, March, and Olsen, 1972: 2)

Under conditions of organized anarchy, the ambiguity of choice present in all decision-making situations reaches its apex. Here problems, solutions, participants, and choice opportunities are viewed as flows that more relatively independently into and out of the decision arena—metaphorically labeled a "garbage can." Which solutions get attached to which problems is largely determined by chance—by what participants with what goals happened to be on the scene, by when the solutions or the problems entered, and so on. Although the system described seems bizarre and even pathological when compared with the conventional model of rational decision making, it does produce decisions under conditions of high uncertainty: that is, some solutions do get attached by some participants to some problems.

Cohen, March, and Olsen (1972) have developed and examined some of the implications of their garbage-can model under varying assumptions by using computer-simulation techniques. However, this model of decision making was originally suggested to them on the basis of observations of decision-making processes in colleges and universities:

> Opportunities for choice in higher education can easily become complex "garbage cans" into which a striking variety of problems, solutions, and participants may be dumped. Debate over the hiring of a football coach can become connected to concerns about the essence of a liberal education, the relations of the school to ethnic minorities, or the philosophy of talent. (Cohen and March, 1976: 175)

Perhaps it is due specifically to the characteristics of universities, or perhaps they intend their comments to apply more generally to all organized anarchies, but unlike Thompson and Tuden, Cohen and March (1974: 1976) do not look for a charismatic leader to ride in on horseback bringing inspiration for new goals. They perceive the role of leaders—for example, university presidents—in such situations in much more problematic and pessimistic terms. They do suggest that leaders can improve their performance if they take into account the unusual nature of decision-making situations in these organizations. By carefully timing issue creation, by being sensitive to shifting interests and involvement of participants, by recognizing the status and power implications of choice situations, by abandoning initiatives that have become hopelessly entangled with other, originally unrelated problems, by realizing that the planning function is largely symbolic and chiefly provides excuses for interaction, leaders in organized anarchies can maintain their sanity and, sometimes, make a difference in the decision made.

One major factor often accounting for the absence of clearly specified goals is the unstable nature of some organizational environments. If environments are turbulent, then it is difficult to establish clear and specific objectives around which to design a structure and orient participant activities. Under unsettled conditions, tents may be preferable to palaces:

> In constant surroundings, one could confidently assemble an intricate, rigid structure combining elegant and refined components—an organizational palace. . . .
>
> However, systematic procedures offer weak protection against unpredictability, just as increased rigidity does not effectively prepare a building for earthquakes. Some flaws of systematic procedures are inherent in the concept of strategic planning: drafting plans, dismantling an old structure, and erecting a new structure take so long that designers need to forecast how the environment will shift. Since forecasts are only conjectures derived from past experiences, greater reliance on forecasts induces greater design errors. Systematic procedures also sap an organization's flexibility by strengthening its rationality.

> ... Residents of changing environments need a tent. An organizational tent placed greater emphasis on flexibility, creativity, immediacy, and initiative than on authority, clarity, decisiveness, or responsiveness; and an organizational tent neither asks for harmony between the activities of different organizational components, nor asks that today's behavior resemble yesterday's or tomorrow's. Why behave more consistently than one's world does? (Hedberg, Nystrom, and Starbuck, 1976: 44–45)

Unstable environments undermine clear and consistent goals, just as they unsettle rigid formalized structures. (See Chapter 9.)

Still, some elements of consistency can be found in the goal structures of organizations operating under unstable conditions. If, following Mintzberg and McHugh (1985), strategies are defined as "a pattern in a stream of decisions or actions," then it may be possible to retrospectively identify underlying motifs. Not all intended strategies are realized, and those that are realized may be emergent rather than deliberate. In their case study of the National Film Board (NFB) of Canada from its inception in 1939, Mintzberg and McHugh were able to discern a number of patterns in its products and approach that although unplanned, nevertheless provided a fabric with discernible designs. The film makers provided the warp, but the environment furnished the woof.

> ... the NFB had an ironic relationship with its environment. In one sense, it was highly responsive—to social trends, new fashions, new media, social turmoil. Ultimately, the NFB found its purpose—when it did—in the world around it, not in itself: it truly was a mirror for its society. ... Yet in another sense, this was truly an organization that "did its own thing." Except during the war years, the NFB as a whole catered largely to its own needs, for the most part selecting those parts of the environment to which it cared to respond. ...
>
> The essence of adhocracy, in contrast to machine bureaucracies that seek to control their environments in order to support their standardized systems of mass production, would seem to be rapid and continuous responsiveness to the environment, with minimal organizational momentum. (Mintzberg and McHugh, 1985: 191)

Organizations such as the NFB that rely less on long-term strategic planning and more on ad hoc, emergent strategies may also be said to replace coventional rational decision-making techniques with *experiential learning*. (See Hedberg, 1981; March, 1981.) Whereas rational system models assume that goals are stable, learning modes assume that they are subject to change, that many choices are not guided by preestablished intentions but result in the discovery of new purposes. And whereas rational systems models propose that technologies are known, learning models stress that they must be continuously invented, shaped, and modified in the light of feedback from the environment. Learning approaches embrace the open system conception of organizations:

> Learning in open, cognitive systems takes the form of positive feedback which changes the systems or their knowledge, whereas learning in closed, natural systems is the function of negative feedback which aims at maintaining the genotype unchanged (Hedberg, 1981: 5).

Learning that "changes the system," that results not simply in new decisions but in new rules and methods for deciding, is what Argyris and

Schon (1978) term *double-loop learning*. It requires the "unlearning" of the old ways as well as the acquisition of new ones.

It should be clear, however, that we should not underestimate how difficult it is for organizational systems to learn anything useful, given a rapidly changing environment, selective attention and inattention processes, enactment processes, inertia, cognitive limits, and ambiguity of feedback.

## CONTROL SYSTEMS

It is one thing to set goals; it is another to see that energies are directed toward their accomplishment. To this end, control must be exercised. Of course, all collectivities control their members. As we have previously argued in defining them, if collectivities do not show evidence of a distinctive normative structure and some regular patterns of participant behavior, we cannot even establish their existence. But, as Etzioni has argued, the problems of control in organizations are especially acute:

> The artificial quality of organizations, their high concern with performance, their tendency to be far more complex than natural units, all make informal control inadequate and reliance on identification with the job impossible. Most organizations most of the time cannot rely on most of their participants to internalize their obligations to carry out their assignments voluntarily, without additional incentives. Hence, organizations require formally structured distribution of rewards and sanctions to support compliance with their norms, regulations, and orders. (Etzioni, 1964: 59)

Perhaps this explains why so many of the topics discussed in connection with organizations relate more or less directly to the subject of control. Consider the following list: administration, authority, automation, boundaries, bureaucratization, centralization, contracts, coordination, decision premises, discipline, evaluation, formalization, hierarchy, incentives, integration, internalization, performance programs, power, procedures, routinization, rules, sanctions, socialization, supervision—these are some of the specific manifestations and instruments of control.

We begin this section by discussing the interpersonal control system— the structure of power and authority in organizations. Then we consider how these arrangements are supplemented and, in some measure, replaced by various impersonal control mechanisms. Finally, we discuss culture as a mode of control prevalent in some types of organizations.

### Power

A great many pages have been filled with discussions of power, and many definitions of this important concept have been proposed (see Cartwright, 1965; Schopler, 1965). One of the simplest and most satisfactory approaches to this topic is that of Emerson (1962: 32):

> It would appear that the power to control or influence the other resides in control over the things he values, which may range all the way from oil

resources to ego-support, depending upon the relation in question. In short, power resides implicitly in the other's dependency.[3]

Emerson views power as relational, situational, and at least potentially reciprocal. Thus, his approach emphasizes that power is to be viewed not as a characteristic of an individual but rather as a property of a social relation. To say that a given person has power is meaningless unless we specify over whom he or she has power. We must take into account the characteristics of both the superordinate and the subordinate individual in describing a power relation. The power of superordinates is based on their ability and willingness to sanction others—to provide or withhold rewards and penalties—but we must recognize that what constitutes a reward or a penalty is ultimately determined by the goals or values of subordinates in the relation. To use two extreme examples, a gunman has no power over the individual who does not value his or her life, nor does a person with money have power over another who does not value money or the things it will buy. Emerson's formulation also provides a means of determining the degree of power in a relation: recall his suggestion that A's power over B is (1) directly proportional to the importance B places on the goals mediated by A, and (2) inversely proportional to the availability of these goals to B outside the A–B relation (1962: 32).

It is consistent with this approach that power can have many bases. An individual's power is based on all the resources—money, skills, knowledge, strength, sex appeal—that he or she can employ to help or hinder another in the attainment of desired goals. What types of resources will function as sanctions will vary from one individual to another and from situation to situation. Thus, if workers in an office value the quality of their technical decisions, then expertise becomes an important resource that can be used as a sanction by them (see Blau, 1955); if boys at a camp prefer to avoid black eyes and to be on winning teams, then such characteristics as strength and athletic prowess will become important bases of power for them (see Lippitt et al., 1953).

Emerson's formulation also allows for the possibility of mutual dependency. Power relations can be reciprocal: one individual may hold resources of importance to another in one area but be dependent on the same person because of resources held by the latter in a different area. And just as the degree of individual dependence may vary by situation, so may the degree of mutual dependence, or interdependence.

We will define interpersonal *power* as the potential for influence that is based on one person's ability and willingness to sanction another person by manipulating rewards and punishments important to the other person. That is, power has its origin in the dependency of one person on resources controlled by another, but power itself is best defined as a potential for influence. We turn now to discuss briefly the emergence of power structures in informal and formal systems.

---

[3]An important advantage to this approach is that it is applicable to relations among varying types of units: individuals, groups, organizations. Here we apply the conception to relations among individuals; in Chapter 8, we used it to examine power relations among organizations.

***Power in informal groups***    During the late 1950s a large number of studies examined the operation of power in informal groups and, in particular, the emergence of power differences in previously undifferentiated task groups. The emergence of power was examined in field studies (Lippitt et al., 1953; Sherif and Sherif, 1953) as well as in the laboratory (Bales, 1952; Bales and Slater, 1955). These studies describe the way in which certain personal qualities that differ among members become the basis for differences in sanctioning ability. As analyzed by Homans (1961) and Blau (1964), the process of differentiation occurs through a series of exchanges among group participants. Over time, some members emerge who are both more willing and more able to make important contributions to goal attainment, whether to the goals of individual members of to those of the group as a whole: they can manipulate sanctions of importance to others. As Blau notes, "a person who commands services others need, and who is independent of any at their command, attains power over others by making the satisfaction of their need contingent on their compliance" (1964: 22). Both Blau and Homans see the origin of power structures as a product of unequal exchange relations that occur when some individuals become increasingly dependent on others for services required in reaching their objectives. A person lacking resources to repay the other for these services, who is unwilling to forgo them and unable to find them in other relations, has but one alternative: "he must subordinate himself to the other and comply with his wishes, thereby rewarding the other with power over himself as an inducement for furnishing the needed help" (Blau, 1964: 21–22). In this manner, exchange processes that involve asymmetries give rise to a differentiated power structure.

***Power in formal organizations***    Power in informal groups is based on the characteristics of individuals—individual differences that can function as resources allowing some to reward and punish others. It is the differential distribution and use of such characteristics or resources that give rise in informal groups to a power structure. By contrast, power in formal organizations is determined at least in part by design. Most organizations are designed in such a manner that a hierarchy of positions is created: one position is defined as controlling another. A supervisory position, for example, is defined as being more powerful than that of a worker, and in accordance with this definition, sanctioning powers are attached to the position. Thus, supervisors may be allowed to evaluate the work of their subordinates, determining by these evaluations who receives what rate of pay and who is to be recommended for promotion. Such powers are attached to the position: they are available to any individual who occupies it, regardless of his or her personal qualities.

Rational system theorists emphasize the importance of formal power structures in the functioning of organizations. They argue that it is possible to design power structures in such a manner that sanctioning power may be made commensurate with responsibilities and distributed so as to facilitate the organization's requirements for coordination and control of participants' contributions. They also note that although the theoretical range of subordinates' values and, hence, of power bases is quite broad, the actual range is quite narrow: certain values are widely shared, so that it is possible to identify resources, such as money and status, that will function as sanctions for most participants most of the time. They further note the quite palpable advantages associated with the formalization process itself, which results in the "domestication" of power. Thus, tensions associated with the generation of power differences are avoided; the organization is freed from the necessity of finding "superior" individuals to fill superior positions; and power is more readily transferred from one person to another as position occupants come and go (see Chapter 2). Formalization is one of the important ways in which the "personal" element is removed from interpersonal control systems.

Natural systems theorists insist, on the other hand, that no organization ever succeeds in completely controlling all sources of power or in rationally allocating power among its positions. There are two reasons for this. First, we come again to the chief thesis of the natural system perspective: positions are filled by persons, and persons possess diverse and variable characteristics, some of which may become the basis for informal power differences in formal organizations. Differences among individuals in intelligence, motivation, training, skills, attractiveness, and other respects can serve as resources that sometimes supplement and sometimes contradict and erode the formal distribution of power. Second, in the organization's allocation of resources to positions, some participants inevitably obtain access to resources that can be used in ways not intended by the organizational designers. For example, access to information is an important resource that can become the basis for sanctioning and controlling others. A position such as secretary can make its occupants privy to sensitive information that they can use to enhance their own power and influence (see Mechanic, 1962). And, as we have learned from Hickson and associates (1971), a strategic location in the structure—a high degree of uncertainty confronted or the centrality of the work performed—can be an important, unanticipated source of sanctioning ability and hence of influence.

Research by Tannenbaum and associates (Tannenbaum, 1968; Tannenbaum et al., 1974) supplies evidence for the general expectation that amount of control or influence is positively associated with position in the formal hierarchy. If individuals are asked to describe how much influence is associated with each type of position in the organization, then it is possible to construct a "control graph" that depicts how centralized or decentralized is the distribution of power in the organization. The centralization of power varies from organization to organization, largely as a function of differences in ideology or goals that directly affect the formal definitions of how power is to be distributed: for example, power was more evenly distributed in the League of Women Voters, a voluntary agency emphasizing member participation, and in Yugoslavian companies emphasizing worker participation than in more traditional United States business and industrial concerns. (However, as Tannenbaum emphasizes, power was somewhat centralized in all of these organizations, ideology and preferences notwithstanding.) Of more interest is Tannenbaum's demonstration that aside from its distribution, the *total amount* of control exercised varies from one organization to another. That is, in some organizations none of the positions is perceived as exercising very much influence over others, whereas in other organizations all of the positions are seen to exercise considerable power. This finding underlines our earlier point that organizations may be expected to vary in the amount of mutual dependence or interdependence they display.

### Authority

Weber has pointed out that in his experience no organization

> voluntarily limits itself to the appeal to material or affectual motives as a basis for guaranteeing its continuance. In addition, every such system attempts to establish and to cultivate the belief in its "legitimacy" (Weber, 1947 trans.: 325)

In other words, no organization is likely to be content with establishing a power structure; in addition, it will attempt to create an authority structure. Most social scientists define authority as legitimate power. *Legitimacy* is the property of a situation or behavior that is defined by a set of social norms as correct or appropriate. Thus, to speak of legitimate power is to indicate (1) a set of persons or positions linked by power relations and (2) a set of norms or rules governing the distribution and exercise of power and the response to it.

In the case of informal groups, we refer to the exercise of power as legitimate to the extent that there emerges a set of norms and beliefs among the members subordinate to the power wielder that the distribution and exercise of power is acceptable to them and is regarded as appropriate. The emergence of such norms significantly alters the control structure, as Blau and I have argued:

> Given the development of social norms that certain orders of superiors ought to be obeyed, the members of the group will enforce compliance with these orders as part of their enforcement of conformity to group norms. The group's demand that orders of the superior be obeyed makes obedience partly independent of his coercive power or persuasive influence over individual subordinates and thus transforms these other kinds of social control into authority. (Blau and Scott, 1962: 29)

In sum, a set of dyadic power relations between the superior and each subordinate is transformed by the emergence of legitimacy norms into a multiperson control structure in which each subordinate now participates in the control of each of his or her colleagues. Peer-group controls are harnessed in the support of the power structure. Another way of describing these important developments is to say that a stable role structure has emerged that guides the expectations of participants, making it possible for a leader to lead and for followers to follow without the generation of disruptive emotional responses. Further, the emergence of legitimacy norms helps to render power relations more impersonal and reduces the tensions associated with the exercise of interpersonal power. As Thibaut and Kelley (1959: 129) suggest, in an authority structure, in contrast with a power structure,

> nonadherence is met with the use of power to attempt to produce conformity, but the influence appeal is to a supra-individual value ("Do it for the group" or "Do it because it's good") rather than to personal interests ("Do it for me" or "Do it and I'll do something for you").

For all of these reasons—involvement of subordinate participants in the control system, development of differentiated expectations among participants, depersonalization of power processes with consequent reduction of interpersonal tensions—authority structures tend to be much more stable and effective control systems than power structures. Like formalization, authority helps to clothe personal power in impersonal garb.

There is, however, another equally important consequence of the legitimation process. The emergence of social norms not only allows a greater measure of control of subordinates by the power wielder but also regulates and circumscribes his or her exercise of power. Emerson (1962) points out that the emergence of legitimacy norms among subordinates allows them to act as a coalition vis-à-vis the power wielder, defining the arena within which he or she can appropriately exercise power. Subordinates are individually weaker but collectively stronger than the superior, allowing them to place some limits on his or her power. Legitimacy norms specify the orders to which subordinates are expected to comply—and hence support the exercise of power—but also identify demands that the power wielder cannot appropriately make of subordinates—and hence limit the exercise of power. In sum, legitimacy norms cut both ways: they permit greater and more reliable control of subordinates within certain limits defined as appropriate areas of control—Barnard (1938) referred to these areas as the "zone of indifference"—and they restrict the exercise of power to these areas. We conclude that *authority is legitimate power* and that *legitimate power is normatively regulated power.*

**Two types of authority: endorsed and authorized power**   Dornbusch and I (Dornusch and Scott, 1975) have raised a question that has not been explicitly asked by previous students of authority. Having determined that social norms that regulate power relations provide the basis for legitimate control structures, we sought to determine who—what group of participants—defines and enforces these norms. In most informal groups, there is only one possible source: the set of participants who are subject to the exercise of power and hence are subordinates of the power wielder. We have noted how, by acting as a coalition, this subordinate group can limit and regulate the exercise of power over them by a superordinate. We label this type of situation *endorsed power,* or authority by endorsement. A number of theorists—in particular, Barnard (1938)—view the enforcement of norms by subordinates, or endorsement, as the basic mechanism underlying authority in formal organizations. While we do not deny this process operates in organizations, in our opinion it is secondary to another process.

An important characteristic of formal organizations is the presence of persons superordinate to as well as persons subordinate to a given power wielder. Most hierarchies are multi-level, so that norms may be developed and enforced by persons superior to the power wielder. Indeed, this is one of the primary features of hierarchy of offices. As Weber states,

> the principles of office hierarchy and of levels of graded authority mean a firmly ordered system of super- and subordination in which there is a supervision of the lower offices by the higher ones (Weber, 1946 trans.: 197).

A familiar safeguard built into most hierarchies is the principle of appeal, by which subordinates who feel that their immediate superior is making unfair or unreasonable demands on them, may turn to their superior's boss with the expectation that he or she will enforce authority norms that curb the superior's power. We label a situation in which power is regulated by those superior to the power wielder *authorized power,* or authority by authorization.[4]

For authorization to operate as a source of normative control, there must be a level of the hierarchy above that of the person or position whose exercise of power is at issue. What happens at the very top of the hierarchy, where there is no superordinate level to regulate the exercise of power? In the usual case, as Parsons (1960) has pointed out, the managerial hierarchy ends with its top position being responsible to a different type of office: the institutional level, exemplified by the board of directors or board of trustees. These offices are defined as being legitimated by—normatively regulated by—some different, nonhierarchical principle. Often, they are legitimated by some type of electoral process (for example, election of officers by stockholders), or officers are appointed to represent the interests of the ultimate beneficiaries—for example, the owners or the citizenry.

It is important to emphasize that a principle function of the institutional level—one noted serveral times throughout this volume—is to secure the legitimation of the organization's hierarchy. This is accomplished by linking the norms and values supporting the hierarchy to broader institutionalized normative systems, demonstrating their congruence and consistency. Weber's famous typology of authority systems, described in Chapter 2, is based on differences in the types of norms that legitimate power systems. Recall that he distinguished between traditional, charismatic, and bureaucratic systems, each of which justifies and regulates an existing structure of power on a different basis. Both Weber (1947 trans.) and Bendix (1956) have examined how these broadly accepted normative beliefs change over time, causing and reflecting changes in power arrangements within specific administrative systems. For example, the legitimacy of the nation-state is no longer likely to be justified by the doctrine of the divine right of kings, but is instead supported by beliefs in its consistency with constitutional documents or the "people's will." Similarly, the authority systems of more limited organizations are justified by beliefs in property rights, or procedural correctness, or the legitimacy of specialized expertise.

Returning to our basic distinction, it is possible for some control attempts to be authorized—that is, supported by superiors of the power wielder—but not endorsed—that is, not supported by subordinates of the power wielder—or vice versa. It is also possible for control attempts to be both authorized and endorsed. An instance of the first type would be the authority exercised by a police officer in an urban neighborhood whose residents are suspicious or hostile toward police activities; the second type is illustrated by the authority exercised by an informal leader in a work

---

[4]Another possible source of the creation and enforcement of norms in organizations is the colleagues or equals of the power wielder—those occupying the same formal position in the organization. This source may be expected to be of particular importance in professional organizations, and is labeled *collegial power.*

group. The third type—authority that is both authorized and endorsed—is represented by an individual serving as a supervisor who is also a natural leader. Authority that is both authorized and endorsed may be said to enjoy greater legitimacy and may be expected to be more effective and more stable than that which receives support from only one source (Dornbusch and Scott, 1975: 56–64).[5]

We do not equate formal with authorized and informal with endorsed power systems: these pairs of concepts are analytically distinct. However, we would expect them to be empirically associated. Consider the relation between authorized and formal power. Managers attempting to regulate the control attempts of the supervisors under their charge are more likely to attempt to treat them equally—to emphasize the power of position rather than the power of person—partly because of equity and precedent and partly because the possibility of turnover in personnel is always present. By contrast, subordinates typically relate to only a single superior and are likely to have some difficulty in separating personal from official characteristics. If comparisons are made, they are more likely to focus on those features that differentiate their own supervisor from others of whom they have knowledge. For these reasons, informal power is likely to be associated with endorsed power. It is striking that virtually all of the empirical studies of supervision and control in organizations tend to focus on informal and endorsed power, often termed *leadership,* to the neglect of formal and authorized systems of control.[6]

### Structural Control

Authority and power are usually regarded as personal or interpersonal control systems, but as we have noted, in moving from informal to formalized power and from power to authority, we introduce more impersonal supports. Formal power is attached to positions rather than persons, and authority is power justified—authorized or endorsed—by normative beliefs.

As Edwards (1979) has pointed out, simple and more personal power systems tend to give way over time to more complex and impersonal forms—to technical and bureaucratic structures. (See Chapter 8.) Controls are built into technical production systems in the form of machine pacing or, in the case of continuous-flow systems, in the layout and speed of the assembly line. These "built-in" controls reduce the need for personal direction and in this manner change the role of supervisors from overseer to troubleshooter. (See Walker and Guest, 1952; Blau and Scott, 1962: 176–83.) Similar functions are performed by statistical records of performance and increased automation for white-collar work. (See Blau, 1955; Whisler, 1970.) Even more elaborate and less visible controls are embedded in the organization structure itself—in the layout of offices,

---

[5]The distinction between authorization and endorsement and their contribution to stabilizing authority systems have been pursued in experimental research. (See Zelditch and Walker, 1984.)

[6]The manner in which authority rights are linked to evaluation processes to provide a basis for the control of task performances in organizations is described at length in Dornbusch and Scott (1975) and is summarized in the first edition of this text. (See Scott, 1981: 283–86)

functions, rules, and policies. Edwards (1979: 145–46) emphasizes that the force of these bureaucratic arrangements resides in their seemingly impersonal character.

> Above all else, bureaucratic control institutionalized the exercise of capitalist power, making power appear to emanate from the formal organization itself. Hierarchical relations were transformed from relations between (unequally powerful) people to relations between jobholders or relations between jobs themselves, abstracted from the specific people or the concrete work tasks involved. "Rule of law"—the firm's law—replaced rule by supervisor command. And indeed, the replacement was not illusory. To the extent that firms were successful in imposing bureaucratic control, the method, extent, and intensity of sanctions imposed on recalcitrant workers were specified by organizational rules. . . .
>
> By establishing the overall structure, management retained control of the enterprise's operations. Once the goals and structure had been established, the system could operate under its own steam. . . . the ability to establish rules provided the capitalist with the power to determine the terrain, to set the basic conditions around which the struggle [with workers] was to be fought. . . . The capitalist's power was effectively embedded in the firm's organization.

Technical and bureaucratic control structures thus represent important instances of *structural controls*. Differences in power are built into the definition of relations among positions, and these power differences are normatively justified. There are two major advantages to power wielders in gaining structural control. The first is that one's power advantages are partially concealed: all participants—both those with greater power and those with lesser power—appear to be commonly subordinated to a normative framework exercising control over all. The second advantage is that those with structural power do not need to mobilize in order to have their interests taken into account. It is automatically assumed that they are "entitled" to be represented in any matter affecting their interests. By contrast, interests that are not structured have to become mobilized if they are to be heard. (See Alford, 1975.) It is in this sense that power can function less as a "wild card" and more like a "trump suit" in the game of politics within organizations. (See Heilbroner, 1980: 146.)

But it is not only capitalists whose power is coded into structural arrangements. As labor's power has increased and as unions have been organized and recognized as legitimate bargaining agents, worker interests have received structural support. More generally, as Selznick (1969) has argued, participants in organizations increasingly enjoy generalized legal supports as "citizenship" rights are coded into the unwritten constitutions of "private governments"—that is, private organizations and associations. As organizations become larger and more powerful, and as their effects on individual participants—on their security, income, and life chances—becomes more potent, the protection of individual rights becomes a matter of public concern. Various due-process protections— the right to a review of decisions, to access to records, to hearings and appeals—are increasingly made available to individual participants of organizations, and are supported by the power of larger political and legal institutions. Such structural protections have spread widely across many types of organizations in recent decades. (See Dobbin et al., in press.)

### Culture

Some types of organizations, as described in Chapter 9, rely primarily on internalized controls. Although a formal control structure is in place and there are expectations that rewards will be distributed according to performance, the organization relies primarily on an informal structure and on individual participants' embracing of common norms and values that can orient and govern their contributions. These types of controls are described as denoting an organizational culture. Pointing to culture as the basis of control should come as no surprise, since anthropologists have long believed most of the orderliness and patterning found in social life is accounted for by cultural systems, but such views have only recently been widely employed by students of organizations.

Smircich (1983: 339) points out that the concept of culture is used in two quite different ways by organizational analysts: "as a critical variable and as a root metaphor." In the first usage, culture is something that an organization *has*. Employed in this manner,

> the term "culture" describes an attribute or quality internal to a group. We refer to an organizational culture or subculture. In this sense culture is a possession—a fairly stable set of taken-for-granted assumptions, shared beliefs, meanings, and values that form a kind of backdrop for action. (Smircich, 1985: 58)

Culture so defined may be employed either as an external independent variable that may affect the organization—for example, organizations in France are molded by a distinctive set of cultural beliefs unique to that society (Crozier, 1964)—or as an internal variable that characterizes the values or style of one or more organizations: organizations possess a culture just as they possess a distinctive technology.

Employed in the second sense, as a root metaphor, culture is something an organization *is*. To view organizations as cultures is to shift from a mechanical or organic to a cognitive or symbolic model. "Organizations are understood and analyzed not mainly in economic or material terms, but in terms of their expressive, ideational and symbolic aspects" (Smircich, 1983: 347–48). Clearly this second perspective embraces a more subjectivist or phenomenological view (see Burrell and Morgan, 1979) and has much in common with the open system conception as developed by Boulding, Pondy and Mitroff, and Weick; with Strauss's conception of organizations as negotiated orders; and with the views of the institutional theorists.

Both conceptions of culture contribute to the analyses of the ways in which culture functions as a control system. Every organization necessarily has a culture, but some create *strong* cultures—belief systems that define a general mission sustaining commitment to something larger than self; that provide guidelines by which participants can choose appropriate activities; that create sources of meaning and identification such that participants not only know what they are to do for the good of the organization but want to do it. Such beliefs are inculcated and reinforced by rituals and ceremonies that provide collective occasions for expressing solidarity and commitment; by the raising up of heroes that personify common goals; and by the creation of slogans and symbols that signify shared values. (Deal and Kennedy, 1982; Peters and Waterman, 1982) Precisely how such strong cultures are created and maintained is the subject of much current study. (See Jelinek, Smircich, and Hirsch, 1983; Frost et al., 1985.)

Culture as a control mechanism closely resembles what Lindblom (1977) has termed a *preceptoral system*. He argues that there are three basic types of control systems: markets based on exchange, authority based on legitimated power, and preceptoral systems based on persuasion and indoctrination. As in a strong culture,

> in a preceptoral system rationality rests on an ideology which once taught to the individual gives him both a "correct" understanding of the social world and guidelines for his own decisions. Although a preceptoral system depends on simple moral and emotional appeals to supplement the rational, the core element in the creation of the new man is his idological education, a genuine attempt to raise the level of his conscious, thoughtful, deliberated understanding. (Lindblom, 1977: 59)

Lindblom also comments on the creation of cultural heroes:

> In social organization great feats can be accomplished in either of two ways. By a finely tuned coordination of individual efforts, which is an accomplishment prized both in market theory and administrative theory. Or by somehow inducing each only loosely coordinated participating individual to rise to unusual levels of individual accomplishment and innovation. (p. 60)

Preceptoral systems stress the latter approach to excellence, and in so doing—like those who emphasize the virtures of strong cultures—they are highly critical of overly formalist, bureaucratic approaches.

Lindblom's central illustration of the full-blown preceptoral system is the Chinese political regime under Mao. This example suggests a major concern raised by the cultural control model: its potential development into an authoritarian system that is subject to abuse precisely because its controls are internalized and individual participants are unconstrained in the demands that they place on themselves. Peters and Waterman (1982: 77) describe this darker side of cultural controls in the corporate setting:

> So strong is the need for meaning, . . . that most people will yield a fair degree of latitude or freedom to institutions that give it to them. The excellent companies are marked by very strong cultures, so strong that you either buy into their norms or get out.

This high level of commitment to special-purpose organizations is of concern in a society based on pluralism and committed to democratic institutions. We regard this kind of commitment as a potential source of pathology and comment further on its implications in the next chapter.

## SUMMARY

Goals are put to many uses by organizational participants. They serve cognitive functions, guiding the selection of alternative courses of action; they have cathectic properties, serving as a source of identification and commitment for participants and as symbolic properties appealing to external constituencies; they provide present justifications for actions taken in the past; they provide criteria for the evaluation of performances, participants, and programs of action; and under some conditions they provide ideological guidance for the contributions of participants. Moreover, individual participants bring their own private goals or motives with them into the organization, and these rarely coincide with those of the organization.

The concept of a dominant coalition that determines goals in organizations solves some of the mysteries of goal setting. It helps to avoid reification of the organization as a single purposeful actor but at the same time allows the organization's goals or preference structures to differ from those of all its human agents. The concept allows for the possibility that groups and individual participants have different interests and agendas and indicates how, through negotiation and the making of side payments, bargains are struck and a basis for common action developed. The concept of dominant coalitions also reminds us that individual participants do not have equal power in decision making and that the preferences and interests of some will receive more attention than those of others. Although individuals and groups bring preferences and interests with them into the organization, organizations are more than a setting where existing interests come together: they are places where new interests are created.

The size and shape of the dominant coalition changes over time in response to the changing external conditions to which the organization must adapt. As new sources of uncertainty and challenge develop in its environment, the organization creates offices to deal with them. Officers who can successfully cope with such problems may be expected to acquire power within the organization, since others are dependent on them for critical services. As environments become more complex and turbulent, the dominant coalition grows and its shape changes to incorporate more and different specialists capable of managing one or another boundary problem. And as the composition of the membership of the dominant coalition changes, the goals of the organization also change, reflecting these shifts in power.

Some organizations lack clear goals or efficacious technologies. Such conditions are not very hospitable to the formation and maintenance of organizations, but when they exist several alternative strategies are possible. Organizations may suffer and hope for the millennium, awaiting the appearance of a charismatic leader who will clarify ends and supply means. They may attune themselves to high ambiguity, recognizing that almost-random connections among streams of problems, participants, and solutions will produce some decisions. Some will seek to institutionalize themselves such that meaning and matter are supplied by rationalized myths. And still others may rely on experiential learning, reading environmental cues in order to improvise changing strategies.

All collectivities control their members, but some distinctive control arrangements are to be found in organizations. Power is the potential for influence based on sanctioning ability, and authority is normatively regulated power. In informal groups authority tends to exist as endorsed power—power constrained by norms enforced by subordinates—but in formal organizations authority exists primarily as authorized power—power circumscribed and supported by norms enforced by officers superior to the power wielder. Most organizations attempt to regulate the contributions of participants by developing evaluation systems that link performances to organizational sanctions. Although such control systems are ubiquitous, they are often cumbersome and complex, and many are flawed. This is particularly so as the goals pursued by organizations and the tasks allocated to participants become increasingly difficult in definition and uncertain in performance. In some types of organizations, control may reside more in organizational cultures—that is, in shared, internalized beliefs and norms that provide meaning and guidance to individual members engaged in collective action.

# ORGANIZATIONS AND SOCIETY

**PART FOUR**

We have emphasized throughout this volume that organizations are only subsystems of larger social systems and are connected in numerous and vital ways to them. What differentiates the focus of the next two chapters from previous ones is not a concern with these connecting links but a shift in reference. Thus far, the organization itself has served as the primary point of reference. We have explored goals, structures, technologies, and participants from the standpoint of what they can reveal about the system of which they are parts. Now we adopt a different benchmark: that of the host society. We ask in these two concluding chapters what organizatins can do to and for the societies that support them. We examine unintended as well as intended effects.

Chapter 12 explores some of the problems and dangers associated with the operation and growth of organizations. In particular, we focus on power and its potential misuse. Organizations generate power as a consequence of their functioning. Previous chapters have examined how power can be employed in the service of organizational goals—whether those goals be certain outputs or the survival of the organization. Chapter 12 investigates the side effects of the power that is generated—its unanticipated consequences for both internal participants and external publics. As might be imagined, these are issues raised primarily by the natural system perspective on the functioning of organizations.

From the rational system perspective, organizations are instruments for the attainment of goals. We have asked numerous questions about the implications of this view for the organization. However, a crucial question for the larger society within which organizations operate is how effective and efficient they are in meeting their goals. Are they sufficiently adept in their functions—in achieving their respective goals—that they merit social support in spite of problems they raise? Although the question of effectiveness is most readily addressed from the rational system perspective, we shall quickly discover that different questions regarding organizational effectiveness are raised by natural and open systems points of view. These queries and issues are addressed in Chapter 13.

# 12 organizational pathologies

Bureaucracy has been and is a power instrument of the first order. . . . The individual bureaucrat cannot squirm out of the apparatus in which he is harnessed. . . . In the great majority of cases, he is only a single cog in an ever-moving mechanism which prescribes to him an essentially fixed route of march. . . .

The ruled, for their part, cannot dispense with or replace the bureaucratic apparatus of authority once it exists. For this bureaucracy rests upon expert training, a functional specialization of work, and an attitude set for habitual and virtuoso-like mastery of single, yet methodically integrated functions. . . . This holds for public administration as well as for private economic management. More and more the material fate of the masses depends upon the steady and correct functioning of the increasingly bureaucratic organizations of private capitalism. The idea of eliminating these organizations becomes more and more utopian.

Max Weber (1947 trans.)

Weber was aware of the use and the possible misuse of power in modern organizations. Inappropriate applications can occur both internally, when participants are exploited or stunted or in other ways damaged by their involvement, and externally, when publics who rely on organizations for goods and services find that organizations are unresponsive to their needs or interests. Internal problems may appear to be an issue only for the individuals involved, but a moment's reflection will convince us that damage done to organizational participants is a social, and not simply a personal, problem. As has been noted, individuals are only partially involved in any given organization: injury inflicted on participants in one setting may be expected to affect their performance in others. Two types of problems for individual participants are frequently cited: the problem of alienation and that of overconformity or ritualism. Both are examined in the first section of this chapter.

Turning to problems involving publics, we will first examine the issue of responsiveness. What can be done to ensure that organizations are attentive to the needs and interests of external constituencies? This is a particularly acute problem for public organizations, which are expected to be oriented primarily to public interests, but is by no means restricted to them. We also examine the broader issue of corporate versus individual interests, which raises more general questions about the distribution and use of power in contemporary society.

Throughout this chapter, we endeavor to show that it is not necessary to develop new concepts or arguments to explain organizatonal pathologies. There is a close correspondence between many of the best and the worst features of organizations. In some cases, similar processes, with slight variations, produce both an organization's strengths and its weaknesses. In other cases, the organization's strengths *are* its weaknesses, when viewed from a different perspective.

## PROBLEMS FOR PARTICIPANTS

### Alienation

Much time and attention has been devoted over the years to the impact of organizations on the personal characteristics of their participants. There are many claims and considerable evidence regarding these effects—and most of them are conflicting! At least since the time of Adam Smith and down to the present, observers have pointed to the debilitating consequences of organizational involvement, and in particular, employment, for individual participants. These destructive processes are often summarized under the concept of alienation—a concept with enough facets and varied interpretations to serve as an adequate umbrella under which to gather a quite varied set of criticisms.

Even Marx, who more than any other theorist called attention to the importance of alienation of workers, identified several possible forms of alienation (see Marx, 1963 trans.; Faunce, 1968). Workers may be alienated from the *product* of their labor. Labor gives value to the objects it creates, but as a worker loses control over his product, it comes to exist "independently, outside himself, and alien to him and . . . stands opposed to him as an autonomous power" (Marx, 1963 trans.: 122–23). Workers can also be alienated from the *process* of production. This occurs to the extent that

> the work is external to the worker, that it is not part of his nature, and that, consequently, he does not fulfil himself in his work but denies himself, has a feeling of misery rather than well-being, does not develop freely his mental and physical energies but is physically exhausted and mentally debased. . . . His work is not voluntary but imposed, forced labor. (Marx, 1963 trans.: 124–25)

As a consequence of the first two processes, workers become alienated from others in the work setting. Marx explains:

> The alien being to whom labour and the product of labour belong, to whose service labour is devoted, and to whose enjoyment the product of labour

goes, can only be man himself. If the product of labour does not belong to the worker, but confronts him as an alien power, this can only be because it belongs to a man other than the worker. (1963 trans.: 130)

Enter the capitalist. And enter the argument that it is not work that alienates, but exploitation of workers by the misuse of power.

Before turning to some evidence regarding the pervasiveness and distribution of alienation, a second influential formulation deserves mention. Like Marx, Seeman (1959; 1975) views alienation as a multi-faceted concept; he identifies six varieties: (1) powerlessness—the sense of little control over events; (2) meaninglessness—the sense of incomprehensibility of personal and social affairs; (3) normlessness—commitment to socially unapproved means for the achievement of goals; (4) cultural estrangement—rejection of commonly held values and standards; (5) self-estrangement—engagement in activities that are not intrinsically rewarding; and (6) social isolation—the sense of exclusion or rejection. Seeman has argued that powerlessness and self-estrangement are the two types of alienation that have most meaning in the workplace, and these seem most consistent with Marx's distinctions. A great many measures, including several multiple-item scales, have been developed to assess one or the other of these dimensions (see Seeman, 1975); most of them treat these conditions as internal, social psychological states. Israel (1971) has taken strong exception to this practice, insisting that alienation is more accurately and usefully viewed as an objective condition of the social structure, not a subjective attitude or disposition. Individuals may not be able to recognize that they are alienated: sentiments may not accurately reflect circumstances.

In spite of Israel's concerns, most empirical studies on alienation are based on data obtained from individual respondents who report their feelings or attitudes—for example, work satisfaction and dissatisfaction, levels of interest or commitment—or their behavior—for example, turnover, absenteeism, physical and mental health symptoms. Most surveys conducted in this country over the past half century report (1) generally high levels of worker satisfaction and morale but (2) large variation in satisfaction and symptoms across differing occupational strata and work situations. These surveys also show that higher satisfaction tends to be associated with such factors as intrinsic interest of the work, level of control, level of pay and economic security, and opportunities for social interaction (see Blauner, 1960; Sheppard and Herrick, 1972; Special Task Force, 1973).

Such clear and expected results do not hold up very well in more detailed and limited investigations of the relation between job characteristics and worker attitudes. As discussed in Chapter 9, research on such job characteristics as variety, autonomy, interaction, and level of skills required have not found strong or consistent associations with worker satisfaction or absenteeism. And efforts to introduce measures of worker "needs" or other assessments of personality have not clarified the situation, indeed have raised more questions than they have resolved. (See Cummings, 1982; Staw, 1984.)

A number of analysts have claimed that the impact of organizations on their participants extends far beyond the walls of the organization itself. Argyris (1957; 1973) summarizes several studies that indicate that workers who experience "constraint and isolation" on the job carry these attitudes into their free time: such workers are less involved in organized leisure, community, or political activities. Kanter (1977*b*) reviews a number of studies that suggest that both men's and women's occupational experiences have important implications for their family roles. She asserts that these studies contradict the "myth of separate worlds" perpetuated by companies that do not wish to assume responsibility for the effects of their policies and practices on the "personal" lives of their employees (and also by social scientists who tend to specialize in studying organizations or families but not their interdependence). Similarly, Ouchi (1979: 36–37) argues that organizations have a vested interest in failing to recognize their psychological casualties:

> The costs of psychological failure are not borne entirely by the firm, but rather are externalized to the society generally. That is, employees who reach the point of emotional disability, who become unsatisfactory workers, are the first to be laid off during depressions or, in extreme cases, are fired. The firm which has "used up" people emotionally does not have to face the cost of restoring them. In much the same manner that firms were able until recently to pollute the air and the water without paying the costs of using up these resources, they continue to be able to pollute our mental health with impunity.

And Kanter concludes that "a major social welfare issue of the decades to come" is likely to be focused on the question "Can organizations more fully and responsibly take into account their inevitable interface with the personal lives of their participants?" (1977*b:* 89). Our own view is much closer to that of Seeman (1975: 108), whose survey of research on alienation leads him to conclude,

> Given the tendency to assume that work is of primary importance in defining the self and in connecting the individual with the larger society, and given the centrality of work in the Marxian sources on alienation, it seems surprising how limited the demonstration has actually been concerning this purported generalization (from the job proper to the extra-job milieu) of alienated labor.

That is, we do not question the importance of the issues raised, but only the quality of the evidence produced thus far.

We are most concerned, however, with one of the proposed solutions for dealing with the problem of alienation. This solution, endorsed by a long and distinguished list of social analysts, is that organizations should absorb more aspects of the personalities of their participants; that they should become the primary focus of social integration, personal identity, and meaning; that they should function as the new communities, or *Gemeinschaften,* of modern society. From Saint-Simon (1952 trans.) and Durkheim (1949 trans.) through Barnard (1938), and Mayo (1945), and Selznick (1957) to Ouchi (1981) and Peters and Waterman (1982), organization theorists have looked to production organizations as a primary source of social integration in a social structure that is judged to be increasingly anomic and disorganized. Wolin calls attention to the underlying conservative and elitist stance that nurtures this point of view:

> The fondness for large scale organization displayed by contemporary writers largely stems from anxieties provoked by the emergence of the mass. They see organizations as mediating institutions, shaping disoriented individuals to socially useful behavior and endowing them with a desperately needed sense of values. These large entities supply the stabilizing centers, which not only integrate and structure the amorphous masses, but control them as well. (Wolin, 1960: 427)

That organizations have some impact on the personal characteristics and the mental health of their participants we do not dispute. That these effects often are detrimental to participants and, hence, to the larger society is a hypothesis that calls for more investigation. But that organizations should be viewed as the principal centers of moral and social integration in modern society we cannot accept.

As indicated in Chapter 7, we see the emergence of organizations as special-purpose systems as being closely associated with the emergence of the ideology of individualism, including the doctrine of natural rights and the value of individual freedom. The development of the rational-legal out of the traditional forms, to use Weber's terms, signals the emergence of norms and structures that place restrictions on the hierarchy of the organization and reduce the leverage of the organization in relation to the individual. We endorse these developments and view with alarm proposals to expand the power and influence of organizations over individuals. This argument will be amplified at the end of this chapter.

### Overconformity

In his justly famous essay "Bureaucratic Structure and Personality," Merton calls attention to a set of processes by which "the very elements which conduce toward efficiency in general produce inefficiency in specific instances" (1957: 200). He argues that structural devices established to ensure reliability and adequacy of performance—rules, discipline, a graded career—can "also lead to an over-concern with strict adherence to regulations which induces timidity, conservatism, and technicism" (1957: 201). Merton also argues that

> adherence to the rules, originally conceived as a means, becomes transformed into an end-in-itself; there occurs the familiar process of *displacement of goals* whereby an instrumental value becomes a terminal value (1957: 199).

Other possible sources of goal displacement are described by natural system analysts, such as Selznick (1949) and Dalton (1959), who emphasize the commitments individuals develop to their tools, working arrangements, procedures, and work groups (see Chapter 3). Rational system analysts March and Simon (1958: 150–58) examine the manner in which means-ends chains designed to support rationality of decision making (see Chapters 2 and 4) also foster goal displacement, which they refer to as *sub-goal formation*. They point out that cognitive processes operating at the individual, group, and organizational levels all contribute to such developments, supplementing the cathectic process emphasized by Merton, Selznick, and Dalton. Since goals are divided and factored among individuals and groups, goal displacement is encouraged by selective perception and attention processes among individuals, the selective content of in-group communication, and the selective exposure to information occasioned by the division of labor within the larger organization. Goals assigned to individuals and groups as means are viewed as ends in themselves. Scientists in research and development units emphasize creativity without regard to feasibility: manufacturing units emphasize producibility without attention to marketability; and so on.

If we take a somewhat larger view, however, we will see that goal displacement is not confined to organizations but is quite widespread in modern societies. Indeed, we would argue that it is synonymous with differentiation of the social structure and elaboration of the cultural system. As societies and cultures develop, activities formerly regarded as means become ends in themselves: eating becomes dining; buildings and garments needed for protection from the elements take on symbolic importance and give rise to architecture and fashion; sexual relations intended "by Nature" as a means to the survival of the species become a terminal value, elaborated in romantic love and sex as play. The myriad occupations that emerge in modern societies may be viewed as instances of means transformed into ends: scientists pursue truth for its own sake; physicians prolong life as an ultimate value; and teachers devote their lives to socialization of the young. And we have noted, time and again, that the goals of organizations can be viewed as specialized functions or means from the perspective of the larger society.

Once we realize that goal displacement is the hallmark of any advanced civilization, it seems unfair and somewhat disingenuous to single out bureaucrats and accuse them of unique vices. They are involved in a process in which we all participate.

It appears to us that the basis for concern is not the displacement of ends by means but the continued pursuit of means that have somehow become disconnected from, or are at odds with, the ends they were designed to serve. In times of rapid change, we can easily imagine such dislocations becoming more common: ultimate goals change, but it is difficult to rapidly design and implement necessary adjustments down the chains of means-ends connections. Efforts to modify organizational structures to enable them to process information more rapidly—augmenting the hierarchy and developing lateral connections (see Chapter 9)—may be interpreted as attempts to shorten and improve the consistency of these chains. Similarly, emphasizing the overriding importance of collectively valued goals as a basis for decision making and action provides another approach to counteracting the disassociation of subgoals and goals (see Chapter 11).

To return to the narrower topic of rigidity or overconformity, results from two large surveys suggest that rather than increasing rigidity, participation in organizations encourages individual flexibility and openness to new ideas. The first study, conducted by Inkeles (1969), reports the results of a cross-national survey of 1000 men from each of six developing societies. The study identified a series of interrelated attitudes labeled *modernity,* which included such specific attitudes as openness to new experiences, assertion of increasing independence from the authority of traditional figures, abandonment of passivity and fatalism, interest in planning and punctuality, and interest in political issues and in keeping abreast of the news. The two most important influences on individuals' development of "modern" attitudes were school attendance and work in a factory. On the role of schools, Inkeles (1969: 213) comments,

> These effects of the school, I believe, reside not mainly in its formal, explicit, self-conscious pedagogic activity, but rather are inherent in the school as an *organization*. . . . It teaches ways of orienting oneself toward others, and of conducting oneself, which could have important bearings on the performance of one's adult roles in the structure of modern society.

And as for the factory experience:

> Just as we view the school as communicating lessons beyond reading and arithmetic, so we thought of the factory as training men in more than the minimal lessons of technology and skills necessary to industrial production. We conceived of the factory as an organization serving as a general school in attitudes, values, and ways of behaving which are more adaptive for life in a modern society. (1969: 213)

Inkeles found organizational participation to be a liberating, consciousness-expanding experience for individuals in developing societies.

Kohn (1971) used survey data from a sample of over 3000 men employed in a variety of civilian occupations to examine the effect of bureaucratic employment on individuals' attitudes. Characteristics of employment settings were measured simply in terms of the number of levels of supervision and the size of the organization; individual attitudes were assessed in terms of three dimensions: (1) emphasis placed on conformity or respectability, (2) intolerance or rigid conformity and resistance to change, and (3) intellectual rigidity. The resulting associations were not particularly strong but were consistent. Kohn found that

> men who work in bureaucratic firms or organizations tend to value, not conformity, but self-direction. They are more open-minded, have more personally responsible standards of morality, and are more receptive to change than are men who work in nonbureaucratic organizations. They show greater flexibility in dealing both with perceptual and with ideological problems. (Kohn, 1971: 465)

Controlling for educational differences reduced but did not eliminate the positive relation between organizational employment and individual flexibility. The data also suggest that such "bureaucratic" factors as greater job security, somewhat higher levels of income, and substantively more complex work contributed to these attitudinal differences.[1] Like Inkeles, Kohn emphasizes the liberalizing effects of organizational involvement on individual participants.

Lest we begin to feel overly sanguine at this point, we need only

---

[1]The argument relating complexity of work to psychological functioning is pursued in Kohn and Schooler (1973), who show that although there is a reciprocal relation between substantive complexity of work and intellectual flexibility of the performer, the job characteristics have a stronger effect on the person's psychological functioning than the reverse.

confront Milgram's (1973: 1974) series of experiments on conformity. Milgram's design called for a three-person situation in which a scientist-teacher is assisted by a second person in attempting to teach a student a series of word pairs. The experiment is described as examining the effects of punishment on learning, and it is the task of the assistant to administer punishments—electrical shocks—to the student when he or she gives an incorrect answer. Intensity of the shocks administered increased systematically throughout the experiment, from a low of 15 volts to a maximum of 450 volts: the upper end of the scale on the generator is labeled "Extreme Intensity/Shock; Danger, Severe Shock," and the final position, "XXX." In reality, the assistant is the true subject of the experiment; both the teacher and the student are actors, and no real shocks are administered. The true purpose of the study is to determine how much (apparent) pain one individual will inflict on another when ordered to do so.

The results are unsettling, to say the least. Across a wide variety of types of subjects—from Yale undergraduates to adult professionals and blue-collar workers to individuals from many different countries—approximately 60 percent of the subjects conformed to the demands of the scientist and administered shock at the highest levels possible to the student. The possibility that all these subjects were sadists was ruled out: left to their own devices, with no instruction from the scientist as to "appropriate" shock levels, the great majority of subjects administered very low, apparently painless shocks.

On examination, the experimental setting is a powerful one: many factors induce conformity. The scientist-teacher enjoys the authority of office as well as of expertise. The setting—a university laboratory—exudes propriety and legitimacy. The subject is a temporary, short-term assistant—not ostensibly the focus of the study but only a supportive or auxiliary figure. To disrupt the experiment by refusing to carry out orders is, apparently, a difficult thing to do. In authority structures, the orientation tends to be directed upward. As Milgram (1973: 77) notes,

> the person feels responsible *to* the authority directing him but feels no responsibility *for* the content of the actions that the authority prescribes. Morality does not disappear—it acquires a radically different focus: the subordinate person feels shame or pride depending on how adequately he has performed the actions called for by authority.

Other experimental variations suggest factors that affect the level of conformity observed. Distance from the punitive action affected conformity: assistants who were asked to force the subject's hand down on an electric plate were less likely to conform than those who simply selected the shock level and pulled a switch; assistants who were asked only to read the word list were more likely to conform than those who were more directly involved in administering the punishment. Pertaining to this latter group, Milgram (1973: 77) observes,

> Predictably, they excused their behavior by saying that the responsibility belonged to the man who actually pulled the switch. This may illustrate a dangerously typically arrangement in a complex society: it is easy to ignore responsibility when one is only an intermediate link in a chain of action.

The terrible consequences that may be associated with "simply following orders" are graphically illustrated by the behavior of officials in Hitler's death camps. It is to stress such simple bases for these heinous crimes that Arendt (1963) subtitles her analysis of the actions of Adolf Eichmann, chief executor of Hitler's "final solution," "A Report on the Banality of Evil."

Although we would not presume to entirely account for the complex problem of overconformity in organizations, one variable of apparent importance can be singled out: insecurity, or uncertainty. Recall that Kohn reported that greater job security of workers was associated with higher flexibility and less resistance to change. We would argue that Milgram's experimental subjects were highly insecure, recognizing that they were amateur, temporary contributors to a professional, ongoing, scientific study. And numerous analysts (Arendt, 1951; Neumann, 1942) have emphasized that totalitarian states such as Nazi Germany are characterized by duplications of office, divisions of power between state and party, and arbitrary acts by charismatic leaders, so that the entire system creates great anxiety and insecurity among its officeholders. Two case studies of organizations—Blau's (1955) study of a law-enforcement agency and Kanter's (1977a) study of a large industrial corporation—lend support to this thesis. Blau reports that the least secure agents were the most resistant to change and the most susceptible to ritualistic adherence to existing procedures. And Kanter asserts that most of the pressures for conformity in business corporations can be attributed to uncertainty. Writing of managers, for example, Kanter asserts,

> It is the uncertainty quotient in managerial work, as it has come to be defined in the large modern corporation, that causes management to become so socially restricting: to develop tight inner circles excluding social strangers; to keep control in the hands of socially homogenous peers; to stress conformity and insist upon a diffuse, unbounded loyalty; and to prefer ease of communication and thus social certainty over the strains of dealing with people who are "different." (Kanter, 1977a: 49)

Finally, Fox and Staw (1979) report that subjects in an experiment who were told that their assignment to an office was temporary and dependent on the quality of their performance were more likely to rigidly adhere to an earlier poor decision than were subjects told that they had permanent assignments. Similarly, the more resistance a decision encountered, the more likely subjects were to reaffirm it. Fox and Staw (1979: 465) summarize and generalize from their series of experiments:

> The results demonstrate the effect of political vulnerability upon commitment to a course of action. When an administrator is worried about keeping his job or fending off critics within an organization, he is less likely to be flexible in his decision making. Thus, the trapped administrator can be thought of as one who is most likely to increase rather than decrease his commitment to a previously chosen policy and most likely to become inflexible in his defense of such positions.

Insecurity and uncertainty appear to produce overconformity and rigidity.

### Uncertainty, Alienation and Overconformity

Uncertainty again! We have asked this concept to bear a heavy burden for us throughout this volume. Uncertainty is the source of variety and power, and it is the enemy of rationality and planning. Too much uncertainty can cause individuals to seek protection in ritualism and oversimplification of alternatives; too little uncertainty can cause individuals to wither in boredom and alienation.

Organizations and individuals are forever seeking to reduce uncertainty. Organizations attempt to buffer it out, and individuals are always programming themselves and others "out of a challenging and novel situation, and then losing interest" (Leavitt, 1964: 546). Fortunately for both, however, they never completely succeed. Uncertainty floods the barriers, bringing variety and challenge. And, as Goldner (1970: 97–98) observes,

> what starts out as a search for ways to reduce problems and uncertainties in organizations leads . . . to the increase of other uncertainties. Rationalization sows the seeds of increased complexity and hence of pressures for yet new forms of rationalization.

How to avoid levels of uncertainty that are too high or too low and to seek out levels that are "just right" in their mix of security and stimulation— this search for the "Goldilocks" standard is a central challenge to all organizations and all participants within them.

## PROBLEMS FOR PUBLICS

### Unresponsiveness

All organizations must provide benefits to external publics—customers, clients, citizens—as a condition for their continued existence. The contributions required from these publics vary according to the nature of the organization but may involve direct payments for products or services received, indirect support in the form of taxes, and normative support in the form of goodwill and legitimacy. A concern with organizational responsiveness to the demands of external publics is most often raised in connection with public organizations, since the public is expected to be the primary beneficiary of their activities. However, problems can also develop in the relations between publics and organizations in the private sector. We will examine both situations.

***Public sector organizations*** Weber, in company with many other past and present political analysts, believed that the most serious challenge facing contemporary societies was to maintain control over the expanding state bureaucracies. Numerous observers before Weber, including Mill, Bagehot, Le Play, and Mosca, noted the growth in numbers and power of paid government officials, but Weber's analyses provide the most complete and systematic conceptualization of this major change in governmental systems (see Albrow, 1970). Unlike some of the previous critics, Weber insisted that the primary problem with the growth of bureaucracy was not that of inefficiency or mismanagement. Indeed, Weber cogently argued that in comparison with earlier administrative forms, the bureaucratic structures were highly efficient and reliable (see Chapter 2). But for Weber, these characteristics—the administrative virtues—also constituted bureaucracies' most serious threat.[2] Accompanying increased bureaucratization was the strong likelihood of growth in the power of public officials. Weber (1946 trans.: 232–33) argued,

> Under normal conditions, the power position of a fully developed bureaucracy is always overpowering. The "political master" finds himself in the position of the "dilettante" who stands opposite the "expert," facing the trained official who stands within the management of administration. This holds whether the "master" whom the bureaucracy serves is a "people" . . . or a parliament. . . . It holds whether the master is an aristocratic, collegiate body, legally or actually based on self-recruitment, or whether he is a popularly elected president, a hereditary and "absolute" or a "constitutional" monarch.

Weber's explanation for this development was quite straightforward: "More and more the specialized knowledge of the expert became the foundation for the power position of the officeholder" (1946 trans.: 235). Recall in this connection Weber's description of the transition from patrimonial to bureaucratic administrative forms (see Chapter 2). As a ruler's territory increased, it would increasingly become necessary to decentralize operations and delegate authority to members of the administrative staff. The division of labor among the staff members becomes more fixed; specialized competence of officers increases, and, at the same time, the ruler's ability to oversee each operation is reduced. Relative to the ruler, each staff member becomes more knowledgeable in each specific area of operation. The staff also becomes more aware of itself as a distinct social group with common interests. We have, in brief, a classic instance of a shift in power-dependence relations: each subordinate is individually less powerful than the ruler, but collectively the subordinates have become more powerful, and by acting in concert they can impose conditions on the ruler's exercise of power (see Chapter 11). These constraints on the ruler's power, which developed slowly and haltingly over long periods, include such bureaucratic "safeguards" as civil service commissions and elaborate codes of conduct. Rosenberg (1958: 180) has described the effects of these developments in his analysis of the evolution of the Prussian state:

> The raising of standardized prerequisites for admission had a profound effect upon the bureaucracy as a social elite and as a political group. Whatever the motives and ostensible objectives of the ministerial sponsors of the

---

[2]Weber was not alone in admitting the likely efficiency of the bureaucracy but expressing reservations about the use of this instrument. Thus, in one of his celebrated essays on bureaucracy, the poet Ezra Pound responds to the claim that bureaucrats are active and attentive to their duty by noting that "the idea of activity as a merit is, when applied to bureaucrats, as deadly as the idea of activity among tuberculous bacillae" (1973: 219).

reformed merit system, the new service tests turned out to be, in the hands of the bureaucratic nobility, a wonderful device for consolidating its control over personnel recruitment and for gaining greater freedom from royal molestations in this crucial area.

The increasing dependence of the dilettante on the expert goes a long way toward accounting for the shift of power "down" from titular rulers to the nominal subordinates—the administrative officials.[3]

In the case of democratic systems, where power is expected to reside in the hands of the governed, other factors operate to shift power "up" from the people to administrative elites. The most influential analysis of these processes is that provided by Michels (1949 trans.) Rather than focusing exclusively on state bureaucracies, Michels insists that processes that withdraw power from the people and place it in the hands of bureaucrats can be studies equally well in organizations such as political parties that are expected to serve the interests of their rank and file.[4] Michels's (1949 trans.) major work is based on a case study of the Social Democratic Party in pre–World War I Germany (see Chapter 3). His famous aphorism "Who says organization, says oligarchy" summarizes his central argument that oligarchic tendencies to shift power from the majority and place it in the hands of an elite minority are built into the very structure of organization. They are an unintended consequence of organization. He points to the division of functions, which creates specialized knowledge; to the hierarchy of offices, which fosters and legitimates the uneven distribution of information and decision-making privileges; and to the structure of incentives, which encourages officials to remain in office but discourages rank-and-file members from involvement in the day-to-day business of the party. Michels's theoretical formulation emphasizes the internal factors giving rise to oligarchical processes; his descriptive account of the development of the Social Democratic party, however, places equal importance on the organization's relation with its environment. Throughout the period from 1890 to 1910, this party, the first of the strong working-class parties, was fighting for its existence. Leaders emphasized the need to present a unified front; internal disagreement and dissent were viewed as a luxury to be forgone until the party came to power; and leaders were reluctant to engage in any activities that weakened the strength of the organization in relation to its external environment.

Michels thus poses the following dilemma: a party or a union must build a strong organization and ensure its survival to achieve its objectives, yet preoccupation with such organizational problems leads to the surrender of these very objectives. "Thus, from a means, organization becomes an end" (1949 trans.: 390). Experience since Michels's time tends to

---

[3]Note that the same arguments were used in Chapter 11 to account for the increasing shift of power in individual organizations—both governmental and nongovernmental—from the owners and general managers to the technical experts and specialist managers. This process results, as noted, in increases in the size of the dominant coalition within organizations.

[4]Lipset (1960: 357) refers to such organizations as *private governments*. Blau and I (Blau and Scott, 1962: 45) refer to them as *mutual benefit associations*. They include such organizations as political parties, unions, and professional associations. Since they are formed to serve the interests of their members, most such organizations develop ideologies and procedures that support the participation of the majority in setting organizational goals.

confirm his thesis. Most unions, most professional associations and other types of voluntary associations, and most political parties exhibit oligarchical leadership structures; the democratic machinery established to prevent such arrangements functions primarily as a feeble device allowing rank-and-file participants to rubber-stamp executive decisions and "elect" slates of nominees running in uncontested elections (see Barber, 1950; Editors of the Yale Law Journal, 1954; Wilson, 1973). Even the well-known study by Lipset, Trow, and Coleman (1956) of a "deviant case," a democratically run union, suggests that although such processes are not inevitable, the conditions—both internal and external—causing the drift of power from the rank-and-file to the upper levels of the organization are sufficiently widespread to vindicate Michels's pessimistic generalization.

Lest we forget, the focus of the present discussion is on representativeness: the degree to which administrative and political bodies reflect the interests of those whom they are presumed to serve. Michels insists that the leaders of the German Social Democratic party forsook the values and interests of its membership, betraying socialist values and working-class interests for bourgeois values and selfish interests. Although it is true that the party's goals shifted over time, it is not obvious that this process was resisted by the members or was contrary to their interests. Thus, Coser (1951) has argued that the shift to the right in the party's program may not have resulted primarily from the bureaucratic conservatism of the leaders but from the rapid improvement in the social and economic situation of the working class during this period. Gouldner (1955) endorses this general line of argument by insisting that there is as much evidence to support an "iron law of democracy" as an "iron law of oligarchy." Gouldner's law asserts that political and administrative elites in both nations and organizations cannot endure for long without some support from the governed. Gouldner (1955: 506) also counters on logical grounds:

> Even as Michels himself saw, if oligarchical waves repeatedly wash away the bridges of democracy, this eternal recurrence can happen only because men doggedly rebuild them after each inundation.

Before leaving the topic of democratic processes within organizations, we wish to make one additional point. We have consciously shifted the level of analysis from the larger society and its bureaucratic apparatus to the individual organization and its administrative staff. In so doing, we agreed with Michels that processes operating at the organizational level may be applicable to the societal level, and vice versa. However, we need to be aware of Lipset's (1960: 395) conclusion regarding the relation between the two levels:

> Institutionalized democracy within private governments is not a necessary condition for democracy in the large society, and may in fact at times weaken the democratic process of civil society.

Specifically, Lipset notes that processes that act to incorporate members more fully in the life of their association and hence activate them in its political processes may also serve to isolate them from the larger community and make them more rigid and single-minded in their commitments. Lipset (1960: 396) summarizes the dilemma:

> Integration of members within a trade-union, a political party, a farm or-
> ganization, a professional society, may increase the chances that members of
> such organizations will be active in the group and have more control over its
> policies. But extending the functions of such organizations so as to integrate
> their members may threaten the larger political system because it reduces
> the forces making for compromise and understanding among conflicting
> groups.

Arguments such as these support our earlier conclusions concerning the dangers of treating individual organizations as if they were the primary centers of moral and social—and political—integration.

With respect to the problem of ensuring responsiveness of governmental officials in the larger society, political analysts generally agree that formal safeguards such as constitutions and legal codes are not in themselves sufficient to curb the power of officeholders. Additional mechanisms are needed to ensure responsiveness. In an instructive historical survey of governmental institutions in the United States, Kaufman (1956; 1969) has identified several "principles" for securing responsiveness that have come to the fore during differing periods of this nation's history. He argues that the public first puts its faith in the principle of *representativeness,* placing great confidence in electoral institutions and granting broad powers to the legislatures, both state and federal. However, as ballots grew longer, voters were unable to choose intelligently and legislatures proved highly vulnerable to the corrupting pressures of special interests. During the second, post–Civil War period, the public endorsed the principle of *neutral competence:* a host of independent boards and commissions were created, the Civil Service Commission was created (in 1883), and the watchword became "take administration out of politics" (Kaufman, 1956: 1060). The major drawback to this approach was, and continues to be, that it led to the fragmentation of government, to the creation of "highly independent islands of decision-making." Further, because administration was protected from politics, the impact of elections on the conduct of government was minimized.

Concerned with this new source of recalcitrance, the public supported, beginning during the 1930s and 1940s, the principle of *executive leadership.* The specific mechanisms utilized during this third phase have been the introduction of the executive budget as a tool of centralized planning and control; the frequent use of administrative reorganization, as executives struggled to reduce the number of independent agencies and centralize them in some meaningful pattern; and the growth of the executive staff.[5] At first glance the last of these mechanisms appears to reflect simply the need for increased information processing on the part of governmental executives: it is a case of the augmentation of hierarchies in political systems (see Chapter 9). Such needs are involved, but they are

[5]Not only has there been a large increase in recent decades in the president's own executive staff at the national level. In addition, the number of "supergrade" political appointees to positions of authority over civil service bureaucrats has also increased dramatically. (See Heclo, 1977.)

subordinate to other requirements. The central function of the enlarged executive staffs is to increase political control over the *line* administrators—the civil servants. To do this, the executive must recruit staff members possessing two qualities: in order of importance, loyalty and specialized expertise. Expertise is required to defend the "dilettante" (executive) from the specialized knowledge of public officials; loyalty is essential to ensure that the expertise will be harnessed in the service of the executive's goals. In many ways this development may be seen as an attempt to repoliticize administration, in belated recognition of the truth that expertise may be neutral, but experts never can be.[6]

Kaufman (1969) argues that the late 1960s witnessed a return to the principle of representation, with the introduction of different mechanisms to breathe new life into this old value. Electoral reforms extended the franchise to new groups of voters and, more important, attempted to reform the systems by which elected officials were nominated and their campaigns financially supported. And for the first time, there were attempts to allow public representatives to participate not only in the creation but in the administration of federal programs. As noted in Chapter 8, a new generation of federal agencies, which stressed decentralized decision making and the inclusion of representation from the affected groups, developed between 1960 and 1980. It is characteristic of all these programs that broad discretionary powers are delegated to the administrative units: the language of the statutes sets overall policy directions but does not provide precise legal guidelines for administrative action. As Lowi notes, "broad discretion makes a politician out of a bureaucrat" (1969; 300–301). And since administrators help to set policy, the public is legitimately concerned about the influences to which they are subject. "The further down the line one delegates power, the further into the administrative process one is forced to provide representation" (1969: 233).

From the earliest days of the Republic, our forefathers were wary of the abuse of power by public servants and took pains to limit and divide power—among the three traditional branches of government as well as within each branch among various offices, commissions, bureaus, and agencies. Executive offices forge political alliances with congressional committees, and commissions and bureaus became linked to special interests both inside and outside the government. Although there are many diagnoses of our current plight, the most prevalent complaints heard from contemporary students of bureaucratic politics are (1) that public power is so fragmented that elected officials cannot ordinarily count on individual agencies to support and implement their policy initiatives (see Pressman and Wildavsky, 1973), and (2) that private special interests have so penetrated public agencies that officials are incapable of acting to support the larger public interest (see Lowi, 1969; Weiss and Barton, 1980). In sum, it is alleged that today's bureaucrats are insufficiently responsive to their political superiors and overly responsive to special interests.

[6]It is of some interest to observe that the fullest development of this structural arrangement is to be found in totalitarian systems such as Nazi Germany and the communist regimes. The so-called parallel structures in which the state bureaucracy is duplicated (and penetrated) by a party bureaucracy is a widely recognized feature of such politican systems (see Friedrich and Brzezinski, 1956).

This overly cozy relation between political bureaus and private inter- ests has already been discussed in a different context. In Chapter 8, considerable attention was devoted to describing bridging strategies as an important means of increasing the security of organizations in their task environments. As we noted, the increasing scale and scope of governmen- tal activity encourages organizations of all types to view public agencies as salient features of ther environments and as targets of co-optation. Gov- ernment officials, for their part, are vulnerable to influences from such groups for many reasons: they must relate to these organized interests on a regular basis, and they may become dependent on them for informa- tion, cooperation, political support, and even future employment (See Heclo, 1977). Thus, contemporary governmental bureaus appear to have insufficient social insulation from specific sources of power in their envi- ronment; they are often unresponsive to the public interest because they are overly responsive to the interests of special publics.

**Private sector organizations**     Much more briefly, we must note that recent analysts are increasingly concerned with the responsiveness of pri- vate organizations to the interests of their clients and the larger public. In an important and influential essay, *Exit, Voice, and Loyalty,* Hirschman (1970) distinguishes between two general options open to disgruntled publics wishing to express dissatisfaction with the types and quality of services received. The first, *exit,* involves the withdrawal of patronage. Dissatisfied customers simply withdraw from a relation with one firm and seek another that is expected to serve their interests more adequately. Exit is the typical economic response; it is typified in the relations between private firms and their customers and presumes the existence of alterna- tives. The second option, *voice,* is broadly defined as "any attempt at all to change, rather than to escape from, an objectionable state of affairs" (Hirschman, 1970: 30). Voice is the typical political option—expressed through elections, petitions, complaints, protests, and riots—because it is more likely to be exercised in situations in which a monopoly exists. Voice is a more costly option than exit, demanding at a minimum the invest- ment of time and energy; in extreme cases, its exercise can entail personal risk and sacrifice.

Hirschman argues that private firms can greatly benefit from publics who take the trouble to exercise the option of voice rather than exit. He notes that the quality of services provided by firms can deteriorate when alternative suppliers are available to some, since the more discerning cus- tomers withdraw their business, leaving those who are less quality-con- scious—or who have no alternatives—to endure substandard service. Such problems are especially characteristic of "lazy monopolies," such as subsid- ized railroads or public educational systems. Hirschman argues that publics would benefit from the use of mixed options. Incentives need to be pro- vided to encourage quality-conscious customers to exercise voice before resorting to exit—this is one of the major functions of *loyalty;* and public organizations should be encouraged to develop exit options—for example, the use of educational vouchers enabling students to seek alternative sup- pliers of educational services.

Lindblom (1977) enlarges Hirschman's comparisons of the varying controls available to publics in regulating public and private organizations. He points out that the most frequently employed voice options—elections—are relatively blunt control devices: the selection of a decision maker, especially one who will be placed in a complex political and organizational arena and subjected to varying cross-pressures on numerous issues, may provide little real control to the voter. By contrast, the exit options of buying or refusing to buy an organization's products or services can be exercised frequently and provide a direct signal to producers about what customers think of their products. On closer examination, however, it turns out that the public's control over private companies is "limited to saying yes or no on what is to be produced and in what quantities" (Lindblom, 1977: 154). On a broad range of other decisions, which Lindblom refers to as *delegated decisions*, private corporations exercise broad discretion:

> The delegated decisions are all the other decisions instrumental to production: among others, on technology, organization of the work force, plant location, and executive prerogatives. Even in an idealized market system, consumer control over them ranges from weak to nonexistent. (1977: 154)

A moment's reflection will suggest that these decisions can be of profound significance for the public interest:

> The discretionary decision of a single large corporation (to move in or out) can create or destroy a town, pollute the air for an entire city, upset the balance of payments between countries, and wipe out the livelihood of thousands of employees. (1977: 155).

Some observers have been content to rely on the development of a sense of "social responsibility" among corporate executives (see Berle, 1963; Cheit, 1964). Others, such as Lindblom, insist that market (exit) incentives must be supplemented with political (voice) controls if social responsibility is to become a reality.

### Inefficiency

In Chapter 7 we encountered Olson's (1965) analysis of the perverse incentives associated with organizing to produce some public good. Because the benefits produced are available to all regardless of their contributions, "rational" actors will not contribute to their production unless compelled to do so—the solution for most public agencies—or unless more selective incentives are developed.

More recently, Olson (1982) has suggested a somewhat parallel and equally problematic dilemma operating at an organizational level in the incentive structure of associations that have been created to produce benefits for their members—associations such as labor unions, professional societies, farmers' organizations, manufacturers' and trade associations, and special interest lobbies. Generally speaking, such associations can provide benefits for their members in one of two ways. First, they can enable members to operate more efficiently and effectively, thus expanding the economic resources of the society as a whole and hence their own welfare as constituent groups within the society. Second, they can facilitate the efforts of their members to secure a larger share for themselves of existing economic resources, by restricting the supply or raising the price of the goods and services they offer or by obtaining special protections or subsidies. Olson argues that "rational" associations will always pursue the second of these two options. For an association to pursue the first alternative is not in the best interests of its membership, since the benefits produced are public—available to and enjoyed by all—but the costs are borne by the membership alone. By contrast, the second alternative provides benefits for association members only; although there are costs created because overall efficiency of the economy has been reduced, these costs do not rest on the association's members alone but are spread across all sectors of the society. In short, the structure of incentives operating in associations created to advance the interests of their membership penalizes efforts to increase their overall productive efficiency and rewards attempts to use their power and influence to secure special privileges for themselves, even at the expense of others. Olson (1982: 47) labels these associations *distributive coalitions* because their primary focus is on influencing the distribution of resources to their members, not on the production of resources by their members. He concludes that "the great majority of special-interest organizations redistribute income rather than create it, and in ways that reduce social efficiency and output."

Olson asserts that these associations do not serve simply to reduce efficiency in the sector involved, but create additional disturbances—for example, drawing capital from other sectors because investors wish to share in the special benefits created, or reducing incentives to adopt new technologies to increase productivity—that magnify the dysfunctional consequences for the society as a whole. As special interests proliferate, tax laws and regulatory structures become more complex, and over time many actors—politicians, lawyers, consultants—gain a vested interest in maintaining if not magnifying this nonproductive machinery.

Olson proceeds to combine the two levels of his argument in order to provide a general explanation for the "rise and decline of nations." According to his 1965 thesis, collective organizations producing indivisible goods are difficult to create. Smaller groups can be more easily organized than larger ones because they can more readily detect beneficiaries who are not contributors—that is, opportunists—and they have at their disposal a wider range of sanctions. Larger groups are more difficult to organize and usually require the creation of some selective incentives. (Of course, once established, such associations are quite resilient, since they almost always provide "selective incentives" (salaries) to an administrative staff, which thereby acquires a vested interest in the survival of the association.) Other things being equal, over time, more and more interests finally succeed in becoming organized into associations, so that older, politically stable societies gradually tend to accumulate more collective associations. The growing numbers of these associations, each attempting to maximize its own share of the wealth by securing special advantages for its members even at the expense of the general welfare, is proposed as a central cause of economic stagnation among developed societies.

Thus, Olson suggests, the democratic stability that has characterized Great Britain since the early eighteenth century is a prime cause of its economic decline. And the economic miracles enjoyed by Germany and

Japan during the past three decades are attributed to the destruction of the congeries of special interests in these societies in the aftermath of World War II. Olsen suggests that his general arguments also help to account for the more rapid recent growth of the southern and western states in the United States in comparison with the more settled, over-organized Northeast and Midwest.

Although there is undoubtedly no satisfactory single-factor theory of economic growth and decline, Olson provides persuasive support for this thesis with examples drawn from many societies and over broad periods of history. The collective organization of special interests is shown to have important effects on the economic well-being of a society.

On the other hand, like many economists, Olsen takes a relatively narrow view of the political process. He tends to see political organizations only as vehicles for expressing existing economic interests; a broader view would recognize that such organizations also shape the ends of their participants. As Reich (1983: 28) argues,

> it is precisely through broadly political activities—within local trade unions, civic groups, grass-roots political movements, town meetings, professional associations, chambers of commerce, shop floor organizations, charitable organizations, and election campaigns—that individuals discover the subtler dimensions of their own needs and learn about the needs of others. They begin to understand the relationship between self and society; the encounter itself shapes their social values. If political organization is understood as a source of social values as well as conduit for political demands, there is no inherent conflict between interest-group politics and economic growth.

While recognizing the power of Olson's argument, Reich emphasizes the need to preserve special-interest groups as an important component of—and contributor to—democratic political institutions.

### Relentlessness

A final concern to be raised about the functioning of organizations in relation to publics is the relentlessness of their behavior. This problem, though neglected by most critics and analysts, is in our view the most serious one raised by the existence of organizations. It consists not in a malfunction of the organization but in the pathological aspects of "normal" organizational activities.

Coleman's (1974) analysis is most compelling. As noted earlier (see Chapter 7), Coleman distinguishes between natural persons, like you and me, and corporate actors—organizations. Organizations are composed not of persons but of positions, and persons are not completely contained within organizations. Persons contribute to and invest in organizations specific resources over which they lose full control. (The corporate actor is empowered to make decisions concerning the use of the resources available to it, and except in the rare and debilitating case in which an individual retains veto power over the use of his or her resources, individuals must be willing to give up a measure of control over their resources as the price for collective action.) With the creation of a corporate actor, a new set of interests comes into existence.

From the perspective of the natural actor, organizations are agencies for achieving desired objectives. However, from the point of view of the corporate actor, individuals are agents hired to pursue the goals of the collective actor. Individual actors are means for attaining corporate ends. Coleman (1974: 49) clearly spells out the implications of this view:

> It is the corporate actors, the organizations that draw their power from persons and employ that power to corporate ends, that are the primary actors in the social structure of modern society.
> What does this mean in practice? It means a peculiar bias in the direction that social and economic activities take. It means that among the variety of interests that men have, those interests that have been successfully collected to create corporate actors are the interests that dominate society.

Unorganized interests of persons are neglected in a society dominated by corporate actors. Further, corporate interests differ from those of natural persons in being more narrow, more intense, more refined, and more single-minded.

> . . .decisions about the employment of resources are more and more removed from the multiplicity of dampening and modifying interests of which a real person is composed—more and more the resultant of a balance of narrow intense interests of which corporate actors are composed (1974: 29).

Individual administrators are constrained by organizational goals and the definitions of their roles. They are expected to act as agents of the organization and as stewards of its resources. University trustees cannot in good conscience use the resources of their institution to relieve poverty or to build low-cost housing for members of the surrounding community. Pentagon officials are expected to build our armaments and strengthen our defenses regardless of the deleterious effects of such activities on the national economy or on the long-range prospects for survival of the human race. Organizations do not speak with one voice, as we have seen, and they are frequently loosely coupled coalitions of interests, but compared with natural persons, they are relatively specialized in their purposes and organized so as to pursue them relentlessly.

Ashby, the noted general system theorist, has pointed out that all "synthetic" organisms, including organizations, exhibit this tendency toward specialization of a sort likely to be dysfunctional for those who create them:

> There is no difficulty, in principle, in developing synthetic organisms as complex, and as intelligent as we please. But we must notice two fundamental qualifications: first, their intelligence will be an adaptation to, and a specialization toward, their first particular environment, with no implication of validity for any other environment such as ours; and secondly, their intelligence will be directed toward keeping their own essential variables within limits. They will be fundamentally selfish. (Ashby, 1968: 116)

Given the expectation that organizations will take a relatively narrow band of interests and pursue them unremittingly, our reluctance to enshrine organizations as the social and moral centers of the new society may seem more intelligible. This reluctance is shared. For example, Hart and W. G. Scott express alarm at the growing acceptance of a new set of values they label "the organizational imperative," which presumes that "whatever is good for man can only be achieved through modern organization" and "therefore, all behavior must enhance the health of such modern organizations" (1975: 261; see also Scott and Hart, 1979).

In a more extreme form, corporate pressures may not only cause participants to pursue a limited set of goals without regard to their effect on other values; they may induce participants to engage in actions that are illegal or immoral. Corporate crime is a matter of growing concern. And much of the deviant behavior identified is encouraged by such "normal" organizational conditions as limitations on information, circumscribed responsibilities, and strong performance pressures. (See Clinard and Yeager, 1980; Ermann and Lundman, 1982)

In our introduction to Part Four, we commented that all of the pathologies of organizations to be identified relate in some manner to the problem of power. This statement applies to the current topic. Coleman (1974) points out that in a social structure containing both natural persons and corporate actors, it is possible for one natural person to lose power without a corresponding gain on the part of another person. Persons can lose power to corporate actors. Coleman argues that this loss or transfer is currently going on at a rapid rate, a situation giving rise to a widespread feeling of powerlessness among individuals. And Coleman (1974: 39) points out that as a result of this transfer

> the outcome of events is only partly determined by the interests of the natural persons, giving a society that functions less than fully in the interests of the persons who make it up.

This seems to us to represent the ultimate form of alienation. In Marx's simpler world, power stripped from one person (the worker) belonged to another (the capitalist). In today's more complex world, power lost by one person may not be gained by any similar person but absorbed by a corporate actor and employed in pursuit of its specialized purposes.

## SUMMARY

Pathologies in the operation of contemporary organizations afflict both individual participants and external publics. We emphasize those that are based on the abuse of power.

Problems affecting individual participants include alienation and overconformity. Alienation can be defined either subjectively as a sense of powerlessness and self-estrangement or objectively as a condition under which workers lose control over the products of their labor or the value created by it. Most empirical studies are based on the subjective conception and reveal that the level of alienation among workers in this country is not high but that it varies greatly by the type of occupation, and that similar objective positions are experienced and reacted to differently by individuals. Although it is suspected that worker alienation will affect nonwork situations such as family life, there are few convincing studies establishing such relationships. We criticize the proposal that work organizations should function as the primary center of social and moral integration for individuals.

Organizational participants are frequently castigated for ritualism in the sense that they convert means into ends. Such transformations are, however, widespread throughout highly differentiated societies and do not become problematic unless there is a disjunction between means and ends. Studies reveal that organizational participation can be a source of flexibility and liberation as well as of timidity and overconformity. Job insecurity and uncertainty appear to be powerful factors governing conformity. Designers of organizational positions should seek to set uncertainty levels such that a proper mix of security and stimulation is achieved.

The responsiveness of organizations to the needs of external publics is of concern for all types of organizations, but especially those in which the public is designated as the prime beneficiary. The central problem with the growth of public organizations is that of maintaining their responsiveness to public interests. Responsiveness may be curtailed by the specialization and increasing expertise of administrative officials, the developing class interests of the administrative cadre, the uneven distribution of information and incentives for participation, and pressures for unity in the face of external threats. Responsiveness is sought through such mechanisms as securing representativeness, promoting neutral competence, and stressing executive leadership. It is suggested that some of the difficulties that beset public organizations are also created by their *over*responsiveness to public interests—the interests of *special* publics.

Private sector organizations are expected to be responsive to economic signals—for example, the withdrawal of business by customers searching for better quality or lower prices. Such options are not available to customers lacking alternatives, who must attempt through political means to change organizations from which they cannot escape. It is increasingly suggested that both private and public organizations should be made susceptible to both economic and political signals.

The structure of economic incentives can be an important source of pathology if there is a lack of incentives to motivate individuals to contribute to the production of public goods and a surplus of incentives to reward associations for pursuing their special interests. It has been proposed that the increasing inefficiency and economic stagnation that characterizes the more stable, advanced societies may be the result of the gradual accumulation of more and more associations representing special interests that may be expected to pursue advantages for their own members even at the expense of damaging those of the larger socioeconomic structure in which they participate.

Thus, even when organizations perform effectively and efficiently, they may nevertheless cause difficulties for the larger society because of their tendency to embody and mobilize support for relatively narrow goals. Individual interests that happen to coincide with organizational domains are well served; those that do not are liable to be seriously neglected. Our interests as individuals may be alienated not only by the actions of powerful others who strip us of our rights and resources but also by the normal functioning of impersonal organizations to whom we bequeath our resources and over which we lose control.

# 13 organizational effectiveness

There is no such thing as "good organization" in any absolute sense. Always it is relative; and an organization that is good in one context or under one criterion may be bad under another.

W. Ross Ashby (1968)

In recent years organizational analysts have become increasingly interested in the topic of organizational effectiveness. During the 1950s and early 1960s, the topic was generally neglected, in part because of the belief that considerations of effectiveness represented only an applied or practical, not a theoretical, concern.[1] Gradually, however, analysts began to perceive that there could be as much theoretical justification in examining the consequences of varying structural arrangements as in probing their determinants. And an important boost to the topic occurred when contingency theorists began to argue that some types of structures were better suited than others to certain tasks or environments. The question was raised, Better suited in what sense? and the answer given was often couched in terms of effectiveness. In this sense, effectiveness is argued by some theorists to be a determinant as well as a consequence of organizational structure.

The topic of organizational effectiveness is eschewed by some analysts on the ground that it necessarily deals with values and preferences that cannot be determined objectively. Such criticisms, however, apply not to the general topic but only to certain formulations of it. We will not seek to determine, for example, whether a given organization is or is not effective in some general sense. Rather, we shall attempt to learn what types of criteria of effectiveness are suggested by what constituencies and what types of indicators of effectiveness are proposed with what implications for organizational assessment. In sum, as was the case in our discussions of such value-loaded topics as decision making, goal setting, and power, we will attempt to remain descriptive and analytic in our approach rather than normative and perspective. (We confess that some of our comments in the previous chapter on pathologies were prescriptive.)

[1]This belief has been reaffirmed by Hannan and Freeman, who regard effectiveness as "a concept of applications and engineering but not of abstract theory and research." (See Goodman and Pennings, 1977: 108.)

Three major questions are addressed in the following discussion: What are the major criteria that have been proposed to define effectiveness? What are the approaches to assessing effectiveness? and What types of explanations are given to account for differences in effectiveness? As we will see, each of these topics is affected by the type of organization examined, and in particular by whether the organization is or is not responsive to market mechanisms.

## DETERMINING CRITERIA
## OF EFFECTIVENESS[2]

To the novice, defining and determining the effectiveness of an organization must seem a relatively straightforward affair: to inquire into effectiveness is to ask how well an organization is doing, relative to some set of standards. This is not wrong, but by this time, we experts in organizational analysis know that the pursuit of this simple question will lead us into some complex and controversial issues. There are many possible bases for generating criteria of effectiveness, and as we would expect, many different constituencies have an interest in the effectiveness of any organization and will want to propose criteria that reflect this interest.

### Multiple Criteria

Price (1968), Steers (1975; 1977), Campbell (1977), and Cameron and Whetten (1982) as well as others have assembled lengthy lists of criteria that have been used by one or more analysts in measuring effectiveness. Campbell, for example, lists thirty different criteria, ranging from productivity and profits to growth, turnover, stability, and cohesion. Steers (1975) limited his attention to seventeen studies of organizational effectiveness in which multiple criteria of effectiveness were devised. Noting that many differing criteria of effectiveness were used in these studies, Steers (1975: 547, 549) points out,

> One of the most apparent conclusions emerging from a comparison of these multivariate models is the lack of consensus as to what constitutes a useful and valid set of effectiveness measures. While each model sets forth its three or four defining characteristics for success, there is surprisingly little overlap across the various approaches.

In attempting to understand why so many and such varied criteria of effectiveness have been proposed, we do not need to search very far beyond the thesis of this volume; quite diverse conceptions of organizations are held by various analysts, and associated with each of these conceptions will be a somewhat distinctive set of criteria for evaluating the effectiveness of organizations. Although several schemata for differentiating among these conceptions have been proposed, we will argue that our

[2]Some of the discussion in this section draws on my papers on organizational effectiveness (Scott, 1977a; Scott et al., 1978).

old friends—the rational, natural, and open systems perspectives—account for much of the variance in measures of effectiveness.

Under a rational system model, since organizations are viewed as instruments for the attainment of goals (see Chapter 2), the criteria emphasized focus on the number and quality of outputs and the economies realized in transforming inputs into outputs. General criteria include measures of total output and of quality, productivity, and efficiency. More so than for the other two models, measures of effectiveness from a rational system perspective take the specific goals of the organization as the basis for generating effectiveness criteria. Thus, automobile companies focus on how many cars are manufactured during a given period in absolute numbers or in relation to cost measures; employment bureaus emphasize how many clients are placed in positions, perhaps in relation to the number of persons processed.[3]

As we know, the natural system model views organizations as collectivities that are capable of achieving specified goals but are engaged in other activities required to maintain themselves as a social unit. Thus, natural system analysts insist on adding a set of support goals to the output goals emphasized by the rational system model. Further, these support goals are expected to dominate output goals if the two do not coincide: organizations are governed by the overriding goal of survival (see Chapter 3). The criteria generated by this conception include measures of participant satisfaction and morale (indicators of whether the organization's inducements are sufficient to evoke contributions from participants adequate to ensure survival), the interpersonal skills of managers, and survival itself.

The open systems perspective views organizations as being highly interdependent with their environments and engaged in system-elaborating as well as system-maintaining activities. Information acquisition and processing is viewed as an especially critical activity, since an organization's long-term well-being is dependent on its ability to detect and respond to subtle changes in its task environment (see Chapter 4). Yuchtman and Seashore specify one criterion that they argue is most appropriate for assessing the effectiveness of organizations from the open systems perspective: "bargaining position, as reflected in the ability of the organization, in either absolute or relative terms, to exploit its environment in the acquisition of scarce and valued resources" (1967: 898). Criteria such as profitability, which may be viewed as the excess of returns over expenditures, are also emphasized by open systems analysts. And a great many theorists stress the importance of adaptability and flexibility as critera of effectiveness. Weick (1977) emphasizes these dimensions when he insists that effective organizations are characterized by a diversity of linguistic forms, techniques for breaking out of normal cognitive and normative constraints, means of simultaneously crediting and discrediting information received,

---

[3]Because of its focus on goals, the rational system is virtually synonymous with the *goals model* described by Etzioni (1960). Several critics have pointed out that because of the emphasis placed by the rational system or goals model on the specific types of goals pursued, these models do not provide an adequate basis for comparing the effectiveness of differing types of organizations (see Yuchtman and Seashore, 1967).

and structural units that are loosely articulated so as to maximize sensitivity to the environment and diversity of response.[4]

Analysts' diverse conceptions of organizations are not the only source of variation in effectiveness criteria. Other important bases of diversity include time perspective and level of analysis. Time considerations enter into the generation and application of effectiveness criteria in two senses. First, the criteria employed may vary depending on whether a relatively shorter or longer time frame is adopted. Steers (1975: 553) provides an example of this distinction:

> If current production, a short-run effectiveness criterion, is maximized at the expense of research and development investments in future products, an organization may ultimately find itself with an outmoded product and threatened for its very survival, a long-run criterion.

How critical a time frame is may depend on how rapidly the environment is changing. Hannan and Freeman (1977: 116), working from an ecological perspective, point out that highly specialized organizations well adapted to their environment may outperform generalist organizations at a given point in time, but may fare much less well over a longer period to the extent that the environment has changed. Second, organizations are necessarily at different stages of their life cycles, and criteria appropriate for assessing effectiveness at one stage may be less so for another. As Seashore has noted, "the meaning of growth for the health, survival, and overall effectiveness of the organization was very different at different stages of the organizational life cycle" (1962). And Cameron and Whetten (1981), in a study of eighteen simulated organizations, found that participants were more apt to stress the effectiveness of acquiring inputs at earlier stages in the history of their organization and the effectiveness of producing outputs at later stages.

We have stressed the importance of level of analysis throughout this volume, and it is a critical factor in accounting for variations in effectiveness criteria. Our conclusions concerning the relative effectiveness of organizations will vary greatly depending on whether we emphasize their impact on individual participants, on the organization itself, or on broader, external societal systems. Cummings argues for the first, social psychological–level criteria for assessing organizational effectiveness. He proposes that

> an effective organization is one in which the greatest percentage of participants perceive themselves as free to use the organization and its subsystems as instruments for their own ends (Cummings, 1977: 60).

Most analysts take the organization itself as the appropriate level of analysis for assessing effectiveness. Yuchtman and Seashore (1967: 896) explicitly adopt this posture, suggesting that a relevant view of effectiveness answers the question How well is the organization doing for itself? Still other investigators adopt a more ecological framework and propose that

[4]In his inimitable fashion, Weick summarizes his criteria as follows: "Specifically, I would suggest that the effective organization is (1) garrulous, (2) clumsy, (3) superstitious, (4) hypocritical, (5) monstrous, (6) octopoid, (7) wandering, and (8) grouchy" (1977: 193–94).

organizations should be evaluated in terms of their contributions to other, more general systems. Parsons's (1960) approach to the study of organizations exemplifies this functionalist type of criteria.

Variations in theoretical perspectives on organizations, in time horizons and developmental stage, and in level of analysis—these help to account for the diversity of criteria proposed in analyzing effectiveness. Yet another source of diversity is to be found in the varying sets of participants and constituents associated with organizations. (See Zammuto, 1982.)

### Participants, Constituents, and Criteria

Whether organizations are viewed as rational, natural, or open systems, our conceptions of their goals, participants, and constituencies have become progressively more complex. We have been instructed by Simon to view even "simple" output goals as complex and multi-faceted (see Chapters 2 and 11), and we have learned from Etzioni and Perrow to add support or maintenance goals to output goals (see Chapter 3). This more complex conception of goals is reinforced by viewing organizations as collections of subgroups of participants who possess various social characteristics, are in different social locations, and exhibit divergent views and interests regarding what the organization is and what it should be doing (see Chapters 4 and 11). This conception of the organization as a political system can be expanded to include outside constituencies who hold goals "for" the organization (Thompson, 1967: 127), and who attempt to impose these goals on the organization.

It is important to emphasize that when we speak of goals in relation to ascertaining the effectiveness of organizations, we are focusing on the use of goals to supply evaluation criteria. As argued in Chapter 11, goals are used to evaluate organizational activities as well as to motivate and direct them. In a rational world, we would expect the criteria that are developed to direct organizational activities to be the same as those employed to evaluate them, but as we have emphasized, events in organizations are not always as rational and tightly coupled as some theorists would have us believe. Instead, we must be prepared to observe different criteria employed by those who assign tasks and those who evaluate performance (see Dornbusch and Scott, 1975). Discrepancies are more likely to occur when the control system becomes differentiatied and these functions are assigned to different actors, but they can occur when the same persons or groups perform both directing and evaluating activities. An oft-cited problem in organizations develops when vague and broad criteria are used to direct task activities but very explicit criteria are employed to evaluate them, with the consequence that evaluation criteria deflect attention and effort from the original stated objectives to a different or narrower set of goals embodied in the evaluation system. Evaluation criteria often focus on the more easily measured task attributes and ignore others less readily assessed. Thus, social workers may be directed by their supervisors to provide therapeutic casework services but be evaluated primarily on the basis of the number and timeliness of their visits to clients and the correctness of their calculation of budgets (see Scott, 1969). Such discrepancies are likely to result in a displacement of goals as participants come to realize what criteria are used to determine evaluations and to dispense rewards (see also Blau, 1955; Dalton, 1959; Dornbusch and Scott, 1975).

Varying goals—viewed both as directive and as evaluative criteria—will be held by different participant groups and constituencies in organizations. The managers of organizations may not speak with one voice but with many, since they may be composed of a shifting coalition of interests. Similarly, top managers' goals for directing and evaluating activities may not coincide with or be completely reflected in the criteria used by middle-level personnel such as supervisors or technical specialists. Performers vary in the extent to which their own conceptions of their work coincide with those of their superiors, and also in their capacity to enforce their preferences. Finally, many "external" constituencies—stockholders, clients, suppliers and buyers, regulators, community leaders, and news media—have genuine interests in the functioning of an organization and may be expected to attempt to advocate and, if possible, impose their own effectiveness criteria on the organization. In general, the number of persons and groups who propose criteria for evaluating the performance of an organization will be much larger than the number who explicitly seek to direct its activities. "A cat may look at a king," and a reporter for the hometown newspaper may scrutinize the performance of the town's leading industry.

According to this conception of organizations, we would expect little commonality in the criteria employed by the various parties who assess organizational effectiveness. This expectation is shared by Friedlander and Pickle (1968), who impute appropriate interests to such groups as owners, employees, creditors, suppliers, customers, governmental regulators, and the host community. Their data on a sample of small business organizations show that performance assessed by these varying criteria results in a pattern of low and often negative correlation coefficients: to do well on a criterion preferred by one constituency is to do poorly on a criterion favored by another. Friedlander and Pickle conclude that "organizations find it difficult to fulfill simultaneously the variety of demands made upon them" (1968: 302–3).

Another consideration complicating the examination of effectiveness is the recent challenges to the assumption that organizations necessarily exhibit a unified or consistent set of performances. The political models just reviewed allow for divergence and conflict of interests among participants but presume their resolution through negotiation and power processes. In the end, the organization is presumed to pursue a single program. Alternative models that we have explored in earlier chapters suggest the utility of viewing some organizations as "organized anarchies" or as loosely coupled systems containing subunits that exhibit a high degree of autonomy and are capable of pursuing inconsistent objectives. This conception admits the possibility that, with respect to any specific criterion of effectiveness, an organization can be both effective and ineffective depending on what components are being evaluated!

Given the wide variety of participants groups and constituencies that can attempt to set criteria for organizational effectiveness, what generalizations, if any, can be suggested to guide investigations in this area? We offer three predictions. First, the criteria proposed by each group will be self-interested ones. Customers will desire higher quality at lower cost, supplier will wish to sell more dearly and wholesalers to buy more cheaply, workers will prefer higher wages and greater fringe benefits, and managers will seek higher profits and lower costs. We should not look for heroes or villians but for parties with varying interests. And all parties will evaluate the performance of the organization in terms of criteria that benefit themselves. Second, although no criteria are disinterested—each will benefit some groups more than others—all will be stated so as to appear universalistic and objective. This generalization receives support from Pfeffer and Salancik's (1974) study of the allocation of resources among university departments. They report that the stronger departments succeed in budget allocation contests not by imposing particularistic criteria on decisions but by ensuring that the universalistic criteria selected favor their own position. For example, strong departments that have larger graduate-student enrollments will favor this criterion in allocating resources while departments with larger numbers of undergraduate majors will seek to impose this criterion as a distribution rule. Third, given multiple sets of actors pursuing their own interests and a situation of scarce resources, we would expect little commonality or convergence and some conflicts in the criteria employed by the various parties to assess organizational effectiveness, a prediction supported by the study conducted by Friedlander and Pickle (1968).

One final constituency remains to be considered. Researchers who attempt to assess the effectiveness of organizations are not immune to these political processes. Which, and whose, criteria we choose to emphasize in our studies of organizations will depend on our own interests in undertaking the study. We must be willing to state clearly what criteria we propose to employ, recognizing that whatever they are and whoever espouses them, they are always normative conceptions, serving some interests more than others, and likely to be both limited and controversial.

## Market and Nonmarket Organizations

The distinction between market-based and nonmarket organizations is especially salient when the question of effectiveness is raised. When properly functioning, the market provides a mechanism for linking the interests of organizational participants and external constituencies in such a manner that the former do not prosper unless they serve the interests of the latter. The effectiveness of market-controlled organizations is directly determined by their customers: if their interests are satisfied, then they will continue to supply the inputs required by the organization; if not, then they can withhold their contributions, causing the organization to suffer and perhaps ultimately to fail. Under ideal market conditions an organization's output goals and system-maintenance goals are tightly linked. However, for reasons explored in Part Three, many organizations have bargained or bridged their way out of competitive market situations and are increasingly the target of governmental regulation.[5]

---

[5]As noted in Chapter 8, although instituted as a mechanism to protect the interests of the public, regulatory agencies are often "captured" by the organizations they were empowered to control, and operate in the latter's interests (see Stigler, 1971; Pfeffer and Salancik, 1978; Noll, 1985).

Other organizations, primarily government agencies, operate from the outset in nonmarket environments. Thus, Downs employs as his major criterion for defining a bureau the condition that "the major portion of its output is not directly or indirectly evaluated in any markets external to the organization by means of voluntary *quid pro quo* transactions" (1967: 25). As Downs emphasizes, an important implication of this condition is that "there is no direct relationship between the services a bureau provides and the income it receives for providing them" (1967: 30). As governments have come under pressure from hard-pressed taxpayers to make every tax dollar count, new techniques have been developed to ascertain the effectiveness of governmental agencies and, more specifically, government-funded programs. The emergence of evaluation research, both as a set of developing methodologies and as a collection of new professional service organizations, may be viewed as a response to this demand. Evaluation research attempts to provide a basis for assessing the effectiveness and efficiency of governmental programs and thus helps to inform decisions concerning what programs are to be closed, continued, or expanded. Although these efforts began with quite naive assumptions regarding techniques for assessing program and agency effectiveness, they have rapidly become more sophisticated, both technically and politically (see Suchman, 1967; Weiss, 1972; Cronbach et al., 1980).

Evaluation research has proved to be no panacea, however, and general discontent with the effectiveness of public organizations has continued to mount.

> Just as the widespread perception of the failures of private enterprise and the market system in the 1930s generated the political impetus for the creation of the welfare state, which reached its climax in the Great Society programs of the 1960s, so have the recent critiques of federal efforts gradually generated a new reaction back toward belief in the magic of the marketplace and the virtues of private sector dynamism and local initiative (Brooks, 1984: 5).

The drive toward "privatization" of the public sector has taken several routes. Increasingly, publicly owned and operated services are expected at least in part to "pay their own way"—to take in enough revenue to cover most if not all the services provided. Indeed, the variety of organizational forms allowing some degree of governmental ownership or sponsorship combined with some degree of reliance on the marketplace is quite remarkable. These forms range from fully owned governmental corporations (such as the U.S. Postal Service) to a wide variety of government-sponsored enterprises (for example, COMSAT— the Communications Satellite Corporation—and the Corporation for Public Broadcasting). (See Seidman, 1975.) Alternatively, many organizations supplying public services are supported by public funds but are privately owned. This is the case, for example, with defense contractors. A large and increasing proportion of public services—health care, education, police and fire protection—are contracted to private agencies. (See Brooks, Liebman, and Schelling, 1984; Hanrahan, 1983) It is argued that contracting out goods and services fosters competition and hence greater efficiency and effectiveness, but small number of suppliers and the widespread use of sole-source bidding greatly reduce the utility of such safeguards, as has been demonstrated by recurrent overpricing and mismanagement scandals involving weapons procurement by the Pentagon. Reliance on the market also presumes that consumers can evaluate the quality of products and services being purchased. But such an assumption is not tenable for many types of services; indeed, this is one of the major reasons why nonmarket organizations came into existence!

Nonmarket organizations are particularly likely to lack clear output measures. When the goals are to provide for an adequate defense, to negotiate advantagious treaties with other countries, or to fight poverty, it is difficult to determine how effective performances are. Of course, other types of organizations also pursue goals that are vague and difficult to assess. Two problems are involved: how to select indicators—the evidence to employ in evaluating performances—and how to set standards—the criteria to be used in judging whether a given performance is good or poor. Issues of standard setting and indicator selection are discussed in the following section.

## ASSESSING EFFECTIVENESS

In order for an evaluation of a performance to occur, criteria must be selected, including the identification of properties or dimensions and the setting of standards; work must be sampled, with decisions made concerning the types of indicators to be employed and the nature of the sample to be drawn; and sampled values must be compared with the selected standards (see Dornbusch and Scott, 1975). In our view, the same components are applicable whether the intent is to evaluate an individual performer or an entire organization. To this point, we have discussed only the problems encountered in determining the properties or dimensions of the organizational performance to be evaluated. In the current section, we discuss the setting of standards and the selection of indicators for assessing organization effectiveness and briefly comment on decisions regarding selection of the sample.

### Setting Standards

The setting of standards is a central component in establishing criteria for evaluating the effectiveness of an organization. By definition, standards are normative and not descriptive statements. The problem of how standards for assessing organizations are set is an interesting one but has received relatively little attention from social scientists. Cyert and March have attempted to adapt the psychological concept of aspiration level to explain how organizations establish goals for use as evaluative standards. They argue that

> organizational goals in a particular time period are a function of (1) organizational goals of the previous time period, (2) organizational experience with respect to that goal in the previous time period, and (3) experience of comparable organizations with respect to the goal dimension in the previous time period (Cyert and March, 1963: 123).

Thompson (1967: 84–87) proposes a somewhat more complex model in which types of assessment are viewed as a function of a combination of two factors: (1) whether the standards of desirability are relatively clearly formulated or ambiguous, and (2) whether the beliefs about cause-effect relations are relatively complete or are incomplete.[6] He argues that when standards are clear and cause-effect relations are known, then *efficiency* tests are appropriate. Such tests assess not simply whether a desired effect was produced but whether it was done so efficiently—that is, with a minimum of inputs. If standards are clear but cause-effect relations are uncertain, then *instrumental* tests are suitable. These tests ascertain only whether the desired state was achieved and do not demand conservation of resources. When standards of desirability are themselves ambiguous, then the organization must resort to *social* tests. Social tests are those validated by consensus or by authority. Their validity depends on how many or on who endorses them. Organizations operating in institutionalized environments are likely to depend on social tests for assessing their effectiveness. Such organizations

> become sensitive to, and employ, external criteria of worth. Such criteria include, for instance, such ceremonial awards as the Nobel Prize, endorsements by important people, the standard prices of professionals and consultants, or the prestige of programs or personnel in external social circles. (Meyer and Rowan, 1977: 350)

Thompson's typology is far from definitive, but it calls attention not only to the diversity of standards employed in assessing organizations but also to factors that help to account for these differences.

### Selecting Indicators

Among the most critical decisions to be made in attempting to assess organizational effectiveness is the choice of the measures or indicators to be employed. Three general types of indicators have been identified: those based on outcomes, those based on processes, and those based on structures (see Donabedian, 1966; Suchman, 1967; Scott, 1977a). The advantages and disadvantages of each type will be reviewed.

**Outcomes**   Outcome indicators focus on specific characteristics of materials or objects on which the organization has performed some operation. Examples of outcome indicators are changes in the knowledge or attitudes of students in educational organizations, or changes in the health status of patients in medical institutions. Outcomes are often regarded as the quintessential indicators of effectiveness, but they also may present serious problems of interpretation. Outcomes are never pure indicators of quality of performance, since they reflect not only the care and accuracy with which work activities are carried out but also the current state of the technology and the characteristics of the organization's input and output environments. These matters are of little import when cause-

---

[6]This second factor is a measure of knowledge of the technology utilized during the throughput process; it is similar to the dimension of predictability (see Chapter 9).

effect knowledge is relatively complete and when organizations are able to exercise adequate controls over their input and output sectors—that is, when the organization is well buffered from its environment. In such situations, represented by the manufacture of standardized equipment in competitive markets, outcomes serve as safe indexes of quality and quantity of organizational performance. However, many types of organizations lack such controls over their work processes and task environments. For example, a patient's medical condition following surgery will reflect not only the quality of care rendered by the surgical staff and the hospital personnel but also the development of medical science with respect to the particular condition treated, as well as the patient's general physical condition and extent of surgical disease at the time of the operation. Such problems are too much for some analysts, who dismiss the attempt to use outcome measures to assess effectiveness under these circumstances. Thus, Mann and Yett (1968: 196–97) reason,

> There are those who argue that the output of a health facility should be specified in terms of its effect on the patient. . . . We reject this definition of hospital output for the same reason that we do not regard the output of a beauty salon as beauty.

In our view, the use of outcome measures presents difficult, but not unsolvable, problems in assessing effectiveness of organizations such as hospitals and schools. The problem of inadequate knowledge of cause-effect relations can be handled by the use of relative rather than absolute performance standards, so that the performance of an organization is compared against others carrying on similar work. This approach presumes that the organizations assessed can—or should—participate in the same cultural system and have access to the same general knowledge pool. A particular organization possessing more relevant knowledge—for example, having better-trained personnel—would be expected to perform better than one possessing less knowledge, but the use of relative standards ensures that an organization is not penalized for lacking knowledge that no one has.

The problem posed by the contribution of variations among input characteristics to variations in outcomes experienced is less easily resolved. Although we can safely assume that organizations have access to the same knowledge, we cannot assume that they have access to the same client pool or supply sources. Indeed, one of the principal ways in which organizations vary is in the amount and quality of inputs they are able to garner. The pattern of inputs characterizing various types of organizations is not as simple as might appear on superficial examination. For example, as might be expected, prestigious universities recruit highly intelligent students, as indicated by scores on standard entrance examinations or past performance in academic settings, whereas less highly regarded institutions accept higher proportions of less qualified students. By contrast, highly regarded teaching hospitals focus primarily on the care of the very sick or on those whose problems pose the greatest challenge to medical science. In these organizations, there is an inverse relation between presumed quality of institution and patient condition. We would expect organizations to seek to take credit for acquiring inputs that enhance their outcomes—a widely used indicator of quality for universities is the characteristics of the student body they are able to attract—but to resist being held accountable for inputs that negatively affect outcomes. Thus, teaching hospitals insist that if patient outcome measures are employed as indicators of performance quality, they be standardized to take account of differences in patient mix. Statistical techniques are available that allow analysts to adjust outcome measures to take into account differences in characteristics of inputs.[7]

Outcome measures may also be affected by the characteristics of output environments. For example, indicators of outcomes relating to sales for products, or to placement or rehabilitation for prisoners or mental patients, will reflect not simply organizational performance but also market conditions or the receptivity of community groups external to the organization. As with inputs, we would expect organizations to prefer to take credit for conditions enhancing outcomes but insist that conditions having a negative effect be taken into account if outcomes are evaluated.

More generally, the decision as to how to treat input characteristics and output environments is not primarily a methodological but a theoretical issue. Do we wish to adjust for differences in student intelligence among universities in assessing student performance, or do we wish to regard student recruitment as an important aspect of a university's performance? Do we wish to adjust for market conditions in assessing a firm's retail sales, or do we wish to consider ability to build a solid market niche an important component of the firm's performance? Answers to these and similar questions depend on whether we seek to concentrate simply on the organization's throughput processes—its technical-core activities—or to include in our assessment the performance of the organization's bridging units—its input and output components.

Still other issues are involved in the use of outcome measures to assess organizational effectiveness. Briefly, it is difficult to determine the appropriate timing of such measures. Some organizations insist that their full effects may not be apparent for long period following their performance. For example, some educators claim that relevant academic outcomes can only be assessed long after the students have left school and have attempted to apply their knowledge in the "real world." And when is the appropriate time to assess a hospital's effect on a patient's health—immediately following a major therapeutic intervention such as surgery, at discharge, or following a post-hospitalization recovery period? Another problem in employing outcome indicators is the lack of relevant information. Many types of organizations have little or no data on outcomes achieved: they quickly lose contact with their "products"—whether these be human graduates or manufactured commodities. The collection of relevant outcome data can become very costly indeed if it entails tracking down such products after they are distributed throughout the environment.

Partly because of these quite formidable difficulties in assessing and interpreting outcome measures, other types of indicators of organiza-

---

[7]My colleagues and I have developed methods for adjusting patient outcome measures in order to assess the relative effectiveness of hospitals in providing surgical services. (See Scott et al., 1978; Flood and Scott, 1987).

tional effectiveness are often preferred. These measures—of processes and structures—can be more briefly described.

**Processes**  Process measures focus on the quantity or quality of activities carried on by the organization. As Suchman (1967: 61) notes, this type of indicator

> represents an assessment of input or energy regardless of output. It is intended to answer the questions, "What did you do?" and "How well did you do it?"

Process measures assess effort rather than effect. Some process measures assess work quantity—for example, staying with our hospital illustration, we may ask how many laboratory tests were conducted during a given period or how many patients were seen in the emergency room. Others assess work quality—for example, hospitals might be rated by the frequency with which medication errors occur or by the proportion of healthy tissue removed from patients during surgery. Still other measures assess the extent of quality-control efforts—for instance, the autopsy rate in hospitals or the proportion of X rays reviewed by radiologists.

In some respects, process measures are more valid measures of the characteristics of organizational performance. Rather than requiring inferences from outcomes to performance characteristics, process measures directly assess performance values. On the other hand, it is important to emphasize that all process measures evaluate efforts rather than achievements, and when the focus is on quality of performance rather than quantity, they assess conformity to a given standard but not the adequacy or correctness of the standards themselves. Process measures are based on the assumption that it is known what activities are required to ensure effectiveness. Students of medical care are currently challenging the assumption that there is a strong correlation between conformity to current standards of medical practice and improvements in patient outcomes (see Brook, 1973), as well as the assumption that higher levels of medical care result in improved health status (see Fuchs, 1974). More generally, social critics such as Illich (1972; 1976) claim that the substitution of process for outcome is one of the great shell games perpetrated by modern institutions against individuals. Illich (1972: 1) argues that contemporary individuals are trained

> to confuse process and substance. Once these become blurred, a new logic is assumed: the more treatment there is, the better are the results; or, escalation leads to success. The pupil is thereby "schooled" to confuse teaching with learning, grade advancement with education, a diploma with competence, and fluency with the ability to say something new. His imagination is "schooled" to accept service in place of value. Medical treatment is mistaken for health care, social work for the improvement of community life, police protection for safety, military poise for national security, the rat race for productive work. Health, learning, dignity, independence, and creative endeavor are deigned as little more than the performance of the institutions that claim to serve these ends, and their improvement is made to depend on allocating more resources to the management of hospitals, schools, and other agencies in question.

Recognizing that Illich's broad accusations have some merit, we would, however, express two sorts of reservations. The first relates to an argument we made in Chapter 12. Focusing on processes rather than outcomes represents a type of goal displacement. However, as noted earlier, goal displacement is a very widespread phenomenon and need not be regarded as pathological. Only when means and ends become disconnected is there cause for distress. Our second demurring relates to the case of organizations in institutionalized environments, in which, to a large extent, process *is* substance. In these organizations, conformity to ritually defined procedures produces a successful outcome, by definition. Ceremony is substance in many contemporary organizations, including religious bodies, legal firms, and many professionally staffed organizations.

Organizations are more likely to compile data on work processes than on outcomes. Performance quality and quantity are often regularly monitored. Gathering information on work processes, however, can still be problematic. Inspections based on observation of ongoing performances are both expensive and reactive—that is, likely to influence the behavior observed. In most work situations there are numerous barriers to work visibility, and workers often resist attempts to directly observe their work in process. Many kinds of work occur under circumstances that render routine inspection impossible, and other kinds, such as those emphasizing mental activities, are by their nature difficult to observe. Because of such difficulties, organizations may rely on self-reports of activities performed. However, such data are likely to be both biased and incomplete representations of work processes (see Dornbusch and Scott, 1975: 145–62). Because of these and related difficulties in obtaining process measures, many organizations rely on structural indicators of effectiveness.

**Structures**    Structural indicators assess the capacity of the organization for effective performance. Included within this category are all measures based on organizational features or participant characteristics presumed to have an impact on organizational effectiveness. Manufacturing organizations can be assessed by the value and age of their machine tools; hospitals are assessed by the adequacy of their facilities and equipment and by the qualifications of the medical staff as reflected in past training and certification; and schools are assessed by the qualities of their faculties measured in terms of types of degrees acquired, and by such features as the number of volumes in their libraries. These types of measures form the basis of accreditation reviews and organizational certification systems.

If process measures are once removed from outcomes, then structure indicators are twice remote, for these measures index not the work performed by structures but their *capacity* to perform work—not the activities carried out by organizational participants but their qualifications to perform the work. Structural indicators focus on organizational inputs as surrogate measures for outputs. Economists warn us that quality of outputs should not be confused with quality (or cost) of inputs, but Yuchtman and Seashore (1967) are close to embracing this position in their influential paper on organizational effectiveness. As noted above, they suggest that the effectiveness of an organization can be defined in terms of its ability to acquire scarce and valued resources—for example, expensive facilities and highly qualified personnel. They make the explicit assumption that an organization's bargaining position in its input environment is "a function of all the three phases of organizational behavior—the importation of resources, their use (including allocating and processing), and their exportation in some output form that aids further input" (Yuchtman and Seashore, 1967: 898).

As was the case with measures of organizational process, a number of observers have suggested that an emphasis on structural measures may have detrimental consequences for quality of outcomes. For example, numerous observers have argued that personnel licensure requirements have become a major obstacle to innovation in work procedures and to the optimal deployment of workers (see Somers, 1969; Tancredi and Woods, 1972). Thus, we have the interesting situation in which some measures of organizational effectiveness based on the assessment of process or of structure are argued to adversely affect other measures of effectiveness based on outcomes.

## Selecting Samples

Once indicators have been selected, decisions must still be made regarding the gathering of information relevant to these measures. We leave aside here discussion of specific techniques of data gathering as well as decisions pertaining to sample size, ensuring of representativeness, and other technical considerations, in order to emphasize the critical importance of the definition of the universe from which the sample is to be drawn. A basic decision confronting the analyst who assesses the effectiveness of any organization is whether to focus on the actual work performed by the organization or instead to ask whether the organization is attending to the appropriate work. The first option takes as given the current program of the organization—its structures, processess, or outcomes—and seeks to ascertain its quality or effectiveness. The second option assumes a broader perspective, asking whether the organization is engaged in the right program. Never mind whether the organization is doing things right; is it doing the right things? Reinhardt (1973) labels the first criterion *microquality* and the second, *macroquality*. If this distinction were applied to a service organization, an assessment of microquality would focus on the quality of structures, processes, or outcomes actually experienced by clients who were the recipients of the organization's services. By contrast, an assessment of macroquality would seek to determine whether the appropriate services were being provided or, more critically, whether the proper clients were receiving services. The effectiveness of a medical care organization might be assessed in terms of the health status of the clients who had received services (microqualitiy) or by the health status of the population residing within the organization's service area (macroquality).

## Participants, Constituents, and Measures

Just as with evaluation criteria, we would expect differing participant and constituency groups to prefer some types of measures over others. Generally, we expect organizational managers to emphasize structural measures of effectiveness, in part because these reflect factors that are more under their control than other types of indicators. Thus, organizational administrators are likely to have considerable influence over the types of facilities provided or the standards used in hiring personnel. By contrast, we would expect performers or rank-and-file participants to emphasize process measures of effectiveness. Skilled and semiskilled workers, who have little or no discretion in the selection of their activities, will prefer to be evaluated on the basis of their conformity to their performance programs rather than on the basis of the efficacy of these programs. And professional personnel, who are granted discretion in their choice of activities, will also usually prefer to be evaluated on the basis of process measures—their conformity to "standards of good practice"— since inadequacies in the knowledge base mean that they lack full control over outcomes.

Clients who use the products or receive the services are likely to focus primarily on outcome measures of effectiveness. They will evaluate the organization's product in terms of the extent to which it has met their own needs and expectations. Did the motor run? Was something of interest or use learned? Was pain relieved or functioning improved? In addition, clients who receive personal services are likely to place considerable value on process measures having to do with promptness, courtesy, and sensitivity of treatment. In circumstances where outcomes are difficult to evaluate, process measures will receive more weight from clients than outcome indicators. The most extreme cases involve institutionalized environments in which no outcomes at all can be demonstrated to occur regularly—although they are alleged to occur—so that both performers and recipients devote attention to evaluating conformity to established norms of practice.

All of the interest groups considered to this point—organizational managers, performers, and consumers—are likely to focus on microquality indicators of effectiveness. They will prefer to focus on the structures, processes, and outcomes associated with the work that the organization is actually performing. But another interest group consisting of the public at large, including some public regulatory bodies, will be more likely to emphasize measures of macroquality. Is the organization concentrating its attention and resources on the proper products or problems? Do eligible clients have access to its services? Is the community as a whole benefiting from its operation?

Our final constituency are the researchers dedicated to the objective, scientific analysis of organizational effectiveness. We would hope to find this group busily engaged in analyzing *all* types of indicators of effectiveness, exploring their interrelation, and employing criteria variously drawn from all of the interested parties. Although we have not conducted the type of systematic survey of the literature required to support such a conclusion, it appears that we analysts have emphasized the structural and process measures of effectiveness—those measures preferred by organizational managers and performers—to the neglect of outcome measures— those preferred by clients and the larger public. Both ideological and economic factors help to produce this bias in orientation. It is our belief that organizational analysts are more likely to identify with organizational managers and professional performers than with client and public interests. Indeed, most of the research on organizations is conducted by persons who train future managers while consulting for present ones. Also, most of the data available to us for analysis are collected by the organizations for their own purposes or are based on information supplied by organizational managers. Organizations, as noted above, are much less likely to collect data on outcomes than data based on their structural features and processes. If we want data on outcomes—and especially on outcomes that represent measures of macroquality—we will have to collect them for ourselves, or persuade governmental agencies to collect them for us. We should not minimize the cost or the value of such data in correcting the bias that currently exists in indicators of organizational effectiveness.

## EXPLAINING EFFECTIVENESS

Given the multiple possible meanings and measures of effectiveness that have been proposed, our comments on explanations of effectiveness can be brief since they are mostly by way of warning. When effectiveness can be viewed as comprising such varied criteria as flexibility, low turnover, and growth, we must seek explanatory variables as varied as what they are asked to account for. Given that many of the proposed measures of effectiveness are uncorrelated or even negatively correlated, we should not expect to find general explanations that will distinguish effective from ineffective organizations. We must agree to settle for modest and limited measures of specific aspects of organizational structures, processes, and outcomes.

Also given the complexity and openness of organizations as detailed in this volume, we would not expect any single set of factors to account for organizational effectiveness. This is the major defect, in our opinion, of some recent best sellers in the organizational literature. For example, such studies as Ouchi's *Theory Z* and Peters and Waterman's *In Search of Excellence*, while they provide valuable insights into new managerial techniques, convey the message that organizational performance is primarily a matter of management effectiveness—of management's capacity to create the right culture and motivational structure. Overlooked or underemphasized are such factors as industrial location, positioning in various markets—resource, labor, capital, sales—critical alliances and connections, information systems, and institutional supports. Effective organizations require more than enthusiastic managers and motivated workers.

Since the appearance of the open systems perspective, a popular approach to explaining variations in effectiveness has involved the use of contingency models: organizations whose internal features best match the demands of their technologies or task environments are expected to be most effective (see Chapter 4). The adequacy of such models depends, among other things, on the quality of our ideas about the appropriate relation (match) between task or environmental demands and organizational arrangements. We have attempted to summarize some of these evolving principles in Chapters 8 through 10, and while we do not apologize for the state of our knowledge, we readily admit that there is much room for improvement. The principles developed are generally vague and need to be carefully adapted for application to specific settings. That this is not a straightforward task is illustrated by Perrow's critique of Neuhauser's attempt to apply these ideas to the organization of doctors' work in hospitals. Neuhauser (1971) embraces the widely accepted design principle that when work is complex and uncertain, attempts to control performance with the use of highly specified procedures—high formalization—will lower work quality. Perrow would certainly subscribe to this general principle, but he takes issue with Neuhauser's specific application of it to the hospital setting:

> Tasks are complex on the medical side of the hospitals, so when dealing with doctors, specification of procedures should be low. But the specifications of what kind of procedures? Any, it seems. For example, he includes the number of tests required at admissions . . . and the number of limitations placed upon the surgery that people can perform (a general practitioner cannot do heart surgery). Using knee-jerk theorizing, he says that if there are a lot of specifications of these kinds, quality should be low. Presumably he could have included scrubbing before surgery as a specification of procedures that would lower quality when tasks are complex. (Perrow, 1972: 420)

Perrow's tone is overly caustic, but his point is well taken, and the problem illustrated is all too common in organizational analysis. We are too often in thralldom before a general principle, applying it mindlessly to situations whose complexity swamps whatever truth might have been revealed by a more thoughtful approach. Let us not be misunderstood. We need the guidance of general principles. But we also require sufficiently detailed knowledge of the organizations and their technologies and environments to be able to select valid indicators of the variables to be assessed. Surgeons do need to be able to exercise discretion in some critical areas of their work, but this requirement need not be inconsistent with the precise specification of other aspects of their performance. If we wish to explain effects, there is no substitute for a knowledge of the specific causal processes linking them with relevant inputs, technologies, and work arrangements.

Contingency models often overlook the open systems concept of equifinality: that many different causal paths can lead to the same effect. In particular, it is often presumed that an organization's ability to maximize its productivity or its profits is due to the superior design of its production structures and the resulting technical efficiency. However, we should know by this time that organizations are technical systems but not simply technical systems. As Katz and Kahn (1978: 249) remind us,

> the textbook path to organizational survival is internal efficiency: build the better mousetrap or build the old trap less expensively. There is, however, a whole class of alternative or supplementary solutions—the political devices that maximize organizational return at some cost to other organizations or individuals.

Pfeffer and Salancik stress the importance of these political solutions throughout their analysis of organizational functioning, concluding: that "the effectiveness of an organization is a sociopolitical question" (1978:

11). Consumers and (some) regulators seek ways to link an organization's effectiveness in goal attainment to its effectiveness in resource acquisition and survival. Sometimes they succeed but often they fail: an organization's resource acquisition and survival are not always tightly linked with the quality of its services to the publics it claims to benefit.

## SUMMARY

Criteria for evaluating organizational effectiveness cannot be produced by some objective, apolitical process. They are always normative and often controversial, and they are as varied as the theoretical models used to describe organizations and the constituencies that have some interest in their functioning. Similarly, the indicators to be used in assessing organizational effectiveness must also be chosen from among several possible types, and data gathered from several possible sampling frames. Measures based on outcomes, processes, and structural features of organizations are likely to produce inconsistent conclusions and are differently favored by various constituencies. We should not seek explanations for organizational effectiveness in general, since such general criteria are not available, and we must be cautious in celebrating the truism that organizations that are better adapted to their environments are more likely to survive. Adaptation can be achieved in numerous ways, many of which contribute to the survival of the organization but fail to serve the interests of external constituencies.

# references

ABEGGLEN, JAMES C. (1958). *The Japanese Factory: Aspects of Its Social Organization.* Glencoe, Ill.: Free Press.

ADAMS, J. STACEY (1965). "Inequity in Social Exchange," in *Advances in Experimental Social Psychology,* vol. 2, pp. 267–300, ed. Leonard Berkowitz. New York: Academic Press.

AIKEN, MICHAEL, and JERALD HAGE (1968). "Organizational Interdependence and Intraorganizational Structure," *American Sociological Review,* 33 (December), 912–29.

ALBROW, MARTIN (1970). *Bureaucracy.* New York: Praeger.

ALCHIAN, A. A., and H. DEMSETZ (1972) "Production, Information Costs, and Economic Organization," *American Economic Review,* 62 (December), 777–95.

ALDRICH, HOWARD E. (1972). "Technology and Organizational Structure: A Reexamination of the Findings of the Aston Group," *Administrative Science Quarterly,* 17 (March), 26–43.

——— (1976). "Resource Dependence and Interorganizational Relations: Local Employment Service Offices and Social Services Sector Organizations," *Administration and Society,* 7 (February), 119–54.

——— (1979). *Organizations and Environments.* Englewood Cliffs, N.J.: Prentice-Hall.

ALDRICH, HOWARD E., and SERGIO MINDLIN (1978). "Uncertainty and Dependence: Two Perspectives on Environment," in *Organization and Environment,* pp. 149–70, ed. Lucien Karpit, Beverly Hills, Calif.: Sage Publications, Inc.

ALDRICH, HOWARD E., and JEFFREY PFEFFER (1976). "Environments of Organizations," *Annual Review of Sociology,* 2, 79–105.

ALDRICH, HOWARD E., and DAVID A. WHETTEN (1981). "Organization-Sets, Action-Sets, and Networks: Making the Most of Simplicity," in *Handbook of Organizational Design,* vol. 1, pp. 385–408, ed. Paul C. Nystrom and William H. Starbuck. New York: Oxford University Press.

ALFORD, ROBERT R. (1975). *Health Care Politics.* Chicago: University of Chicago Press.

ALFORD, ROBERT R. and ROGER FRIEDLAND (1975). "Political Participation and Public Policy," *Annual Review of Sociology,* 1, 429–79.

ALLISON, GRAHAM T. (1971). *Essence of Decision: Explaining the Cuban Missile Crisis,* Boston: Little, Brown.

ALTHAUSER, ROBERT P., and ARNE L. KALLEBERG (1981). "Firms, Occupations, and the Structure of Labor Markets: A Conceptual Analysis and Research Agenda," in *Sociological Perspectives on Labor Markets,* pp. 119–49, ed. Ivan Berg. New York: Academic Press.

ALTHUSSER, LOUISE (1969 trans.). *For Marx.* Harmondsworth, England: Penguin.

AMBER, G. H., and P. S. AMBER (1962). *Anatomy of Automation.* Englewood Cliffs, N.J.: Prentice-Hall.

ANDERSON, BO, JOSEPH BERGER, BERNARD P. COHEN, and MORRIS ZELDITCH, JR. (1966). "Status Classes in Organizations," *Administrative Science Quarterly,* 11 (September) 264–83.

ARENDT, HANNAH (1951). *The Origins of Totalitarianism.* New York: Harcourt, Brace.

——— (1963). *Eichmann in Jerusalem.* New York: Viking.

ARGOTE, LINDA (1982). "Input Uncertainty and Organizational Coordination in Hospital Emergency Units," *Administrative Science Quarterly,* 27 (September), 420–34.

ARGYRIS, CHRIS (1957). *Personality and Organization.* New York: Harper.

——— (1962). *Interpersonal Competence and Organizational Effectiveness.* Homewood, Ill.: Richard D. Irwin.

——— (1973). "Personality and Organization Theory Revisited," *Administrative Science Quarterly,* 18 (June), 141–67.

ARGYRIS, CHRIS, and DONALD A. SCHON (1978). *Organization Learning.* Reading, Mass.: Addison-Wesley.

ARMOUR, HENRY O., and DAVID J. TEECE (1978)."Organization Structure and Economic Performance: A Test of the Multidivisional Hypothesis," *Bell Journal of Economics,* 9 (Spring), 106–22.

ARROW, KENNETH J. (1974). *The Limits of Organization.* New York: W. W. Norton & Co., Inc.

ASHBY, W. Ross (1952). *A Design for a Brain.* New York: John Wiley.

——— (1956). "The Effect of Experience on a Determinant System," *Behavioral Science,* 1 (January), 35–42.

——— (1968) "Principles of the Self-Organizing System," in *Modern Systems Research for the Behavioral Scientist,* pp. 108–18, ed. Walter Buckley. Chicago: Aldine.

ASTLEY, W. GRAHAM (1985). "The Two Ecologies: Population and Community Perspectives on Organizational Evolution," *Administrative Science Quarterly,* 30 (June), 224–41.

ASTLEY, W. GRAHAM, and ANDREW H. VAN DE VEN (1983). "Central Perspectives and Debates in Organization Theory," *Administrative Science Quarterly*, 28 (June), 245–73.
AVERITT, RICHARD T. (1968). *The Dual Economy: The Dynamics of American Industry Structure.* New York: W. W. Norton & Co., Inc.

BABER, WALTER F. (1983). *Organizing the Future: Martix Models for the Postindustrial Polity.* Birmingham: University of Alabama Press.
BACHRACH, PETER, and MORTON S. BARATZ (1962). "The Two Faces of Power," *American Political Science Review,* 56 (December), 947–52.
BAKER, ALTON W., and RALPH C. DAVIS (1954). *Ratios of Staff to Line Employees and Stages of Differentiation of Staff Functions.* Columbus: Bureau of Business Research, Ohio State University.
BALES, ROBERT F. (1952). "Some Uniformities of Behavior in Small Social Systems," in *Readings in Social Psychology* (2nd ed.), pp. 146–59, ed. Guy E. Swanson, Theodor M. Newcomb, and Eugene L. Hartley. New York: Holt, Rinehart & Winston.
——— (1953). "The Equilibrium Problem in Small Groups," in *Working Papers in the Theory of Action,* pp. 111–61 by Talcott Parsons, Robert F. Bales, and Edward A. Shils. Glencoe, Ill.: Free Press.
BALES, ROBERT F., and PHILIP E. SLATER (1955). "Role Differentiation in Small Decision-Making Groups,: in *Family, Socialization and Interaction Process,* pp. 259–306, ed. Talcott Parsons and Robert F. Bales. New York: Free Press.
BARBER, BERNARD (1950). "Participation and Mass Apathy in Associations," in *Studies in Leadership,* pp. 477–504, ed. Alvin W. Gouldner. New York: Harper.
BARDACH, EUGENE, and ROBERT A. KAGAN (1982). *Going by the Book: The Problem of Regulatory Unreasonableness.* Philadelphia: Temple University Press.
BARKER, E. (1944). *The Development of Public Services in Western Europe, 1660–1930.* New York: Oxford University Press.
BARNARD, CHESTER I. (1938). *The Functions of the Executive.* Cambridge, Mass.: Harvard University Press.
——— (1948). *Organization and Management.* Cambridge, Mass.: Harvard University Press.
BARNES, JOHN A. (1972). *Social Networks.* Reading, Mass.: Addison-Wesley.
BARON, JAMES N. (1984). "Organizational Perspectives on Stratification," *Annual Review of Sociology,* 10, 37–69.
BARON, JAMES N., and WILLIAM T. BIELBY (1980). "Bringing the Firms Back In: Stratification, Segmentation, and the Organization of Work," *American Sociological Review,* 45 (October), 737–65
——— (1984). "The Organization of Work in a Segmented Economy," *American Sociological Review* 49 (August), 454–73.
BATESON, GREGORY (1972). *Steps to an Ecology of Mind.* New York: Ballantine.
BAVELAS, ALEX (1951). "Communication Patterns in Task-Oriented Groups," in *The Policy Sciences,* pp. 193–202, ed. Daniel Lerner and Harold D. Lasswell. Stanford, Calif.: Stanford University Press.
BECKHARD, RICHARD (1972) "Organizational Issues in the Team Delivery of Comprehensive Health Care, *Milbank Memorial Fund Quarterly* 50 (July) part 1, 287–316.
BEDEIAN, ARTHUR G. (1984). *Organizations: Theory and Analysis* (2nd ed.) Chicago: Dryden Press.
BEER, STAFFORD (1964). *Cybernetics and Management.* New York: John Wiley.
BELKNAP, IVAN (1956). *The Human Problems of a State Mental Hospital.* New York: McGraw-Hill.
BELL, DANIEL (1960). Work and Its Discontents: The Cult of Efficiency in America," in *The End of Ideology,* pp. 222–62, by Daniel Bell. Glencoe, Ill.: Free Press.
——— (1973). *The Coming of Post-Industrial Society.* New York: Basic Books.
BELL, GERALD D. (1967). "Determinants of Span of Control," *American Journal of Sociology,* 73 (July), 100–109.
BEN-DAVID, JOSEPH (1963). "Professions in the Class System of Present-Day Societies," *Current Sociology,* 12, 247–330.
BENDIX, REINHARD (1956). *Work and Authority in Industry.* New York: John Wiley.
——— (1960). *Max Weber: An Intellectual Portrait.* Garden City, N.Y.: Doubleday, 1960.
BENDIX, REINHARD, and LLOYD H. FISHER (1949). "The Perspectives of Elton Mayo," *Review of Economics and Statistics,* 31 (November), 312–19.
BENDIX, REINHARD, and SEYMOUR MARTIN LIPSET (1966). "Karl Marx's Theory of Social Classes," in *Class, Status and Power* (rev. ed.) pp. 6–11, ed. Reinhard Bendix and Seymour Martin Lipset. New York: Free Press.
BENNIS, WARREN G. (1959). "Leadership Theory and Administrative Behavior," *Administrative Science Quarterly,* 4 (December), 259–301.
——— (1966). *Changing Organizations.* New York: McGraw-Hill.
BENNIS, WARREN G., and PHILIP E. SLATER (1968). *The Temporary Society.* New York: Harper & Row, Pub.
BENSON, J. KENNETH (1977). "Organizations: A Dialectical View," *Administrative Science Quarterly,* 22 (March), 1–21.
——— (1982). "A Framework for Policy Analysis," in *Interorganizational Coordination,* pp. 137–76, ed. David L. Rogers and David A. Whetten. Ames: Iowa State University Press.
BERG, IVAR (1971). *Education and Jobs: The Great Training Robbery.* New York: Praeger.
BERGER, PETER L., BRIGITTE BERGER, and HANSFRIED KELLNER (1973). *The Homeless Mind: Modernization and Consciousness.* New York: Random House, Vintage Books.
BERGER, PETER L., and THOMAS LUCKMANN (1967). *The Social Construction of Reality.* New York: Doubleday.

BERGER, SUZANNE, ed. (1981). *Organizing Interests in Western Europe: Pluralism, Corporatism and the Transformation of Politics.* New York: Cambridge University Press.

BERLE, A. A. (1963). *The American Economic Republic.* New York: Harcourt, Brace & World.

BERLE, A. A., and GARDINER C. MEANS (1932). *The Modern Corporation and Private Property.* New York: Macmillan.

BERTALANFFY, LUDWIG VON (1956). "General System Theory," in *General Systems: Yearbook of the Society for the Advancement of General Systems Theory,* ed. Ludwig von Bertalanffy and Anatol Rapoport, 1, 1–10.

——— (1962). "General System Theory: A Critical Review," in *General Systems: Yearbook of the Society for General Systems Research,* ed. Ludwig von Bertalanffy and Anatol Rapoport, 7, 1–20.

BEYER, JANICE M., and HARRISON M. TRICE (1979). "A Reexamination of the Relations between Size and Various Components of Organizational Complexity," *Administrative Science Quarterly,* 24 (March), 48–64.

BIDWELL, CHARLES E. (1965). "The School as a Formal Organization," in *Handbook of Organizations,* pp. 972–1022, ed. James G. March. Chicago: Rand McNally.

BITTNER, EGON (1967). "The Police on Skid Row: A Study of Peace Keeping," *American Sociological Review,* 32 (October), 699–715.

BLAKE, R. R., and J. S. MOUTON (1964). *The Managerial Grid.* Houston: Gulf.

BLAKE, R. R., H. A. SHEPHARD, and J. S. MOUTON (1964). *Intergroup Conflict in Organizations.* Ann Arbor, Mich.: Foundation for Research on Human Behavior.

BLAU, PETER M. (1955). *The Dynamics of Bureaucracy.* Chicago: University of Chicago Press (rev. 1963).

——— (1956). *Bureaucracy in Modern Society.* New York: Random House.

——— (1957). "Formal Organization: Dimensions of Analysis," *American Journal of Sociology,* 63 (July), 58–69.

——— (1960). "Structural Effects," *American Sociological Review,* 25 (April) 178–93.

——— (1964). *Exchange and Power in Social Life.* New York: John Wiley.

——— (1968). "The Hierarchy of Authority in Organizations," *American Journal of Sociology,* 73 (January), 453–67.

——— (1970). "A Formal Theory of Differentiation in Organizations," *American Sociological Review,* 35 (April), 201–18.

——— (1973). *The Organization of Academic Work.* New York: John Wiley.

BLAU, PETER M., and OTIS DUDLEY DUNCAN, *The American Occupational Structure.* New York: John Wiley. (1967).

BLAU, PETER M. CECILIA McHUGH FALBE, WILLIAM McKINLEY, and PHELPS K. TRACY (1976). "Technology and Organization in Manufacturing," *Administrative Science Quarterly,* 21 (March) 20–40.

BLAU, PETER M., WOLF V. HEYDEBRAND, and ROBERT E. STAUFFER (1966). "The Structure of Small Bureaucracies," *American Sociological Review,* 31 (April), 179–91.

BLAU, PETER M., and RICHARD A. SCHOENHERR (1971). *The Structure of Organizations.* New York: Basic Books.

BLAU, PETER M., and W. RICHARD SCOTT (1962). *Formal Organizations.* San Francisco: Chandler.

BLAUNER, ROBERT (1960). "Work Satisfaction and Industrial Trends in Modern Society," in *Labor and Trade Unionism,* pp. 339–60 ed. Walter Galenson and Seymour Martin Lipset. New York: John Wiley.

BLUMBERG, PAUL (1968). *Industrial Democracy: The Sociology of Participation.* New York: Schocken Books.

BOAS, MAX, and STEVE CHAIN (1977). *Big Mac: The Unauthorized Story of McDonald's.* New York: New American Library.

BOGUSLAW, ROBERT (1965). *The New Utopians: A Study of System Design and Social Change.* Englewood Cliffs, N.J.: Prentice-Hall.

BOORMAN, SCOTT, and HARRISON C. WHITE (1976). "Social Structures from Multiple Networks: II. Role Structures," *American Journal of Sociology,* 81 (May) 1384–446.

BOULDING, KENNETH E. (1953). *The Organizational Revolution.* New York: Harper & Brothers.

——— (1956). "General Systems Theory: The Skeleton of Science," *Management Science,* 2 (April), 197–208.

BRAVERMAN, HARRY (1974). *Labor and Monopoly Capital: The Degradation of Work in the Twentieth Century.* New York: Monthly Review Press.

BRAYFIELD, ARTHUR H., and WALTER H. CROCKETT (1955). "Employee Attitudes and Employee Performance," *Psychological Bulletin,* 52 (September), 396–424.

BRIEF, ARTHUR P., and RAMON J. ALDAG (1975). "Employee Reactions to Job Characteristics: A Constructive Replication," *Journal of Applied Psychology,* 60 (April), 182–86.

BRIGHT, CHARLES, and SUSAN HARDING, eds. (1984). *Statemaking and Social Movements.* Ann Arbor: University of Michigan Press.

BRITTAIN, JACK, and JOHN FREEMAN (1980). "Organizational Proliferation and Density-Dependent Selection," in *Organizational Life Cycles,* pp. 291–338, ed. John Kimberly and Robert Miles. San Francisco: Jossey-Bass.

BROOK, ROBERT H. (1973). *Quality of Care Assessment: A Comparison of Five Methods of Peer Review.* Washington, D.C.: Bureau of Health Services Research and Evaluation.

BROOKS, HARVEY (1984). "Seeking Equity and Efficiency: Public and Private Roles," in *Public-Private Partnership: New Opportunities for Meeting Social Needs.* pp. 3–29, ed. Harvey Brooks, Lance Liebman, and Corinne S. Schelling. Cambridge, Mass.: Ballinger.

BROOKS, HARVEY, LANCE LIEBMAN, and CORINNE S. SCHELLING, eds. (1984). *Public-Private Partnership: New Opportunities for Meeting Social Needs.* Cambridge, Mass.: Ballinger.

BROWN, RICHARD HARVEY (1978). "Bureaucracy as Praxis: Toward a Political Phenomenology of Formal Organizations," *Administrative Science Quarterly*, 23 (September), 365–82.

BRUNSSON, NILS (1985). *The Irrational Organization.* New York: John Wiley.

BUCHER, RUE, and ANSELM STRAUSS (1961). "Professions in Process," *American Journal of Socioogy*, 66 (January), 325–34.

BUCKLEY, WALTER (1967). *Sociology and Modern Systems Theory.* Englewood Cliffs, N.J.: Prentice-Hall.

BURAWOY, MICHAEL (1979). *Manufacturing Consent: Changes in the Labor Process under Monopoly Capitalism.* Chicago: University of Chicago Press.

——— (1982). "Introduction: The resurgence of Marxism in American Sociology," in *Marxist Inquiries: Studies of Labor, Class, and States.* Supplement to *American Journal of Sociology*, 88, S1–S30, ed. Michael Burawoy and Theda Skocpol. Chicago: University of Chicago Press.

——— (1985). *The Politics of Production.* London: Verso.

BURNS, TOM, and GEORGE M. STALKER (1961). *The Management of Innovation.* London: Tavistock.

BURRELL, GIBSON, and GARETH MORGAN (1979). *Sociological Paradigms and Organizational Analysis.* London: Heinemann.

BURT, RONALD S. (1980). "Models of Network Structure," *Annual Review of Sociology*, 6, 79–141.

——— (1983). *Corporate Profits and Cooptation.* New York: Academic Press.

BURT, RONALD S., KENNETH P. CHRISTMAN, and HAROLD C. KILBURN, Jr. (1980). "Testing a Structural Theory of Corporate Cooptation: Interorganizational Directorate Ties as a Strategy for Avoiding Market Constraints on Profits," *American Sociological Review*, 45 (October), 821–41.


CAMERON, KIM S., and DAVID A. WHETTEN (1981). "Perceptions of Organizational Effectiveness over Organizational Life Cycles," *Administrative Science Quarterly*, 26 (December), 525–44.

——— eds. (1982). *Organizational Effectiveness: A Comparison of Multiple Models.* New York: Academic Press.

CAMPBELL, DONALD (1969). "Variation and Selective Retention in Socio-Cultural Evolution," *General Systems: Yearbook of the Society for General Systems Research*, 16, 69–85.

CAMPBELL, JOHN P. (1977). "On the Nature of Organizational Effectiveness," in *New Perspectives on Organizational Effectiveness*, pp. 13–55, ed. Paul S. Goodman and Johannes M. Pennings. San Francisco: Jossey-Bass.

CAREY, ALEX (1967). "The Hawthorne Studies: A Radical Criticism," *American Sociological Review*, 32 (June), 403–16.

CARROLL, GLEN R. (1984). "Organizational Ecology," *Annual Review of Sociology*, 10, 71–93.

CARROLL, GLEN R., and JACQUES DELACROIX (1982). "Organizational Mortality in the Newspaper Industries of Argentina and Ireland: An Ecological Approach," *Administrative Science Quarterly*, 27 (June), 169–98.

CARTER, LAUNOR, WILLIAM HAYTHORN, BEATRICE SHRIVER, and JOHN LANZETTA (1953). "The Behavior of Leaders and Other Group Members," in *Group Dynamics*, pp. 551–60, ed. Dorwin Cartwright and Alvin Zander. Evanston, Ill.: Row, Peterson.

CARTWRIGHT, DORWIN (1965). "Influence, Leadership, Control," in *Handbook of Organizations*, pp. 1–47, ed. James G. March. Chicago: Rand McNally.

CARZO, ROCCO, JR., and JOHN N. YANOUZAS (1967). *Formal Organization: A Systems Approach.* Homewood, Ill.: Richard D. Irwin; Dorsey.

CHANDLER, ALFRED D., JR. (1962) *Strategy and Structure: Chapters in the History of the American Industrial Enterprise.* Cambridge, Mass.: M.I.T. Press.

——— (1977). *The Visible Hand: The Managerial Revolution in American Business.* Cambridge, Mass.: Harvard University Press, Belknap Press.

CHEIT, EARL F. (1964). "The New Place of Business: Why Managers Cultivate Social Responsibility," in *The Business Establishment*, pp. 152–92, ed. Earl F. Cheit. New York: John Wiley.

CHILD, JOHN (1972). "Organizational Structure, Environment and Performance: The Role of Strategic Choice," *Sociology*, 6 (January), 1–22.

——— (1981). "Culture, contingency and capitalism in the cross-national study of organizations," in *Research in Organizational Behavior*, vol. 3, pp. 303–56, ed. L. L. Cummings and Barry M. Staw. Greenwich, Conn.: JAI Press.

CHILD, JOHN, and ROGER MANSFIELD (1972). "Technology, Size and Organization Structure," *Sociology*, 6 (September), 369–93.

CHRISTIE, L. S., R. S. LUCE, and J. MACY, JR. (1952). "Communication and Learning in Task-Oriented Groups," Technical Report No. 231. Cambridge: Research Laboratory of Electronics, Massachusetts Institute of Technology.

CICOUREL, AARON (1968). *The Social Organization of Juvenile Justice.* New York: John Wiley.

CLARK, BURTON R. (1956). *Adult Education in Transition.* Berkeley: University of California Press.

——— (1963). "Faculty Organization and Authority," in *The Study of Academic Administration*, pp. 37–51, ed. Terry F. Lunsford. Boulder, Colo.: Western Interstate Commission for Higher Education.

——— (1965) "Interorganizational Patterns in Education," *Administrative Science Quarterly*, 10 (September), 224–37.

——— (1970). *The Distinctive College: Antioch, Reed and Swarthmore.* Chicago: Aldine.

——— (1972). "The Organizational Saga in Higher Education," *Administrative Science Quarterly*, 17 (June), 178–183.

——— (1983). *The Higher Education System.* Berkeley: University of California Press.

CLARK, PETER M., and JAMES Q. WILSON (1961). "Incentive Systems: A Theory of Organizations," *Administrative Science Quarterly*, 6 (September), 129–66.

CLEMMER, DONALD (1940). *The Prison Community*. Boston: Christopher.

CLINARD, MARSHALL B. and PETER C. YEAGER (1980). *Corporate Crime*. New York: Free Press.

CLOUGH, DONALD J. (1963). *Concepts in Management Science*. Englewood Cliffs, N.J.: Pentice-Hall.

COASE, R. H. (1937). "The Nature of the Firm," *Economica*, N.S., 4 (November), 386–405.

COCH, L., and J. R. P. FRENCH, JR. (1948). "Overcoming Resistance to Change," *Human Relations*, 1:4, 512–32.

COHEN, BERNARD P. (1972). "On the Construction of Sociological Explanations," *Synthese*, 24 (December), 401–9.

COHEN, MICHAEL D., and JAMES G. MARCH (1974). *Leadership and Ambiguity: The American College President*. New York: McGraw-Hill.

——— (1976). "Decisions, Presidents, and Status," in *Ambiguity and Choice in Organizations*, pp. 174–205, ed. James G. March and Johan P. Olsen. Bergen, Norway: Universitetsforlaget.

COHEN, MICHAEL D., JAMES G. MARCH, and JOHAN P. OLSEN (1972). "A Garbage Can Model of Organizational Choice," *Administrative Science Quarterly*, 17 (March), 1–25.

——— (1976). "People, Problems, Solutions and the Ambiguity of Relevance," in *Ambiguity and Choice in Organizations*, pp. 24–37, ed. James G. March and Johan P. Olsen. Bergen, Norway: Universitetsforlaget.

COLE, ROBERT E. (1979). *Work, Mobility, and Participation*. Berkeley: University of California Press.

COLEMAN, JAMES S. (1974). *Power and the Structure of Society*. New York: W. W. Norton & Co., Inc.

——— (1975). "Social Structure and a Theory of Action," in *Approaches to the Study of Social Structure*, pp. 76–93, ed. Peter M. Blau. New York: Free Press.

COLLINS, ORVIS (1946). "Ethnic Behavior in Industry: Sponsorship and Rejection in a New England Factory," *American Journal of Sociology*, 21, 293–98.

COLLINS, RANDALL (1971). "Functional and Conflict Theories of Educational Stratification," *American Sociological Review*, 36 (December), 1002–19.

——— (1979). *The Credential Society*. New York: Academic Press.

COMMONS, JOHN R. (1924). *Legal Foundations of Capitalism*. New York: Macmillan.

COMSTOCK, DONALD E., and W. RICHARD SCOTT (1977). "Technology and the Structure of Subunits: Distinguishing Individual and Workgroup Effects," *Administrative Science Quarterly*, 22 (June), 177–202.

COSER, ROSE LAUB (1951). "An Analysis of the Early German Socialist Movement," Unpublished M.A. thesis, Department of Sociology, Columbia University.

CRONBACH, LEE J. and ASSOCIATES (1980). *Toward Reform of Program Evaluation*. San Francisco: Jossey-Bass.

CROZIER, MICHEL (1964). *The Bureaucratic Phenomenon*. Chicago: University of Chicago Press.

CUMMINGS, LARRY L. (1977). "Emergence of the Instrumental Organization," in *New Perspectives on Organizational Effectiveness*, pp. 56–62, ed. Paul S. Goodman and Johannes M. Pennings. San Francisco: Jossey-Bass.

——— (1982). "Organizational Behavior," *Annual Review of Psychology*, 33, 541–79.

CYERT, RICHARD M., and JAMES G. MARCH (1963). *A Behavioral Theory of the Firm*. Englewood Cliffs, N.J.: Prentice-Hall.

DAHL, ROBERT A. (1970). *After the Revolution?* New Haven: Yale University Press.

DAHRENDORF, RALF (1959 trans.). *Class and Class Conflict in Industrial Society*. Stanford, Calif.: Stanford University Press (first published in 1957).

DALTON, MELVILLE (1950). "Conflicts between Staff and Line Managerial Officers," *American Sociological Review*, 15 (June), 342–51.

——— (1959). *Men Who Manage*. New York: John Wiley.

DAVIS, KINGSLEY (1949). *Human Society*. New York: Macmillan.

DAVIS, STANLEY M., and PAUL R. LAWRENCE (1977). *Matrix*. Reading, Mass.: Addison-Wesley.

DEAL, TERRENCE E., and ALLAN A. KENNEDY (1982). *Corporate Cultures*. Reading, Mass.: Addison-Wesley.

DELANY, WILLIAM (1963). "The Development and Decline of Patrimonial and Bureaucratic Administrations," *Administrative Science Quarterly*, 7 (March), 458–501.

DERTHICK, MARTHA (1972). *New Towns In-Town*. Washington, D.C.: Urban Institute.

DESS, GREGORY G., and DONALD W. BEARD (1984). "Dimensions of Organizational Task Environments," *Administrative Science Quarterly*, 29 (March), 52–73.

DIAMOND, SIGMUND (1958). "From Organization to Society," *American Journal of Sociology*, 63 (March), 457–75.

DIBBLE, VERNON K. (1965). "The Organization of Traditional Authority: English County Government, 1558 to 1640," in *Handbook of Organizations*, pp. 879–909, ed. James G. March. Chicago: Rand McNally.

DILL, WILLIAM R. (1958). "Environment as an Influence on Managerial Autonomy," *Administrative Science Quarterly*, 2 (March), 409–43.

DiMAGGIO, PAUL (1983). "State Expansion and Organizational Fields," in *Organizational Theory and Public Policy*, pp. 147–61, ed. Richard H. Hall and Robert E. Quinn. Beverly Hills, Calif.: Sage Publications, Inc.

DiMAGGIO, PAUL J., and WALTER W. POWELL (1983). "The Iron Cage Revisited: Institutional Isomorphism and Collective Rationality in Organizational Fields," *American Sociological Review*, 48 (April), 147–60.

DOBBIN, FRANK, LAUREN EDELMAN, JOHN W. MEYER, W. RICHARD SCOTT, and ANN SWIDLER (in press). "Legalization in Organizations: The Expansion of Due Process Protections," in *Institutional Patterns and Organizations: Culture and Environment*, ed. Lynne G. Zucker. New York: Academic Press.

DOERINGER, PETER B., and MICHAEL J. PIORE (1971). *Internal Labor Markets and Manpower Analysis*. Lexington, Mass.: Heath.

DOMHOFF, G. WILLIAM (1983). *Who Rules America Now? A View for the 80s*. Englewood Cliffs, N.J.: Prentice-Hall.

DONABEDIAN, AVEDIS (1966). "Evaluating the Quality of Medical Care," *Milbank Memorial Fund Quarterly*, 44 (July), part 2, 166–206.

DORE, RONALD (1973). *British Factory–Japanese Factory*. Berkeley: University of California Press.

DORNBUSCH, SANFORD M., and W. RICHARD SCOTT, with the assistance of BRUCE C. BUSCHING and JAMES D. LAING (1975). *Evaluation and the Exercise of Authority*. San Francisco: Jossey-Bass.

DOWNS, ANTHONY (1967). *Inside Bureaucracy*. Boston: Little, Brown.

DRUCKER, PETER (1970). "The New Markets and the New Capitalism," *Public Interest*, 21 (Fall), 44–79.

——— (1976). "What Results Should You Expect? A User's Guide to MBO," *Public Administration Review*, 36 (January-February), 1–45

DUBIN, ROBERT, ed. (1968). *Human Relations in Administration* (3rd ed.). Englewood Cliffs, N.J.: Prentice-Hall.

DUNCAN, ROBERT B. (1972). "Characteristics of Organizational Environments and Perceived Environmental Uncertainty," *Administrative Science Quarterly*, 17 (September), 313–27.

DURKHEIM, EMILE (1949 trans.) *Division of Labor in Society*. Glencoe, Ill.: Free Press (first published in 1893).

ECCLES, ROBERT G., and HARRISON C. WHITE (1983). "Firm and Market Interfaces of Profit Center Control," unpublished paper, Harvard University.

EDITORS OF THE YALE LAW JOURNAL (1954). "The American Medical Association: Power, Purpose, and Politics in Organized Medicine," *Yale Law Journal*, 63 (May), 938–1022.

EWARDS, RICHARD (1979). *Contested Terrain: The Transformation of the Workplace in the Twentieth Century*. New York: Basic Books.

EISENSTADT, S. N. (1958). "Bureaucracy and Bureaucratization: A Trend Report and Bibliography," *Current Sociology*, 7:2, 99–164.

——— (1981). "Interactions between Organizations and Societal Stratification," in *Handbook of Organizational Design*, Vol. 1, pp. 309–22, ed. Paul C. Nystrom and William H. Starbuck. Oxford: Oxford University Press.

ELLUL, JACQUES (1964 trans.). *The Technological Society*. New York: Knopf (first published in 1954).

EMERSON, RICHARD M. (1962). "Power-Dependence Relations," *American Sociological Review*, 27 (February), 31–40.

EMERY, FRED E. (1959). *Characteristics of Socio-Technical Systems*. Tavistock Document 527. London: Tavistock.

EMERY, FRED E., and E. THORSRUD (1969 trans.) *Form and Content in Industrial Democracy*. London: Tavistock (first published in 1964).

——— (1976). *Democracy at Work*. Leiden: Martinus Nijhoff.

EMERY, FRED E., and E. L. TRIST (1965). "The Causal Texture of Organizational Environments," *Human Relations*, 18 (February), 21–32.

ERMANN, M. DAVID and RICHARD J. LUNDMAN (1982). *Corporate Deviance*. New York: Holt, Rinehart and Winston.

ETZIONI, AMITAI (1960). "Two Approaches to Organizational Analysis: A Critique and a Suggestion," *Administrative Science Quarterly*, 5 (September), 257–78.

——— (1961). *A Comparative Analysis of Complex Organizations*. New York: Free Press of Glencoe (rev. 1975).

——— (1964). *Modern Organizations*. Englewood Cliffs, N.J.: Prentice-Hall.

———, ed. (1969). *The Semi-Professions and Their Organization*. New York: Free Press.

EVAN, WILLIAM M. (1966). "The Organization Set: Toward a Theory of Interorganizational Relations," in *Approaches to Organizational Design*, pp. 173–88, ed. James D. Thompson. Pittsburgh: University of Pittsburgh Press, 1966.

EVANS, PETER B. (1981). "Recent Research on Multinational Corporations," *Annual Review of Sociology*, 7, 199–223.

EVANS, PETER B., DIETRICH RUESCHEMEYER and THEDA SKOCPOL, ed. (1986). *Bringing the State Back In*. Cambridge: Cambridge University Press.

FAMA, EUGENE F. (1980). "Agency Problems and the Theory of the Firm," *Journal of Political Economy*, 88 (April), 288–307.

FAUNCE, WILLIAM A. (1968). *Problems of an Industrial Society*. New York: McGraw-Hill.

FAYOL, HENRI (1949 trans.). *General and Industrial Management*. London: Pitman (first published in 1919).

FENNELL, MARY L. (1980). "The Effects of Environmental Characteristics on the Structure of Hospital Clusters," *Administrative Science Quarterly*, 25 (September), 485–510.

FERGUSON, KATHY E. (1984). *The Feminist Case against Bureaucracy*. Philadelphia: Temple University Press.

FESTINGER, LEON (1957). *A Theory of Cognitive Dissonance*. Evanston, Ill.: Row, Peterson.

FIEDLER, FRED E. (1964). "A Contingency Model of Leadership Effectiveness," in *Advances in Experimental Social Psychology*, ed. Leonard Berkowitz. New York: Academic Press.

——— (1971). "Validation and Extension of the Contingency Model of Leadership Effectiveness: A Review of Empirical Findings," *Psychological Bulletin*, 76 (August), 128–48.

FLIGSTEIN, NEIL (1985a). "The Spread of the Multidivisional Form among Large Firms, 1919–1979," *American Sociological Review*, 50 (June), 377–91.

——— (1985b). "The Intraorganizational Firm Power Struggle: The Rise of Finance Presidents in Large Firms, 1919–1979," presented at the annual meetings of the American Sociological Association, Washington, D.C.

FLOOD, ANN BARRY, and W. RICHARD SCOTT (1987). *Hospital Structure and Performance*. Balitmore: Johns Hopkins.

FOLEY, HENRY A., and STEVEN S. SHARFSTEIN (1983). *Madness and Government: Who Cares for the Mentally Ill?* Washington, D.C.: American Psychiatric Press.

FOLLETT, MARY PARKER (1942). *Dynamic Administration*. New York: Harper.

FOX, FREDERICK V., and BARRY M. STAW (1979). "The Trapped Administrator: Effects of Job Insecurity and Policy Resistance upon Commitment to a Course of Action," *Administrative Science Quarterly*, 24 (September), 449–71.

FOX, RENÉE (1959). *Experiment Perilous*. Glencoe, Ill.: Free Press.

FREEDMAN, MARCIA (1976). *Labor Markets: Segments and Shelters*. Montclair, N.J.: Allanheld, Osmun.

FREEMAN, JOHN H. (1978). "The Unit of Analysis in Organizational Research," in *Environments and Organizations*, pp. 335–51, ed. Marshall W. Meyer. San Francisco: Jossey-Bass.

FREEMAN, JOHN H., and JACK W. BRITTAIN (1977). "Union Merger Process and Industrial Environment," *Industrial Relations*, 16 (May), 173–85.

FREEMAN, JOHN H., and MICHAEL T. HANNAN (1975). "Growth and Decline Processes in Organizations," *American Sociological Review*, 40 (April), 215–28.

——— (1983). "Niche Width and the Dynamics of Organizational Populations," *American Journal of Sociology*, 88 (May), 1116–45.

FREIDSON, ELIOT (1970a). *Professional Dominance: The Social Structure of Medical Care*. Chicago: Aldine.

——— (1970b). *Profession of Medicine*. New York: Dodd, Mead.

——— (1975). *Doctoring Together: A Study of Professional Social Control*. New York: Elsevier.

FREIDSON, ELIOT, and BUFORD RHEA (1963). "Processes of Control in a Company of Equals," *Social Problems*, 11 (Fall), 119–31.

FRIEDLAND, ROGER (1980). "Corporate Power and Urban Growth: The Case of Urban Renewal," *Politics and Society*, 10:2, 203–24.

——— (1983). *Power and Crisis in the City: Corporations, Unions and Urban Policy*. New York: Schocken Books.

FRIEDLAND, ROGER, and DONALD PALMER (1984). "Park Place and Main Street: Business and the Urban Power Structure," *Annual Review of Sociology*, 10, 393–416.

FRIEDLANDER, FRANK, and HAL PICKLE (1968). "Components of Effectiveness in Small Organizations," *Administrative Science Quarterly*, 13 (September), 289–304.

FRIEDRICH, CARL J., and ZBIGNIEW K. BRZEZINSKI (1956). *Totalitarian Dictatorship and Autocracy*. Cambridge, Mass.: Harvard University Press.

FROST, PETER J., LARRY F. MOORE, MERYL REIS LOUIS, CRAIG C. LUNDBERG, and JOANNE MARTIN, eds. (1985). *Organizational Culture*. Beverly Hills, Calif.: Sage Publications, Inc.

FUCHS, VICTOR R. (1974). *Who Shall Live? Health, Economics, and Social Choice*. New York: Basic Books.

GALASKIEWICZ, JOSEPH (1979). "The Structure of Community Organizational Networks," *Social Forces*, 57 (June), 1346–64.

——— (1985). "Interorganizational Relations," *Annual Review of Sociology*, 11, 281–304.

GALBRAITH, JAY (1973). *Designing Complex Organizations*. Reading, Mass.: Addison-Wesley.

——— (1977). *Organization Design*. Reading, Mass.: Addison-Wesley.

GALBRAITH, JOHN KENNETH (1952). *American Capitalism*. Boston: Houghton Mifflin.

——— (1967). *The New Industrial State*. Boston: Houghton Mifflin.

GALL, JOHN (1978). *Systemantics*. New York: Simon & Schuster, Pocket Books.

GAMSON, WILLIAM (1975). *The Strategy of Protest*. Homewood, Ill.: Dorsey.

GARFINKEL, HAROLD (1967). *Studies in Ethnomethodology*. Englewood Cliffs, N.J.: Prentice-Hall.

GEORGOPOULOS, BASIL S. (1972). "The Hospital as an Organization and Problem-Solving System," in *Organization Research on Health Institutions*, pp. 9–48, ed. Basil S. Georgopoulos. Ann Arbor: Institute for Social Research, University of Michigan.

GEORGOPOULOS, BASIL S., and ALEX MATEJKO (1967). "The American Hospital as a Complex Social System," *Health Services Research*, 2 (Summer), 76–112.

GIDDENS, ANTHONY (1983). *Profiles and Critiques in Social Theory*. Berkeley: University of California Press.

GILBRETH, F. B., and L. M. GILBRETH (1917). *Applied Motion Study*. New York.

GIULIANO, VINCENT (1982). "The Mechanization of Office Work," *Scientific American*, 247 (September), 148–65.

GLASBERG, DAVITA SILFEN, and MICHAEL SCHWARTZ (1983). "Ownership and Control of Corporations," *Annual Review of Sociology*, 9, 311–32.

GLASSMAN, ROBERT (1973). "Persistence and Loose Coupling in Living Systems," *Behavioral Science*, 18 (March), 83–98.

GLENNON, LYNDA M. *Women and Dualism.* New York: Longman, 1979.

GOFFMAN, ERVING (1961). *Asylums.* Garden City, N.Y.: Doubleday, Anchor Books.

—— (1974). *Frame Analysis.* Cambridge, Mass.: Harvard University Press.

GOLDMAN, PAUL, and DONALD R. VAN HOUTEN (1977). "Managerial Strategies and the Worker: A Marxist Analysis of Bureaucracy," *Sociological Quarterly,* 18 (Winter), 108–25.

GOLDNER, FRED H. (1970). "The Division of Labor: Process and Power," in *Power in Organizations,* pp.97–143, ed. Mayer N. Zald. Nashville, Tenn.: Vanderbilt University Press.

GONOS, GEORGE (1977). " 'Situation' versus 'Frame': The 'Interactionist' and the 'Structuralist' Analyses of Everyday Life," *American Sociological Review,* 42 (December), 854–67.

GOODMAN, PAUL (1968). *People or Personnel* and *Like a Conquered Providence.* New York: Random House, Vintage.

GOODMAN, PAUL S., and JOHANNES M. PENNINGS, eds. (1977). *New Perspectives on Organizational Effectiveness.* San Francisco: Jossey-Bass.

GORAN, M. J., J. S. ROBERTS, M. A. KELLOG, J. FIELDING, and W. JESSEE (1975). "The PSRO Hospital Review System," *Medical Care,* 13 (Supplement to April), 1–32.

GORDON, DAVID M., RICHARD EDWARDS, and MICHAEL REICH (1982). *Segmented Work, Divided Workers.* Cambridge: Cambridge University Press, 1982.

GOSNELL, HAROLD F. (1937). *Machine Politics: Chicago Model.* Chicago: University of Chicago Press.

GOSS, MARY E. W. (1961). "Influence and Authority among Physicians in an Outpatient Clinic," *American Sociological Review,* 26 (February), 39–50.

GOULDNER, ALVIN W. (1954). *Patterns of Industrial Bureaucracy.* Glencoe, Ill.: Free Press.

—— (1955). "Metaphysical Pathos and the Theory of Bureaucracy," *American Political Science Review,* 49 (June), 496–507.

—— (1959). "Organizational Analysis," in *Sociology Today,* pp. 400–428, ed. Robert K. Merton, Leonard Broom, and Leonard S. Cottrell, Jr. New York: Basic Books.

GRAMSCI, ANTONIO (1971 trans.). *Selections from the Prison Notebooks of Antonio Gramsci,* ed. Quinton Hoare and Geoffrey Nowell Smith. New York: International Publishers (first published 1948–1951).

GRANOVETTER, MARK (1985). "Economic Action and Social Structure: The Problem of Embeddedness," *American Journal of Sociology,* 91 (November), 481–510.

GREINER, LARRY E. (1972). "Evolution and Revolution as Organizations Grow," *Harvard Business Review,* 50 (July-August), 37–46.

GRIMES, A. J., and S. M. KLEIN (1973). "The Technological Imperative: The Relative Impact of Task Unit, Modal Technology, and Hierarchy on Structure," *Academy of Management Journal,* 16 (December), 583–97.

GROSS, EDWARD (1953). "Some Functional Consequences of Primary Controls in Formal Work Organizations," *American Sociological Review,* 18 (August), 368–73.

—— (1968). "Universities as Organizations: A Research Approach," *American Sociological Review,* 33 (August), 518–44.

GROSS, EDWARD, and AMITAI ETZIONI (1985). *Organizations in Society.* Englewood Cliffs, N. J.: Prentice-Hall.

GROSS, NEAL, WARD S. MASON, and ALEXANDER W. McEACHERN (1958). *Explorations in Role Analysis.* New York: John Wiley.

GUETZKOW, HAROLD (1965). "Communications in Organizations," in *Handbook of Organizations,* pp. 534–73, ed. James G. March. Chicago: Rand McNally.

GUETZKOW, HAROLD, and HERBERT A. SIMON (1955). "The Impact of Certain Communication Nets upon Organization and Performance in Task-Oriented Groups," *Management Science,* 1 (April-July), 233–50.

GULICK, LUTHER, and L. URWICK, eds. (1937). *Papers on the Science of Administration.* New York: Institute of Public Administration, Columbia University.

GUSFIELD, JOSEPH R. (1968). "The Study of Social Movements," *International Encyclopedia of the Social Sciences,* vol. 14, pp. 445–52. New York: Macmillan.

GYLLENHAMMAR, P. G. (1977). *People at Work.* Reading, Mass.: Addison-Wesley.


HABERMAS, JURGEN (1971 trans.). *Toward A Rational Society.* London: Heinemann.

HABERSTROH, CHADWICK J. (1965). "Organization Design and Systems Analysis," in *Handbook of Organizations,* pp. 1171–211, ed. James G. March. Chicago: Rand McNally.

HACKMAN, J. RICHARD, and GREG R. OLDHAM (1980). *Work Redesign.* Reading, Mass.: Addison-Wesley.

HAGE, JERALD (1965). "An Axiomatic Theory of Organizations," *Administrative Science Quarterly,* 10 (December), 289–320.

HAGE, JERALD, and MICHAEL AIKEN (1969). "Routine Technology, Social Structure, and Organization Goals," *Administrative Science Quarterly,* 14 (September), 366–76.

HALL, A. D., and R. E. FAGEN (1956). "Definition of System," *General Systems: The Yearbook of the Society for the Advancement of General Systems Theory,* 1, 18–28.

HALL, RICHARD H. (1963). "The Concept of Bureaucracy: An Empirical Assessment," *American Journal of Sociology,* 69 (July), 32–40.

—— (1967). "Some Organizational Considerations in the Professional-Organizational Relationship," *Administrative Science Quarterly,* 12 (December), 461–78.

—— (1968). "Professionalization and Bureaucratization," *American Sociological Review,* 33 (February), 92–104.

HALL, RICHARD H., J. EUGENE, HAAS, and NORMAN J. JOHNSON (1967). "Organizational Size, Complexity, and Formalization," *American Sociological Review*, 32 (December), 903–12.

HALL, RICHARD H., and CHARLES R. TITTLE (1966). "Bureaucracy and Its Correlates," *American Journal of Sociology*, 72 (November), 267–72.

HANNAN, MICHAEL T., and JOHN FREEMAN (1977). "The Population Ecology of Organizations," *American Journal of Sociology*, 82 (March), 929–64.

——— (1984). "Structural Inertia and Organizational Change," *American Sociological Review*, 49 (April), 149–64.

HANRAHAN, JOHN D. (1983). *Government by Contract*. New York: W. W. Norton & Co., Inc.

HART, DAVID K., and WILLIAM G. SCOTT (1975). "The Organizational Imperative," *Administration and Society*, 7 (November), 259–85.

HARVEY, EDWARD (1968). "Technology and the Structure of Organizations," *American Sociological Review*, 33 (April), 247–59.

HAWLEY, AMOS (1950). *Human Ecology*. New York: Ronald Press.

HECLO, HUGH (1977). *A Government of Strangers: Executive Politics in Washington*. Washington D. C.: Brookings Institution.

HEDBERG, BO (1981). "How Organizations Learn and Unlearn," in *Handbook of Organizational Design*, vol. 1, pp. 3–27, ed. Paul C. Nystrom and William H. Starbuck. Oxford: Oxford University Press.

HEDBERG, BO L. T., PAUL C. NYSTROM, and WILLIAM H. STARBUCK (1976). "Camping on Seesaws: Prescriptions for a Self-Designing Organization," *Administrative Science Quarterly*, 21 (March), 41–65.

HEILBRONER, ROBERT L. (1980). *An Inquiry into the Human Prospect* (rev. ed.). New York: W. W. Norton and Co., Inc.

HEMPEL, C. (1959). "The Logic of Functional Analysis," in *Symposium on Sociological Theory*. pp. 271–307, ed. Llewellyn Gross, Evanston, Ill.: Row, Peterson.

HENDERSON, LAWRENCE J. (1935). *Pareto's General Sociology*. Cambridge, Mass.: Harvard University Press.

HERMAN, E. S. (1981). *Corporate Control, Corporate Power*. Cambridge: Cambridge University Press.

HERZBERG, FREDERICK (1966). *Work and the Nature of Man*. Cleveland: World Publishing.

HEYDEBRAND, WOLF V. (1973). "Autonomy, Complexity, and Non-Bureaucratic Coordination in Professional Organizations," pp. 158–189, in *Comparative Organizations*, ed. Wolf V. Heydebrand. Englewood Cliffs, N.J.: Prentice-Hall.

HICKSON, DAVID J., C. R. HININGS, C. A. LEE, R. E. SCHNECK, and J. M. PENNINGS (1971). "A Strategic Contingencies' Theory of Intraorganizational Power," *Administrative Science Quarterly*, 16 (June), 216–29.

HICKSON, DAVID J., D. S. PUGH, and DIANA C. PHEYSEY (1969). "Operations Technology and Organization Structure: An Empirical Reappraisal," *Administrative Science Quarterly*, 14 (September), 378–97.

HILL, RAYNARD E., and BERNARD J. WHITE (1979). *Matrix Organization and Project Management*. Ann Arbor: University of Michigan Press.

HILLERY, GEORGE A., JR. (1968). *Communal Organizations: A Study of Local Societies*. Chicago: University of Chicago Press.

HIND, ROBERT R., SANFORD M. DORNBUSCH, and W. RICHARD SCOTT (1974). "A Theory of Evaluation Applied to a University Faculty," *Sociology of Education*, 47 (Winter), 114–28.

HININGS, C. R., D. J. HICKSON, J. M. PENNINGS, and R. E. SCHNECK (1974). "Structural Conditions of Intraorganizational Power," *Administrative Science Quarterly*, 19 (March), 22–44.

HIRSCH, PAUL M. (1972). "Processing Fads and Fashions: An Organization-Set Analysis of Cultural Industry Systems," *American Journal of Sociology*, 77 (January), 639–59.

——— (1975). "Organizational Effectiveness and the Institutional Environment," *Administrative Science Quarterly*, 20 (September), 327–44.

——— (1985). "The Study of Industries," in *Research in the Sociology of Organizations*, vol. 4 pp. 271–309, ed. Samuel B. Bacharach and Stephen M. Mitchell. Greenwich, Conn.: JAI Press.

HIRSCHMAN, ALBERT O. (1970). *Exit, Voice, and Loyalty*. Cambridge, Mass.: Harvard University Press.

HOBSBAWM, ERIC, and TERENCE RANGER, eds. (1983). *The Invention of Tradition*. Cambridge: Cambridge University Press.

HODSON, RANDY D., and ROBERT L. KAUFMAN (1982). "Economic Dualism: A Critical Review," *American Sociology Review*, 47 (December) 727–39.

HOFSTADTER, RICHARD (1945). *Social Darwinism in American Thought, 1860–1915*. Philadelphia: University of Pennsylvania Press.

HOFSTEDE, GEERT (1984). *Culture's Consequences: International Differences in Work-Related Values* (abridged ed.). Beverly Hills, Calif.: Sage Publications, Inc.

HOFSTEDE, GEERT, and M. S. KASSEM, eds. (1976). *European Contributions to Organization Theory*. Assen, The Netherlands: Van Gorcum.

HOLDAWAY, EDWARD A., and THOMAS A. BLOWERS (1971). "Administrative Ratios and Organizational Size: A Longitudinal Examination," *American Sociological Review*, 36 (April), 278–86.

HOLLANDER, EDWIN P., and JAMES W. JULIAN (1969). "Contemporary Trends in the Analysis of Leadership Processes," *Psychological Bulletin*, 71 (May), 387–97.

HOMANS, GEORGE C. (1950). *The Human Group*. New York: Harcourt.

——— (1961). *Social Behavior: Its Elementary Forms*. New York: Harcourt, Brace & World.

HOPKINS, TERENCE K. (1961). "Bureaucratic Authority: The Convergence of Weber and Barnard," in *Complex Organizations: A Sociological Reader*, pp. 82–100, ed. Amitai Etzioni. New York: Holt, Rinehart & Winston.

HOUSE, WILLIAM C., ed. (1971). *The Impact of Information Technology on Management Operation.* Princeton, N.J.: Auerbach Publishers.

HREBINIAK, LAWRENCE G. (1974). "Job Technology, Supervision and Work Group Structure," *Administrative Science Quarterly,* 19 (September), 395–410.

HUGHES, EVERETT C. (1946). "The Knitting of Racial Groups in Industry," *American Sociological Review,* 11 (October), 512–19.

——— (1958). *Men and Their Work.* Glencoe, Ill.: Free Press.

HULIN, CHARLES L., and MILTON R. BLOOD (1968). "Job Enlargement, Individual Differences, and Worker Responses," *Psychological Bulletin,* 69 (January), 41–55.

HUNTINGTON, SAMUEL P. (1966). "Political Modernization: American vs. Europe," *World Politics,* 18 (April), 378–414.


IANNI, FRANCIS A. J. (1972). *A Family Business: Kinship and Social Control in Organized Crime.* New York: Russell Sage Foundation.

ILLICH, IVAN (1972). *Deschooling Society.* New York: Harper & Row, Pub., Harrow Books.

——— (1976). *Medical Nemesis.* New York: Random House.

INKELES, ALEX (1969). "Making Men Modern: On the Causes and Consequences of Individual Change in Six Developing Countries," *American Journal of Sociology,* 75 (September), 208–25.

ISRAEL, JOACHIM (1971). *Alienation: From Marx to Modern Sociology.* Boston: Allyn & Bacon.


JACOBS, DAVID (1974). "Dependency and Vulnerability: An Exchange Approach to the Control of Organizations," *Administrative Science Quarterly,* 19 (March), 45–59.

JACOBY, HENRY (1973). *The Bureaucratization of the World,* trans. Eveline L. Kanes. Berkeley: University of California Press.

JAMES, HENRY (1907). Preface to *Roderick Hudson.* New York: Scribner's.

JAQUES, ELLIOTT (1951). *The Changing Culture of a Factory.* London: Tavistock.

JELINEK, MARIANN, LINDA SMIRCICH, and PAUL HIRSCH eds. (1983). "Organizational Culture," *Administrative Science Quarterly,* 28 (September), entire issue.

JENKINS, J. CRAIG (1979). "What Is to Be Done: Movement or Organization?" *Contemporary Sociology,* 8 (March), 222–28.

JENSEN, MICHAEL C., and WILLIAM H. MECKLING (1976). "Theory of the Firm: Managerial Behavior, Agency Costs and Ownership Structure," *Journal of Financial Economics,* 3 (October) 305–60.

JURKOVICH, RAY (1974). "A Core Typology of Organizational Environments," *Administrative Science Quarterly,* 19 (September), 380–94.


KAHN, ROBERT L., D. M. WOLFE, R. P. QUINN, J. D. SNOEK, and ROBERT A. ROSENTHAL (1964). *Organizational Stress.* New York: John Wiley.

KAHNEMAN, DANIEL, P. SLOVIC, and AMOS TVERSKY (1982). *Judgment under Uncertainty: Heuristics and Biases.* Cambridge: Cambridge University Press.

KALLEK, SHIRLEY (1975). "Potential Applications of Census Bureau Economic Series in Microdata Analysis," *American Economic Review,* 65 (May), 257–62.

KANTER, ROSABETH MOSS (1972). *Commitment and Community: Communes and Utopias in Sociological Perspective.* Cambridge, Mass.: Harvard University Press.

——— (1977a). *Men and Women of the Corporation.* New York: Basic Books.

——— (1977b). *Work and Family in the United States: A Critical Review and Agenda for Research and Policy.* New York: Russell Sage Foundation.

KASARDA, JOHN D. (1974). "The Structural Implications of Social System Size: A Three-Level Analysis," *American Sociological Review,* 39 (February), 19–28.

KATZ, DANIEL, and ROBERT L. KAHN (1952). "Some Recent Findings in Human Relations Research in Industry," in *Readings in Social Psychology* (2nd ed.), pp. 650–65, ed. Guy E. Swanson, Theodor M. Newcomb, and Eugene L. Hartley. New York: Holt.

——— (1966). *The Social Psychology of Organizations.* New York: John Wiley (rev. 1978).

KATZ, DANIEL, N. MACCOBY, G. GURIN, and L. FLOOR (1951). *Productivity, Supervision and Morale among Railroad Workers.* Ann Arbor: Institute for Social Research, University of Michigan.

KATZ, DANIEL, N. MACCOBY, and N. MORSE (1950). *Productivity, Supervision and Morale in an Office Situation.* Ann Arbor: Institute for Social Research, University of Michigan.

KATZ, ELIHU, and S. N. EISENSTADT (1960). "Some Sociological Observations on the Response of Israeli Organizations to New Immigrants," *Administrative Science Quarterly,* 5 (June), 113–33.

KAUFMAN, HERBERT (1956). "Emerging Conflicts in the Doctrines of Public Administration," *American Political Science Review,* 50 (December), 1057–73.

——— (1969). "Administrative Decentralization and Political Power," *Public Administration Review,* 29 (January-February), 3–15.

——— (1975). "The Natural History of Human Organizations," *Administration and Society,* 7 (August), 131–49.

——— (1976). *Are Government Organizations Immortal?* Washington, D. C.: Brookings Institution.

KENDALL, PATRICIA L., and PAUL F. LAZARSFELD (1950). "Problems of Survey Analysis," in *Continuities in Social Research: Studies in the Scope and Method of "The American Soldier,"* pp. 133–96, ed. Robert K. Merton and Paul F. Lazarsfeld. Glencoe, Ill.: Free Press.

KENNEDY, ROBERT F. (1969). *Thirteen Days: A Memoir of the Cuban Missile Crisis.* New York: W. W. Norton & Co., Inc.

KERR, CLARK (1954). "The Balkanization of Labor Markets," in *Labor Mobility and Economic Opportunity,* pp. 92–110, ed. E. Wight Bakke. Cambridge, Mass.: M.I.T. Press.

KERR, CLARK, JOHN T. DUNLOP, FREDERICK HARBISON, and CHARLES A. MYERS (1964). *Industrialism and Industrial Man (2nd ed.).* New York: Oxford University Press.

KHANDWALLA, PRADIP N. (1974). "Mass Output Orientation of Operations Technology and Organizational Structure," *Administrative Science Quarterly,* 19 (March), 74–97.

——— (1977). *The Design of Organizations.* New York: Harcourt Brace Jovanovich.

KIMBERLY, JOHN (1976). "Organizational Size and the Structuralist Perspective: A Review, Critique and Proposal," *Administrative Science Quarterly,* 21 (December) 571–97.

KIMBERLY, JOHN R., ROBERT H. MILES, and ASSOCIATES (1980). *The Organizational Life Cycle.* San Francisco: Jossey-Bass.

KING, NATHAN (1970). "Clarification and Evaluation of the Two-Factor Theory of Job Statisfaction," *Psychological Bulletin,* 74 (July), 18–31.

KMETZ, JOHN L. (1984). "An Information Processing Study of a Complex Workflow in Aircraft Electronics Repair," *Administrative Science Quarterly,* 29 (June), 255–80.

KNOKE, DAVID (1982). "The Spread of Municipal Reform: Temporal, Spatial, and Social Dynamics," *American Journal of Sociology,* 87 (May), 1314–39.

KNOKE, DAVID, and EDWARD O. LAUMANN (1982). "The Social Organization of National Policy Domains," in *Structure and Network Analysis,* pp. 255–70, ed. Peter V. Marsden and Nan Lin. Beverly Hills, Calif.: Sage Publications, Inc.

KOHN, MELVIN L. (1971). "Bureaucratic Man: A Portrait and an Interpretation," *American Sociological Review,* 36 (June), 461–74.

KOHN, MELVIN L., and CARMI SCHOOLER (1973). "Occupational Experience and Psychological Functioning: An Assessment of Reciprocal Effects," *American Sociological Review,* 38 (February), 97–118.

KORNHAUSER, WILLIAM (1962). *Scientists in Industry: Conflict and Accommodation.* Berkeley: University of California Press.

KRASNER, STEPHEN D. (1984). "Approaches to the State: Alternative Conceptions and Historical Dynamics," *Comparative Politics,* (January), 223–46.

KRAUSE, ELLIOTT A. (1968). "Functions of a Bureaucratic Ideology: 'Citizen Participation,' " *Social Problems,* 16 (Fall), 129–43.

KRUPP, SHERMAN (1961). *Pattern in Organization Analysis.* Philadelphia: Chilton.

KUHN, THOMAS S. (1962). *The Structure of Scientific Revolutions.* Chicago: University of Chicago Press.

LAMMERS, CORNELIS J., and DAVID J. HICKSON (1979a). "A Cross-National and Cross-Institutional Typology of Organizations," in *Organizations Alike and Unlike: International and Interinstitutional Studies in the Sociology of Organizations.* pp. 420–34, ed. Cornelis J. Lammers and David J. Hickson. London: Routledge & Kegan Paul.

———, eds. (1979b). *Organizations Alike and Unlike: International and Interinstitutional Studies in the Sociology of Organizations.* London: Routledge & Kegan Paul.

LANDSBERGER, HENRY A. (1958). *Hawthorne Revisited.* Ithaca, N.Y.: Cornell University Press.

——— (1961). "Parsons' Theory of Organizations," in *Social Theories of Talcott Parsons,* pp. 214–49, ed. Max Black. Englewood Cliffs, N.J.: Prentice-Hall.

——— (1970). *Comparative Perspectives on Formal Organizations.* Boston: Little, Brown.

LARSON, MAGALI SARFATTI (1977). *The Rise of Professionalism.* Berkeley: University of California Press.

LAUMANN, EWARD O., JOSEPH GALASKIEWICZ, and PETER V. MARSDEN (1978). "Community Structure as Interorganizational Linkages," *Annual Review of Sociology,* 4, 455–84.

LAUMANN, EDWARD O., DAVID KNOKE, and YONG-HAK KIM (1985). "An Organizational Approach to State Policy Formation," *American Sociological Review,* 50 (February), 1–19.

LAUMANN, EWARD O., PETER V. MARSDEN, and DAVID PRENSKY (1983). "The Boundary Specification Problem in Network Analysis," in *Applied Network Analysis,* pp. 18–34, ed. Ronald S. Burt and Michael J. Minor. Beverly Hills, Calif.: Sage Publications, Inc.

LAUMANN, EDWARD O., and FRANZ U. PAPPI (1976). *Networks of Collective Action.* New York: Academic Press.

LAWRENCE, PAUL R., and JAY W. LORSCH (1967). *Organization and Environment: Managing Differenciation and Integration.* Boston: Graduate School of Business Administration, Harvard University.

LAZARSFELD, PAUL F. (1959). "Problems in Methodology," in *Sociology Today,* pp. 39–78, ed. Robert K. Merton, Leonard Broom, and Leonard S. Cottrell, Jr. New York: Basic Books.

LAZARSFELD, PAUL F., and HERBERT MENZEL (1961). "On the Relation between Individual and Collective Properties," in *Complex Organizations: A Sociological Reader,* pp. 422–40, ed. Amitai Etzioni. New York: Holt, Rinehart & Winston.

LAZARSFELD, PAUL F., and WAGNER THIELENS, JR. (1958). *The Academic Mind.* Glencoe, Ill.: Free Press.

LEAVITT, HAROLD J. (1951). "Some Effects of Certain Communication Patterns on Group Performance," *Journal of Abnormal and Social Psychology.* 46, 38–50.

——— (1964). "Unhuman Organizations," in *Readings in Managerial Psychology,* pp. 542–56, ed. Harold J. Leavitt and Louis R. Pondy. Chicago: University of Chicago Press.

——— (1965). "Applied Organizational Change in Industry: Structural, Technological and Humanistic

Approaches," in *Handbook of Organizations,* pp. 1144–70, ed. James G. March. Chicago: Rand McNally.

LEAVITT, HAROLD J., WILLIAM R. DILL, and HENRY B. EYRING (1973). *The Organizational World.* New York: Harcourt Brace Jovanovich.

LEVENSON, BERNARD (1961). "Bureaucratic Succession," in *Complex Organizations: A Sociological Reader,* pp. 362–75, ed. Amitai Etzioni. New York: Holt, Rinehart & Winston.

LEVINE, SOL, and PAUL E. WHITE (1961). "Exchange as a Conceptual Framework for the Study of Interorganizational Relationships," *Administrative Science Quarterly,* 5 (March), 583–601.

LEWIN, KURT (1948). *Resolving Social Conflicts.* New York: Harper.

LIGHT, IVAN H. (1972). *Ethnic Enterprise in America.* Berkeley: University of California Press.

LIKERT, RENSIS (1961). *New Patterns of Management.* New York: McGraw-Hill.

LIKERT, RENSIS, and JANE C. LIKERT (1976). *New Ways of Managing Conflict.* New York: McGraw-Hill.

LILIENTHAL, DAVID E. (1944). *TVA: Democracy on the March.* New York: Harper & Brothers.

LINCOLN, JAMES R. (1979). "Organizational Differentiation in Urban Communities: A Study in Organizational Ecology," *Social Forces,* 57 (March), 915–29.

――― (1982). "Intra-(and Inter-) Organizational Networks," in *Research in the Sociology of Organizations,* vol. 1, pp. 1–38, ed. Samuel B. Bacharach. Greenwich, Conn.: JAI Press.

LINDBLOM, CHARLES E. (1959). "The 'Science' of Muddling Through," *Public Administration Review,* 19 (Spring), 79–88.

――― (1977). *Politics and Markets.* New York: Basic Books.

LIPPITT, RONALD, NORMAN POLANSKY, FRITZ REDL, and SIDNEY ROSEN (1953). "The Dynamics of Power," in *Group Dynamics,* pp. 462–82, ed. Dorwin Cartwright and Alvin Zander. Evanston, Ill.: Row, Peterson.

LIPSET, SEYMOUR MARTIN (1960). *Political Man.* New York: Doubleday.

LIPSET, SEYMOUR MARTIN, MARTIN A. TROW, and JAMES S. COLMAN (1956). *Union Democracy.* Glencoe, Ill.: Free Press.

LITTERER, JOSEPH A., ed (1963). *Organizations: Structure and Behavior.* New York: John Wiley.

LITWAK, EUGENE (1961). "Models of Bureaucracy Which Permit Conflict." *American Journal of Scoiology,* 67 (September), 177–84.

――― (1968). "Technological Innovation and Theoretical Functions of Primary Groups and Bureaucratic Structures," *American Journal of Sociology,* 73 (January), 468–81.

LITWAK, EUGENE, and LYDIA F. HYLTON (1962). "Interorganizational Analysis: A Hypothesis on Coordinating Agencies," *Administrative Science Quarterly,* 6 (March), 395–420.

LITWAK, EUGENE, and HENRY J. MEYER (1966). "A Balance Theory of Coordination between Bureaucratic Organizations and Community Primary Groups," *Administrative Science Quarterly,* 11 (June), 31–58.

LOWI, THEODORE J. (1969). *The End of Liberalism.* New York: W. W. Norton & Co., Inc.

LOWIN, AARON, and JAMES R. CRAIG (1968). "The Influence of Level of Performance on Managerial Style: An Experimental Object-Lesson in the Ambiguity of Correlational Data," *Organizational Behavior and Human Performance,* 3 (November), 440–58.

LUKACS, GEORG (1971 trans.). *History and Class Consciousness.* London: Merlin (first published in 1923).

LYDEN, F. J. (1975). "Using Parsons' Functional Analysis in the Study of Public Organizations," *Administrative Science Quarterly,* 20 (March), 59–70.

LYNCH, BEVERLY P. (1974). "An Empirical Assessment of Perrow's Technology Construct," *Administrative Science Quarterly,* 19 (September), 338–56.

McCARTHY, JOHN D., and MAYER N. ZALD (1973). *The Trends of Social Movements in America: Professionalization and Resource Mobilization.* Morristown, N.J.: General Learning Press.

――― (1977). "Resource Mobilization and Social Movements: A Partial Theory," *American Journal of Sociology,* 82 (May), 1212–41.

McEWEN, C. A. (1980). "Continuities in the Study of Total and Nontotal Institutions," *Annual Review of Sociology,* 6, 143–85.

McGREGOR, DOUGLAS (1960). *The Human Side of Enterprise.* New York: McGraw-Hill.

MacIVER, ROBERT M. (1947). *The Web of Government.* New York: Macmillan.

McKELVEY, BILL (1982). *Organizational Systematics.* Berkeley: University of California Press.

McKELVEY, BILL, and HOWARD ALDRICH (1983). "Populations, Natural Selection, and Applied Organizational Science," *Administrative Science Quarterly,* 28 (March), 101–28.

McLEAN, ALAN (1970). *Mental Health and Work Organizations.* Chicago: Rand McNally.

McLUHAN, MARSHALL (1964). *Understanding Media: The Extensions of Man.* New York: Signet.

McMILLAN, CHARLES J., DAVID J. HICKSON, CHRISTOPHER R. HININGS, and RODNEY E. SCHNECK (1973). "The Structure of Work Organizations across Societies," *Academy of Management Journal,* 16 (December), 555–69.

McNEIL, KENNETH, and JAMES D. THOMPSON (1971). "The Regeneration of Social Organizations," *American Sociological Review,* 36 (August), 624–37.

MAIER, NORMAN R. F. (1952). *Principles of Human Relations.* New York: John Wiley.

MAILER, NORMAN (1968). "The Steps of the Pentagon," *Harper's,* 236 (March), 47–142.

MAINES, DAVID R. (1977). "Social Organization and Social Structure in Symbolic Interactionist Thought," *Annual Review of Sociology,* 3, 235–59.

MAJONE, GIANDOMENICO (1980). "Process and Outcome in Regulatory Decision-Making," in *Making Bu-*

*reaucracies Work*, pp. 235–58, ed. Carol H. Weiss and Allen H. Barton. Beverly Hills, Calif.: Sage Publications, Inc.

MALINOWSKI, BRONISLAW (1939). "The Group and the Individual in Functional Analysis," *American Journal of Sociology*, 44, 938–64.

MANN, JUDITH K., and DONALD E. YETT (1968). "The Analysis of Hospital Costs: A Review Article," *Journal of Business*, 41 (April), 191–202.

MANNHEIM, KARL (1950 trans.) *Man and Society in an Age of Reconstruction*, trans. Edward Shils. New York: Harcourt Brace Jovanovich (first published 1935).

MANSFIELD, ROGER (1973). "Bureaucracy and Centralization: An Examination of Organizational Structure," *Administrative Science Quarterly*, 18 (December), 77–88.

MARCH, JAMES G., (1976). "The Technology of Foolishness," in *Ambiguity and Choice in Organizations*, pp. 69–81, ed. James G. March and Johan P. Olsen. Bergen, Norway: Universitetsforlaget.

——— (1978). "Bounded Rationality, Ambiguity, and the Engineering of Choice," *Bell Journal of Economics*, (Autumn), 587–608.

——— (1981). "Decisions in Organizations and Theories of Choice," in *Perspectives on Organization Design and Behavior*, pp. 205–44, ed. Andrew H. Van de Ven and William F. Joyce. New York: John Wiley, Wiley-Interscience.

——— ed. (1965). *Handbook of Organizations*. Chicago: Randy McNally.

MARCH, JAMES G., and JOHAN P. OLSEN (1976). *Ambiguity and Choice in Organizations*. Bergen, Norway: Universitetsforlaget.

MARCH, JAMES G., and HERBERT A. SIMON (1958). *Organizations*. New York: John Wiley.

MARGLIN, STEPHEN (1974). "What the Bosses Do: The Origins and Functions of Hierarchy in Capitalist Production," *Review of Radical Political Economics*, 6 (Summer), 60–112.

MARTIN, JOANNE (1981). "Relative Deprivation: a Theory of Distributive Injustice for an Era of Shrinking Resources," in *Research in Organizational Behavior*, vol. 3, pp. 53–107, ed. L. L. Cummings and Barry M. Staw. Greenwich, Conn.: JAI Press.

MARX, KARL (1954 trans.). *Capital*. Moscow: Foreign Languages Publishing House (first published in 1867).

——— (1963 trans.). *Karl Marx: Early Writings*. trans. and ed. T. B. Bottomore. London: C. A. Watts (first published as *Economic and Philosophical Manuscripts*, 1844).

——— (1972 trans.). "Economic and Philosophic Manuscripts of 1844: Selections," in *the Marx-Engels Reader*, ed. Robert C. Tucker. New York: W. W. Norton & Co., Inc.

——— (1973 trans.). *Grundrisse: Foundations of the Critique of Political Economy*. Harmondsworth, England: Penguin (first published in 1939–1941).

MARX, KARL, and FREDERICK ENGELS (1955 trans.). *Manifesto of the Communist Party*. Moscow: Foreign Languages Publishing House (first published in 1848).

MASLOW, ABRAHAM (1954). *Motivation and Personality*. New York: Harper.

MASSIE, JOSEPH L. (1965). "Management Theory," in *Handbook of Organizations*, pp. 387–422, ed. James G. March. Chicago: Rand McNally.

MAYO, ELTON (1945). *The Social Problems of an Industrial Civilization*. Boston: Graduate School of Business Administration, Harvard University.

MEAD, GEORGE HERBERT (1934). *Mind, Self and Society*. Chicago: University of Chicago Press.

MECHANIC, DAVID (1962). "Sources of Power of Lower Participants in Complex Organizations," *Administrative Science Quarterly*, 7 (December), 349–62.

MELMAN, SELMOUR (1951). "The Rise of Administrative Overhead in the Manufacturing Industries of the United States, 1899–1947," *Oxford Economic Papers*, 3, 62–112.

MERTON, ROBERT K. (1957). *Social Theory and Social Structure* (2nd ed.). Glencoe, Ill.: Free Press.

MERTON, ROBERT K., AILSA P. GRAY, BARBARA HOCKEY, and HANAN C. SELVIN, eds. (1952). *Reader in Bureaucracy*. Glencoe, Ill.: Free Press.

MESSINGER, SHELDON L. (1955). "Organizational Transformation: A Case Study of a Declining Social Movement," *American Sociological Review*, 20 (February), 3–10.

MEYER, JOHN W. (1977). "The Effects of Education as an Institution," *American Journal of Sociology*, 83 (July), 55–77.

——— (1978). "Strategies for Further Research: Varieties of Environmental Variation," in *Environments and Organizations*, pp. 352–68, ed. Marshall W. Meyer. San Francisco: Jossey-Bass.

——— (1983). "Institutionalization and the Rationality of Formal Organizational Structure," in *Organizational Environments: Ritual and Rationality*, pp. 261–82, by John W. Meyer and W. Richard Scott. Beverly Hills, Calif.: Sage Publications, Inc.

——— (1985). "Institutional and Organizational Rationalization in the Mental Health System," *American Behavioral Scientist*, 28 (May/June), 587–600.

MEYER, JOHN W., and BRIAN ROWAN (1977). "Institutionalized Organizations: Formal Structure as Myth and Ceremony," *American Journal of Sociology*, 83 (September), 340–63.

——— (1978). "The Structure of Educational Organizations," in *Environments and Organizations*, pp. 78–109, ed. Marshall W. Meyer. San Francisco: Jossey-Bass.

MEYER, JOHN W., and W. RICHARD SCOTT, with the assistance of BRIAN ROWAN and TERRENCE E. DEAL (1983). *Organizational Environments: Ritual and Rationality*. Beverly Hills, Calif.: Sage Publications, Inc.

MEYER, JOHN W., W. RICHARD SCOTT, SALLY COLE, and JO-ANN K. INTILI (1978). "Instructional Dissensus and Institutional Consensus in Schools," in *Environments and Organizations*, pp. 233–63, ed. Marshall W. Meyer. San Francisco: Jossey-Bass.

MEYER, JOHN W., W. RICHARD SCOTT, and TERRENCE E. DEAL (1981). "Institutional and Technical Sources of Organizational Structure: Explaining the Structure of Educational Organizations," in *Organization and the Human Services: Cross-Disciplinary Reflections*, pp. 151–79, ed. Herman D. Stein. Philadelphia: Temple University Press.
MEYER, MARSHALL W. (1972). "Size and the Structure of Organizations: A Causal Analysis," *American Sociological Review*, 37 (August), 434–41.
—— (1979a). "Organizational Structure as Signaling," *Pacific Sociological Review*, 22 (October), 481–500.
—— (1979b). *Change in Public Bureaucracies*. Cambridge: Cambridge University Press.
MICHELS, ROBERT (1949 trans.). *Political Parties*, trans. Eden and Cedar Paul. Glencoe, Ill.: Free Press (first published in 1915).
MILES, MATTHEW B. (1964). "On Temporary Systems," in *Innovations in Education*, pp. 437–90, ed. Matthew B. Miles. New York: Teachers College, Columbia University.
MILES, ROBERT H. (1982). *Coffin Nails and Corporate Strategies*. Englewood Cliffs, N.J.: Prentice-Hall.
MILGRAM, STANLEY (1973). "The Perils of Obedience," *Harper's* (December), 62–66; 75–77.
—— (1974). *Obedience to Authority*. New York: Harper & Row, Pub.
MILIBAND, RALPH (1969). *The State in Capitalist Society*. New York: Basic Books; Harper Colophon Books.
MILLER, E. J., and A. K. RICE (1967). *Systems of Organization*. London: Tavistock.
MILLER GEORGE A. (1953). "What Is Information Measurement?" *American Psychologist*, 8, 3–12.
MILLER, JAMES GRIER (1978). *Living Systems*. New York: McGraw-Hill.
MILLS, C. WRIGHT (1956). *The Power Elite*. New York: Oxford University Press.
MINER, ANNE S. (1985). "The Strategy of Serendipity: Ambiguity, Uncertainty and Ideosyncratic Jobs." Unpublished Ph.D. dissertation, Graduate School of Business, Stanford University.
MINER, ANNE S., and SUZANNE E. ESTLER (1985). "Accrual Mobility: Job Mobility in Higher Education through Responsibility Accrual," *Journal of Higher Education*, 56 (March/April), 121–43.
MINTZ, BETH, and MICHAEL SCHWARTZ (1983). *Bank Hegemony, Corporate Networks and Intercorporate Power: A study of Interlocking Directorates in American Business*. Chicago: University of Chicago Press.
MINTZBERG, HENRY (1971). "Managerial Work: Analysis from Observation,: *Management Science*, 18 (October), B97–B110.
—— (1973). *The Nature of Managerial Work*. New York: Harper & Row, Pub.
—— (1979). *The Structure of Organizations*. Englewood Cliffs, N.J.: Prentice-Hall.
—— (1983). *Power in and around Organizations*. Englewood Cliffs, N.J.: Prentice-Hall.
MINTZBERG, HENRY, and ALEXANDRA McHUGH (1985). "Strategy Formation in an Adhocracy," *Administrative Science Quarterly*, 30 (June), 160–97.
MISES, LUDWIG VON (1944). *Bureaucracy*. New Haven: Yale University Press.
MIZRUCHI, MARK (1982). *The American Corporate Network, 1904–1974*. Beverly Hills, Calif.: Sage Publications, Inc.
MIZRUCHI, MARK, and MICHAEL SCHWARTZ, eds. (1986). *The Structural Analysis of Business*. Cambridge: Cambridge University Press.
MOE, EDWARD O. (1959). "Consulting with a Community System: A Case Study," *Journal of Social Issues*, 15:2, 28–35.
MOHR, LAWRENCE B. (1971). "Organizational Technology and Organizational Structures," *Administrative Science Quarterly*, 16 (December), 444–59.
MOLOTCH, HARVEY (1976). "The City as a Growth Machine: Toward a Political Economy of Place," *American Journal of Sociology*, 82 (September), 309–32.
MONTAGNA, PAUL D. (1968). "Professionalization and Bureaucratization in Large Professional Organizations," *American Journal of Sociology*, 72 (September), 138–45.
MONTEVERDE, KIRK, and DAVID J. TEECE (1982). "Supplier Switching Costs and Vertical Integration in the Automobile Industry," *Bell Journal of Economics*, 12 (Spring), 206–13.
MOONEY, JAMES D. (1937). "The Principles of Organization," in *Papers on the Science of Administration*, pp. 89–98, ed. Luther Gulick and L. Urwick. New York: Institute of Public Administration, Columbia University.
MOONEY, JAMES D., and ALLAN C. REILEY (1939). *The Principles of Organization*. New York: Harper.
MORRISSEY, JOSEPH P., RICHARD H. HALL, and MICHAEL L. LINDSEY (1982). *Interorganizational Relations: A Sourcebook of Measures for Mental Health Programs*. National Institute of Mental Health, Series BN No. 2. DHHS Pub. No. (ADM) 82-1187. Washington, D. C.: Government Printing Office.
MORSE, CHANDLER (1961). "The Functional Imperatives," in *Social Theories of Talcott Parsons*, pp. 100–52, ed. Max Black. Englewood Cliffs, N.J.: Prentice-Hall.
MOUZELIS, NICOS P. (1968). *Organization and Bureaucracy: An Analysis of Modern Theories*. Chicago: Aldine.
MOYNIHAN, DANIEL P. (1970). *Maximum Feasible Misunderstanding*. New York: Free Press.
MYERS, CHARLES A., ed. (1967). *The Impact of Computers on Management*. Cambridge, Mass.: M.I.T. Press.

NAGEL, ERNEST (1961). *The Structure of Science*. New York: Harcourt, Brace & World.
NAISBITT, JOHN (1982). *Megatrends*. New York: Warner Books.
NATIONAL TRAINING LABORATORIES (1953). *Explorations in Human Relations Training*. Washington, D.C.: National Training Laboratories.
NEUHAUSER, DUNCAN (1971). *The Relationship between Administrative Activities and Hospital Performance*. Research Series 28. Chicago: Center for Health Administration Studies, University of Chicago.
—— (1972). "The Hospital as a Matrix Organization," *Hospital Administration*, 17 (Fall), 8–25.

NEUMANN, FRANZ (1942). *Behemoth*. London: Victor Follancz, 1942.
NEWMAN, KENNETH (1975). "Voluntary Associations in a British City," *Journal of Voluntary Action Research*, 4 (January-April), 43–62.
NISBETT, RICHARD, and LEE ROSS (1980). *Human Inference: Strategies and Shortcomings of Social Judgment*. Englewood Cliffs, N.J.: Prentice-Hall.
NOLL, ROGER G., ed. (1985). *Regulatory Policy and the Social Sciences*. Berkeley: University of California Press.
NUTTER, G. WARREN (1968). "Concentration," *International Encyclopedia of the Social Sciences*, vol. 3, pp. 218–22. New York: Crowell Collier and Macmillan.

OBERSCHALL, ANTHONY (1973). *Social Conflict and Social Movements*. Englewood Cliffs, N.J.: Prentice-Hall.
O'CONNOR, JAMES (1973). *The Fiscal Crisis of the State*. New York: St. Martin's Press.
ODIONE, GEORGE S. (1965). *Management by Objective*. New York: Pitman.
OKIMOTO, DANIEL I. (1984) *Competitive Edge: The Semiconductor Industry in the United States and Japan*. Stanford, Calif.: Stanford University Press.
OLSEN, JOHAN P. (1983). *Organized Democracy: Political Institutions in a Welfare State—The Case of Norway*. Bergen, Norway: Universitetsforlaget.
OLSON, MANCUR, JR. (1965). *The Logic of Collective Action*. Cambridge, Mass.: Harvard University Press.
—— (1982). *The Rise and Decline of Nations: Economic Growth, Stagflation, and Social Rigidities*. New Haven: Yale University Press.
O'TOOLE, J., ed. (1972). *Work in America: A Report to the Secretary of State for Health, Education and Welfare*. Cambridge, Mass.: M.I.T. Press.
OUCHI, WILLIAM G. (1979). "Markets, Bureaucracies and Clans." Unpublished paper, Graduate School of Management, University of California, Los Angeles.
—— (1980). "Markets, Bureaucracies and Clans," *Administrative Science Quarterly*, 25 (March), 129–41.
—— (1981). *Theory Z*. Reading, Mass.: Addison-Wesley.
OUCHI, WILLIAM G., and ALFRED M. JAEGER (1978). "Type Z Organization: Stability in the Midst of Mobility," *Academy of Management Review*, 3 (April), 305–14.

PALMER, DONALD (1983). "Broken Ties: Interlocking Directorates and Intercorporate Coordination," *Administrative Science Quarterly*, 28 (March), 40–55.
PALMER, DONALD, ROGERT FRIEDLAND, P DEVEREAUX JENNINGS, and MELANIE E. POWERS (1985). "The Determinants of the Multidivisional Form in Large U.S. Corporations," presented at the annual meeting of the American Sociological Association, Washington, D.C.
PARKINSON, C. NORTHCOTE (1957). *Parkinson's Law and Other Studies in Administration*. Boston: Houghton Mifflin.
PARSONS, TALCOTT (1947). Introduction to *The Theory of Social and Economic Organization*, pp. 3–86, by Max Weber. Glencoe, Ill.: Free Press.
—— (1951). *The Social System*. Glencoe, Ill.: Free Press.
—— (1953). "A Revised Analytical Approach to the Theory of Social Stratification," in *Class, Status and Power: A Reader in Social Stratification*, pp. 92–129, ed. Reinhard Bendix and Seymour M. Lipset. Glencoe, Ill.: Free Press.
—— (1960). *Structure and Process in Modern Societies*. Glencoe, Ill.: Free Press.
—— (1966). *Societies: Evolutionary and Comparative Perspectives*. Englewood Cliffs, N.J.: Prentice-Hall.
PARSONS, TALCOTT, ROBERT F. BALES, and EDWARD A. SHILS (1953). *Working Papers in the Theory of Action*. Glencoe, Ill.: Free Press.
PATCHEN, MARTIN (1961). *The Choice of Wage Comparisons*. Englewood Cliffs, N.J.: Prentice-Hall.
PELZ, DONALD C. (1952). "Influence: A Key to Effective Leadership in the First-Line Supervisor," *Personnel*, 29, 209–17.
PENNINGS, J. (1973). "Measures of Organizational Structure: A Methodological Note," *American Journal of Sociology*, 79 (November), 686–704.
—— (1975). "The Relevance of the Structural-Contingency Model for Organizational Effectiveness," *Administrative Science Quarterly*, 20 (September), 393–410.
—— (1981). "Strategically Interdependent Organizations," in *Handbook of Organizational Design*, vol. 1, pp. 433–55, ed. Paul C. Nystrom and William H. Starbuck. Oxford: Oxford University Press.
PERROW, CHARLES (1961). "The Analysis of Goals in Complex Organizations," *American Sociological Review*, 26 (December), 854–66.
—— (1965). "Hospitals: Technology, Structure, and Goals," in *Handbook of Organizations*, pp. 910–71, ed. James G. March. Chicago: Rand McNally.
—— (1967). "A Framework for the Comparative Analysis of Organizations," *American Sociological Review*, 32 (April), 194–208.
—— (1970). *Organizational Analysis: A Sociological View*. Belmont, Calif.: Wadsworth.
—— (1972). "Review of Neuhauser, D.: *The Relationship between Administrative Activities and Hospital Performance*," *Administrative Science Quarterly*, 17 (September), 419–21.
—— (1973). "The Short and Glorious History of Organizational Theory," *Organizational Dynamics*, 2 (Summer), 2–15.
—— (1979). *Complex Organizations: A Critical Essay* (2nd ed.). Glenview, Ill.: Scott, Foresman.
—— (1982). "Three Mile Island: A Normal Accident," in *The International Yearbook of Organizational Studies 1981*, pp. 1–25, ed. David Dunkerley and Graeme Salaman. London: Routledge & Kegan Paul.
—— (1984). *Normal Accidents: Living with High-Risk Technologies*. New York: Basic Books.

PETERS, THOMAS J., and ROBERT H. WATERMAN, JR. (1982). *In Search of Excellence*. New York: Harper & Row, Pub.

PFEFFER, JEFFREY (1972*a*). "Size and Composition of Corporate Boards of Directors: The Organization and Its Environment," *Administrative Science Quarterly*, 17 (June), 218–28.

——— (1972*b*). "Merger as a Response to Organizational Interdependence," *Administrative Science Quarterly*, 17 (September), 382–92.

——— (1973). "Size, Composition, and Function of Hospital Boards of Directors: A Study of Organization-Environment Linkage," *Administrative Science Quarterly*, 18 (September), 349–64.

——— (1978). "The Micropolitics of Organizations," in *Environments and Organizations*, pp. 29–50, ed. Marshall W. Meyer. San Francisco: Jossey-Bass.

——— (1981). *Power in Organizations*. Marshfield, Mass.: Pitman.

——— (1982). *Organizations and Organization Theory*. Boston: Pitman.

——— (1983). "Organizational Demography," in *Research in Organizational Behavior*, vol. 5, pp. 299–357, ed. L. L. Cummings and Barry M. Staw. Greenwich, Conn.: JAI Press.

PFEFFER, JEFFREY, and YINON COHEN (1984). "Determinants of Internal Labor Markets in Organizations," *Administrative Science Quarterly*, 29 (December), 550–72.

PFEFFER, JEFFREY, and PHILLIP NOWAK (1976). "Joint Ventures and Interorganizational Dependence," *Administrative Science Quarterly*, 21 (September), 398–418.

PFEFFER, JEFFREY, and GERALD R. SALANCIK. (1974). "Organizational Decision Making as a Political Process: The Case of a University Budget," *Administrative Science Quarterly*, 19 (June), 135–51.

——— (1978). *The External Control of Organizations*. New York: Harper & Row, Pub.

PIVEN, FRANCES FOX, and RICHARD A. CLOWARD. (1971). *Regulating the Poor*. New York: Pantheon.

——— (1977). *Poor People's Movements: Why They Succeed, How They Fail*. New York: Pantheon.

POLANYI, KARL (1944). *The Great Transformation*. New York: Holt.

PONDY, LOUIS R., and IAN I. MITROFF (1979). "Beyond Open System Models of Organization," in *Research in Organizational Behavior*, vol. 1, pp. 3–39, ed. Barry M. Staw. Greenwich, Conn.: JAI Press.

PORTER, LYMAN W., and EDWARD E. LAWLER, III (1968). *Managerial Attitudes and Performance*. Homewood, Ill.: Richard D. Irwin.

PORTER, LYMAN W., EDWARD E. LAWLER, and J. R. HACKMAN (1975). *Behavior in Organizations*. New York: McGraw-Hill.

PORTER, MICHAEL E. (1980). *Competitive Strategy*. New York: Free Press.

POUND, EZRA (1973). *Selected Prose, 1909–1965*, ed. William Cookson. New York: New Directions.

POWELL, WALTER W. (1985). *Getting into Print: The Decision-Making Process in Scholarly Publishing*. Chicago: University of Chicago Press.

PRESSMAN, JEFFREY L., and AARON WILDAVSKY (1973). *Implementation*. Berkeley: University of California Press.

PRICE, JAMES L. (1968). *Organizational Effectiveness*. Homewood, Ill.: Richard D. Irwin.

PUGH, D. S., and D. J. HICKSON (1976). *Organizational Structure in Its Context: The Aston Programme I*. Lexington, Mass.: Heath, Lexington Books.

PUGH, D. S., D. J. HICKSON, and C. R. HININGS (1969). "An Empirical Taxonomy of Structures of Work Organizations," *Administrative Science Quarterly*, 14 (March). 115–26.

——— (1985). *Writers on Organizations* (3rd ed.). Beverly Hills, Calif.: Sage Publications, Inc.

PUGH, D. S., D. J. HICKSON, C. R. HININGS, K. M. MACDONALD, C. TURNER, and T. LUPTON (1963). "A Conceptual Scheme for Organizational Analysis," *Administrative Science Quarterly*, 8 (December), 289–315.

PUGH, D. S., D. J. HICKSON, C. R. Hinings, and C. TURNER (1968). "Dimensions of Organization Structure," *Administrative Science Quarterly*, 13 (June), 65–91.

——— (1969). "The Context of Organization Structures," *Administrative Science Quarterly*, 14 (March), 91–114.

RACKHAM, JEFFREY, and JOAN WOODWARD (1970). "The Measurement of Technical Variables," in *Industrial Organization: Behaviour and Control*, pp. 19–36, ed. Joan Woodward. London: Oxford University Press.

RADCLIFFE-BROWN, A. R. (1952). *Structure and Function in Primitive Society*. Glencoe, Ill.: Free Press.

REED, THEODORE L. (1978). "Organizational Change in the American Foreign Service, 1925–1965: The Utility of Cohort Analysis," *American Sociological Review*, 43 (June), 404–21.

REEVES, WILLIAM JOSEPH (1980). *Librarians as Professionals*. Lexington. Mass.: Heath, Lexington Books.

REICH, ROBERT B. (1983). "Why Democracy Makes Economic Sense," *New Republic* (December 19), 25–32.

REINHARDT, UWE E. (1973). "Proposed Changes in the Organization of Health-Care Delivery: An Overview and a Critique," *Milbank Memorial Fund Quarterly*, 51 (Spring), 169–222.

RICE, A. K. (1958). *Productivity and Social Organization: The Ahmedabad Experiment*. London: Tavistock.

ROBERTS, KARLENE H., and WILLIAM GLICK (1981). "The Job Characteristics Approach to Task Design: A Critical Review," *Journal of Applied Psychology*, 66 (April), 193–217.

ROBOCK, STEFAN H., and KENNETH SIMMONDS (1973). *International Business and Multinational Enterprises*. Homewood, Ill.: Richard D. Irwin.

ROETHLISBERGER, F. J., and WILLIAM J. DICKSON (1939). *Management and the Worker*. Cambridge, Mass.: Harvard University Press.

ROGERS, DAVID L., and DAVID A. WHETTEN (1982). *Interorganizational Coordination: Theory, Research, and Implementation*. Ames: Iowa State University Press.

ROGERS, EVERETT M., and REKHA AGARWALA-ROGERS (1976) *Communication in Organizations*. New York: Free Press.
ROSENBERG, HANS (1958). *Bureaucracy, Aristocracy and Autocracy: The Prussian Experience 1660–1815*. Cambridge, Mass.: Harvard University Press.
ROSZAK, THEODORE (1969). *The Making of a Counter Culture*. Garden City, N.Y.: Doubleday, Anchor Books.
ROTHSCHILD-WHITT, JOYCE (1979). "The Collectivist Organization: An Alternative to Rational Bureaucratic Models," *American Sociological Review*, 44 (August), 509–27.
ROTHSCHILD-WHITT, JOYCE, and A. WHITT (1986). *Work without Bosses: Conditions and Dilemmas of Organizational Democracy in Grassroots Cooperatives*. New York: Cambridge University Press.
ROWAN, BRIAN (1981). "The Effects of Institutionalized Rules on Administrators," in *Organizational Behavior in Schools and School Districts*, pp. 47–55, ed. Samuel B. Bacharach. New York: Praeger.
———— (1982). "Organizational Structure and the Institutional Environment: The Case of Public Schools," *Administrative Science Quarterly*, 27 (June), 259–79.
ROY, DONALD (1952). "Quota Restriction and Goldbricking in a Machine Shop," *American Journal of Sociology*, 57 (March), 427–42.
RUSHING, WILLIAM A. (1966a). "Organizational Rules and Surveillance: Propositions in Comparative Organization Analysis," *Administrative Science Quarterly*, 10 (March), 423–43.
———— (1966b). "Organizational Size and Administration," *Pacific Sociological Review*, 9 (Fall), 100–108.
———— (1968) "Hardness of Material as an External Constraint on the Division of Labor in Manufacturing Industries," *Administrative Science Quarterly*, 13 (September), 229–45.

SAGE, ANDREW P. (1981). "Designs for Optimal Information Filters," in *Handbook of Organizational Design*, vol. 1, pp. 105–21, ed. Paul C. Nystrom and William H. Starbuck. London: Oxford University Press.
SAINT-SIMON, HENRI COMTE DE (1952 trans.). *Selected Writings*, trans. F. M. H. Markham. New York: Macmillan (first published in 1859).
SALAMAN, GRAEME, and KENNETH THOMPSON, eds. (1980). *Control and Ideology In Organizations*. Cambridge, Mass.: M.I.T. Press.
SALANCIK, GERALD R., and JEFFREY PFEFFER (1977). "An Examination of Need-Satisfaction Models of Job Attitudes," *Administrative Science Quarterly*, 22 (September), 427–56.
SATOW, ROBERTA LYNN (1975). "Value-Rational Authority and Professional Organizations: Weber's Missing Type," *Administrative Science Quarterly*, 20 (December), 526–31.
SAYLES, LEONARD R. (1958). *Behavior of Industrial Work Groups*. New York: John Wiley.
———— (1976). "Matrix Organization: The Structure with a Future," *Organizational Dynamics*, (Autumn), 2–17.
SCHMITTER, PHILIPPE C. (1974). "Still the Century of Corporatism?" in *The New Corporatism: Social-Political Structures in the Iberian World*, pp. 85–131, ed. Frederick B. Pike and Thomas Stritch. Notre Dame, Ind.: University of Notre Dame Press.
SCHOONHOVEN, CLAUDIA BIRD (1981). "Problems with Contingency Theory: Testing Assumptions Hidden within the Language of Contingency Theory," *Administrative Science Quarterly*, 26 (September), 349–77.
SCHOPLER, JOHN (1965). "Social Power," in *Advances in Experimental Social Psychology*, vol. 2, pp. 177–219, ed. Leonard Berkowitz. New York: Academic Press.
SCHRÖDINGER, ERWIN (1945). *What Is Life?* Cambridge: Cambridge University Press.
SCHUMPETER, JOSEPH A. (1947). *Capitalism, Socialism and Democracy* (2nd ed.). New York: Harper.
SCHUTZ, ALFRED (1962 trans.). *Collected Papers*, vols. 1 and 2. The Hague: Nijhoff.
SCHWAB, DONALD P., and LARRY L. CUMMINGS (1970). "Theories of Performance and Satisfaction: A Review," *Industrial Relations*, 9 (October), 408–30.
SCHWAB, J. J. (1960). "What Do Scientists Do?" *Behavioral Science*, 5 (January), 1–27.
SCOTT, JOHN (1979). *Corporations, Classes and Capitalism*. New York: St. Martins Press.
SCOTT, W. RICHARD (1964). "Theory of Organizations," in *Handbook of Modern Sociology*, pp. 485–529, ed. Robert E. L. Faris. Chicago: Rand McNally.
———— (1965a). "Field Methods in the Study of Organizations," in *Handbook of Organizations*, pp. 261–304, ed. James G. March. Chicago: Rand McNally.
———— (1965b). "Reactions to Supervision in a Heteronomous Professional Organization," *Administrative Science Quarterly*, 10 (June), 65–81.
———— (1969). "Professional Employees in a Bureaucratic Structure: Social Work," in *The Semi-Professions and Their Organization*, pp. 82–144, ed. Amitai Etzioni. New York: Free Press.
———— (1970). *Social Processes and Social Structures: An Introduction to Sociology*. New York: Holt, Rinehart & Winston.
———— "Professionals in Hospitals: Technology and the Organization of Work," in *Organization Research on Health Institutions*, pp. 139–58, discussion, pp. 173–89, ed. Basil S. Georgopoulos. Ann Arbor: Institute for Social Research, University of Michigan.
———— (1975). "Organizational Structure," *Annual Review of Sociology*, 1, 1–20.
———— (1977a). "Effectiveness of Organizational Effectiveness Studies," in *New Perspectives on Organizational Effectiveness*, pp. 63–95, ed. Paul S. Goodman and Johannes M. Pennings. San Francisco: Jossey-Bass.
———— (1977b). "Some Problems in the Study of Organization Structure," *Mid-American Review of Sociology*, 2 (Spring), 1–16.

—— (1978). "Theoretical Perspectives," in *Environments and Organizations*, pp. 21–28, ed. Marshall W. Meyer. San Francisco: Jossey-Bass.

—— (1981). *Organizations: Rational, Natural and Open Systems.* Englewood Cliffs, N.J.: Prentice-Hall. (First edition)

—— (1982). "Managing Professional Work: Three Models of Control for Health Organizations," *Health Services Research*, 17 (Fall), 213–40.

—— (1983). "The Organization of Environments: Network, Cultural, and Historical elements," in *Organizational Environments: Ritual and Rationality*, pp. 155–75, by John W. Meyer and W. Richard Scott. Beverly Hills, Calif.: Sage Publications, Inc.

—— (1985a). "Conflicting Levels of Rationality: Regulators, Managers, and Professionals in the Medical Care Sector," *Journal of Health Administration Education*, 3 (Spring), 113–31.

—— (1985b). "Systems within Systems: The Mental Health Sector," *American Behavioral Scientist*, 28 (May/June), 601–18.

—— (1986). "The Sociology of Organizations: Crisis or Continuum?" in *Sociology: The Aftermath of Crisis*, ed. Ulf Himmelstrand. Beverly Hills, Calif.: Sage Publications, Inc.

SCOTT, W. RICHARD, SANFORD M. DORNBUSCH, BRUCE C. BUSHING, and JAMES D. LAING (1967). "Organizational Evaluation and Authority," *Administrative Science Quarterly*, 12 (June), 93–117.

SCOTT, W. RICHARD, SANFORD M. DORNBUSCH, CONNIE J. EVASHWICK, LEONARD MAGNANI, and INGER SAGATUN (1971). "Task Conceptions and Work Arrangements." Technical Report 47, Laboratory for Social Research. Stanford, Calif.: Stanford University.

SCOTT, W. RICHARD, ANN BARRY FLOOD, WAYNE EWY, and WILLIAM H. FORREST, JR. (1978). "Organizational Effectiveness and the Quality of Surgical Care in Hospitals," in *Environments and Organizations*, pp. 290–305, ed. Marshall W. Meyer. San Francisco: Jossey-Bass.

SCOTT, W. RICHARD, and JOHN W. MEYER (1983). "The Organization of Societal Sectors," in *Organizational Environments: Ritual and Rationality*, pp. 129–54, by John W. Meyer and W. Richard Scott. Beverly Hills, Calif.: Sage Publications, Inc.

—— (1984). "Environmental Linkages and Organizational Complexity: Public and Private Schools," (Project Report no. 84-A16) Stanford, Calif.: Institute for Research on Educational Finance and Governance, Stanford University.

SCOTT, WILLIAM G., and DAVID K. HART. (1979) *Organizational America.* Boston: Houghton Mifflin.

SEASHORE, STANLEY E. (1954). *Group Cohesiveness in the Industrial Work Group.* Ann Arbor: Institute for Social Research, University of Michigan.

—— (1962). *The Assessment of Organizational Performance.* Ann Arbor: Survey Research Center, University of Michigan.

SEEMAN, MELVIN (1959). "On the Meaning of Alienation," *American Sociological Review*, 24 (December), 783–91.

—— (1975). "Alienation Studies," *Annual Review of Sociology*, 1, 91-123.

SEIDMAN, HAROLD (1975). "Government-Sponsored Enterprise in the United States," in *The New Political Economy: The Public Use of the Private Sector*, pp. 83–108, ed. Bruce L. R. Smith. New York: John Wiley.

SELZNICK, PHILIP (1948). "Foundations of the Theory of Organization," *American Sociological Review*, 13 (February), 25-35.

—— (1949). *TVA and the Grass Roots.* Berkeley: University of California Press.

—— (1957). *Leadership in Administration.* New York: Harper & Row, Pub.

—— (1969). *Law, Society, and Industrial Justice.* New York: Russell Sage Foundation.

SEWELL, WILLIAM H., and ROBERT M. HAUSER (1975). *Education, Occupation and Earnings: Achievement in the Early Career.* New York: Academic Press.

SHANNON, CLAUDE E., and WARREN WEAVER (1963). *The Mathematical Theory of Communication.* Urbana: University of Illinois Press.

SHAW, M. E. (1954). "Some Effects of Problem Complexity upon Problem Solution Efficiency in Various Communication Nets," *Journal of Experimental Psychology*, 48, 211–17.

—— (1964). "Communication Networks," in *Advances in Experimental Social Psychology*, vol. 1, pp. 111–47, ed. Leonard Berkowitz. New York: Academic Press.

SHEPPARD, HAROLD L., and NEAL HERRICK (1972). *Where Have All the Robots Gone?* New York: Free Press.

SHERIF, MUZAFER, and CAROLINE W. SHERIF (1953). *Groups in Harmony and Tension.* New York: Harper & Row, Pub.

SHILS, EDWARD E. (1960). *Political Development in the New States.* The Hague: Mouton.

SILVERMAN, DAVID (1971). *The Theory of Organizations.* New York: Basic Books.

SIMMEL, GEORG (1955 trans.). *Conflict and The Web of Group-Affiliations.* Glencoe, Ill.: Free Press. (The firs essay was first published in 1908, the second in 1922.)

SIMON, HERBERT A. (1957). *Administrative Behavior* (2nd ed.). New York: Macmillan (1st ed., 1945).

—— (1966). *The New Science of Management Decision.* New York: Harper.

—— "The Architecture of Complexity," *Proceedings of the American Philosophical Society*, 106 (December), 467–82.

—— (1964) "On the Concept of Organizational Goal," *Administrative Science Quarterly*, 9 (June), 1–22.

—— (1979). "Rational Decision Making in Business Organizations," *American Economic Review*, 69 (September), 493–513.

SIMON, HERBERT A., DONALD W. SMITHBERG, and VICTOR A. THOMPSON (1950). *Public Administration.* New York: Knopf.

SIMON, WILLIAM H. (1983). "Legality, Bureaucracy, and Class in the Welfare System," *Yale Law Journal*, 92 (June), 1198–1269.

SKOWRONEK, STEPHEN (1982). *Building a New American State: The Expansion of National Administrative Capacities.* New York: Cambridge University Press.

SLATER, PHILIP E. (1955). "Role Differentiation in Small Groups," *American Sociological Review*, 20 (June), 300–310.

SMIGEL, ERWIN O. (1964). *The Wall Street Lawyer: Professional Organization Man?* New York: Free Press.

SMIRCICH, LINDA (1983). "Concepts of Culture and Organizational Analysis," *Administrative Science Quarterly*, 28 (September), 339–58.

——— (1985). "Is the Concept of Culture a Paradigm for Understanding Organizations and Ourselves?" in *Organizational Culture*, pp. 55–72, ed. Peter J. Frost, Larry F. Moore, Meryl Reis Louis, Craig C. Lundberg, and Joanne Martin. Beverly Hills, Calif.: Sage Publications, Inc.

SMITH, ADAM (1957). *Selections from the Wealth of Nations*, ed. George J. Stigler. New York: Appleton Century Crofts (originally published in 1776).

SMITH, BRUCE L. R. (1966). *The Rand Corporation.* Cambridge, Mass.: Harvard University Press.

SMITH, THOMAS SPENCE, and R. DANFORTH ROSS (1978). "Cultural Controls on the Demography of Hierarchy: A Time-Series Analysis of Warfare and the Growth of the United States Army, 1960–68." Unpublished paper, University of Rochester.

SNYDER, DAVID, and CHARLES TILLY (1972). "Hardship and Collective Violence in France, 1830 to 1960," *American Sociological Review*, 37 (October), 520–32.

SOMERS, ANNE R. (1969). *Hospital Regulation: The Dilemma of Public Policy.* Princeton, N.J.: Industrial Relations Section, Princeton University.

SPECIAL TASK FORCE TO THE SECRETARY OF HEALTH, EDUCATION AND WELFARE (1973). *Work in America.* Cambridge, Mass.: M.I.T. Press.

SPROULL, LEE S. (1981). "Response to Regulation: An Organizational Process Framework," *Administration and Society*, 12 (February), 447–70.

STABER, UDO (1985). "A Population Perspective on Collective Action as an Organizational Form: The Case of Trade Associations," in *Research in the Sociology of Organizations*, vol. 4, pp. 181–220, ed. Samuel B. Bacharach and Stephen M. Mitchell. Greenwich, Conn.: JAI Press.

STABER, UDO, and HOWARD ALDRICH (1983). "Trade Association Stability and Public Policy," in *Organizational Theory and Public Policy*, pp. 163–78, ed. Richard H. Hall and Robert E. Quinn. Beverly Hills, Calif.: Sage Publications, Inc.

STANTON, ALFRED H., and MORRIS S. SCHWARTZ (1954). *The Mental Hospital.* New York: Basic Books.

STARK, DAVID (1980). "Class Struggle and the Transformation of the Labour Process: A Relational Approach," *Theory and Society*, 9 (January), 89–130.

STAW, BARRY M. (1980). "Rationality and Justification in Organizational Life," in *Research in Organizational Behavior*, vol. 2, pp. 45–80, ed. Barry M. Staw and Larry L. Cummings. Greenwich, Conn.: JAI Press.

——— (1984). "Organizational Behavior: A Review and Reformulation of the Field's Outcome Variables." *Annual Review of Psychology*, 35, 627–66.

STEERS, RICHARD M. (1975). "Problems in the Measurement of Organizational Effectiveness," *Administrative Science Quarterly*, 20 (December), 546–58.

——— (1977). *Organizational Effectiveness: A Behavioral View.* Pacific Palisades, Calif.: Goodyear.

STEERS, RICHARD M., and DANIEL G. SPENCER (1977). "The Role of Achievement Motivation in Job Design," *Journal of Applied Psychology*, 62 (August), 472–79.

STEINBRUNER, JOHN D. (1974). *The Cybernetic Theory of Decision.* Princeton, N.J.: Princeton University Press.

STEINER, GEORGE A., and WILLIAM G. RYAN (1968). *Industrial Project Management.* New York: Crowell-Collier and Macmillan.

STERN, ROBERT N. (1979). "The Development of an Interorganizational Control Network: The Case of Intercollegiate Athletics," *Administrative Science Quarterly*, 24 (June), 242–66.

STIGLER, GEORGE J. (1971). "The Theory of Economic Regulation," *Bell Journal of Economics and Management Science*, 2 (Spring), 3–21.

STINCHCOMBE, ARTHUR L. (1959). "Bureaucratic and Craft Administration of Production: A Comparative Study," *Administrative Science Quarterly*, 4 (September), 168–87.

——— (1965). "Social Structure and Organizations," in *Handbook of Organizations*, pp. 142–93, ed. James G. March. Chicago: Rand McNally.

——— (1974). *Creating Efficient Industrial Administrations.* New York: Academic Press.

——— (1983). *Economic Sociology.* New York: Academic Press.

——— (1985). "Contracts as Hierarchical Documents," in *Organization Theory and Project Management*, by Arthur Stinchcombe and Carol Heimer. Bergen, Norway: Universitetsforlaget.

STOGDILL, R. M., and A. E. COONS, eds. (1957). *Leader Behavior: Its Description and Measurement.* Research Monograph 88. Columbus, Ohio: Bureau of Business Research, Ohio State University.

STOLZENBERG, ROSS, M. (1978). "Bringing the Boss Back In: Employer Size, Employee Schooling, and Socioeconomic Achievement," *American Sociological Review*, 43 (December), 813–28.

STONE, EUGENE (1978). *Research Methods in Organizational Behavior.* Santa Monica, Calif.: Goodyear.

STONE, EUGENE F., RICHARD T. MOWDAY, and LYMAN W. PORTER (1977). "Higher Order Need Strengths as Moderators of the Job Scope–Job Satisfaction Relationship," *Journal of Applied Psychology*, 62 (August), 466–71.

STRAUSS, ANSELM, LEONARD SCHATZMAN, DANUTA EHRLICH, RUE BUCHER, and MELVIN SABSHIN (1963).

"The Hospital and Its Negotiated Order," in *The Hospital in Modern Society*, pp. 147–69, ed. Eliot Freidson. New York: Free Press of Glencoe.

STREET, DAVID, GEORGE T. MARTIN, JR., and LAURA KRAMER GORDON (1979). *The Welfare Industry: Functionaries and Recipients in Public Aid*. Beverly Hills, Calif.: Sage Publications, Inc.

STREET, DAVID, ROBERT VINTER, and CHARLES PERROW (1966). *Organization for Treatment*. New York: Free Press.

SUCHMAN, EDWARD A. (1967). *Evaluative Research*. New York: Russell Sage Foundation.

SUNDQUIST, JAMES L. (1969). *Making Federalism Work*. Washington, D.C.: Brookings Institution.

SWANSON, GUY E. (1976). "The Tasks of Sociology," *Science*, 192 (May), 665–67.

SWIDLER, ANN (1979). *Organization without Authority: Dilemmas of Social Control in Free Schools*. Cambridge, Mass.: Harvard University Press.

SWINTH, ROBERT L. (1974). *Organizational Systems for Management: Designing, Planning and Implementation*. Columbus, Ohio: Grid.

SYKES, A. J. M. (1965). "Economic Interests and the Hawthorne Researchers: A Comment," *Human Relations*, 18 (August), 253–63.


TALBERT, JOAN, and CHRISTINE E. BOSE. (1977). "Wage-Attainment Processes: The Retail Clerk Case," *American Journal of Sociology*, 83 (September), 403–24.

TANCREDI, LAURENCE R., and J. WOODS (1972). "The Social Control of Medical Practice: Licensure versus Output Monitoring," *Milbank Memorial Fund Quarterly*, 50 (January), part 1, 99–126.

TANNENBAUM, ARNOLD S. (1968). *Control in Organizations*. New York: McGraw-Hill.

TANNENBAUM, ARNOLD S., BOGDAN KAVCIC, MENACHEM ROSNER, MINO VIANELLO, and GEORG WIESER (1974). *Hierarchy in Organizations*. San Francisco: Jossey-Bass.

TAUSKY, CURT (1970). *Work Organizations: Major Theoretical Perspectives*. Itasca, Ill.: F. E. Peacock.

TAYLOR, DONALD W. (1965). "Decision Making and Problem Solving," in *Handbook of Organizations*, pp. 48–86, ed. James G. March. Chicago: Rand McNally.

TAYLOR, FREDERICK W. (1911). *The Principles of Scientific Management*. New York: Harper.

——— (1947). *Scientific Management*. New York: Harper & Brothers.

TERREBERRY, SHIRLEY (1968). "The Evolution of Organizational Environments," *Administrative Science Quarterly*, 12 (March), 590–613.

TERRIEN, FRED W., and DONALD L. MILLS (1955). "The Effect of Changing Size upon the Internal Structure of Organizations," *American Sociological Review*, 29 (February), 11–13.

THIBAUT, JOHN W., and HAROLD H. KELLEY (1959). *The Social Psychology of Groups*. New York: John Wiley.

THOMAS, GEORGE M., and JOHN W. MEYER (1984). "The Expansion of the State," *Annual Review of Sociology*, 10, 461–82.

THOMPSON, JAMES D. (1967). *Organizations in Action*. New York: McGraw-Hill.

THOMPSON, JAMES D., and FREDERICK L. BATES (1957). "Technology, Organization, and Administration," *Administrative Science Quarterly*, 2 (December), 325–42.

THOMPSON, JAMES D., and ARTHUR TUDEN (1959). "Strategies, Structures, and Processes of Organizational Decision," in *Comparative Studies in Administration*, pp. 195–216, ed. James D. Thompson et al. Pittsburgh: University of Pittsburgh Press.

THOMPSON, VICTOR A. (1961). *Modern Organization*. New York: Knopf.

TILLY, CHARLES (1978). *From Mobilization to Revolution*. Reading, Mass.: Addison-Wesley.

——— (1981). *As Sociology Meets History*. New York: Academic Press.

TOFFLER, ALVIN (1970). *Future Shock*. New York: Random House.

——— (1980). *The Third Wave*. New York: Morrow.

TOLBERT, CHARLES M., PATRICK M HORAN, and E. M. BECK (1980). "The Structure of Economic Segmentation: A Dual Economy Approach," *American Journal of Sociology*, 85 (March), 1095–116.

TOLBERT, PAMELA S. (1985). "Institutional Environments and Resource Dependence: Sources of Administrative Structure in Institutions of Higher Education," *Administrative Science Quarterly*, 30 (March), 1–13.

TOLBERT, PAMELA S., and LYNNE G. ZUCKER (1983). "Institutional Sources of Change in the Formal Structure of Organizations: The Diffusion of Civil Service Reform, 1880–1935," *Administrative Science Quarterly*, 28 (March), 22–39.

TOUT, T. F. (1916). *The English Civil Service in the Fourteenth Century*. Manchester, England: University Press.

TRIST, ERIC L. (1981). "The Evolution of Sociotechnical Systems as a Conceptual Framework and as an Action Research Program," in *Perspectives on Organization Design and Behavior*, pp. 19–75, ed. Andrew H. Van de Ven and William F. Joyce. New York: John Wiley, Wiley-Interscience.

TRIST, ERIC L., and K. W. BAMFORTH (1951). "Social and Psychological Consequences of the Longwall Method of Coal-Getting," *Human Relations*, 4 (February), 3–28.

TROW, D. B. (1957). "Autonomy and Job Satisfaction in Task-Oriented Groups," *Journal of Abnormal and Social Psychology*, 54, 204–9.

TSURUMI, Y. (1977). *Multinational Management*. Cambridge, Mass.: Ballinger.

TURK, HERMAN (1970). "Interorganizational Networks in Urban Society: Initial Perspectives and Comparative Research," *American Sociological Review*, 35 (February), 1–19.

——— (1977). *Organizations in Modern Life*. San Francisco: Jossey-Bass.

TURNER, ARTHUR N., and PAUL R. LAWRENCE (1965). *Industrial Jobs and the Worker*. Boston: Harvard Graduate School of Business Administration.

TUSHMAN, MICHAEL L. (1979). "Work Characteristics and Subunit Communication Structure: A Contingency Analysis," *Administrative Science Quarterly*, 24 (March), 82–97.

TVERSKY, AMOS, and DANIEL KAHNEMAN (1974). "Judgment under Uncertainty: Heuristics and Biases," *Science*, 185, (September), 1124–31.

UDY, STANLEY H., JR. (1959a). " 'Bureaucracy' and 'rationality' in Weber's Organization Theory," *American Sociological Review*, 24 (December), 791–95.

—— (1959b). *Organization of Work*. New Haven: Human Relations Area Files Press.

—— (1962). "Administrative Rationality, Social Setting, and Organizational Development," *American Journal of Sociology*, 68 (November), 299–308.

—— (1970). *Work in Traditional and Modern Society*. Englewood Cliffs, N.J.: Prentice-Hall.

USEEM, MICHAEL (1980). "Corporations and the Corporate Elite," *Annual Review of Sociology*, 6, 41–77.

U.S. BUREAU OF THE CENSUS (1984). *Statistical Abstracts of the United States 1985*. Washington, D.C.: Government Printing Office.

U.S. DEPARTMENT OF LABOR, BUREAU OF LABOR STATISTICS (1979). *Employment and Wages, 1976*. Springfield, Va.: National Technical Information Service.

U.S. OFFICE OF THE FEDERAL REGISTER, GENERAL SERVICE ADMINISTRATION (1984/85). *The United States Government Manual*. Washington, D.C.: Government Printing Office.

VAN DE VEN, ANDREW H., and ANDRE DELBECQ (1974). "A Task Contingent Model of Work-Unit Structure," *Administrative Science Quarterly*, 19 (June), 183–97.

VAN DE VEN, ANDREW H., ANDRE L. DELBECQ, and RICHARD KOENIG, JR. (1976). "Determinants of Coordination Modes within Organizations," *American Sociological Review*, 41 (April), 322–38.

VAN DE VEN, ANDREW H., and DIANE L. FERRY (1980). *Measuring and Assessing Organizations*. New York: John Wiley, Wiley-Interscience.

VAN DORN, JACQUES (1979). "Organizations and the Social Order: A Pluralist Approach," in *Organizations Alike and Unlike*, pp. 61–75, ed. Cornelis J. Lammers and David J. Hickson. London: Routledge & Kegan Paul.

VAUPFI, JAMES W., and JOAN P. CURHAN (1969). *The Making of Multinational Enterprise*. Cambridge, Mass.: Harvard University Press.

VEBLEN, THORSTEIN (1904). *The Theory of Business Enterprise*. New York: Scribner's.

VERBA, SIDNEY (1961). *Small Groups and Political Behavior*. Princeton, N.J.: Princeton University Press.

VERBA, SIDNEY, and NORMAN H. NIE (1972). *Participation in America: Political Democracy and Social Equality*. New York: Harper & Row, Pub.

VROOM, VICTOR H. (1969). "Industrial Social Psychology," in *The Handbook of Social Psychology* (2nd ed.), vol. 5, pp. 196–268, ed. Gardner Lindzey and Elliot Aronson. Reading, Mass.: Addison-Wesley.

WALKER, CHARLES R., and ROBERT H. GUEST. (1952). *The Man on the Assembly Line*. Cambridge, Mass.: Harvard University Press.

WALKER, GORDON, and DAVID WEBER (1984). "A Transaction Cost Approach to Make-or-Buy Decisions," *Administrative Science Quarterly*, 29 (September), 373–91.

WALLACE, WALTER L. (1975). "Structure and Action in the Theories of Coleman and Parsons," in *Approaches to the Study of Social Structure*, pp. 121–34, ed. Peter M. Blau. New York: Free Press.

WALTON, RICHARD E. (1969). *Interpersonal Peacemaking: Confrontations and Third Party Consultation*. Reading: Mass.: Addison-Wesley.

WALTON, RICHARD E., and JOHN M. DUTTON (1969). "The Management of Interdepartmental Conflict: A Model and Review," *Administrative Science Quarterly*, 14 (March), 73–84.

WALTON, RICHARD E., JOHN M. DUTTON, and H. GORDON FITCH (1966). "A Study of Conflict in the Process, Structure, and Attitudes of Lateral Relationships," in *Some Theories of Organization* (rev. ed.), pp. 444–65, ed. Chadwick J. Haberstroh and Albert H. Rubenstein. Homewood, Ill.: Richard D. Irwin; Dorsey.

WAMSLEY, GARY L., and MAYER N. ZALD (1973). *The Political Economy of Public Organizations*. Lexington, Mass.: Heath.

WARD, JOHN WILLIAM (1964). "The Ideal of Individualism and the Reality of Organization," in *The Business Establishment*, pp. 37–76, ed. Earl F. Cheit. New York: John Wiley.

WARNER, W. LLOYD, and J. O. Low (1947). *The Social System of the Modern Factory*. New Haven: Yale University Press.

WARREN, ROLAND L. (1963). *The Community in America*. Chicago: Rand McNally (rev. ed., 1972).

—— (1967). "The Interorganizational Field as a Focus for Investigation," *Administrative Science Quarterly*, 12 (December), 396–419.

WEBER, MAX (1946 trans.). *From Max Weber: Essays in Sociology*, ed. Hans H. Gerth and C. Wright Mills. New York: Oxford University Press. (first published in 1906–24).

—— (1947 trans.). *The Theory of Social and Economic Organization*, ed. A. H. Henderson and Talcott Parsons, Glencoe, Ill.: Free Press (first published in 1924).

—— (1958 trans.). *The Protestant Ethic and the Spirit of Capitalism*. trans. Talcott Parsons. New York: Scribner's (first published in 1904–5).

WEICK, KARL E. (1969). *The Social Psychology of Organizing*. Reading, Mass.: Addison-Wesley (2nd ed., 1979).

—— (1974). "Middle Range Theories of Social Systems," *Behavioral Science*, 19 (November), 357–67.

—— (1976). "Educational Organizations as Loosely Coupled Systems," *Administrative Science Quarterly*, 21 (March), 1–19.

—— (1977). "Re-Punctuating the Problem," in *New Perspectives on Organizational Effectiveness*, pp. 193–225, ed. Paul S. Goodman and Johannes M. Pennings. San Francisco: Jossey-Bass.

WEISS, CAROL H. (1972). *Evaluation Research*. Englewood Cliffs, N.J.: Prentice-Hall.

WEISS, CAROL H., and ALLEN H. BARTON, eds. (1980). *Making Bureaucracies Work*. Beverly Hills, Calif.: Sage Publications, Inc.

WHISLER, THOMAS (1970). *The Impact of Computers on Organizations*. New York: Praeger.

WHITE, HARRISON C., SCOTT A. BOORMAN, and RONALD L. BREIGER (1976). "Social Structure from Multiple Networks: 1. Blockmodels of Roles and Positions," *American Journal of Sociology*, 81 (January) 730–80.

WHITE, RALPH, and RONALD LIPPITT (1953). "Leader Behavior and Member Reaction in Three 'Social Climates,'" in *Group Dynamics*, pp. 586–611, ed. Dorwin Cartwright and Alvin Zander. Evanston, Ill.: Row, Peterson.

WHITEHEAD, ALFRED NORTH (1929). *The Aims of Education*. New York: Macmillan.

WHYTE, MARTIN KING (1973). "Bureaucracy and Modernization in China: The Maoist Critique," *American Sociological Review*, 38 (April), 149–63.

WHYTE, WILLIAM FOOTE, ed. (1946). *Industry and Society*. New York: McGraw-Hill.

—— (1948). *Human Relations in the Restaurant Industry*. New York: McGraw-Hill.

—— (1951). "Small Groups and Large Organizations," in *Social Psychology at the Crossroads*, pp. 297–312, ed. John H. Rohrer and Muzafer Sherif. New York: Harper.

—— (1959). *Man and Organization*. Homewood, Ill.: Richard D. Irwin.

WHYTE, WILLIAM FOOTE, et al. (1955). *Money and Motivation: An Analysis of Incentives in Industry*. New York: Harper.

WHYTE, WILLIAM H., JR. (1956). *The Organization Man*. New York: Simon & Schuster.

WIELAND, GEORGE F., and ROBERT A. ULLRICH (1976). *Organizations: Behavior, Design, and Change*. Homewood, Ill.: Richard D. Irwin.

WIENER, NORBERT (1956). *I Am a Mathematician*. New York: Doubleday.

WILDAVSKY, AARON B. (1959). "A Methodological Critique of Duverger's *Political Parties*," *Journal of Politics*, 21, 303–18.

—— (1979). *Speaking Truth to Power: The Art and Craft of Policy Analysis*. Boston: Little, Brown.

WILLIAMS, LAWRENCE K., WILLIAM F. WHYTE, and CHARLES S. GREEN (1966). "Do Cultural Differences Affect Workers' Attitudes?" *Industrial Relations*, 5 (May), 105–17.

WILLIAMSON, OLIVER E. (1975) *Markets and Hierarchies: Analysis and Antitrust Implications*. New York: Free Press.

—— (1981). "The Economics of Organization: The Transaction Cost Approach," *American Journal of Sociology*, 87 (November) 548–77.

—— (1985). *The Economic Institutions of Capitalism*. New York. Free Press.

WILLIAMSON, OLIVER E., and WILLIAM G. OUCHI (1981). "The Markets and Hierarchies and Visible Hand Perspectives," in *Perspectives on Organization Design and Behavior*, pp. 347–70, ed. Andrew H. Van de Ven and William F. Joyce. New York: John Wiley.

WILSON, JAMES Q. (1962). *The Amateur Democrat*. Chicago: University of Chicago Press.

—— (1973). *Political Organizations*. New York: Basic Books.

—— (1978). *The Investigators: Managing FBI and Narcotics Agents*. New York: Basic Books.

——, ed. (1980). *The Politics of Regulation*. New York: Basic Books.

WOLFE, ALAN (1977). *The Limits of Legitimacy: Political Contradictions of Contemporary Capitalism*. New York: Free Press.

WOLIN, SHELDON S. (1960). *Politics and Vision: Continuity and Innovation in Western Political Thought*. Boston: Little, Brown.

WOODWARD, JOAN (1958). *Management and Technology*. London: H. M. S. O.

—— (1965). *Industrial Organization: Theory and Practice*. New York: Oxford University Press.

——, ed. (1970). *Industrial Organization: Behaviour and Control*. London: Oxford University Press.

WUTHNOW, ROBERT, JAMES DAVISON HUNTER, ALBERT BERGESEN, and EDITH KURZWEIL (1984). *Cultural Analysis*. Boston: Routledge & Kegan Paul.

YUCHTMAN, EPHRAIM, and STANLEY E. SEASHORE (1967). "A System Resource Approach to Organizational Effectiveness," *American Sociological Review*, 32 (December), 891–903.

ZALD, MAYER N (1970). "Political Economy: A Framework for Comparative Analysis," in *Power in Organizations*, pp. 221–61, ed. Mayer N. Zald. Nashville: Vanderbilt University Press.

ZALD, MAYER N., and ROBERTA ASH (1966). "Social Movement Organizations: Growth, Decay and Change," *Social Forces*, 44 (March), 327–40.

ZALD, MAYER N., and PATRICIA DENTON (1963). "From Evangelism to General Service: The Transformation of the YMCA," *Administrative Science Quarterly*, 8 (September), 214–34.

ZAMMUTO, RAYMOND F. (1982). *Assessing Organizational Effectiveness*. Albany: State University of New York Press.

ZEITLIN, MAURICE (1974). "Corporate Ownership and Control: The Large Corporation and the Capitalist Class," *American Journal of Sociology*, 79 (March), 1073–119.

ZELDITCH, MORRIS, JR. (1969). "Can You Really Study an Army in the Laboratory?" in *A Sociological*

*Reader on Complex Organizations* (2nd ed.), pp. 528–39, ed. Amitai Etzioni. New York: Holt, Rinehart & Winston.

ZELDITCH, MORRIS, JR., and HENRY A. WALKER (1984). "Legitimacy and the Stability of Authority," in *Advance in Group Processes: Theory and Research,* vol. 1, pp. 1–25, ed. Edward J. Lawler. Greenwich, Conn.: JAI Press.

ZEY-FERRELL, MARY, and MICHAEL AIKEN, eds. (1981). *Complex Organizations: Critical Perspectives.* Glenview, Ill.: Scott, Foresman.

ZIMBALIST, ANDREW, ed. (1979). *Case Studies in the Labor Process.* New York: Monthly Review Press.

ZIMMERMAN, DON H. (1970). "The Practialities of Rule Use," in *Understanding Everyday Life,* ed. J. D. Douglas. Chicago: Aldine.

ZIMMERMAN, DON H., and D. WIEDER (1970). "Ethnomethodology and the Problem of Order," in *Understanding Everyday Life,* pp. 287–95, ed. J. D. Douglas. Chicago: Aldine.

ZUCKER, LYNNE G. (1977). "The Role of Institutionalization in Cultural Persistance," *American Sociological Review,* 42 (October), 726–43.

—— (1983). "Organizations as Institutions," in *Research in the Sociology of Organizations,* vol. 2, pp. 1–47, ed. Samuel B. Bacharach. Greenwich, Conn.: JAI Press.

ZUCKER, LYNNE G., and CAROLYN ROSENSTEIN (1981). "Taxonomies of Institutional Structure: Dual Economy Reconsidered," *American Sociological Review,* 46 (December), 869–84.

*Acknowledgments, continued*

Fig. 7–1. Adapted from Oliver E. Williamson, *Markets and Hierarchies: Analysis and Antitrust Implications,* p. 40. New York, The Free Press, Copyright © 1975 by The Free Press; A Division of Macmillan Publishing Co., Inc. Reprinted by permission.

Fig. 9–1. From George A. Steiner and William G. Ryan, *Industrial Project Management,* p. 10. New York, The Trustees of Columbia University of the City of New York, 1968. Reprinted by permission.

Fig. 10–1. Reprinted from Alfred D. Chandler, Jr., *Strategy and Structure,* p. 10. by permission of the MIT Press, Cambridge, Massachusetts. Copyright © 1962 by Massachusetts Institute of Technology.

Table 5–1. Adapted from W. Richard Scott, Theoretical perspectives, in Marshall W. Meyer and Associates, *Environments and Organizations,* Table 1, p. 22, San Francisco, California, Jossey-Bass, Inc. 1978. Reprinted by permission.

Table 9–1. Adaptation reproduced, with permission, from W. Richard Scott, Organizational structure. *Annual Review of Sociology,* 1 (1975): 5–6. Copyright © 1975 by Annual Reviews Inc.

p. 3. From Guy E. Swanson, The tasks of sociology, *Science* 192 (May 1976): 666. Copyright © 1976 by the American Association for the Advancement of Science. Reprinted by permission.

p. 31. From John William Ward, The ideal of individualism and the reality of organization, in Earl F. Cheit (ed.) *The Business Establishment,* p. 62. New York: John Wiley & Sons, Inc., 1964. Reprinted by permission.

p. 51. From Peter M. Blau, *Bureaucracy in Modern Society,* p. 58. New York: Random House, 1956. Copyright © 1956 by Random House, Inc. Reprinted by permission.

p. 76. From Walter Buckley, *Sociology and Modern Systems Theory,* p. 50. Englewood Cliffs, New Jersey: Prentice-Hall, Inc., 1967. Copyright © 1967 by Prentice-Hall, Inc. Reprinted by permission.

p. 93. Reprinted from *The Structure of Scientific Revolutions* by Thomas S. Kuhn, by permission of the University of Chicago Press. Copyright © 1962 by The University of Chicago. All rights reserved.

p. 143. From Arthur L. Stinchcombe, *Creating Efficient Industrial Administrations,* p. 46. New York: Academic Press, 1974. Reprinted by permission.

p. 119. From A. D. Hall and R. E. Fagen, Definition of system, *General Systems: Yearbook of the Society for the Advancement of General Systems Theory* 1 (1956): 20. Washington, D.C.: Society for General Systems Research. Reprinted by permission.

p. 170. Excerpt from The natural history of human organizations by Herbert Kaufman is reprinted from *Administration and Society* Vol. 7, No. 2 (August 1975) p. 143 by permission of the Publisher, Sage Publications, Inc.

p. 210. From Henry Mintzberg, *The Structuring of Organizations,* p. 2. Englewood Cliffs, New Jersey: Prentice-Hall, Inc., 1979. Copyright © 1979 by Prentice-Hall, Inc. Reprinted by permission.

p. 240. From Erwin Schrödinger, *What Is Life?,* p. 75. New York: Cambridge University Press, 1945. Reprinted by permission.

p. 267. From John Kenneth Galbraith, *The New Industrial State,* 2nd edition, p. 65. Boston, Massachusetts: Houghton Mifflin Company. 1971 (rev.). Copyright © 1967, 1971 by John Kenneth Galbraith. Reprinted by permission of the publisher and Andre Deutsch, Ltd., England.

p. 297. From Max Weber, *From Max Weber: Essays in Sociology,* pp. 228–229, H. H. Gerth and C. Wright Mills, eds. New York: Oxford University Press, 1946. Reprinted by permission.

p. 319. From W. Ross Ashby, Principles of the self-organizing system, in Heinz von Foerster and George W. Zopf, eds. Oxford, England, Pergammon Press, 1962. Reprinted by permission.

Quotes reprinted from *Organizations in Action* by James D. Thompson with permission of the McGraw-Hill Book Company. Copyright © 1967 by McGraw-Hill Book Company. Reprinted by permission.

# name index

# subject index